Key Issues

LEVIATHAN
Contemporary Responses to the Political Theory of
Thomas Hobbes

Key Issues

LEVIATHAN

Contemporary Responses to the Political Theory of THOMAS HOBBES

Edited and Introduced by

G. A. J. Rogers
Keele University

Series Editor
Andrew Pyle
University of Bristol

THOEMMES PRESS

© Thoemmes Press 1995

Published in 1995 by
Thoemmes Press
11 Great George Street
Bristol BS1 5RR
England

ISBN
Paper: 1 85506 406 5
Cloth: 1 85506 407 3

Leviathan:
Contemporary Responses to the Political Theory of Thomas Hobbes
Key Issues No. 5

British Library Cataloguing-in-Publication Data

A catalogue record of this title is available
from the British Library

Printed in Great Britain by Antony Rowe Ltd., Chippenham

CONTENTS

The reviews reprinted in this book have been taken from original copies and the different grammatical and stylistic arrangement of each has been preserved.

INTRODUCTION

Perhaps no work of philosophy has ever generated such a strong reaction as did Thomas Hobbes's *Leviathan* in the decades after its publication in 1651. The response was so widespread and so sustained that it would be very difficult to give an accurate number to the works of criticism – for they were overwhelmingly critical – that appeared in the next fifty years alone.[1] Since its recognition as a classic – which took some time to achieve and was certainly not before the end of the century – that criticism has mellowed. But Hobbes's claims remain both contentious and rewarding and continue to generate an enormous amount of literature, not least through the modern scholarly editions of his many works.[2] This collection brings together some of those early reactions, now

1 Samuel I. Mintz, in his *The Hunting of Leviathan* (Cambridge University Press: Cambridge, 1962) lists in an Appendix over 100 anti-Hobbes works written between 1650 and 1700. But many are omitted, including some of those reprinted in this volume, and it cannot be regarded as in any sense comprehensive.

2 Of these the two most important are (i) the Clarendon Edition of the Works of Thomas Hobbes which currently include the English and Latin editions of *De Cive*, edited by Howard Warrender (Oxford, 1983) and *The Correspondence of Thomas Hobbes*, edited by Noel Malcolm in two volumes, (Oxford, 1994), and (ii) the French edition of his works published by Vrin under the direction of Yves Charles Zarka of which so far the following have appeared: *Béhémoth*, edited by Luc Borot (Paris, 1990), *Dialogue des Common Laws*, edited by Lucien et Paulette Carrive (Paris, 1990), *De la Liberté et de la Nécessité*, edited by Franck Lessay (Paris, 1993), *Hérésie et Histoire*, edited by Franck Lessay (Paris, 1993). Important recent individual editions of *Leviathan* are the French edition with Introduction, traduction et notes de François Tricaud, (Editions Sirey: Paris, 1971) – the first French translation of *Leviathan*, and the first one to include variants introduced by Hobbes in the Latin edition of 1668; that of Richard Tuck in the Cambridge Texts in the History of Political Thought series (Cambridge University Press: Cambridge, 1991), and that edited by Edwin Curley (Hackett: Indianapolis, 1994) which includes important variants from the Latin edition of 1668. The standard edition of Hobbes's works remain *The English Works of Thomas Hobbes*, edited by William Molesworth, eleven volumes, (London, 1839–45, reprinted Routledge/ Thoemmes Press, London, 1992) and *Opera Latine*, also edited by Molesworth (London, 1839–45) five volumes.

published mostly for the first time since the seventeenth century.

One of the reasons for Hobbes's notoriety amongst his contemporaries was because *Leviathan*, and to a lesser extent his earlier work *De Cive* (1642), challenged many deeply held assumptions on several fronts. Not only did it reject the central tenets of contemporary political theory, in itself posing a challenge at many different levels to the fragile consensus of post-Civil War and post-Restoration England, but it also argued a materialist account of the natural world which represented the unacceptable face of the mechanical philosophy that was in process of replacing the traditional Aristotelian natural philosophy of the schools. Furthermore, that uncompromising materialism not only challenged many of the philosophical assumptions of the age but also, and more seriously, the theological assumptions as well. One of these was the widely accepted belief that human beings were not part of a deterministic physical system but could exercise free will in a way which allowed for the notion of human responsibility and divine rewards and punishments. Hobbes's account seemed to point inevitably to quite contrary conclusions. It is perhaps not wholly surprising that in the Restoration, a time which was in part an attempt to return to earlier values discarded in the Commonwealth period, Hobbes's philosophy was seen as a threat that needed to be resisted with intellectual and even, if necessary, physical force. When in 1666, shortly after the plague and the Great Fire of London, the House of Commons proposed to consider a 'Bill against Atheism and Profaneness' which would consider such books as tended in that direction, including Thomas White's *Of the Middle State of Souls* (1659, first published in Latin in 1652) and *Leviathan*,[3] Hobbes believed himself in serious danger and, according to Aubrey, burned some of his papers.[4] There can also be little doubt that, despite his famous timorous nature – in his Latin autobiography he tells us that 'fear and I were born twins' – Hobbes in many ways enjoyed his notoriety. Just as Charles II's courtiers enjoyed 'baiting the bear' of Malmesbury so Hobbes in his turn obtained pleasure from shocking the Establishment.

[3] George Croom Robertson: *Hobbes* (Blackwood: London, 1886) p. 194.

[4] *Brief Lives*, edited by Oliver Lawson Dick (Penguin: Harmondsworth, 1949, reissued 1962) p. 235.

Sir Robert Filmer and the First Published assault on 'Leviathan'
Filmer, the son of a Kentish landowner, was probably born in
1588, the same year as Hobbes. Educated at Trinity College,
Cambridge and Lincoln's Inn, he was knighted in 1619 and ten
years later at his father's death he took over the responsibilities
of the family estate. He continued to maintain his London
contacts, many of which were intellectual and political, and
began to set some of his ideas down on paper as they related
primarily to the contemporary issues which were troubling him
and his neighbours. Of these writings the most famous has
come down to us as *Patriarcha: A Defence of the Natural
Power of Kings against the Unnatural Liberty of the People*, a
manuscript that circulated amongst his friends, but which was
not published until twenty seven years after its author's death
in 1680.[5] It has become known as the work which John Locke
so famously attacked in the first of his two *Treatises of
Government* (1689), an assault that has tended to colour our
view of Filmer and to underestimate his merit as a thinker.

Filmer was a committed Royalist and for his pains spent
much of the Civil War as a prisoner in Leeds Castle. It was a
few years later that, in response to the growing literature
defending the Puritan Revolution, he wrote and published
*Observations Concerning the Original of Government, Upon
Mr Hobs Leviathan, Mr Milton against Psalmists, H. Grotius
De Juri Belli*, which was published in London by R. Royston in
1652. It is the section on Hobbes that is reprinted below.

Filmer completely agreed with Hobbes on one thing: the
right of sovereignty. He accepted absolutely that there was no
power within a community that could justly challenge the
sovereign authority. But he totally rejected Hobbes's account of
how that authority arose. For Hobbes it could only be
explained as arising from a contract between the autonomous
individuals that existed in the State of Nature. They must agree
with each other to accept some individual or one group of
individuals as the ruler who must be obeyed. The compelling
reason for establishing such an authority was that only through
such a sovereign was it possible for there to be a condition of
peace. For the state of nature was, said Hobbes, a condition of
war, where the life of man would be, in his memorable words,

[5] Cf. Peter Laslett's Introduction to *Patriarcha or, the Natural Power of the
Kings of England Asserted and Other Political Works of Sir Robert Filmer*
(Basil Blackwell: Oxford, 1949).

'solitary, poor, nasty, brutish and short'. Since peace, and with it security, was the single most desirable state for human beings it would be wholly irrational for anybody not to want it. And the only way to guarantee it was to agree with others to accept a government with power to make and enforce laws.

Filmer has a quite different account of the origins and justification of sovereignty. He first of all takes Hobbes to task because he says that Hobbes's account assumes that men sprung from the earth 'like mushrooms' without any obligations one to another. Yet we know full well that human beings have natural obligations which arise from their roles as parents and children. A parent's obligation to its child cannot have arisen by contract, Filmer points out, because it predates the child's ability to enter into such agreements. On another tack, Filmer challenges Hobbes's use of the Bible to support his argument. Hobbes had claimed that the people of Israel had entered into a contract – 'covenant' – with God. But, Filmer argues, the contract had been entered into only by Abraham, not by the people. Furthermore, it was not possible for them (or anybody else) to enter into a contract to agree to accept Yahweh as their God for He must inevitably occupy that position no matter what they might say or do.

Filmer's objections to Hobbes's argument, and in particular his entering into dispute in matters of biblical exegesis, reflect the close ties that Hobbes himself built between his theory and the Christian religion, which at first seems surprising for a man who was so often accused of being an atheist. But it also reflects the important fact that in mid-seventeenth century England it was not possible to write a work of political theory, even if one had so wished, that did not have religious implications. Whether Hobbes himself wanted to establish an entirely secular argument for the exercise of sovereign power is itself a mute question about the interpretation of his work but he surely knew that *Leviathan*'s implications for much Christian theology were bound to be a major issue in its reception. As we shall see it was an aspect of his position that was to be echoed in the views of later critics as well.

George Lawson's Examination of 'Leviathan'
George Lawson was born in Yorkshire in 1598 and after attending Emmanuel College in Cambridge, famous as a Puritan college and strongly associated with the revival of

Platonism through Benjamin Whichcote, he was ordained in
1624. From 1637 he was rector of More in Shropshire where
he remained until his death in 1678. His most important work
on which his fame rests is *Politica Sacra & Civilis; or A Modell
of Civil and Ecclesiasticall Government* (London, 1660, second
edition 1689).[6] His attack on Hobbes, *An Examination of the
Political Part of Mr Hobbs his Leviathan*, was published in
London in 1657. It is a book of some 214 pages, written as a
running commentary on quotations and summaries of
Hobbes's claims, of which the largest part, the first 155 pages,
and reprinted here, is concerned with the first two books. In
the Preface he makes very clear that it is the interaction
between the political and religious implications of *Leviathan*
that particularly concern him. He tells us that he has
undertaken his examination because he has come to realize that
Hobbes's work is an evil threat that had become dangerously
fashionable with the young. He is particularly concerned to
reveal Hobbes's inconsistency with scripture and right reason,
but he also draws on history, including recent British history,
to argue his case.

Lawson, like Filmer, makes clear from the outset his total
rejection of the Hobbist view of the origin of government in a
contract. Lawson's position, not surprisingly, is providential.
Civil government is part of God's government over mankind.
Furthermore, the state of nature is far from being a state of
war, as Hobbes claims, but is one governed by the two Laws of
Nature: 'Love thy neighbour as thyself' and 'Do as you would
be done unto'.

From there Lawson goes on to attack Hobbes for his
inadequate and misleading definitions, his muddled reasoning
and his unacceptable conclusions. Drawing on his education in
Aristotelian logic and his knowledge of the Bible Lawson
proceeds to give his critical analysis and to offer his
alternatives. A central theme is that although there must indeed
be a supreme secular power it is itself always subordinate to
'Godliness and Honesty' (1. Timothy 2.1). Although Lawson

6 A recent new edition, the first since 1689, is in the Cambridge Texts in the
   History of Political Thought series edited by Conal Condren (Cambridge
   University Press: Cambridge, 1992). For discussion of the *Politica* see:
   Julian H. Franklin: *John Locke and the Theory of Sovereignty* (Cambridge
   University Press: Cambridge, 1978) and Conal Condren: *George Lawson's
   Politica and the English Revolution* (Cambridge University Press: Cam-
   bridge, 1989).

thinks that tyranny is better than anarchy there could be times when a subject would be right not to obey a monarch and rebel against his unjust acts and commands. As for the authority of covenants without a temporal power to enforce them, which Hobbes dismisses as mere words, Lawson takes this to be firm evidence that Hobbes is indeed an atheist, for a theist would accept the power of God to act in an afterlife against those who break their promises in this. In reply to Hobbes's claim that monarchy is the best form of government, Lawson, writing in 1657, is more circumspect. Monarchy is far from perfect, Lawson tells us, and the only true monarchical government is that of the Deity. The power of any earthly ruler is never absolute and always circumscribed by 'the Law of Reason, Nature, God'. Similar arguments apply to the ownership of property which is not determined merely by the sovereign's decision. Civil power was never given by the citizens to any ruler so that he may destroy their property but to protect it, Lawson tells us.

Lawson goes on to contrast his beliefs with those of Hobbes on a large number of topics including those of punishment, conscience, and the origin and nature of God's authority which lies, Lawson says, not in God's irresistible power but in his infinitely superior wisdom.

How widely read Lawson's attack was is unclear but we can be certain that he spoke for many in his criticisms. The whole tone and nature of his argument is consistent with much political thinking in England in the remainder of the century and it is not surprising that he is now widely seen as having anticipated important features of Locke's political theory.[7]

John Bramhall's 'The Catching of Leviathan'
John Bramhall (1594–1663) is another cleric who strongly criticised Hobbes's philosophy. He went to Sidney Sussex College, Cambridge in 1609 and entered the church in about 1616. In 1633, by which time he was a rising young clergyman, he went to Ireland where he soon distinguished himself as a church administrator. In the Civil War he supported the King and was in Ireland and England until 1644 when he was under severe threat and so, like so many other Royalists, withdrew to Paris. It was there in 1645 that he met Hobbes and enjoyed

[7] See, for example, Julian H. Franklin: *John Locke and the Theory of Sovereignty*, esp. Ch. 3.

discussion and disagreement with him about, amongst other topics, free will, exchanges which were later continued in print. He returned to England at the Restoration and was made Archbishop of Armagh in 1661. He soon became speaker of the Irish House of Lords, and retained both positions until his death.

Bramhall's *The Catching of Leviathan or the Great Whale* (London, 1658) was originally published as an appendix to his second volume attacking Hobbes on liberty and necessity. That work, *Castigations of Mr Hobbes his last animadversions, in the Case concerning liberty, and universal necessity*, followed Bramhall's *A Defence of True Liberty of Human Actions from Antecedent or Extrinsic Necessity* (London, 1655) and the first published work in their debate, *Of Libertie and Necessitie* (London, 1654). The last named work had a complicated history. It was a record of their Paris discussions which both Hobbes and Bramhall had agreed to put in writing for the benefit of Hobbes's patron, William Cavendish, Marquis, later Duke, of Newcastle, who had been present at the debates.[8] Unknown to Hobbes a copy of that discussion came into the hands of one of his admirers who published it without consulting either party, but who slanted the presentation in Hobbes's favour. Bramhall, who knew nothing of this, supposed that Hobbes had authorised publication and was naturally angry. It is hardly surprising that the tone of the later exchanges sometimes leaves something to be desired.

Bramhall's *The Catching of Leviathan* begins aggressively with the accusation that Hobbes's philosophy destroys all religion. It is notable for Bramhall's unambiguous commitment to the position that we have an innate knowledge of God and the law of nature. That being so, any failure to acknowledge either cannot, as Hobbes argues, be excused as an omission of ignorance. He also totally rejects Hobbes's conjecture that God is corporeal: either He is incorporeal or he is no God. Hobbes's treatment of other central theological concepts is also unacceptable: his accounts of the Trinity, prophecy, angels, eternal punishment, idolatry, are all fatally flawed. And, like many another of Hobbes's critics, Bramhall completely repudiates what he takes to be Hobbes's rejection of the supremacy of divine law and the espousal of a subjectivist ethics.

---

[8]   To be found in Hobbes's *English Works*, Vol. 5.

After savaging Hobbes's religious claims Bramhall turns to the political theory. A central weakness is taken to be his dismissal of covenants which are not supported by the sword, for this destroys all possibility of international agreement. Further, Hobbes makes self-defence override any other duty, which allows him to take his sovereign 'for better' but not 'for worse'. And according to Hobbes unjust laws are impossible, which is absurd. On the domestic front Hobbes's principles destroy relationships within the family. Parents have no natural right over their children and wives are not naturally subordinate to their husbands. Finally, and according to Bramhall, conclusively, Hobbes's principles are inconsistent: sometimes the laws of nature are taken to be God's laws and sometimes the laws of men; children may and may not be justly punished; the sovereign is free but also tied by Scripture. At the close, Bramhall concludes with heavy irony, that although Hobbes's system was inappropriate for Europe, he should be allowed to set up his form of government in America 'as being calculated and fitted for that meridian'.

Bramhall's book apparently did not come to Hobbes's attention until 1668, ten years after its publication. When it did he was not prepared to allow it to go unanswered, especially as it raised the serious charge of heresy, a matter which Hobbes was well aware had already been, as we have already noted, the recent concern of Parliament. He wrote a reply immediately but it was not published until after Hobbes's death.[9]

Clarendon's 'Survey'

The longest and most interesting and important critique of *Leviathan* to be published in the seventeenth century was that of Edward Hyde, Earl of Clarendon (1609–1674). Hyde was the greatest and most cultivated of all the seventeenth century Royalist politicians and occupied centre stage through crucial years of the Civil War, the Interregnum and the early years of the Restoration. He was educated at Magdalen Hall, Oxford, where Hobbes had been almost a generation before, and the

---

[9]   Hobbes tells us that he would have replied to Bramhall sooner if he had known the work was extant. He had, he tells us, only heard of it three months before: 'To the Reader', *An Answer to a Book Published by Dr Bramhall. . .Called the Catching of Leviathan. Together with an Historical Narration Concerning Heresie*, London, 1682, (*English Works*, Vol. IV, p. 282).

Middle Temple. His profession was the law but he always maintained a deep interest in history and many of his friends were scholars and churchmen associated with the group around Lucius Cary, Lord Falkland, which gathered regularly at Great Tew, eighteen miles north of Oxford.[10] Having entered Parliament he soon made his mark on important committees. He stood strong in defence of the established Anglican episcopal church against Puritan pressures and urged faith in the law against parliamentary enthusiasms. It is not surprising, therefore, that he placed himself more and more firmly in the Royalist camp, though his advice, either immediately before or during the conflict, was not always successful or accepted. After the war was lost and the king executed Hyde was summoned to the exiled court in Paris and soon became the young king's principal adviser, despite having many powerful enemies, including the old queen, around him. It was here in 1658 that he was declared Lord Chancellor.

At the Restoration Hyde was raised to the title of Earl of Clarendon. At first he remained a powerful force. But his enemies were always scheming against him and the secret marriage of his daughter Anne to the Duke of York in 1660 had only confirmed and inflamed hostility, even though Hyde was no party to it. On the matter of toleration, too, Clarendon and the king found themselves at odds: the king was for toleration whilst the earl preferred comprehension. The opposition in the country and Parliament reached such a peak in 1667 that the king required Clarendon to go into exile. He spent his last years in France, mostly in Montpellier, where he wrote his most famous works, his great *History of the Rebellion and Civil Wars in England*, his biography and his *A Brief View and Survey of the Dangerous and pernicious Errors to Church and State in Mr Hobbes's Book, Entitled Leviathan*, which was published three years after the author's death in 1676.

Clarendon and Hobbes were well acquainted, though when exactly they met is unclear. In the Introduction to the *Survey* Clarendon tells us that:

---

10 For an excellent account of the Great Tew circle see Hugh Trevor-Roper, 'The Great Tew Circle' in his *Catholics, Anglicans and Puritans. Seventeenth Century Essays* (Secker and Warburg: London, 1987) pp. 166–230.

> Mr Hobbes is one of the most ancient acquaintance I have in
> the World, and of whom I have always had a great esteem, as
> a Man who besides his eminent parts of learning and
> knowledg, hath bin alwais looked upon as a Man of Probity,
> and a life free from scandal; and it may be that there are few
> Men now alive, who have bin longer known to him then I
> have bin in a fair and friendly conversation and sociable-
> ness. . . (p. 3)

Although they knew each other well in Paris in the exile
generated by the Civil War Clarendon's words imply a longer
acquaintanceship than that. It is almost certain that Hobbes
was not himself a member of the Great Tew circle, despite
Aubrey's claim to the contrary. But it is likely that they knew
each other in London well before the Civil War. *Leviathan* was
dedicated to Francis Godolphin, brother of Sydney, who had
been killed in the war and who had been a friend of both
Clarendon and Hobbes. Despite such overlaps in their lives
there is little evidence that they had actually spent a great deal
of time in each other's company, partly at least because they
were rarely in the same place. And even when they were
Clarendon was no doubt often too taken with affairs of state to
devote time to social exchanges.

There was also a much deeper reason why they were unlikely
to become close friends. It is that their intellectual stances were
so very different. As Clarendon makes clear in the *Survey*, he
believed that the method employed by Hobbes in his analysis of
the state had little to do with the real world. It was not
deductively generated models but history and a knowledge of
law which he believed gave insight into the nature of society
and the state. Hobbes, he held, with his geometrical method
had constructed an account of the essence of political society
which made contact with reality only intermittently. Hobbes
claimed to have turned politics into a science. This was a task
that Clarendon believed to be quite impossible. What then we
are given in the *Survey* is an entirely different way of looking at
the state and its institutions. Furthermore, it is viewed from
entirely within the intellectual framework of a profoundly
religious man who sees nothing but catastrophe in the adoption
of the Hobbesian account of the state, law and obligation.
Clarendon's total rejection of Hobbes's view is neatly summar-
ised in his closing words to Part II: 'And surely if these articles

of Mr Hobbes's creed be the product of right reason, and the effects of Christian obligations, the Great Turk may be looked upon as the best philosopher, and all his subjects as the best Christians'. The differences between Hobbes and Clarendon reflect two profoundly different ways of looking at intellectual issues. Clarendon's is the mind of the great historian and practical man of affairs, always conscious of the subtle differences that mark one event from another and give each one its own unique place in history. Hobbes, on the other hand, attempts to capture the essences of the furniture of the universe both natural and institutional, in his definitions and deductions. Comparing their works is an exercise in enlightenment about two of the most fruitful methods to emerge in the history of civilization.

G. A. J. Rogers
University of Keele, 1995

OBSERVATIONS ON
MR HOBBES'S LEVIATHAN
Robert Filmer

THE PREFACE

With no small content I read Mr. Hobbes's book *De Cive*, and his *Leviathan*, about the rights of sovereignty, which no man, that I know, hath so amply and judiciously handled: I consent with him about the rights of exercising government, but I cannot agree to his means of acquiring it. It may seem strange I should praise his building, and yet mislike his foundation; but so it is, his *Jus Naturae*, and his *Regnum Institutivum*, will not down with me: they appear full of contradiction and impossibilities; a few short notes about them, I here offer, wishing he would consider whether his building would not stand firmer upon the principles of *Regnum Patrimoniale* (as he calls it) both according to scripture and reason. Since he confesseth the 'Father being before the institution of a commonwealth was originally an absolute sovereign with power of life and death', and that 'a great family, as to the rights of sovereignty is a little monarchy'. If according to the order of nature he had handled paternal government before that by institution, there would have been little liberty left in the subjects of the family to consent to institution of government.

In his pleading the cause of the people, he arms them with a very large commission of array; which is, a right in nature for every man, to war against every man when he please: and also a right for all the people to govern. This latter point, although he affirm in words, yet by consequence he denies, as to me it seemeth.

He saith a representative may be of all, or but of a part of the people. If it be of all he terms it a democracy, which is the government of the people. But how can such a commonwealth be generated? for if every man covenant with every man, who shall be left to be the representative? if all must be representatives, who will remain to covenant? for he that is sovereign makes no covenant by his doctrine. It is not all that will come together, that makes the democracy, but all that have power by covenant; thus his democracy by institution fails.

The same may be said of a democracy by acquisition; for if all be conquerors, who shall covenant for life and liberty? and if all be not conquerors, how can it be a democracy by conquest?

A paternal democracy I am confident he will not affirm, so that in conclusion the poor people are deprived of their government, if there can be no democracy by his principles.

Next, if a representative aristocratical of a part of the people be free from covenanting, then that whole assembly (call it what you will) though it be never so great, is in the state of nature, and every one of that assembly hath a right not only to kill any of the subjects that they meet with in the streets, but also they all have a natural right to cut one another's throats, even while they sit together in council by his principles. In this miserable condition of war is his representative aristocratical by institution.

A commonwealth by conquest he teacheth, is, then acquired, when the vanquished to avoid present death covenanteth that so long as his life, and the liberty of his body is allowed him, the victor shall have the use of it, at his pleasure: here I would know how the liberty of the vanquished can be allowed, if the victor have the use of it at pleasure, or how is it possible for the victor to perform his covenant, except he could always stand by every particular man to protect his life and liberty?

In his review and conclusion he resolves, that an ordinary subject hath liberty to submit, when the means of his life is within the guards and garrisons of the enemy. It seems hereby that the rights of sovereignty by institution may be forfeited, for the subject cannot be at liberty to submit to a conqueror, except his former subjection be forfeited for want of protection.

If his conqueror be in the state of nature, when he conquers he hath a right without any covenant made with the conquered: if conquest be defined to be the acquiring of right of sovereignty by victory, why is it said the right is acquired in the peoples' submission, by which they contract with the victor, promising obedience for life and liberty? hath not every one in the state of nature a right to sovereignty, before conquest, which only puts him in possession of his right? If his conqueror be not in the state of nature, but a subject by covenant, how can he get a right of sovereignty by conquest when neither he himself hath right to conquer, nor subjects a liberty to submit? since a former contract lawfully made cannot lawfully be broken by them.

I wish the title of the book had not been of a commonwealth, but of a weal public, or commonweal, which is the true word carefully observed by our translator of *Bodin de Republica* into English: many ignorant men are apt by the name of commonwealth to understand a popular government, wherein wealth and all things shall be common, tending to the levelling community in the state of pure nature.

OBSERVATIONS ON MR. HOBBES'S *LEVIATHAN*: OR HIS ARTIFICIAL MAN – A COMMONWEALTH

I

If God created only Adam, and of a piece of him made the woman; and if by generation from them two as parts of them all mankind be propagated: if also God gave to Adam not only the dominion over the woman and the children that should issue from them, but also over the whole earth to subdue it, and over all the creatures on it, so that as long as Adam lived no man could claim or enjoy anything but by donation, assignation, or permission from him; I wonder how the right of nature can be imagined by Mr. Hobbes, which he saith, page 64, is a liberty for each man to use his own power as he will himself for preservation of his own life; a condition of war of everyone against everyone; a right of every man to everything, even to one another's body, especially since himself affirms, page 178, that originally the Father of every man was also his Sovereign Lord with power over him of life and death.

II

Mr. Hobbes confesseth and believes it was never generally so, that there was such a *jus naturae*; and if not generally, then not at all, for one exception bars all if he mark it well; whereas he imagines such a right of nature may be now practised in America, he confesseth a government there of families, which government how small or brutish soever (as he calls it) is sufficient to destroy his *jus naturale*.

III

I cannot understand how this right of nature can be conceived without imagining a company of men at the very first to have been all created together without any dependency one of another, or as mushrooms (*fungorum more*) they all on a sudden were sprung out of the earth without any obligation one to another, as Mr. Hobbes's words are in his book *De Cive*, chapter 8, section 3: the scripture teacheth us otherwise, that all men came by succession, and generation from one man: we must not deny the truth of the history of the creation.

IV

It is not to be thought that God would create man in a condition worse than any beasts, as if he made men to no other end by nature but to destroy one another, a right for the Father to destroy or eat his children, and for children to do the like by their parents, is worse than cannibals.* This horrid condition of pure nature when Mr. Hobbes was charged with, his refuge was to answer, that no son can be understood to be in this state of nature: which is all one with denying his own principle, for if men be not free-born, it is not possible for him to assign and prove any other time for them to claim a right of nature to liberty, if not at their birth.

V

But if it be allowed (which is yet most false) that a company of men were at first without a common power to keep them in awe; I do not see why such a condition must be called a state of war of all men against all men: indeed if such a multitude of men should be created as the earth could not well nourish, there might be cause for men to destroy one another rather than perish for want of food; but God was no such niggard in the creation, and there being plenty of sustenance and room for all men, there is no cause or use of war till men be hindered in the preservation of life, so that there is no absolute necessity of war in the state of pure nature; it is the right of nature for every man to live in peace, that so he may tend the preservation of his life, which whilst he is in actual war he cannot do. War of itself as it is war preserves no man's life, it only helps us to preserve and obtain the means to live: if every man tend the right of preserving life, which may be done in peace, there is no cause of war.

VI

But admit the state of nature were the state of war; let us see what help Mr. Hobbes hath for it. It is a principle of his, that 'the law of nature is a rule found out by reason' (I do think it is given by God), page 64, 'forbidding a man to do that which is destructive to his life, and to omit that by which he thinks it may be best preserved'. If the right of nature be a liberty for a

* De Cive, *cap.* I, *sect.* 10.

man to do anything he thinks fit to preserve his life, then in the first place nature must teach him that life is to be preserved, and so consequently forbids to do that which may destroy or take away the means of life, or to omit that by which it may be preserved: and thus the right of nature and the law of nature will be all one: for I think Mr. Hobbes will not say the right of nature is a liberty for a man to destroy his own life. The law of nature might better have been said to consist in a command to preserve or not to omit the means of preserving life, than in a prohibition to destroy, or to omit it.

VII

Another principle I meet with, page 65. 'If other men will not lay down their right as well as he, then there is no reason for any to divest himself of his': hence it follows that if all the men in the world do not agree, no commonwealth can be established, it is a thing impossible for all men in the world every man with every man to covenant to lay down their right. Nay it is not possible to be done in the smallest kingdom, though all men should spend their whole lives in nothing else but in running up and down to covenant.

VIII

Right may be laid aside but not transferred, for page 65, 'he that renounceth or passeth away his right, giveth not to any other man a right which he had not before, and reserves a right in himself against all those with whom he doth not covenant'.

IX

Page 87. 'The only way to erect a common power or a commonwealth, is for men to confer all their power and strength upon one man, or one assembly of men, that may reduce all their wills by plurality of voices to one will; which is to appoint one man or an assembly of men to bear their person, to submit their wills to his will: this is a real unity of them all in one person, made by covenant of every man with every man, as if every man should say to every man, I authorize, and give up my right of governing myself to this man, or this assembly of men, on this condition, that thou give up thy right to him, and authorize all his actions. This done, the multitude so united in one person, is called a commonwealth.'

To authorize and give up his right of governing himself, to confer all his power and strength, and to submit his will to another, is to lay down his right of resisting: for if right of nature be a liberty to use power for preservation of life, laying down of that power must be a relinquishing of power to preserve or defend life, otherwise a man relinquisheth nothing.

To reduce all the wills of an assembly by plurality of voices to one will, is not a proper speech, for it is not a plurality but a totality of voices which makes an assembly be of one will, otherwise it is but the one will of a major part of the assembly, the negative voice of any one hinders the being of the one will of the assembly, there is nothing more destructive to the true nature of a lawful assembly, than to allow a major part to prevail when the whole only hath right. For a man to give up his right to one that never covenants to protect, is a great folly, since it is neither 'in consideration of some right reciprocally transferred to himself, nor can he hope for any other good, by standing out of the way, that the other may enjoy his own original right without hindrance from him by reason of so much diminution of impediments', page 66.

X

The liberty, saith Mr. Hobbes, whereof there is so frequent and honourable mention in the histories and philosophy of the ancient Greeks and Romans, and in the writings and discourse of those that from them have received all their learning in the politics, is not the liberty of particular men, but the liberty of the commonwealth. Whether a commonwealth be monarchical or popular, the freedom is still the same. Here I find Mr. Hobbes is much mistaken: for the liberty of the Athenians and Romans was a liberty only to be found in popular estates, and not in monarchies. This is clear by Aristotle, who calls a city a community of freemen, meaning every particular citizen to be free. Not that every particular man had a liberty to resist his governor or do what he list, but a liberty only for particular men, to govern and to be governed by turns, ἄρχειν and ἄρχεσθαι are Aristotle's words: this was a liberty not to be found in hereditary monarchies: so Tacitus mentioning the several governments of Rome, joins the consulship and liberty

to be brought in by Brutus, because by the annual election of
Consuls, particular citizens came in their course to govern and
to be governed. This may be confirmed by the complaint of our
author, which followeth: 'It is an easy thing for men to be
deceived by the specious name of liberty: and for want of
judgment to distinguish, mistake that for their private inheritance or birthright which is the right of the public only: and
when the same error is confirmed by the authority of men in
reputation for their writings on this subject, it is no wonder if it
produce sedition and change of government. In the western
parts of the world, we are made to receive our opinions
concerning the institution and right of commonwealths from
Aristotle and Cicero, and other men, Greeks and Romans, that
living under popular estates, derived those rights not from the
principles of nature, but transcribed them into their books out
of the practice of their own commonwealths, which were
popular. And because the Athenians were taught (to keep them
from desire of changing their government) that they were
freemen, and all that lived under monarchy slaves: therefore
Aristotle puts it down in his *Politics*. In democracy liberty is to
be supposed, for it is commonly held that no man is free in any
other government. So Cicero and other writers grounded their
civil doctrine on the opinions of the Romans, who were taught
to hate monarchy, at first, by them that having deposed their
sovereign, shared amongst them the sovereignty of Rome. And
by reading of these Greek and Latin authors, men from their
childhood have gotten a habit (under a false show of liberty) of
favouring tumults, and of licentious controlling the actions of
their sovereigns.'

XI

Page 102. 'Dominion paternal not attained by generation but
by contract', which is 'the child's consent, either express or by
other sufficient arguments declared'. How a child can express
consent, or by other sufficient arguments declare it before it
comes to the age of discretion I understand not, yet all men
grant it is due before consent can be given: and I take it Mr.
Hobbes is of the same mind, page 249, where he teacheth that
'Abraham's children were bound to obey what Abraham
should declare to them for God's law: which they could not be
but in virtue of the obedience they owed to their parents'; they

owed, not that they covenanted to give. Also where he saith, page 121, the 'Father and master being before the institution of commonweals absolute sovereigns in their own families', how can it be said that either children or servants were in the state of *jus naturae* till the institutions of commonweals? It is said by Mr. Hobbes in his book *De Cive*, chapter 9, section 7, 'the mother originally hath the government of her children, and from her the Father derives his right, because she brings forth and first nourisheth them'. But we know that God at the creation gave the sovereignty to the man over the woman, as being the nobler and principal agent in generation. As to the objection, that 'it is not known who is the Father to the son but by the discovery of the mother, and that he is his son whom the mother will, and therefore he is the mother's'. The answer is, that it is not at the will of the mother to make whom she will the Father, for if the mother be not in possession of a husband, the child is not reckoned to have any Father at all; but if she be in the possession of a man, the child notwithstanding whatsoever the woman discovereth to the contrary is still reputed to be his in whose possession she is. No child naturally and infallibly knows who are his true parents, yet he must obey those that in common reputation are so, otherwise the commandment of honour thy Father and thy mother were in vain, and no child bound to the obedience of it.

XII

If the government of one man, page 94, and the government of two men, make two several kinds of government, why may not the government of two, and the government of three, do the like, and make a third? and so every differing number a differing kind of commonwealth. If an assembly of all (as Mr. Hobbes saith) that will come together be a democracy, and an assembly of a part only an aristocracy, then if all that will come together be but a part only, a democracy and aristocracy are all one; and why must an assembly of part be called an aristocracy and not a merocracy?

It seems Mr. Hobbes is of the mind that there is but one kind of government, and that is monarchy, for he defines a commonwealth to be one person, and an assembly of men, or real unity of them all in one and the same person, the multitude so united he calls a commonwealth: this his moulding of a multitude into one person, is the generation of his great *Leviathan*, the King of the children of pride page 167. Thus he concludes the person of a commonwealth to be a monarch.

XIII

I cannot but wonder Master Hobbes should say, page 112, the consent of a subject to sovereign power is contained in these words, I authorize and do take upon me all his actions, in which there is no restriction at all of his own former natural liberty. Surely here Master Hobbes forgot himself, for before he makes the resignation to go in these words also, 'I give up my right of governing myself to this man': this is a restriction certainly of his own former natural liberty when he gives it away: and if a man allow his sovereign to kill him which Mr. Hobbes seems to confess, how can he reserve a right to defend himself? And if a man have a power and right to kill himself, he doth not authorize and give up his right to his sovereign, if he do not obey him when he commands him to kill himself.

XIV

Mr. Hobbes saith, page 112, 'No man is bound by the words of his submission to kill himself, or any other man: and consequently that the obligation a man may sometimes have upon the command of the sovereign to execute any dangerous or dishonourable office, dependeth not on the words of our submission, but on the intention which is to be understood by the end thereof. When therefore our refusal to obey, frustrates the end for which the sovereignty was ordained, then there is no liberty to refuse: otherwise there is.' If no man be bound by the words of his subjection to kill any other man, then a sovereign may be denied the benefit of war, and be rendered unable to defend his people, and so the end of government frustrated. If the obligation upon the commands of a sovereign to execute a dangerous or dishonourable office, dependeth not on the words of our submission, but on the intention, which is to be understood by the end thereof; no man, by Mr. Hobbes's rules, is bound but by the words of his submission, the intention of the command binds not, if the words do not: if the intention should bind, it is necessary the sovereign must discover it, and the people must dispute and judge it; which how well it may consist with the rights of sovereignty, Mr.

Hobbes may consider: whereas Master Hobbes saith the intention is to be understood by the ends, I take it he means the end by effect, for the end and the intention are one and the same thing; and if he mean the effect, the obedience must go before, and not depend on the understanding of the effect, which can never be, if the obedience do not precede it: in fine, he resolves refusal to obey, may depend upon the judging of what frustrates the end of sovereignty, and what not, of which he cannot mean any other judge but the people.

XV

Mr. Hobbes puts a case by way of question, page 112: 'A great many men together have already resisted the sovereign power unjustly, or committed some capital crime, for which every one of them expecteth death: whether have they not the liberty then to join together and assist and defend one another? Certainly they have, for they but defend their lives, which the guilty man may as well do as the innocent: there was indeed injustice in the first breach of their duty, their bearing of arms subsequent to it, though it be to maintain what they have done, is no new unjust act, and if it be only to defend their persons it is not unjust at all.' The only reason here alleged for the bearing of arms is this: that it is no new unjust act, as if the beginning only of a rebellion were an unjust act, and the continuance of it none at all: no better answer can be given to this case than what the author himself hath delivered in the beginning of the same paragraph in these words: To resist the sword of the commonwealth in defence of another man, guilty or innocent, no man hath liberty: because such liberty takes away from the sovereign the means of protecting us, and is therefore destructive of the very essence of government. Thus he first answers the question, and then afterwards makes it, and gives it a contrary answer; other passages I meet with to the like purpose. He saith, page 66, A man cannot lay down the right of resisting them that assault him by force to take away his life: the same be said of wounds, chains and imprisonment. Page 69 A covenant to defend myself from force by force is void. Page 68. Right of defending life and means of living can never be abandoned.

These last doctrines are destructive to all government whatsoever, and even to the *Leviathan* itself: hereby any rogue

or villain may murder his sovereign, if the sovereign but offer
by force to whip or lay him in the stocks, since whipping may
be said to be a wounding, and putting in the stocks an
imprisonment: so likewise every man's goods being means of
living, if a man cannot abandon them, no contract among men,
be it never so just, can be observed: thus we are at least in as
miserable a condition of war as Mr. Hobbes at first by nature
found us.

XVI

The kingdom of God signifies, saith Master Hobbes, page 216,
a kingdom constituted by the votes of the people of Israel in a
peculiar manner, wherein they choose God for their King, by
covenant made with him, upon God's promising them Canaan.
If we look upon Master Hobbes's text for this, it will be found
that the people did not constitute by votes, and choose God for
their King; but by the appointment first of God himself the
covenant was to be a God to them: they did not contract with
God, that if he would give them Canaan they would be his
subjects, and he should be their King: it was not in their power
to choose whether God should be their God, yea, or nay: for it
is confessed He reigned naturally over all by his might. If God
reigned naturally He had a kingdom, and sovereign power over
His subjects, not acquired by their own consent. This
kingdom, said to be constituted by the votes of the people of
Israel, is but the vote of Abraham only, his single voice carried
it, he was the representative of the people. For at this vote, it is
confessed, that the name of King is not given to God, nor of
kingdom to Abraham, yet the thing, if we will believe Master
Hobbes is all one. If a contract be the mutual transferring of
right, I would know what right a people can have to transfer to
God by contract. Had the people of Israel at Mount Sinai a
right not to obey God's voice? If they had not such a right,
what had they to transfer?

The covenant mentioned at Mount Sinai was but a
conditional contract, and God but a conditional King, and
though the people promised to obey God's word, yet it was
more than they were able to perform, for they often
disobeyed God's voice, which being a breach of the condition the covenant was void, and God not their King by
contract.

It is complained by God, they have rejected me that I should not reign over them: but it is not said according to their contract; for I do not find that the desiring of a King was a breach of their contract or covenant, or disobedience to the voice of God: there is no such law extant.

The people did not totally reject the Lord, but in part only, out of timorousness, when they saw Nahash King of the Children of Ammon come against them, they distrusted that God would not suddenly provide for their deliverance, as if they had had always a King in readiness to go up presently to fight for them: this despair in them who had found so many miraculous deliverances under God's government, was that which offended the Lord so highly: they did not desire an alteration of government, and to cast off God's laws, but hoped for a certainer and speedier deliverance from danger in time of war. They did not petition that they might choose their King themselves, that had been a greater sin, and yet if they had, it had not been a total rejection of God's reigning over them, as long as they desired not to depart from the worship of God their King, and from the obedience of his laws. I see not that the kingdom of God was cast off by the election of Saul, since Saul was chosen by God himself, and governed according to God's laws. The government from Abraham to Saul is nowhere called the kingdom of God, nor is it said, that the kingdom of God was cast off at the election of Saul.

Mr. Hobbes allows, that Moses alone had next under God the sovereignty over the Israelites, page 252, but he doth not allow it to Joshua, but will have it descend to Eleazar the high priest, Aaron's son. His proof is, God expressly saith concerning Joshua, he shall stand before Eleazar, who shall ask counsel for him before the Lord, (after the judgment of Urim is omitted by Mr. Hobbes) at his word they shall go out, etc., therefore the supreme power of making peace and war was in the priest.

Answer. The work of the high priest was only ministerial not magisterial; he had no power to command in war; or to judge in peace; only when the sovereign or governor did go up to war, he inquired of the Lord by the ministry of the high priest, and, as the Hebrews say, the inquirer with a soft voice as one that prayeth for himself, asked: and forthwith the Holy Ghost came upon the priest, and he beheld the breast-plate, and saw therein by the vision of prophecy, go up, or go not up, in the letters that showed forth themselves upon the breast-plate before his face: then the priest answered him, go up, or go not up. If this answer gave the priest the sovereignty, then neither King Saul nor King David had the sovereignty, who both asked counsel of the Lord by the priest.

AN EXAMINATION OF THE POLITICAL PART OF MR. HOBBS HIS *LEVIATHAN*

[George Lawson]

The Epistle to the Reader

To glorifie God, and benefit man, both by doing good, and preventing and removing evil, should be the endeavour, as its the duty, of every Christian in his station. Upon this account I have undertaken this examination of Mr. *Hobbs*: I was indeed at the first unwilling, though sollicited, to do any such thing; because upon the perusal of the Political part of his *Leviathan*, I conceived, that as little good was to be expected, so little harm was to be feared from that book. Yet after that I understood by divers learned and judicious friends, that it took much with many Gentlemen and young Students in the Universities, and that it was judged to be a rational piece, I wondered; for though I knew the distemper of the times to be great, yet by this I found it to be far greater than I formerly suspected. And upon which considerations I judged it profitable and convenient, if not necessary, to say something to the Gentleman; and did so. After that I had communicated my pains unto divers worthy and learned friends, they pressed me to give way to the Printing of them, which I did, if they after serious perusal should think them worthy the Press. They were at length approved, and again by some desired to be publick; yet by others thought too brief, and I was desired to enlarge. But this I refused to do, both because there is very little, if any thing material at all in Mr. *Hobbs* his Civil and Ecclesiastical Politicks, omitted by me and not examined; and also because I had formerly finished a Treatise of Civil and Ecclesiastical Government, which if it had not been lost by some negligence, after an *Imprimatur* was put upon it, might have prevented and made void the Political part of Mr. *Hobbs*: and though one copy be lost, yet there is another, which may become publick hereafter. When thou hast read this brief Examination, thou maist, if judicious and

impartial, easily judge, whether there be any thing in Mr.
Hobbs which is either excellent or extraordinary: and whether
there be not many things inconsistent, not only with the sacred
Scriptures, but with the rules of right reason. But not wiling to
prepossess thee, I commit thee to God, and remain,

Thine in the Lord,

Geo. Lawson.

CAP. I.

Of Mr. Hobbs *his Leviathan, concerning the Causes, Gene-*
ration, and Definition of a Common-wealth.

Civil Government derives its Being from Heaven: for it is a part
of Gods Government over mankind, wherein he useth the
Ministery of Angels, and the service of men: yet so, as that he
reserves the supreme and universal Power in his own hands,
with a liberty to depose the Rulers of the World at will and
pleasure, and transfer the Government of one Nation to
another; to lay the foundation of great Empires, and again to
destroy them for their iniquity. To think that the sole or
principal Cause of the constitution of a civil State is the consent
of men, or that it aims at no further end then peace and plenty,
is too mean a conceit of so noble an effect. And in this
particular I cannot excuse Mr. *Hobbs*, who in the modelling
both of a Civil, and also of an Ecclesiastical Common-wealth,
proceeds upon principles not only weak, but also false and
dangerous. And for this reason I undertake him. This should
have been done by some wel-skill'd in Political Learning, and
not by me who do not profess, it as being a Divine, and one of
the meanest amongst many. And my intention is not to inform
my Betters, who know the vanity and absurdity of his
discourse, but to undeceive the ignorant Reader, who may too
easily be surprized.

The first Chapter of the second Part, which is the
seventeenth of his Book, doth inform us,

First, *That the end of civil Government, is Security.*

Secondly, *This Security cannot be had in the State of Nature,*
    because it is the state of War; nor by a weak, nor a great
    multitude, except united by one perpetual judgement.

Thirdly, *A great multitude are thus united, when they conferr all their power and strength upon one man or assembly of men, that may reduce all their wils by plurality of voices to one will,* &c. *From whence ariseth a Common-wealth.*
Fourthly, *This Common-wealth is defined and distributed.*
Against all this, some thing may be excepted. For First, That the State of Nature is the State of War, may be doubted, if not denied; For man is a rational creature, and if he act according to his nature, he must act rationally: and though he may seek to preserve himself, and that sometimes with the dammage or destruction of another, yet he cannot, may not do this unjustly, but according to the Laws of Nature; which are two:

The First, *Love thy neighbour as thy self.*
The Second, *Do as thou wouldst be done unto.*

These tend directly unto Peace, not unto War, which is unnatural; and they may be kept by multitudes of men not united in a civil State, or under a form of Government. And this is evident from Divine and profane Histories. For Families and Vicinities, which had no dependance one upon another, and also States both by confederation, and without any such thing, have lived peaceably together. When the Apostle saith, *The Gentiles which have not the Law, by nature do the things contained in the Law*, he doth not mean by [Nature] a Commonwealth, or form of Government civil. Its true, the Apostle brings in a Bill of Indictment against all mankind, and accuseth them, *That their feet are swift to shed blood: Destruction and calamity or misery are in their ways; And the way of peace they have not known*, Rom. 3. 15, 16, 17. Yet he understands this not of Nature, but the corruption of Nature: and the parties here accused, are not men only as in the state of Nature, but also under a Government, and that not only Civil but Ecclesiastical too: For such the Jews here charged, were. So that all that can be either by him evidently proved, or by others granted, is, That if by Nature, he mean corruption of Nature, and the same not only original and native, but also acquired by perpetual acts, so far as to quench the light of Nature, and suppress the vigour of those Principles which God left as reliques of his image, then his Position may be true, That the state of Nature is the state of War. Secondly, That by a well-constituted civil Government, to which Nature inclines man, the Laws of Nature and Peace may be more easily and better observed.

But I hasten to his Definition of a Common-wealth, and it is thus defined by Mr. *Hobbs*.

A Common-wealth is a Person, of whose acts a great multitude by mutual Covenant one with another, have made themselves every one the Author, to the end he may use the strength and means of them all, as he shall think expedient for their peace and common defence.

G. L.

1. This Definition is obscure, and might have been made more plain and easie, and such as we read in other Authors.

2. Its imperfect, and only tels us what [*pars imperans*] is, and that most poorly, if not falsly too.

3. It may agree unto the Head of Captain of a sedition or rebellion, or a company of Thieves and Robbers by Land, or Pirats by Sea; nay but that he speaks of a society or multitude of men, it exactly agrees unto *Belzebub* the prince of Devils. In a word, it agrees to any unlawful multitude, united to do mischief; For here is no mention of reason, or justice, or law; *Aristotle*, and other Authors use to qualifie their Definition of a State, with some such term; For they make it τάξιν κατὰ νομὸν, legitimam ordinationem and do not give up all to the soveraigns judgement, which may be blinded; or his will, which may be corrupted; or his power, which may act more like a beast, then like a man.

4. A Common-wealth may be defined in another manner, thus; It is a community of men orderly subjected to a supreme power civil, that they may live peaceably in all godliness and honesty.

This Definition, or rather Description is not so accurate, yet it is sufficient to inform the Reader of the nature of civil Government somewhat better than the Author hath done. In it we may consider,

1. The community, as the Matter and Subject.
2. The supreme Power civil informing this Matter.
3. The orderly Subjection unto it for peace and a good life.

1. The community is the Matter, of which some things may be observed; as 1. That the name in Greek is [πολις] in Latine [*Civitas*] which is not as the author saith, a Common-wealth in proper sense: for that in Greek is [πολιτεία] in Latine [*Respublica.*] 2. That it is a multitude of reasonable Men, not a

Leviathan, which is an irrational Brute. The number of this multitude may be greater or less, and not certainly determinable. For *Ragusa* a little City, as well as the vast Roman Empire, may be a community to make a perfect State. 3. This community must be associated and united not only in vicinity of place, which is convenient, but also in some stricter bond, before they can be capable of a supreme Power. 4. The Members of this Society are by nature free, and by God, to whom they are subject, left at liberty to choose what Governours or form of Government they please; yet so that they must desire and endeavour the best, and such as shall be most conducing to Peace and Righteousness. 5. Sometimes it fals out, and is so ordered by Providence, that a People who have continued for a certain time under a form of Government, return unto their first liberty; yet even then, when God doth offer them an opportunity to establish the best form and constitution, that they are fearfully divided. Some are for the former Government, others idolize some new Idea framed in their own brains. Others in the mean time get the sword into their hands, and once possessed of Power, are unwilling to part with it. Yet these sometimes are dispossessed again; in the mean time the People like so many waves of the Sea, are tossed this way and that way, by contrary winds, like as in *Daniels* vision, when he saw the four winds strive upon the great Sea, out of which arose the great Empires of the world, *Dan.* 7.2,3, &c. And all this comes to pass through the just Judgement of God, and the wilful folly of men, who are enemies to their own Peace. Lastly, In these many alterations of Governours and forms of Government, the Community abides the same, except it be cut off by the sword, as the *Amalakites* and *Canaanites* were, or destroyed by some extraordinary Judgement, as *Sodom* and *Gomorrha* with fire and brimstone from heaven.

The second part of the Definition is [the Supreme Power] And here we must consider,

1. The Nature of Power ingeneral.
2. The Nature of supreme Power civil.
3. The Original of it.
4. The Subject wherein its fixed.

1. Power, in Latine [*Potestas*] in Greek [εξεσια] is [*Jus imperandi*] a quality inherent in a Superiour as such, whereby he can effectually command or bind any person subject, as subject. *Imperium* or Command is properly an act of a

superiour Will, whereby the person subject is bound to obedience or punishment: It presupposeth the Understanding and practical Judgement, whereby it is directed: and is to no purpose without an executive power and coactive force, sufficient to protect the Subject obeying, and punish him, if he prove disobedient; And because the Judgement may be erroneous, and the command unjust, therefore there can be no *Jus imperandi*, without Divine Wisdom to direct the Understanding, and Justice to regulate the Will, which is to direct the coactive force. And though Superiours may in many things abuse their Superiority, yet they do not cease to be Superiours, though as abusing their power, they are not Superiours; because *Nulla datur Potestas ad malum*; none can have power to bind contrary to Divine Wisdom and Justice.

2. Supreme Power civil, which is in Latine called [*Majestas*] which is [*maxima Potestas in Civitate*] may be defined out of *Rom.* 13. 1, 2, 3, 4, 5, &c. and I *Pet.* 2. 13. to be a Sword committed by God, unto higher Powers, for to punish the bad, and protect the good. For 1. In all Government civil there must be a sword which is an outward coactive strength and force, and the same sufficient for the end it was ordained and given by God. How otherwise can there possibly be any sufficient protection or punishment within the precints of the community and territory. And here two things are to be observed. 1. That one and the same Sword must protect from enemies without, and unjust Subjects within. For the Sword of War and Justice are but one Sword. 2. That there is a plain difference between Civil and Ecclesiastical Power, between the Sword and the Keyes. For what is bound by the civil Power on Earth, is bound and made good on earth by an earthly Sword: But what is bound on earth by the Spiritual Power is bound in heaven, and made good, and executed by Jesus Christ, and that by a Spiritual force upon a Divine Promise.

Secondly this Sword must protect the good, and punish the bad; which implies there must be wise and just Laws. 2. There must be just judgement according to these Laws. For otherwise there can be no true and certain knowledge of good and bad, for to put a difference between them, that the one may be punished for violation, the other protected for the observation of the Laws. And here again we must note, 1. That there is a threefold Power civil, or rather three degrees of that Power. The first is Legislative. The second Judicial. The third Executive. For

Legislation, Judgement, and Execution by the Sword, are the three essential acts of supreme Power civil in the administration of a State. 2. That there is no Power to punish the good and protect the bad. For the Sword must execute according to Judgment, and that must pass according to Laws: and both Judgement and Laws must be regulated by Divine Wisdom and Justice.

Thirdly, This Sword must be in the hands and possession of higher or supereminent Governors. For a Title without the possession of a Sword can neither punish nor protect: Therefore in all States of the world, they who have possession of the Sword do rule, let the Title be what it will; neither can it be otherwise. And no Prince can rule, when God hath taken away his Sword.

It hath been declared in some measure: 1. What Power in General. 2. What Power civil in Particular is. The third thing concerning this supremacy of Power to be examined, is the original of it. And the same Text of the Apostle *Paul* tels us, that it is of God; therefore in the Definition, I said, That the Sword was committed by God to higher Powers, who become such by this Commission, when God gives them possession of the Sword. So that the Original of this Power is from God, both in respect of the Power, and the persons possessed of Power. For it is he that gives Understanding, Will and Power sufficient for to govern: he gives Wisdom and Justice: he commands all Societies that have opportunity, to set up a wise and just Government for Peace and Godliness. In respect of the persons, he designs them either in an ordinary or extraordinary way; he inclines the hearts of the people to submit and obey: he prevents seditions, rebellions, treasons, and such like acts as tend to confusion and the ruin of Common-wealths, according to that of the Psalmist, *Thou hast delivered me from the strivings of the people*, Psal. 18. 43. *And it is God that subdueth the people under me*, Psal. 47. In this designation, God sometimes useth the consent, tacit or express, sometimes the force and consent of Man.

Fourthly, The Subject of this Power is either standing, or movable. The standing Subject by Nature is the community, in whom vertually it resides, and is exercised by a general representative upon extraordinary occasions, or at certain determinate times. And this is the best way to preserve liberty, if these general Assemblies be well ordered, and fit persons rightly qualified be chosen. For its dangerous to trust either one man, or a number of men with too much power, & the constant exercise of the same. This supreme power reserved to the whole community to be exercised as necessity or occasion shall require, might be called [*Realis Majestas*] yet every Community is neither so wise nor so happy. For in most States we find only a personal Majesty, or supreme Power, and the same sometimes Despotical, and too absolute; yet in other Common-wealths, the supreme Governours are limited, and only trusted with the exercise of the power according to certain Rules and fundamental Laws.

Of this Majesty or supreme Power, civil, some Writers have observed, that it must be not only supreme, but also perpetual and above Laws; [*Soluta Legibus*] That it must be supreme, and above all subordinate power within, and independent upon all other soveraigns without its necessary. It must be also perpetual and fixed, that it may be distinguished from the extraordinary and temporary powers trusted in the hands of one or more upon extraordinary occasions. How far it is absolute or above the Laws, I shall examine hereafter.

After the supreme Power civil is determined and fixed in a certain Subject, Subjection to it follows, which is the third thing in the Definition. *Regimen est ordo Imperii & subjectionis.* For in all Government, some must be above and have power to command; some must be below, and be bound to obey. And in a civil State there must be one universal supreme, to which all others in the Community must subject themselves. This Subjection must be rational, free, and orderly, or else the State cannot continue long, nor be well administred. And wisom must determine not only the general order of superiour and inferiour, but also in particular the Community must be divided into parts with a co-ordination of equals and subordination of the unequals, and of every several part unto the whole, that so every one may know his place and rank, that he may keep it. Therefore the Apostle commands every soul, *Rom.* 13. 1 ψωοταάτεως. not barely to be subject any ways but in a certain order, for the Community must be like an Army put in array, that so the supreme Power may the better animate and order it: upon which followeth a more regular motion of this great body both in the whole and every part, tending the more directly to Peace, Godliness and Honesty.

For there is a twofold end of regular civil Government; The first is Peace; The second is Godliness and Honesty, to which

Peace is subordinate. For the Apostle exhorts us *to pray for Kings, and all that are in authority, that we may lead a quiet and peaceable life in all Godliness and Honesty*: 1 Tim. 2. 1. Government is for Peace, Peace for Godliness, and the performance of our duty towards God, and Honesty: That we may live soberly and justly toward men. When God doth bless a people with a setled Government and an happy peace, (for these are Gods blessings) neither Prince nor people must forget their God, or live in Luxury, and deal unjustly one with another. For these things offend him, provoke him to anger, and pull down his Judgements upon them. He expects Piety and Honesty from every one, even from the highest to the lowest. And these earthly States are erected, and subordinated to an higher end then peace and plenty here on earth: they should be so ordered as to prepare men for eternity: otherwise *Regna* are but *latrocinia*, a den of thieves, and a combination of devils. Thus much I thought good to deliver concerning the Nature of a Common-wealth civil. The Distribution followeth.

Mr. Hobbs.

A Common-wealth is either by instutiton or acquisition.

G. L.

This is not the distribution of a Common-wealth either into the integral parts, which are two, 1. The soveraign 2. The subject: not into the kinds: for those are usually taken from the several manners of disposing the supreme power in one or more to make it Monarchical or Polycratical; but its a distinction of the manner of acquiring supreme power. And the ordinary way, or rather means whereby it is acquired, is either by force or consent. Yet this distinction is imperfect: for there be other means besides these: neither when supreme power is obtained either by force or consent, is a Common-wealth framed. The Power is always derived from God, as before: and he takes it from one, and gives to another, either in an extraordinary or an ordinary way of Providence: as by giving a finall victory, or inclining mens hearts, and that upon several reasons to submit, and sometimes so, that if they had liberty and power, they would not consent at all. And though men may be unjust in desiring and seeking, yet he is just in giving it. And by the way its to be observed, 1. That a Power acquired, and held by force, cannot govern without a tacit consent at least, so that all Common-wealths are by consent. 2. No man or men can govern any people long by force, except it be the Will of God to punish and oppress them with an iron rod for their transgressions.

CAP. II

Of the Second Part, and the Eighteenth of the Book: Of the Rights of Soveraigns by Institution.

This Chapter informs us, what the rights of Soveraigns once constituted are. In every Common-wealth there must be a supreme Power fixed in some certain Subject; this is essential to it: yet though this be a principal thing to be done, yet it is not all, neither being done, doth it make a compleat Common-wealth. His Covenant of every one with every one for to design a Soveraign, is but an Utopian fancy. For by the best Histories we may understand that many States have attained to a setled form of Regular Government by degrees in a long tract of time, and that by several alterations intervening; so that the Laws of their constitution are rather customs then any written Charter. Some Communities come under a form of Govermnent more suddenly, and by a way fortuitous unto man, though not so to God. And in this point the practise of former times, not the fancies and speculations of men must instruct us.

T. H.

The first of the twelve Rights of the Soveraign, is, That Subjects cannot change the form of Government.

G. L.

That Community which hath Power and Liberty to alter the form of Government to the better, do not their duty, or are not wise, if they do it not. And it were wisdom in any people to reserve the Power to the whole body, to be used as occasion, opportunity and necessity shall require. As they are bound to reform the State when it is corrupted, so they are bound to alter the form, when without an alteration reformation cannot be obtained.

That the Subjects have no power to alter the form of
Government may be granted: for Subjects as Subjects, must
submit unto the Power established, not take upon them the
highest and most transcendent Prerogative of all others: yet this
is no right of the Soveraign, nor to be reckoned *inter Jura
Majestatis*. For the Soveraign himself hath no right of himself
to change the fundamental constitution: Before this can be
done, the People must return unto the original State of Liberty,
and to a Community, which in *England* is not a Parliament,
but the fourty Counties. Upon this ground some have said that
a Parliament cannot alter the Govermment; what men may do
upon a Dissolution, and in a case of real, not pretended
necessity, is another matter. But let us hear his reasons.

T. H.

*The first upon supposition of no former Obligation, is, That it
is a breach of that Covenant whereby they made themselves
authours of every act the soveraign doth, or shall judge fit to be
done.*

*2. If they depose the Soveraign, that which is his own, and
they had formerly given him, they take away unjustly.*

*3. If any attempting to depose his Soveraign, be killed or
punished, he is Author of his own punishment.*

*4. A new Covenant pretended to be made with God, cannot
free them from offence and injustice in their disobedience unto
their Soveraign; because they can make no Covenant with God,
without his Lieutenant, which is the Prince.*

G. L.

1. I grant as formerly, that a Subject as such, cannot act to
change the Government, or depose his lawful Soveraign.
2. They who set up a Soveraign, and by Covenant advance
him to the Throne, must and ought to be free from all former
superiour obligations, which cannot stand with this. But what
is this to purpose? The question is, whether Subjects cannot
change the form of Government in any case, and whether the
Subjects may not be freed, and that lawfully from their
allegiance, and cease to be in the State of Subjects? That it
many times fals out so to be, is evident: For by civil wars, by
forraign invasions, transmigrations, and other wayes it comes
to pass, that Subjects are free from their Soveraigns, who

cannot protect them; and in such cases, if God give them Power, they may alter the form of Government, if it may be for the best.

But to come more close unto his first reason, let us suppose as he affirmeth, That a people by Covenant have set up a particular person to be a Monarch, and so made themselves authors of all his acts, whether it is lawful for you by a new Covenant to obey another, or cast off Monarchy, or transfer his person upon another without injustice? He saith ye cannot without breach of Covenant do it.

But 1. He here presupposeth his former Utopian fancy of a Covenant of every man with every man; whereas its plain, few States of the world now in power, were thus constituted. 2. Soveraigns are of two sorts; 1. Such as in whom the supreme power doth constantly and immediately abide. 2. Such as are such only for execution and administration. To these latter, the subjects bind themselves to be faithful, so far as they shall be faithful to the Kingdom and the Crown, which is theirs, not [*jure dominii*] by absolute right, with a power to alienate them, or destroy them. For every subject is first bound to be faithful to their Countrey, then unto their King, who swears to maintain the Laws, Liberty and Religion by Law established. These cannot bind us to do any thing against the Laws of God, of Nature, nor against our Countrey. But with this Author every Monarch is absolute, and in particular the Kings of *England* amongst the rest. 3. Suppose a Covenant with a Soveraign, absolute or limited, be against the Laws of God either moral or positive in force, may not the subjects break this Covenant without injustice? Nay is it not injustice for to keep it, seeing [*Nullum juramentum ligas ad illicitum.*] 4. If the Soveraigns Acts be directly contrary to justice, equity, and the fear of God, must the subjects who gave him no such power, be authors of these horrid acts, as murther, incest, adultery, blasphemy, as also of his unjust commands and perverse judgements? 5. To be obedient to another, to transfer his power, to depose him, is not to change the form of government, but to pull down one, and set up another, the form remaining the same. 6. Subjects or rather they who are subjects, as subjects, cannot make any such Covenant, as to make one who was no Soveraign to be their Soveraign; If they can make a Soveraign, they must be equal, and equally free in making that Covenant whereby a supreme Governour is constituted. 7. If they, who were [*æquè liberi*]

before, and in the time of making this Covenant, and after it is
concluded, become subjects, afterwards rebel, they cease to be
subjects, and become [*hostes*] enemies, and are so to be dealt
withall: And what reason can be given why the Soveraign, if he
prove a Tyrant in the administration, and challenge more
power then was given him, or could by the Laws of God or
Nature be conferred upon him, should not cease to be a
Soveraign, and the subjects free from their allegiance to him,
seeing he hath violated the essential part of the Covenant, and
perverted the main end of all Government? Why should it be
othewise in this then in all other pacts and contracts? The
question is the more difficult to be answered by this Author,
because he allows the people a power to make a Soveraign: and
if he be such as is one onely for administration, its unanswerable. This point might have been more clearly determined, if he
had instanced in any particulars.

   In all this I desire to be understood aright. For, 1. That
power which the Bishop of *Rome* doth challenge, and hath
sometimes exercised in the excommunication and deposition of
Princes, and absolving their subjects from allegiance, I detest.
2. I desire all Covenants, that are just and justly made, whilest
they are in force, to be kept, especially by all subjects to their
lawful Soveraigns. For no subjects are to be perswaded or
encouraged to Treason or Rebellion. 3. I would advise all
people to beware how they rise against, or resist the highest
powers, though the cause may be just: and because the remedy
may prove worse then the disease, and often proves so: and the
confusions which follow such commotions, are more mischievous then the former oppressions, and a Tyrannie is better
then an Anarchy.

   His second reason is, because they had given him the right of
Soveraignty, which they cannot take away. Where, 1. He
grants, That the people give the Soveraign his right; and if so,
then they gave it him not as subjects; and when they return to
the same occasion again, they may give the power to another.
2. I deny that subjects do give any such right. 3. Neither can he
prove that there is any such Covenant of every man with every
man in the constitution of civil States. His third reason is not
worth an answer.

   But in the end of this paragraph, he seems to take away the
pretence and allegation of some new Covenanters with God.
What Covenant he means, is not here expressed: If he

understand the National Covenant, as its very likely he doth, then let those who pretend it answer for themselves. For that Covenant could not give the least power either to *England*, or *Scotland*, or any in either Nation, entering into it: and in the same they only engaged to use lawful means, to accomplish what they had promised. Yet with him this and all other Covenants are void, if made with God without his Vicegerent, who is their Soveraign. Yet if this were true, then the Covenant made in Baptism, by the converted Christians or under the heathen Emperours cannot be valid. This is evidently false, because every man may voluntarily bind himself to God in those things wherein the Laws of God and man have left him free, without the consent or express permission of his civil Soveraign.

T. H.

The second right of a Soveraign is, he cannot forfeit; the reasons are,

   1. There is no Covenant made on his part either with them all joyntly or severally: not with them joyntly, because they cannot be one person before they subject unto him: Not with them severally, for they Covenant one with another, not with him, and if any one pretend freedom from subjection, there can be no judge of the controversie.

   2. Words, as all Covenants are, be of no force without a sword publick.

G. L.

This is the substance, though not all the words to prove that Soveraigns cannot forfeit. His 1. Reason takes that for granted, which is false, and cannot be proved. For a community is one person moral by fiction of Law, as they use to speak, or as the Civilians express themselves [*persona conjuncta*] opposed to [*singularis*]. For a community is the immediate subject of a Common-wealth, and must be associate before they can be capable of a form of Government; and without union and communion too, it cannot be *civitas, societas, populus*. As thus united, it may act and covenant by their Deputies, who may be many, or by a Deputy, which may be one: and here they may in the name of the whole, Covenant with the person whom they like for Soveraign, and upon conditions just and reasonable.

Thus *Israel*, a meer community, makes *Moses* their Deputy and Mediator, to Covenant with God in their behalf. Thus the ten Tribes by some of their principal men capitulate with *Jeroboam*. Thus the *Gileadites* by their Messengers offer to contract with *Jephtah*, and some of the Tribes make the same offer unto *Gideon*. Thus a free people may invest one man or more either with original power, or trust him and them only with the administration. And they may put conditions upon them, either to give them an unlimited or limited power, as the wisest men amongst them shall think fit. And there is great reason so to do: For, 1, They are free. 2. He with whom they purpose to contract, hath no right to command them, no power over them before he be made Soveraign: He is but a private person, and they are mad men if they will subject themselves upon unreasonable conditions: They are very unwise, who will make a Butcher their Shepherd, or set a Woolf over their Flocks. And surely its no point of wisdom in any free-people, to trust any one man, or assembly of men, with an absolute unlimited power. If an enemy come in by conquest, they must be content with what conditions he pleaseth, not with such as they desire. For they are not free, because their estates, liberty, lives are in his power; As for the Covenant of every one with every one, its a meer *Chimera*: there was never any such thing, neither can he give any instance of it, and therefore all that he builds upon it must needs fall.

As for his second reason, wherein he affirms Covenants to be but words, and words are but breath and of no force, without a publike sword, its no waies tolerable. By these words he may be proved to be an Atheist, whatsoever he pretends, and to deny the immortality of the soul, all Religion and fear of the Deity, and his providence over the world, and I should be very unwilling to trust his promise upon oath, for any thing I could not recover by Law. The principal force of a Covenant depends upon the will and consent of the immortal soul, which fears a Deity, and believes a supreme Judge of the world, who will render to every man according to their works; yet because Covenants are but words and breath, therefore he inferrs.

T. H.

That a Soveraign cannot be made or receive his power by Covenant or upon condition, for so to think is ignorance.

G. L.

Its true, that we are ignorant fools, if we think, when a Monarch is made such upon condition to which he is sworn, that he will part with his power, though he hath forfeited his right unto it: if he have a long sword, and a broad conscience, he will be possessor as long as he can. And by this passage he seems to affirm, that few Monarchs have any conscience or fear of God: For though they lose their right, yet they will not part with their possession, though their own conscience, Laws of God, and the dictates of nature perswade them to keep their Covenants, and not violate their Oaths. In a word, though Soveraigns be made by Covenant and Oath, yet the Obligation is in vain, because the people cannot force them to the observation thereof: for they have parted with their power, and delivered the sword unto their Governors; Yet they never gave them the sword to maintain their injustice, but to protect the just and punish the unjust. Yet in a popular State this seems to be clear; That the Soveraign cannot be made upon condition; for thus he writes,

T. H.

No man is so dull as to say, for example, The people of Rome *made a Covenant with the* Romans *to hold the Soveraignty on such or such conditions, which not performed, the* Romans *might lawfully depose the* Roman *people. That men see not the reason to be alike in a Monarchy and a Popular Government, proceedeth from the ambition of some,* &c.

G. L.

Men are not so dull as to believe that the reason of not forfeiting the supreme power is alike in a Monarchy and a Popular State; For we know that in such a Common-wealth, the Community and the Soveraign are the same, though in some respect different; but in a Monarchy or Aristocraty its far otherwise. In the State of *Rome*, after that *Tarquin* was deposed, and that Government reduced unto a Republick, every one severally, though never so great, was a subject: and all joyntly was their Soveraign: for in that form [*singuli subduntur universis, & universi præsunt singulis*] yet the universality of the people, as a Community, could not act and exercise the Soveraignty, and therefore Consuls and other Officers were trusted with great power, but not with the supreme: and these might forfeit and be deposed by the people. In all States we must distinguish between the constitution and the administration, or as others use to express themselves [*Inter Statum & exercitium.*] They who are trusted only with the administration, as such, are not supreme, though they will endeavour to usurp and possess that power. Therefore the Author either is very ignorant, or else goes about to delude his ignorant Reader.

The question therefore is, whether a Soveraign may forfeit? That he cannot, is not at all, by so much as a probable argument yet evinced. 1. That he may forfeit unto God there is no doubt. 2. That if any forfeit, God will in his due time take the forfeit, pass Judgement upon the party forfeiting, and execute the same, either by himself, or by Angels, or by forrein forces, or by civil wars, or some other way; and in all this God is just, though men may be unjust. 3. Monarchs and Princes only trusted with the power of Execution and Administration, may forfeit, and justly be restrained, or reduced, or deposed. 4. Absolute Princes may forfeit their right unto the Soveraignty, when they pervert all Laws of God and man, oppress, murther, raise war unjustly against their own subjects, to butcher them as so many wild beasts, violate their Oaths and Covenants without any fear of God or man. For such, as such, are *hostes humani generis*, rebels against God, and agents for the Devil. All powers are ordained of God, and from him they receive Commission to protect their subjects, not destroy them, and to punish the bad, not to protect them and advance them, and use them for the destruction of the good. If any man dare plead for these, let him; I dare not. 5. If the Author had stated the question, and informed us of the several titles of Soveraigns, which are many, or had instanced in particulars, and informed us of their particular titles, it had been easie to determine the controversie; Princes acquire their power many waies, as by Election, Succession, Marriage, the Sword, and by that, either justly, or unjustly, usurping the power which is not due; and that out of revenge, or covetousness, or ambition, with a desire to be great, not do good. The question is not, whether a Soveraign according to the Apostles definition, *Rom.* 13. can forfeit to his subjects, as his subjects; for so he cannot do: but it is this, whether a Soveraign may not cease to be a Soveraign, and the subjects cease to be his subjects: and to this the Author hath said nothing.

T. H.

No man can without injustice protest against the institution of the Soveraign, declared by the major part.

G. L.

1. There are very few Soveraigns thus instituted; and if this be the only way, what title have the greatest part of Soveraigns in the world? 2. If they be not thus instituted, whether is it lawful to protest against them or no? of this the Author saith nothing. 3. Suppose the major part be a faction, and institute one of their own party Soveraign, not for publick good so much as for private interest, whether may not the dissenters protest? 4. In all Assemblies and Societies, which proceed by way of suffrage, the major part concludes and determines for the whole, to avoid confusion and dissention, and to preserve unity and order. Yet so that the major part may err; because they are not infallible: and one good reason being evident, should prevail against ten millions of votes; We find that most men in their suffrages, follow the example of some eminent person or persons, or their own affection; few are determined by reason. And in doubtful matters, men should first debate and throughly examine the thing debated, before they proceed to give their voices; and this is most properly and conveninently done, when after a diligent search, no preponderant reason can be found for either part of the proposition: Mens votes are inferiour to reason and superiour Laws, and are not good because votes, but because agreeable to reason. And whereas he alledgeth two reasons, 1. That to protest against a major part is injustice. 2. It puts the party protesting out of protection; the answer is easie: 1. That a protestation is not unjust, because it is against the major part, except it be against reason and right; and no man will be so mad as to assent unto a major against reason, which is above all votes. 2. Its true, that the party protesting puts himself out of the protection of that Soveraign against whom he protests; but this may be a misery, but no injustice.

T. H.

The Soveraigns actions cannot be accused of injustice by the subject; because he hath made himself Author of all his actions: And no man can do injustice to himself. The Soveraign may do iniquity, but not injustice.

G. L.

1. The Soveraigns actions are to punish the evil and protect the good: as a Soveraign, he can do no other actions, and these cannot be justly accused. 2. Neither can the consent of the people, nor doth a Commission of God give him any power to act contrary to these. 3. When he acts unjustly, (for so he may do, and all iniquity is injustice) neither God nor the people are authors of such actions; for he was set up by them to do justly, and no waies else. 4. Civil justice and injustice, as they consist in formalities, differ much from moral and essential justice and injustice. In this respect a Prince may be civilly just and morally unjust. 5. To accuse may be judicial, or *extra*-judicial. Judically, a Prince as a Prince, cannot be accused by his subject, as such. Yet the subject may represent unto his soveraign his faults, and by way of humble petition, desire them to be reformed.

T. H.

Whatsoever the Soveraign doth is unpunishable by the subject: because if the subject punish him, he punisheth another for his own actions.

G. L.

1. A Soveraign as a Soveraign, cannot be punished by his subject as his subject. 2. Yet he that is supreme only for administration, may be punished and put to death. Thus the *Ephori* might punish the *Lacedæmonian* Kings, and the Justice of *Arragon* the Kings of that Kingdom. 3. Absolute Princes may cease to be such, and then they differ not from other men. And it will be an hard task to prove that any consent of man or humane title, can free one from punishment with death, who is guilty of a crime which God hath determined to be capital, and commanded to be punished with death. 4. Why should it be lawful for a forrein Prince, warring and proving victorious

upon a just quarrel, to put a wicked Prince to death: and not for those who have been his subjects, when they have power to do it, and tends to the publick good, which cannot possibly without this act of justice, be preserved? Yet this cannot warrant any cursed Rebels, or Traytors, or the like, to murther Princes: though their pretences may be coloured with piety and justice.

The *jura Majestatis*, or rights of higher-powers following are truly such. Two things only I take notice of, 1. That the Prince is only Judge of Doctrines taught, so far as either the matter of right, or manner of teaching may be prejudicial to the State, or beneficial to the same: as the Doctrine of the Gospel wisely taught, alwaies is a blessing. 2. Whereas he affirms that there is no propriety before a form of Government be established, its evidently false; and civil Laws determine how every man may keep or recover that which is by justice his own. According to his rules, the institution of a Soveraign takes away all propriety of the subject.

That the rights of Soveraigns are indivisible and incommunicable, is true, if rightly understood. To this purpose Authors distinguish these royalties into the greater and the less, and say, the latter may, the former cannot be divided or communicated. Others affirm, That in a mixt State, they of necessity must; in a pure State, they must not be either divisible, or communicable. This point may be made more clear, if we understand, 1. That these rights or *jura*, are but so many branches of one and the same power supreme civil, as it may act upon several objects. And all these branches are reducible to three; For supreme power civilis, Legislative, Judicial, Executive, as before; and because it extends to these three acts, therefore it may be said to be threefold. And all these rights reckoned up by him, which are such indeed, are contained under these three, though neither he nor other Authors have much observed it. Amongst these the Legislative is the principal, not only the first but the chiefest, yet the other are necessary, because without them its in vain; for what are Laws without Judgement and Execution? yet even the Laws regulate both. And to know who are Soveraign in any act, the only infallible way is by the Legislation. For in whomsoever the Legislative power originally is, he or they are supreme; for it is not the actual making of certain rules to order all things in a State, but the giving of a binding force unto them, which makes the Soveraign.

This power, not only as it is a power, but as supreme, cannot be divided. For if you take any essential part from it, you destroy it, so that its indivisible in it self. 2. In respect of the subject: For whether the subject be the Community, or the Optimates, they must be considered as one person morally, though they be many physically: and the reason is, they must go all together, otherwise there can be no first mover in a State; for it is one supreme power in it self, and must also be in one subject: yet for the administration it may be divided: because the Soveraign doth exercise this power, and acts severally by several Officers, which are but instruments animated and acted by him. This power is also incommunicable within one and the same community and territory, except you will constitute more States then one.

T. H. pag. 93.

If there had not first been an opinion received of the greatest part of England, that these powers were divided between the King, and the Lords and the Commons, the people had never been devided, and fallen into these civil wars.

G. L.

The cause moral of these wars, was our sins: the Political cause was the male-administration; yet so, that all sides have offended through want of wisdom, and many other waies. The ignorance of Politicks in general, and of our own constitution in particular, cannot be excused or excepted; What the ancient constitution was, we know not certainly, though some reliques of the same continued till our times: but the whole frame was strangely altered and corrupted. Many different opinions there be concerning our Government; yet three amongst the rest are most remarkable: For one party conceives the King to be an absolute Monarch: A second determines, the King, Peers, and Commons to be three co-ordinate powers, yet so that some of them grant three Negatives, some only two: A third party give distinct rights unto these three: yet in this they are sub-divided, and they would be thought to be more rational, who give the Legislative Power unto the Lords and Commons in one house; the judicial, to the Lords in a distinct house, and the executive to the King, who was therefore trusted with the Sword both of War and Justice: None of these can give satisfaction. There is another opinion, which puts the supreme power radically in the 40 Counties, to be exercised by King, Peers and Commons, according to certain rules, which by Antiquaries in Law, together with some experienced States-men of this Nation, might be found out, but are not. The seeds of this division were sown and begun to appear before the wars; and the opinion, that all these were only in one man, that is the King absolutely, some say, was the greatest cause, not only of the last, but also of other civil wars in former times: And it hath been observed, that every man liked that opinion best, which was most suitable to his own interest. Our several opinions in Religion have heightened our differences, and hindered our settlement; yet Religion is but pretended; for every party aims at civil power, not spiritual liberty from sin. And the power to settle us thus wofully distracted, is only in God; and if he ever will be thus merciful unto us, the way whereby he will effect it, will be by giving the greatest power to men of greatest wisdom and integrity, not by reducing us unto one opinion, that all the powers civil must be in one, as the Author doth fondly fancy: Let the form be the best in the world, yet without good Governors its in vain.

The subject of this Chapter is [*Majestas*] [*& jura Majestatis*] the Rights of Soveraigns, which this Author hath handled very poorly; and if he had but translated that which others had more excellently written in this particular before him, he might have informed us better, given his Reader more satisfaction, reduced them to a better method, and neither have made such to be Rights which are none, nor omitted those which truly are such, as he hath done.

CAP. III.

Of the Second part, and the Nineteenth of the Book, of the several kinds of Common-wealths by institution, and of succession to the Soveraign power.

By these brief contents it appears, that the subject of this Chapter is the distinction of Common-wealths, and Succession to the Soveraign power, in a successive State. In the first part, he 1. Reduceth all Common-wealths to three kinds. 2. Prefers Monarchy, one of them, before all the rest.

T. H.

Other kind of Common-wealths besides Monarchy, Democracy, Aristocracy, there cannot be.

G. L.

This is conceived to be a distribution into species or kinds; yet if we throughly examine it, it is not so; for its but an accidential difference: For it ariseth only from the distinct and different manner of disposing the supreme power, in one or more. In more, and these are the [Optimates] some of the best and most eminent, or in the whole Community. Yet in all these the essential acts of Government (and so the Soveraign power) are the same in all States: and they are, as you heard before three, Legislation, Judgement and Execution; for its meerly accidental to the supremacy to be disposed more or more. That it must be disposed in some certain such sect is necessary; and that as the Supremacy is one and indivisible, so the subject must be one also, and that either physically or morally: The great variety of Common-wealths, which is such, that there be not two in the whole world in all things like, ariseth not from the constitution, but from the different manner of administration: Though the Author denies all mixt Common-wealths; yet wise and learned men, which without disparagement to him, may be preferred before him, as in other things, so in State-learning, have said, 1. That there is no pure Monarchy, or Aristocracy, or Democracy in the world. 2. That not only some, but all Common-wealths are in some measure mixt or tempered and allayed, because they conceive its hardly possible for any pure State to continue long. Against these I find in Mr. *Hobbs* a verbal contradiction, but no real confutation. And it seems to me he never truly understood them, neither hath he taken notice of the difference between Real and Personal Majesty; or of the Natural or Ethical subject of Supremacy, or of the exercise thereof by certain persons, and the constant inherency of it in a certain subject. And we know by experience, that such as are only trusted with the exercise of supreme power, will by little and little usurp it, and in the end plead prescription. So *Lewis* the II. of *France*, when he violated the Laws of the constitution, removed all such as by right ought to have poysed him, could boast, That he had freed the Crown from Wardship. And this hath been the practice of the Princes of

Europe, which in the end will prove their ruine, as for the present it hath been their trouble. There is no Common-wealth, but may be reduced to one of these three, in some respect; yet so, that Monarchies differ as much from one another, as they differ from the other two. Some are regal, some despotical; and there be several sorts of these. But I do not intend at this time to contest with him about this distribution, but proceed.

T. H.

Tyrannie and Oligarchy are but different names of Monarchy and Aristocracy, not different forms of Governments.

G. L.

These names do not signifie *Chimera's*, but real Entities; and if any have abused them to signifie forms of Government, let them answer for themselves; I know them not, they cannot be men of any note; Tyrannie doth not signifie Monarchy, nor Oligarchy an Aristocracy. They signifie the vicious corruption of States degenerate from their original constitution, and that by the wickedness of a Prince, and the faction of an assembly ingrossing power, and enhancing it above that which is due and just, and so become a multitude of Tyrants; and this hath been the cause, why many Nations, when they had power in their own hands, have altered the form of Government, been jealous of trusting one man or assembly of men long with too much power, and the wisest have set their wits on the rack, to find out a way, how to limit and restrain the power of their Governors.

T. H.

Subordinate Representatives are dangerous: And I know not how that so manifest a truth should of late be so little observed, that in a Monarchy, he that had the Soveraignty from a descent of 600 years, was alone called Soveraign, had the title of Majesty from every one of his subjects, and was unquestion-ably taken by them for their King, was notwithstanding never considered as their Representative: that name without con-tradiction, passing for the title of those men, which at his command, were sent up by the people to carry their petitions, and give him (if he permitted) their advice.

G. L.

This man deserves to be a perpetual slave; his intention is to make men believe, that the Kings of *England* were absolute Monarchs, their subjects slaves, without propriety of goods, or liberty of person, the Parliaments of *England* meerly nothing but shadows, and the members thereof but so many carriers of letters and petitions between home and the Court; What he means by subordinate Representatives, I know not; I think his intention is to oppose those, who affirmed King, Peers, and Commons to be co-ordinate, not subordinate powers, and all of them joyntly to make up one supreme; Subordinate Representatives or powers he may safely and must grant in all States. The word Representative, he either doth not understand, or if he do, he intolerably abuseth his unwary and unlearned Reader by that term. A Representative in the Civil Law, called τοποτηρητης, is one who by his presence supplies the place of another that is absent, for some certain end, as to act that which another should do, but in his own person doth not, yet with the consent of the person represented, so far as that the thing is judged to be done by him. And in this sense, the person representing, is Judged to be one with the person represented by fiction of Law. And one may represent another as a Superior, who may represent another in any act, so far as that other is in his power: or as an inferiour, by a power derived from his superiour; or as an equal by consent, so far as the person represented is willing, and the person representing will undertake to act for him. In all these representations, the *Representee* and the Representer are judged one person. In a free-State, a Parliament is a Representative of the whole body of the people; this we call a general Representative. The reason of this representation is, because the whole body of a people cannot well act personally. What kind of Representative the Parliament of *England* was, is hard to know, except we knew certainly the first institution, which, by tract of time, and many abuses of that excellent Assembly, is now unknown. It was certainly trusted with the highest acts of Legislation, Judgement, Execution. The whole body consisted of several orders and ranks of men, as of King, Peers, Commons, the Clergy. Whether they might meddle with the constitution or no, is not so clear; its conceived they could not alter it, though they might declare it what it was. Their power was great without all doubt, yet not so great, but that it was bounded, and a later Parliament might alter and reform what a former had established, which argues, That the 40. Counties, and the whole body of the people whence all Parliaments have their original and being, as they are Parliaments, were above them. In this great assembly, the Knights and Burgesses did represent the Counties and the Burroughs; the Convocation, the whole body of the Clergy; the Peers, by antient tenure, their Families, Vassals, and Dependants. But whom the King should represent is hard to determine. If the Law did consider him as an infant, and this according to the constitution, he could represent no other person or persons. And if this be so, then there is plain reason why he never should have the title of Representative; yet evident reason there is, why the rest should be called a Representative: and the people are not Representers, as he fondly imagines, but the persons represented.

It is affirmed by the Author,

1. *That our Government is a Monarchy.*
2. *The King had the Soveraignty from a descent of 600. years.*
3. *Was alone called Soveraign.*
4. *Had the title of Majesty from every one of his Subjects.*
5. *Was unquestionably taken by them for their King.*

1. Our Government is called a Monarchy] is true, and he himself is this Chapter confesseth that Elective limited Kings are called Monarchs, and their Kingdoms Monarchies, yet he saith, they are not so. Again, Monarchy is Regal over free-men, Despotical over slaves and servants, not by a Legal but an Arbitrary power. If he say its Regal, then the King is no absolute Monarch as he would have him to be. If he say its Despotical, its false, and we know it so to be false. And the Doctrine of Dr. *Sibthorp*, and *Mannering*, or *Martin*, affirming this, was condemned by a whole Parliament, and that by men who have been as great Zealots of the King in these civil wars as any other.

2. The King of *England* had Soveraignty by a descent of 600. years;] But first, what doth he mean by Soveraignty? If he understand an absolute supreme power, its not true: the Kings of *England* have no such thing. Its true, that many of them did challenge so much power as they could acquire and keep; and as their sword was longer or shorter, so their power in possession was more or less. Yet by the constitution of Law,

and the best custom, it was alwaies determined within certain bounds. Secondly, Whence will he commence the date of 600. years? and how will he derive the Soveraignty? If from the Conqueror, the date of so many years is not yet expired, & the Succession is interrupted, if not cut off by the sword upon a civil war. If he derive this power from the Conqueror as Conqueror; all free English men will deny it; the Kings themselves durst not challenge it upon those terms, and by consent they never had it. Therefore the Soveraignty, the time of the commencement, the title it self doth vanish. He saith something, proves nothing; that he was called Soveraign, doth neither prove that he was really such, nor that he was absolute, and that by his own confession.

3. The King had the title of Majesty from every one of his subjects.] The title or name doth not prove the thing: for we know very well, that the title is constantly given to divers Princes who have not the thing, no more then our Kings had the Kingdom of *France*, though they had the title of the Kings of *France*: *France* was so civil as to grant the title and the word, but never part with the thing. The Dukes of *Venice* (as *Contarene* tells us) had *insignia sed potestatem regis*. *Majestas* is sometimes *maxima dignitas*, and this no subject denyed to the King. He had his Scepter and his Throne, his Robe and Diadem; but all these are far short of supreme power: *Majestas* is *Personalis aut Realis*. Real he had not, Personal he might have. Yet personal Majesty might be his either in respect of dignity, as it was, or in respect of power; and that also two waies; either in respect of the whole power, and all the acts thereof; or 2. in respect of the executive only, so far as that all Commissions, Judgements, Executions determined by Law, should run in his name, as they did. I remember I have read in the *Mirrour* something to this purpose, That in the first constitution of this Government of *England*, in the time of the *Saxons*, the 40. Counts, of the 40. Shires or Counties set up a King above them, so that he had neither any one his Superiour, nor his Peer; Yet *ex obligatione criminis*, by his mis-government the 40. Counts, joyntly together might judge him, whether in their own names, or the name of the 40. Counties, may be a question. And in this sense I believe is to be understood that saying, *Rex singulis major, universis minor.* Let these things be so or no, (for they are out of my sphere) its certain the Kings of *England* had the title of Majesty, yet thats

no argument at all that he was invested with the supreme and universal power.

4. He was unquestionably taken by them for their King.] I grant he both was so taken, and was so truly and indeed. And when our Kings were such as were more tender of the peoples good, then their own greatness, and also governed by the direction of a wise and faithful Council, they found them the most loving and loyal subjects of any in the world. For the English alwaies desired to be governed as men, not as Asses. And this is the quality of all understanding people of other Nations. Some are not capable either of a mild, or moderate power.

Eminent Authors who take upon them to know Law and the power of Kings, have said, 1. That the King of *England* may be judged, so *Horn*. 2. That he is in Law considered as *Infans minorennis*, as a pupil alwaies in nonage; and as his Courts and Officers can do nothing but in his name, so he can do nothing but by their heads and hands, and he cannot take away the formalities of judicial proceedings, nor by all his power revoke or make null the Judgement of any Court. So several Authors. 3. He hath not *Regiam potestatem, sed politicam à populo effluxam*; so *Fortescue* the great Chancellor. 4. That he was a King by Law, not above Law, and could not exercise any power but according to Law. 5. He was sworn *corroborare leges, quas vulgus eligeret*: where *vulgus*, is *populus*, and *populus eligit leges*; and as the Law-giver, so his Oath. 6. No King made a Law without a Parliament, nor could justly impose a Subsidy upon the people without a Parliament. These two things forreign writers could observe. 7. By the manner of their Coronation, which was turned to a Formality, he derived not his power from the first investiture, as some tell us, the princes of *Germany* and the Kings of *France* do; nor from his immediate predecessor, but by Election; and this is agreeable to *Fortescue, A populo effluxam*. 8. King *Henry* 8. desires by an act of Parliament to be empowered to design by will which of his children he should please, for to succeed him. What power either Kings or Parliaments have assumed and exercised *de facto*, and not *de jure*, might be observed by some men, and brought into example, yet to little purpose. From all this every one may see what little credit is to be given to *Arniseus* and *Besoldus*, and some other outlandish writers, who affirm the Kings of *England* to be absolute Monarchs. For they took their information either from partial or ignorant men, or from unlearned Histories, as many of our English be. For few of our Historians have been either Antiquaries in Law, or learned and experienced States-men, such as *Thucidides*, *Xenophon*, *Polybius*, *Livy*, *Tacitus*, *Guiccardine*, *Commeignes*, and such like have been: These are men that could penetrate into the bowels of a State, and discover the inward fabrick of the same.

T. H.

Monarchy is the best form of Government.

G. L.

This is the substance of the next part of this Chapter. And in this particular I will not be tedious, nor answer him word by word. But 1. Its certain there is no absolute Monarch but one, and that is the eternal glorious God. 2. Monarchy well regulated, may be a good Government amongst men. 3. There are several kinds of Monarchies so called, and some better then another. 4. Monarchy may be good for some people, bad for another, and sometimes good for the same people, sometimes not. 5. To infer that Monarchy in general is the best kind of Government alwaies for all people, because some kind of Monarchy is sometimes good, for some kind of people, is very absurd. One of our learned Bishops in his answer to *Bellarmine*, who affirmed Monarchical Government was the best, and therefore the Government of the Church must be such, saith, that purple is the best colour, yet not the best for the Cardinals face, so it is in this case. No man (I think) can demonstrate the Government of Angels to be Monarchical. There may be amongst those blessed spirits *primatus ordinis*, not *jurisdictionis*. We do not read that God did ever immediately institute a form of Government to any people except to *Israel*; yet that was not Monarchical. And though Monarchy were supposed to be the best, yet wise men having the opportunity, did never institute that form of Government which in it self was best, but the best the people were capable of. I am no enemy to Monarchy, and I desire all Christian States to be content with their present form of Government, especially if they may enjoy peace and the Gospel. If divine Providence bring them into such a condition, as that they must, or may lawfully and safely alter, let them use their utmost power to make the alteration so, that it may be a reformation. To endeavour a change in a quiet State, and that out of ambition, or an humour of innovation, or an high conceit of their own State-learning, will much offend God, and bring great misery on man. Alterations in Government, which though they be for the better, if sudden, are dangerous: and should be made insensibly and by little and little; yet so, that if there be any thing in the former old constitution, which is good, it should be retained; what wise Polititians have done in this kind, Histories inform us, as in *England* in the Common-Law, which so many excellent Lawyers have so highly commended, as next unto the eternal Law, were introduced, it would prove a wonderful *compendium* in the regulation of Justice, and cut off a world of useless Statutes, which are rather an impediment, then a furtherance to Justice. There may be many forms of Government, and all good, yet its certain, that is the best, which provides most effectually for good Officers in the administration. If we may believe *Contzen* the Jesuite, There are amongst others, in the constitution of the Empire of *China*, two excellent rules constantly put in practise; The one is an Office or Colledge, whose duty is to inform the King of his errours, and never to cease petitioning in the name of the people, till he reform, and return to the observation of the Laws. These also inform the King of the miscarriage of all other Officers, though never so great. The other rule and practise is, every third year to make a severe and rigid inquisition into the administration of all Magistrates, and to put out and punish the unjust, negligent, and unworthy, and to establish the just.

The Author endeavours to prove the excellency of Monarchy above other forms, because it hath conveniencies proper to it self, and is free from inconveniencies incident to Aristocratical and Democratical States. Yet this is to little purpose. For, 1. The best forms have their imperfections. 2. The inconveniences mentioned, are easily prevented by wise States-men, even in other forms of Government.

The discourse following, concerning elective and limited Monarchies so called, yet are not such, as also concerning succession, I omit. 1. Because others have discussed these points in their Political systems more accurately. 2. Because though some things are both ignorantly and untruly affirmed, yet they are not worthy to be taken notice of, much less of any refutation.

CAP. IV.

Of the Second Part, the twentieth of the Book, of Paternal and Despotical Dominion.

The method of Politicks is miserably perverted by the Author. For whereas power is first acquired before a Common-wealth can be constituted, he first informs us of the several kinds of Constitutions, which arise from the different manner of disposing the power acquired, and after that of several waies how the power is acquired. And further to bewray his ignorance of the rules of Government, he confounds Oeconomical power with Political, so that I may truly say, that he is one of the worst that ever wrote either of Civil or Ecclesiastical Politicks.

In this Chapter he undertakes,

1. To define a Common-wealth by acquisition, and to shew the difference between it, and that by constitution.
2. To declare how dominion is acquired.
3. To prove the Soveraign rights out of Scripture.
4. From thence to demonstrate that all Soveraign power is absolute.

T. H.

A Common-wealth by acquisition, is that where the Soveraign power is acquired by force – And the difference of this from that of Constitution is, that in the former, men subject themselves for fear of the Soveraign: in the latter for fear of one another.

G. L.

This is the substance, though not all his words, where we must observe, That this is no distinction of a Common-wealth, but of the manner how the power, whereby any is made a Soveraign, is acquired: and that all Soveraigns do one way or other acquire their power: for its meerly accidental, no waies essential to any man, for to be invested with power. And howsoever the Soveraignty civil be obtained, it makes no difference in the Common-wealth. For in every state the power is acquired, and so there is no Common-wealth but its both by acquisition and constitution too. So that he hath made a distinction without a difference.

T. H.

Dominion is acquired two waies, by Generation and Conquest: The first is Paternal, the latter is Despotical.

G. L.

This is very defective, as in this place its hetereogeneous and impertinent. What have we to do with Family-power in a Common-wealth? For Familes as they make vicinities, and vicinities a Community civil, are but a remote material part of Politicks. In a Family there is a threefold power acquired; the power of an husband over his wife by marriage, covenant or contract, the power of parents over their children, by generation; the power of Masters over their servants, acquired several waies; for some servants are slaves, some are free; Slaves are *vernæ*, servants born in the Family: or *emptitii*, bought with money: such as are free be *conductitii*: The two former are more subject that the last; and the Master hath more power over the former sort who are born and bought, then over the latter, who are only hired. So that there is a difference of Despotical power even in a Family; the one is more absolute, the other more limited.

Soveraignty civil is acquired several waies, and all may be reduced to two. For men come unto this power either justly or unjustly. Justly, and that either in an extraordinary way, as by special unction and designation from God: thus *Saul*, and *David*, and *Davids* lawful Successors of his Family were made (the two first by particular nomination, the other by a general entail) or in an ordinary manner, and that is either by the Law of Nature, or by institution. By the Law of Nature, when a multitude sufficient for their own protection and government, associate and by union and communion become a Community, the Soveraignty is virtually and eminently in themselves, and in the whole body of the people being free: and this is so natural a subject, that upon the defect of succession, it returns unto them again. By institution and more formal contract; and that is by a free and full election, or by a submission to a Conquerer, which is so far voluntary, that if they had power to protect themselves, they would not submit. Unjustly by usurpation; when he or they who have no right, yet take the possession into their own hands in a way contrary to the Laws of God, and the consent of men: yet such an Usurper cannot be a Soveraign

without some kind of consent of God and man. In this case
fraud or force gets the advantage over the people so far, as that
they must submit or do worse. When any ascend the Throne by
Marriage, Succession, Election, they are made Governors by
institution, with free and full consent. In all this I speak of the
supreme, not the subordinate power, which is by Commission
derived from the supreme. In all these waies of acquiring
power, we must distinguish between power of constitution in
constitution, and in administration; and also take special
notice that there is no power which can govern without consent
not only of man, but also and especially of God, who either in
justice and severity, or in mercy doth change and alter the
Kingdoms of the world at will and pleasure. For he alone doth
rule in heaven and earth at all times.

Thus far concerning the acquisition of power, and of the
[*jura majestatis*] rights of Soveraigns, which he conceives to
have made clear by reason, and now in the next place
undertakes to prove out of Scripture, yet in such a loose and
impious abusive manner, that I verily perswade my self, he
doth not believe them to be revealed and written from heaven,
or that Jesus Christ was an ordinary just man, much less the
Eternal Son of God incarnate.

T. H. *pag.* 105.

*Lets now consider what the Scripture teacheth in the same
point: To* Moses *the children of* Israel *say thus, Speak thou to
us, and we will hear thee: but let not God speak to us, lest we
die. This is absolute obedience to* Moses.

G. L.

This is the first Scripture alledged by him; we read it in *Exod.*
20. 19. To understand these words, we must consider, 1. That
cap. 19. 8. That all the people answered together, and said, All
that the Lord hath said, that will we do. This was an absolute
subjection of themselves to God, and a promise to obey him. 2.
That the Lord said unto *Moses*, Lo, I come unto thee in a thick
cloud, that the people may hear when I speak with thee, and
believe thee for ever, *Verse* 9. This was to procure authority
and credit unto *Moses*, as a Messenger between God and
Israel. 3. That the words of *Exod.* 20. 19. quoted by the
Author, are expounded, *Deut.* 5. 27. For thus there we read,

Go thou near, and hear all that the Lord our God shall say: and speak thou unto us all that the Lord our God shall speak to thee, and we will hear it and do it. From all which it is apparent, 1. That the people had formerly before they spake these words, subjected themselves to God: and he was their Soveraign, not *Moses*. 2. That they promise to obey the words of God declared by *Moses*, not as they were the words and Laws of *Moses*, but of God, they will do them. 3. That they promise to believe *Moses* as a Messenger between God and them, not obey him as their supreme Lord. Its one thing to believe *Moses* as a Prophet from God, and to yield him absolute obedience as a King. Believe him as a Prophet they might, obey him as their King they must not. God was their King, and *Moses* his Messenger and servant. How grossly therefore doth he abuse the place? how absurdly and falsly doth he thence infer the peoples promise of absolute obedience to *Moses*, which was only due and promised unto God?

T. H.

Concerning the right of Kings, God himself by the mouth of Samuel *saith, This shall be the right of the King you will have to raign over you, he shall take your sons,* &c. 1 *Sam.* 8, 11, 12, &c.

G. L.

1. The translation, which he confessed is allowed by his Soveraign and the Church of *England*, is perverted. For instead of This will be the manner of the King, he turns it, This shall be the right of the King. There is a great difference between right which is alwaies just, and manner or custom, which is many times unjust. 2. If this be a prerogative of Soveraigns, then its a very great misery to be subject to a King; and that in two respects. 1. Because he will take away from his subjects unjustly, that which justly is their own, even the best things. 2. Because by doing thus, he will oppress them so grievously, that having no remedy or redress from man, they will cry unto God for deliverance from a King, as a great and intolerable mischief. 3. If it be the right of a King, yet it is but the right of heathen Despotical Princes, and not of the Kings of *Israel*. But how can it be the right of heathen Kings, seeing they had no power to oppress and do wrong? 4. It could not be the right of the Kings

of *Israel*; for they were bound to act and judge according to the Laws God had made; yet these acts here mentioned, are directly contrary to those Laws and Rules of Regal Government, delivered by God himself. For he must have a copy of the Laws, and read in it all his life, that he may fear God, keep his Laws, not exalt himself above his Brethren, *&c. Deut.* 17. 18, 19, 20. Neither did the Kings of *Judah* or *Israel*, no not wicked *Ahab* practice or make use of this power, as is evident in the case of *Naboths* Vineyard. 5. To do according to this power pretended in this place, is directly contrary to the very end of all Government civil, which is to do justice and judgement, to preserve to every one his own, to protect the good, and punish the bad. How shall he punish the Oppressor, when he is the great Oppressor himself? How can he do justice upon thieves, when he is the greatest thief in his Kingdom? 6. If this should be the right of the Kings of *Israel*, and of all Soveraigns, then though the people of *Israel* were a free people, yet if a King was once set over them, they were meer slaves: neither their Lands, nor their goods, nor their children, nor their servants were their own; and also by this reason, there can be no subjects in any state under heaven, that can have propriety or liberty, but all are meer and absolute servants and slaves. Kings may have *potentiam*, but not *potestatem*, force and fraud, but no just power to oppress their subjects, and do such things as are here mentioned. Whereas some say, That God in this place teacheth us what Kings may do, and in *Deut.* 17. 18, 19, 20. what they ought to do, is to little purpose, as being more acute than solid. For *id quisque potest, quod jure potest.* And no man, no not the greatest Princes in the world, have any power to do that which is unjust. 7. Its a question whether they had such a King as they desired. For they desired a King which would offend God, and oppress them: but God gave them such a King as had no power to make Laws, but such as were bound to Judge according to the civil or judicial Laws made by himself; and even in the time of Kings, he reserved the Soveraign Rights in his own hand. It seems they understood not well, what kind of King they had desired; for to maintain the state and pomp of a great Court, and an army in constant pay, was a vast charge, and required such a revenue as could no waies be raised without the great oppression of the people. And this they did not consider, neither would understand till it was too late, and the yoak was upon their necks, and the burden pressed them very sore. When Princes are trusted with an absolute power to raise men and moneys at their will and pleasure, they will not be content with the ordinary Revenue of their Crowns, but what they cannot obtain justly by the Laws, and the constitution of the State, they will force by the sword, and so the Government proves military, and in the end meerly arbitrary. Whereas Mr. *Hobbs* conceives, That to go in and out before them, and Judge the people, contains as absolute a power of the Militia and Judicature, as one man can possibly transfer unto another, he is much deceived. For both these may be had in a despotical, or a Regal way, or by Commission. The first is absolute, the two latter are not so. The Kings of *Sparta*, *Poland*, *Arragon*, might have both these, and yet be no absolute Soveraigns.

T. H.

Solomon *prayed that God would give him understanding to judge his people, and discern between good and evil,* 1 Kings 3. 8. *therefore he had the Judicial and Legislative power supreme and absolute.*

G. L.

This is his meaning, and thus he understands these words, wherein we may observe, 1. *Solomons* place and duty as King of *Israel*, and that was to judge that people. 2. That this duty could not be well performed without wisdom. 3. God doth give wisdom for that purpose: These things are implied. 4. *Solomon* praies for wisdom to that end. Neither from his place or prayer will it follow that he had the supreme, absolute, legislative power in himself alone: Neither indeed had he any such thing at all, for God had made the Laws both Civil and Ecclesiastical. And he could neither alter or abrogate them, but was bound precisely and strictly to judge according to them, and neither depart unto the right hand or the left. And suppose *Solomon* had been invested with this power, doth it therefore follow that all other Kings have the like?

The rest which follow are not worthy any answer. He instanceth, 1. In *Saul*, whom being their Lords annointed, *David* did not slay, though he was in his power. And what follows hence, but only thus much, That no man in *Davids* case, and of *Davids* conscience, dare secretly put to death a

King annointed by Gods special and immediate Word. 2.
Servants must obey their Masters, and Children their Parents
in all things. And what is this to purpose? Doth it hence
follow, that all Kings have absolute power? what impertinent
and absurd illations are these? But, 3. Christs Disciples must
observe and do all that the Scribes and Pharisees bid them, as
sitting in *Moses* Chair. From hence it cannot be concluded,
that they had Soveraign power civil, no more then Ministers
of the Gospel have it, because the people must observe and
do all that they bid them out of the Gospel. 4. *Paul* chargeth
Titus, cap. 3. 2. to warn the people of *Creet*, that they
subject themselves to Princes, and to those that are in
authority, and obey them. And his gloss is, this is simple
obedience. What is this to absolute and supreme power? By
this may be as easily proved, that every petty Officer hath
supreme power, as well as any other; for an Officer must be
obeyed, because he is in Authority. 5. Christ commands to
give to *Cæsar* the things that are *Cæsars*, and paid taxes
himself. All that can be inferred from hence is, That tribute is
to be paid, to whom tribute is due: and that it is due from
Provinces to their supreme Governors. The summ of all these
places amounts to thus much in Politicks, That the chief
commands in war, just Judgement in peace, or the exercise of
Jurisdiction belonged unto the Kings of *Judah*, and tribute to
the *Roman* Emperour. How many plain and express places of
Scripture might have been produced to prove that there is a
Legislative, Judicial, Executive power in every State, and
that it is to be exercised by some certain persons designed for
that purpose? And the Author had no need to lay the weight
of his praise for these things, upon such places as do but
tacitly and by way of intimation, point at some of them. But
why he should falsifie the translation, abuse so many texts,
make such woful illations from some of them, and so
impertinently alledge them, I know no reason: and it seems to
me intolerable, that in the last example he should make Christ
Jesus the civil Soveraign of the Jews in the time of his
humiliation, and by vertue of that civil power, to take another
mans Ass as his own, which he did but desire to borrow, and
use for a little journey with the consent of the owner. That the
sin of our first parents, in desiring to be as Gods, knowing
good and evil, was an ambition to become civil Soveraigns, he
may perswade us to believe, when he can prove it.

T. H. *pag.* 106.

Soveraign power ought in all Common-wealths to be absolute.

G. L.

This I read in the margent; and to his understanding, its plain both from reason and Scripture, that its as great as possibly a man can be imagined to make it: This is plainly ridiculous. For what cannot men imagine; seeing their imaginations can reach to wonders, impossibilities, and many things far above a civil Soveraign power? And here is a fit occasion offered, to examine what absolute power is, and in what resepct Soveraignty is absolute. There is no power, as there is no being absolute, but that of Gods, whose power is his being. Civil supreme power is said to be absolute, because its *soluta legibus*, free from the Laws, and not limited and obliged by them. Yet the Laws from which they are free, as being above them, are only civil Laws made by themselves, for the administration of the States where they are Soveraign. For they are so strictly bound by the Law of Reason, Nature, God, which are but all one divine Law, as they have not the least power to do any thing either as private persons, or publike Soveraigns against them, except they will dethrone themselves, provoke the wrath of God, and bring his Judgements upon them. They are besides, subject to the Law of Nature, which is above any particular Soveraign, though never so great. They are indeed above their own Laws, and many not only alter many things in them, but abrogate them. Yet so as all this tends to the publick good. They may act upon occasion, above and besides them, as the general good shall require it. They are not bound unto formalities, but may omit them. Yet all this is but little, and confined to the narrow compass of things indifferent, as they are subordinate to pure morals. Its true, that their power is in some respect arbitrary; yet if they do any thing which either in it self, or in the circumstances only is unjust, they offend and transgress the bounds God hath put unto their power. And here we must distinguish between the Soveraign for the Constitution, and the Soveraign for Administration. The former hath more power then the later, who only is above the Laws of administration, yet both must be just; for they have no power to be unjust. Its certain that Princes desire to be Gods, absolute, independent, above all Laws, and to have a priviledge to do what they list, and a right to do wrong; and its a dangerous thing to flatter them, and make them believe their power to be greater, then indeed it is; for this is the very high-way unto ruine. Wise men have advised all Princes to observe their own Laws made by themselves, and by their example encourage their subjects to obedience. And this is an effectual means to procure their safety, and confirm them in their power, and the love of their subjects.

CAP. V.

Of the Second Part, the one and twentieth of the Book, Of the liberty of subjects.

The subject of this Chapter is, as in the argument, the liberty of subjects, which follows the power of Soveraigns in this discourse. And because his method is no method, but rather a confusion, I do forbear to reduce the Chapter either to certain Heads or Propositions, and will only observe some few passages, to manifest that he never understood what liberty is. Liberty of subjects is not Natural, nor Moral, nor Theologicall, but Political and Civil. In the Civil Law, and Politicks, is opposed to servitude and bondage, not simply and meerly to obligation by Laws, as he fancieth: for thus he writes.

T. H.

So men have also made artificial Charms, called Civil Laws, which they themselves by mutual Covenants have fastened at one end to the lips of the Soveraign, at the other to their own ears.

G. L.

The Authors meaning is, That so far as Laws bind the subject, so far they take away his liberty: and men by constitution of a Soveraign over them, give a power absolute to make Laws, and so far as they are virtually subject to his power, and actually bound by his Laws, they cannot be free; yet this well examined, will not prove true. For not any kind of Obligation takes it away; for then the Laws of Nature, by which a man is bound, before he be subject to a civil Soveraign, should deprive him of his liberty, yet they leave him as free a man as any possibly in a free-State can be. The Obligation of just Laws and wise Edicts do regulate liberty, keep it within its proper bounds, and no waies destroy it, or take it away. Therefore that which follows is questionable. For he affirms,

T. H.

That the liberty of a subject therefore lieth only in those things, which in regulating their actions, the Soveraign hath pretermitted.

G. L.

But, 1. In things left indifferent, because not defined by Law, the subject is not only *liber, sed dominus*, and hath not only *libertatem*, but *potestatem*. He is not only free, but Lord of those actions, and hath not only liberty, but also an absolute power. 2. Though wise and just Laws do regulate actions, yet they do not make the agent a slave or a servant. For to be a slave or a servant, is to be cast below the condition of a man, and make him subject to some thing below himself. Wisdom and Justice are above the power of the Soveraign, much more above the liberty of a subject. They are particles of the divine perfection, and to be bound by them, is not only a liberty, but an honour. To be free from the dominion of our own base lusts and sins, and the power of Satan, is true liberty divine; and so not to be subject to the lusts and imperious unworthy commands of absolute Soveraigns, whose wills, though ir-rational & contrary to justice, must stand for Laws, is civil liberty. And then a man is Politically free, when he is so far Master of his life, goods, children, and that which is justly his, that they cannot be taken away from him, but for some crime contrary to just Laws, deserving such a penalty. In a word, the liberty of a subject is such a state or condition, as that he is neither by the Soveraign power, nor any Laws, bound to do any thing, which a rational and just man would not willingly do, though there were no Laws or Penalities Civil at all. This is not to be free from Laws. And I do not know, who they are, which he saith demands any such thing. The rude and ignorant people, and also all children of *Belial*, desire to have a licence, not only to do good, but evil too, as they please, and they judge all Laws as heavy burdens, and grievous yoaks. If he mean that the subjects of *England* demanding the benefit of *Magna Charta*, and the Petition of Right, did aim at any such extravagant liberty, he must needs be a slanderer of his own fellow-subjects, and an enemy to the English liberty, as indeed he is, and that through an erroneous notion and conceit of absolute power civil. The liberty of the subjects of this Nation is very great, and such, as if we either consider the laws of the Constitution, or Administration, the ordinary and common subjects of other Nations are but slaves unto them. Our Freeholders have the choice of their Knights and Burgesses for the Parliament, so that neither any Laws can be made, nor moneys imposed upon them, without their verbal consent, given by their Representatives. In all causes, civil, criminal, capital, no Judgement can pass against them but by the verdict of a jury made up of their neighbours, which in it self is an excellent priviledge. The Civilians say, *Libertas est res inestimabilis*, and to be redeemed at any rate; much more the English liberty is to be valued, and ever was by our ancestors, who obtained it, recovered it, kept it, though with the blood of many thousands. But the question is, whether this liberty is consistent with the Soveraigns power. His opinion is,

T. H.

That by the liberty of the subject, the Soveraigns power of life and death, is neither abolished nor limited.

G. L.

Its certain that the Soveraigns power and the subjects liberty are consistent. For the Soveraign may take away the life of his subject, yet according to the evidence of Judgement, agreeable to Law: no otherwise. Yet he presupposeth, 1. That the King is supreme, and the primary subject, owner and possessor of the original power, which sometimes may be, yet with us its far otherwise. 2. That the power of civil Soveraigns is absolute. For with him,

T. H.

Nothing the Soveraign representative can do to a subject on what pretence soever, can properly be called Injustice or Injury,

because every subject is Author of every act the Soveraign doth,
so that he never wanteth right to any thing, otherwise then as
he himself is the subject of God, and bound thereby to observe
the Laws of Nature. When Jephtah *sacrificed his daughter, and*
David *murthered* Uriah, *both innocent, yet, they did them no*
injustice, &c.

G. L.

Here he seems to contradict himself. For he grants two things.
1. That the Soveraign is subject to God. 2. That in that respect
he is bound to observe the Laws of nature; yet he saith, he can
do no injustice to the subject, and that he hath right to any
thing, yet so as he is limited by subjection to God, and the Laws
of Nature. 1. If he be Gods subject, as certainly he is, it
follows, 1. That in that respect he is but trusted as a servant
with the Administration of the power civil. 2. That he is fellow-
subject with his subjects. 3. He may do injustice, as one fellow
subject may wrong another.

Secondly, If he be bound to observe the Laws of Nature,
which are the Laws of God; then, 1. He is not absolute, or
solutus legibus. His power is limited and bounded by these
Laws. 2. Then he hath no power to murther, oppress and
destroy his innocent subjects, who are more Gods then his, and
only trusted by God in his hands for to be protected, righted in
all just causes, and vindicated from all wrongs. 3. No Prince or
Soveraign can assume, or any people give to any person or
persons, any the least power above, or contrary unto the Laws
of Nature. These Laws are the moral precepts of eternal justice
and equity, from which all civil Laws have their rise, and are
either conclusions drawn from them, or certain rules tending to
the better observation of them. Which things well considered,
do make it very evident how little the power of civil Lords and
Princes must needs be. In some few indifferent things, they may
be absolute, have arbitrary power, and be in some respect
above those constitutive Laws which they themselves enact.

His instance in *Jephtah* gives them power above, and
contrary to the Laws of God and Nature. Yet who will grant
him, that *Jephtah* sacrificed his daughter? The text will not
evince it; for it only saith, that whatsoever cometh forth of my
doors to meet me, *&c.* shall be the Lords, or I will offer it up
for a burnt-offering, *Judges* 11. 31. For the particle [*Vau*]

turned by some copulatively for [*and*] is here, as in many other places, dis-junctive, and signifies [*or*]. Again, if *Jephtah* did sacrifice her, he sinned, not only against the Law of Nature, but also the written Law of *Moses*: For God gave no command, permission or toleration to any that we read of, but only to *Abraham*, to sacrifice with humane blood; and that Commandment was but to try him; for he would not suffer him to put him to death. Besides God threatens ruine and destruction to such as did offer their children to *Moloch*, and shed their blood. And their sin was not only because they offered them to Idols and Devils, but also because they shed innocent blood, without any warrant or Commission from God, the only supreme and absolute Lord of life. Further, how could the vow of man, which was but a voluntary Obligation, be above the Law of God, and make that lawful, which by a Superiour Law was unlawful? I verily believe, she was devoted only, not sacrificed. But suppose he did sacrifice her to God, to whom he had vowed her, yet he did not this as a Soveraign of her life, but as a subject to God.

The example of *David* murthering *Uriah*, can much less prove the absolute power of Soveraigns to take away the lives of their innocent subjects. For, *David* hath no such power: for, 1. He was no absolute Prince, but limited both by the written Laws of God, and also the Natural. 2. Neither he nor any other can have any such power, because man cannot, God doth not give any such power. 3. *David* did not only iniquity, but injustice to *Uriah*. 1. As his fellow-subject in respect of God. 2. As his own subject, whom he was bound as innocent to protect, not to destroy. 4. His proof out of *Psal. 51. 4.* [*Against thee only*] is invalid. For, 1. Though it be so translated by some, and so understood by *Ambrose* and others who follow him, yet neither that translation, nor the interpretation thereon, can be evinced either out of the Original, or the Septuagint, or the vulgar, or *Junius*, or *Vatablus*. 2. *Genebrard*, *Vatablus*, *Junius*, *Ainsworth* and others understand it, that God only was privy to, and knew of this sin: and the words following [And done this evil in thy sight] seem to confirm this sense. 5. Yet suppose it should be turned [*against thee only*] yet others interpret [*onely*] to be principally, as supreme Law-giver and Judge, not only to me, but all others; who only hast the Original power of punishing and pardoning, not only me, but others, and that not only temporally, but spiritually and eternally. Yet the exposition of *Ambrose* is taken up, because Princes desire it, to be so absolute; and both Divines and other men are very ready to flatter such as are in present possession of power.

But to make the point more evident, let me digress a little, and search out the reason and cause of the power of life and death, as in the hands of civil Soveraigns. To this end observe, That no man hath absolute power of his own life, as he hath of his goods: Man may have the use and possession, but not the propriety and dominion of it. Therefore its granted on all hands, that though a mans life be said to be his own, yet he may not be *felo de se*, and kill himself; he is not Master of his life so far, as to have any power or liberty to do any such thing. Its true that God, who is Lord of life and death, gives liberty to man in some cases to hazard, in some he commands to lay down his life. He may hazard it in a just war and defence of his own Countrey, and also of himself, against an injust invader. He must lay down his life, and God commands it for the testimony of Christ, in which case he that loseth it shall find it. From all this it follows, that no people can by making a Soveraign, give any absolute power of life and death unto him: For nothing can give that which it hath not: neither can they make themselves Authors of the unjust acts of their Soveraign, much less of his murthers, and taking away the lives of their innocent subjects. *Id enim quisque potest quod jure potest.* If thus it be, then they must have power to take away life, from God who alone hath power of life: and this power he only gives in case the subject be guilty of such crimes as by his Laws are capital.

T. H. *pag.* 110 in the margent.

The liberty which writers praise, is the liberty of Soveraigns, not of private men.

G. L.

By writers, he means the Roman and Greek Historians and Philosophers, who wrote so much of liberty; amongst the rest, especially *Aristotle* and *Cicero*. By this, it seems he never understood these Authors, though he accuse others of ignorance. The liberty which the English have challenged and obtained with so much expence of blood, is not the power of

Kings, much less of absolute Soveraigns, as he would make the world believe, but that which is due unto us by the constitution of the State, *Magna Charta*, the Laws, and the Petition of Right. Its but the liberty of subjects, not Soveraigns, when he hath said all he can; we are not willing to be slaves, or subject our selves to Kings as absolute Lords. Neither are we willing that either flattering Divines, Court-Parasites, or Unjust Ministers of State should wind up the pretended prerogative so high, as to subject our lives and estates, and also our Religion to the arbitrary, absolute, and unreasonable will of one man, whom they did desire to advance so much for their own interest. There is a difference between the subjects liberty, whereby in many things he may command himself, and supreme power which commands others under their Supremacy. By liberty, *Aristotle* & *Cicero* meant such a priviledge as every subject might have in a free-State, not that Soveraignty which belonged to the whole and universal body over several persons; where it is to be noted, that one and the same person, who is a subject, and at the best but a Magistrate, hath a share in the Soveraign power. Yet this he hath, not as a single person, but as one person joyntly with the whole body, or major part at least of the people. So in our Parliaments, every man there is as a single person, and all of them any waies considered but as the joynt Representative of the people in a certain place, at a certain time, acting according to a certain order, are but subjects; yet in the capacity and habitude of a Parliament, they are no subjects, but in the name of the people have a Legislative power, and exercise the highest acts of Government, excepting those of the Constitution. And this may be one reason, why our English Ancestors have been so careful to maintain and preserve this great Court and Assembly of Parliaments, because they knew upon that depended their liberty, in the vacancy and intervals of Parliaments. For take away this, and our liberty is gone. And wise men know, that the liberty of the English subject depends upon these great Assemblies. Some therefore have attempted, either the total extirpation of them, according to the example of *France* and *Spain*; or a diminution of their power and priviledges, so as to make them meer shadows. If any say, and infer from all this, that therefore the form of our Government even under Kings is popular, and hath the nature of a free-State. I say, it hath much of a free-State in the Constitution, but not in the Administration.

Yet its far different from those four kinds of popular Governments mentioned by *Aristotle, Pol. lib. 6. c. 4.* The constitution whereof is little better than levelling. The principal thing aimed at in such forms, as the Author alledgeth out of the Philosopher, *cap. 2. Ejusdem libri*, was liberty, supposing it could be had no where but in such Governments: and this liberty was to do either what they pleased, or to govern by course, fearing lest any person or persons continued long in any eminent place of command, would in time ingross the power. Yet this supposition was false. For liberty might be had without levelling, and free-States might be, and have been better constituted and regulated. For no constitution is good, where provision is not made, that Wisdom and Justice, rather then persons may govern: and the multitude so kept under, as that they may be subjects, not rebels, and cast off all power. To return unto the matter proposed, and conclude this point. 1. The English liberty is their birth-right. 2. Its not the power of Soveraigns. 3. Its not unlimited, but bounded within reasonable bounds. 4. We do not learn it out of the Greek and Roman Histories, nor from the Athenians or Romans, but from our own Laws, which are far different from theirs, and far more agreeable to the written Laws of God, which left the people of *Israel* under their Judges the freest people of the world, and yet no Levellers. 5. Our learning out of Greek and Latine Authors, hath not been bought so dear, or cost so much blood, except out of the breech of School-boyes: And most of those who have controlled the just acts of their Soveraigns, never read, much less understood those authors.

T. H. pages 111, 112, 113.

The liberty of the subject is in such things as are neither determined by his first submission to the Soveraign power, nor by the laws.

G. L.

This is the substance of three pages, and amounts to so much as may easily be comprised in a few words. For when a subject is not bound either by the Laws of the Constitution or Administration, he is free according to Mr. *Hobbs* his judgement. Yet in proper sense in both these cases, he is no subject; but [*Dominus*] and far more then [*liber*]. The Civilians do better determine the liberty of the subject to be [*potestatem agendi sub publicæ defensionis præsidio*] though this be no perfect definition. As before, so now I say, that liberty here is not opposed to obligation but servitude. For to be subject to a wise Soveraign according to just Laws, is so much liberty as any reasonable man can desire: for in this respect he is rather subject to God then man; and to serve him is doubtless perfect freedom. As no Soveraign should be denied so much power as to protect the least, if innocent, and to punish the greatest, if guilty; so no subject should be bound to do evil, which is servitude and bondage indeed, or restrained from doing that good which God commands him. Civil government was never ordained by God, to be destructive either of moral or divine vertues, or of the noble condition of man as a rational creature. Therefore regular submission unto supreme power, will never stand with any obligation unto evil, or contract for protection except in innocency. *Paul* pleading before *Festus* saith, If I be an offender, or have committed any thing worthy of death, I refuse not to die, *Acts 25. 11*. How this can stand with what this Author saith, when he affirmeth that its lawful for a man guilty and condemned to save himself if he can, I leave to others for to examine. From the Apostles words its evident, he desires no protection, even of himself, as worthy of death, neither hath God given any power to man to save in such a case. And though any person by the Law of nature may defend himself, yet this must be done *cum moderamine tutelæ inculpatæ*. In case a subject hath made himself capitally guilty, he hath forfeited his life to his Soveraign as Gods Vicegerent, whom he must not resist in the execution of Justice, though he be not bound to kill himself: neither doth the multitude or strength of any such capital offenders, any waies give them right to resist their Soveraign in their own defence, as the Author would have it. For they cannot defend themselves as men, but they must defend themselves in this case as guilty men, which is not lawful. How the offer of pardon should take away the plea of self-defence, I understand not, seeing they had no right before it was offered. The offer of pardon indeed, if the party offering may be safely trusted, may take away all fear, and so all colour of any plea by force to defend themselves from that death, which pardon will take away or remove.

In the close of this discourse concerning liberty of the subject, he grants it a part of this liberty, That the subject may sue his Soveraign, and before a Judge appointed by the said Soveraign. If this be so, then 1. The subject hath propriety of goods. 2. That he and his Soveraign are two distinct parties, and in this case the Soveraign represents him not as one person. 3. That the Law in this respect is above the supreme Governor. 4. Therefore the Soveraign is not absolute. 5. That the subject may complain of some actions and injustice of the Soveraign, contrary to the Authors fourth right of Soveraigns. 6. That to him belongs not all Judicature, in all Causes, as in the eighth, right of majesty he did affirm. Yet he distinguisheth of the Soveraigns demand as twofold, either by vertue of a Law, or by force; if he demand or take away any thing by power or pretence thereof, there lyeth in that case no action of Law, because the subject is made author of the Soveraigns acts, and therefore the suit against him, is against the Plantiff himself, being his subject. If this answer be good, then the Soveraign may do what he can and will, not what he ought; he may rule according to his strength and power, and not according to Justice: he may borrow, and promise to repay; take away, and engage to restore, and yet do no such thing, but violate his promise and engagement, contrary to the very Law of Nature. He hath a liberty to be unjust and wicked, and that more then any of his subjects, as he hath greater power. I leave him to be a subject of such a Soveraign, and wish all good men a better. The true reason, why a Soveraign may be sued, is, 1. Because in the institution of a Soveraign, especially of administration, the subjects may reserve the propriety of their goods, which may be done without any diminution of a lawful supreme power; and in this case, when a Soveraign takes away or detains that which is his subjects, and an action is brought against him, the subject is not his subject, nor he his Soveraign in that respect. Both of them in this particular are but private persons; and he that is subject to him as he is just in his Government, questions him as he is unjust in his actions. Again, propriety belongs unto the Law of nature, which is above civil power. But he proceeds.

T.H.

If a Monarch, or Soveraign Assembly, grant a liberty to all or any of his subjects, which grant standing, he is disabled to provide for their safety, the grant is void, unless he directly renounce or transfer his Soveraignty to another.

G. L.

By this we easily understand to what purpose the Treaty in the
Isle of *Wight* with the King was. For though the Parliament had
voted his concessions to be satisfactory, in some respect that of
Bishops, and he was ready to close with them, yet in the
judgement of this man, and all that party adhering to the King,
the Parliament was accounted no Parliament, the King an
absolute Monarch, and the Concessions, *ipso facto*, void: and
for this reason, because the King had disabled himself by
granting the Militia to protect his subjects. And the issue of this
Treaty to be expected was this, so far as the King had obtained
liberty and opportunity, he would declare his Concessions void
and unreasonable, and so possess himself of the Militia, and
proceed against the Treators, as Rebels and Enemies; for so
they were accounted.

Yet this was not a meer grant of liberty, but of power, which
in the Treaty is presupposed to be his, though confined and a
prisoner, and vanquished in a civil war. But if we will speak
properly, the grant of liberty may be such as it may amount to
an *exemption* from a sufficient degree of subjection, but it doth
not transfer the Soveraign power to another; And this must
needs be granted, that to pass away any of the greater rights, is
to dethrone. In the conclusion of this *Cap.* we are informed
when the obligation of the subject to the Soveraign doth cease;
and it is then when his power to protect doth cease. And there
is great reason for it. For whatsoever his title may be, and how
unjustly soever it may be taken away, and howsoever his
subjects may stand well affected towards him, yet seeing there
can be no protection from wrong within, nor from invasion of
enemies without, nor administration of Justice, without which
any people returns unto the confusion of Anarchy, except there
be actual possession of power; therefore Obligation for the
present must cease, or at least be suspended. There be many
waies, whereby a Soveraign may cease to be a Soveraign, as by
conquest, death, resignation, cession, *&c.* and when the
Soveraign ceaseth to be such, the Obligation must needs
determine, as to such a particular Governor. And here I might
take occasion to treat of subalternate Governments, and
fiduciary Princes, who are Soveraigns in respect of their
subjects, yet acknowledge a superiour, from whom they hold
their territory. But seeing he is silent, I will be so too.

CAP. VI.

*Of the Second Part, and the two and twentieth of the Book: Of
Systems subject, Political and Private.*

I pass by his divisions and subdivisions of Systems, as being
well known to such as are acquainted either with Politicks, or
Civil Law. For the subject of *Jurisprudentia civilis*, being
communio, or *communitas hominum*; wherein the Lawyers
out of their institutions observe persons, things and actions
both private and publick, that they may the better find out the
several rights determined by Law: They distinguish *personam
in singularem & conjunctam. Persona conjuncta*, consists of
several persons distinct Physically, yet made one by consent
and association Politically. And these Systems and Societies
may be considered as parts of the Community, which is the
immediate subject of a Common-wealth, and a civil Government. Some of these are natural, as a Family, some are
voluntary and by institution. In a Common-wealth once
constituted, all these are subject to the supreme power, and
their actions are so far warrantable, as they derive their power
from the Soveraign, and are agreeable to the Laws.

Some of these are made by division, co-ordination, and
subordination, as Provinces, Counties, Hundreds, Allotments,
Town-ships, Parishes. Some of them are Ecclesiastical, some
Civil. Some are made by Charter and Patent, and have their
special priviledges, and immunnities, and have their Statutes,
and power to make Orders and By-Laws within themselves,
and some have jurisdiction within their liberties. Some are
more noble, as Colledges, and Universities, and Schools, and
all such as are Nurseries of Law and Learning; some less noble,
as Corporations, with their several Companies and Officers.

The end of the Institution of these, is either for the better and
more easie Government of the whole Community: or for the
better education of the subjects in learning or trades; or for the
maintenance, or enriching, or adorning of the State.

And it concerns the supreme Governors of a State, to have a
special care of these Societies, to order, regulate and reform
them, as they shall see occasion or need. For the good of the
Commonwealth doth much depend upon the regulation and
wise ordering of them.

CAP. VII.

*Of the Second Part. Of the Book 23. Of the publick Ministers
of the Soveraign power.*

My intention in the examination of the Author, is to manifest,
1. That where he hath done ill, none hath done worse. And 2.
where he hath done well, many before him have done better.
This latter is my work in this part of his Book, as also in other
passages of his discourse.

The subject of this Chapter is [*The Ministers of State*] which
by some in Latine are called [*Officiales*] in English, Officers;
and by the same generally is understood the same with these,
who are stiled, and that very fitly [Publick Ministers of the
Soveraign Power.] For in all acts of civil Government, the
principal agent is the Soveraign, the instrumental or ministerial
are Officers, who are therefore called by some, *instrumenta
majestatis vicaria*, which words imply much, and contain in
some sort the definition of the Author. For they imply, 1. That
the Soveraign is the principal agent. 2. That they represent the
Soveraign. 3. That they are but his instruments, and act by
power derived from him.

The difference between them and the Soveraign is, 1. That
they are essentially and properly but subjects, and accidentally
Officers. 2. That though they have power, and the same is the
Soveraigns, yet as in him its original, supreme, universal in
respect of the whole state, in them it is derivative, subordinate,
particular, or but a part and particle of it. 3. That whatsoever
the Soveraign acts, is valid immediately in it self; but what they
act is only good and valid as they are one person with him, and
make his will their rule and principle, and do all things in his
name.

The reason why there must be Officers in every State, and
that of necessity, is given, because no Soveraign, whether one
person or more, can see all things with his own eyes, hear all
things with his own ears, do all things with his own hands, or
be present and acting in every place, where he ought to act.
This is proper to God, who yet useth the Ministry both of men
and Angels, in the Government of the world, but not out of any
necessity, but because its his will and pleasure.

There be two parts of Politicks; the 1. Constitution, which
disposeth the supreme power in a certain subject, whether one

or more; and determines the rights both of the Soveraign and subject. The 2. Administration, which is the exercise of that power. In which Administration, the first act is *legislation*; and this is the proper place to speak of Laws concerning the Administration, as different from those of the Constitution; the next is the making of Officers for the execution of these Laws. This is the method, and here is the proper handling of this subject.

These Officers are either extraordinary or ordinary: Extra-ordinary, are such as are trusted with power for a time limited in some extraordinary exigency of the State, as the Dictators amongst the *Romans*. Ordinary, are such as are usual in all States; and they are either such as by which the Soveraign acts and deals with forrein States, or within his own Dominions. The former are Embassadors, Agents, Messengers, Heralds, Intelligencers. These Embassadors are constant and *legier*, or temporary & occasional. They represent Majesty, and act according to the Laws of Nations. The Officers within the Soveraigns Dominions, are either for war or peace. For war either by Sea or Land: hence *Jus Nauticum & Militare*; and these are for defence, and act also according to the Laws of Nations. For peace, and they are either for counsel, or judgement, or execution, or the revenue. Hence Councellers, Judges, Sheriffs, Treasurers, and all their servants or subordi-nate Agents and Assistants. Amongst these there is a subordi-nation, till we come to some general Officer, in every several kind next unto the Soveraign. How to reduce the Officers of this or any other State unto these heads, is not my work; and many have made this reduction in several Common-wealths.

The general rules of these Officers are many, and may be read in several Authors: As 1. Any man fitly qualified may be forced to do service for his Countrey. 2. To avoid confusion and charge, they are to be reduced to a certain number and order. The number should be according to the necessity of the State. 3. No Officer should be trusted too long with great and transcendent power. 4. They should be fitly qualified and advanced for desert, and no other reason. 5. Some should be superintendents over others within a certain precinct, and also generall visitors selected of purpose, to enquire into the carriage of all the rest at certain set times. The Roman Censors had some power in this kind, but no Jurisdiction: As the Visitors of *China* are said to have.

In this Chapter Mr. *Hobbs* seems to make Ministers of the
Gospel, such as the Apostle, *Eph.* 4. 11, calls Pastors and
Teachers, to be publick Ministers and Officers civil; yet though
they be subject to the civil Soveraign as well as other men, yet
as Ministers they derive their power from Christ by the
Church, and not from any civil Governors, as shall be made
good hereafter.

CAP. VIII.

*Of the Second Part, the Twenty fourth of the Book; Of
nutrition and procreation of a Common-wealth*

Two things only in this Cap. I question: the 1. Concerning the
original of propriety. The 2. Concerning a standing revenue of
the Crown. The 1. he deriveth from the Soveraign, in manner
as followeth.

T. H.

*Propriety in all kinds of Common-wealths belongs to the
Soveraign power. And again, propriety is the act only of the
Soveraign, who distributes to every man his own by Law; and
this distribution is first of Land, as of the Land of Promise by*
Eleazer *and* Joshua.

G. L.

This is the summe and brief substance of many more words,
and cannot be true. For 1. we find propriety of goods and lands
in several families, which are of no Common-wealth. 2. The
Constitution of any Common-wealth doth presuppose this
propriety, without which there can be no buying, selling,
exchanging, stealing, restitution; otherwise the eighth Commandment, *Thou shalt not steal*, could not be a Law of nature,
nor bind any man, except in a Common-wealth; and so before
a Common-wealth be instituted in a Community or people,
there could be no sin in stealing. 3. All that may be granted in
this point, is, That the Soveraign may preserve and regulate
propriety, both by Laws and Judgements. Yet the Author
makes all men brutes, nay wild and ravenous beasts, and birds

of prey, until they have made themsleves slaves unto some absolute Soveraign, and such they must be, either beasts by the Law of nature, or slaves by the Laws of a civil State. 4. As for his instance in the Land of *Canaan* divided by lots to be chosen before *Eleazer* the high Priest, and *Joshua* the general, its impertinent and false. For, 1. *Israel* before it was molded into a Common-wealth, had propriety in their goods. 2. The propriety of that Land was at the first, and continued in God; for they were but Gods Tenants, in a special and peculiar manner, so as no people in the world was; therefore no man could alienate nor morgage beyond the year of Jubilee: at which time God seemed to renue their Leases, after the Jubilee-Sabbath. 3. When they had in common conquered, and taken possession of the Land, it was theirs, so far as God had conveyed it, in common. 4. It was for peace and order, as also for to preserve the distinction of Tribes divided, yet so as the Soveraign dividing it was God, who ordered the lot. *Eleazer* and *Joshua* were but Superintendents of the lot, and no Soveraigns; neither had they any the least propriety more then others of the people. The Text expresly saith, That when they had made an end of dividing the Land, they gave *Joshua Timnath Serah* in Mount *Ephra* in for his inheritance, *Joshua* 19. 49, 50. where it is to be observed, That the people gave it him.

T. H.

The propriety of the subject excludes all other subjects from the use of them, and not the Soveraign.

G. L.

It doth not only exclude other subjects, but the Soveraign too. For, 1. The Soveraign is bound to observe the Laws of nature, which are the moral Laws of God; and propriety as by the Law of nature. 2. *Imperium nihil aliud esse sapientes definiunt, nisi curam salutis alienæ,* saith one very well. For civil supreme power was never given by any people to destroy their propriety, but to defend it. Otherwise no intelligent people in the world would advance one person or more to take away their goods, and so put themselves in a worse condition then they were by the Laws of nature. 3. It may be granted, that the Soveraign hath *dominium eminens,* so far as to command not only the estates, but the lives of the subjects for the publike safety; but what is this to propriety properly taken? 4. If his assertion were true, then that distinction of Civilians, and the Authors of Politicks, whereby they put a difference *inter res & possessiones publicas* and *privatas*, were in vain and false; but so it is not. 5. By the Soveraigns in *England*, he means the Kings, who were no Soveraigns at all, nor could at any time raise any moneys, or impose any subsidy upon the people without their consent in Parliament, as not only English men, but forrein Ministers of State, who have either read our Histories, or our Laws, or our practice, do well know, and have made it known to others. 6. There may be a device in Law, to pass all the land in *England* upon the Crown, for to derive all tenures from thence, or to confirm propriety to the subjects, for that every one might not only know, but keep and recover his own the better: Yet this gives the King no more propriety, then a *Feoffee* in trust may have; and that is none.

T. H.

The publick is not to be dieted: in the Margint.

G. L.

His meaning is, that the Soveraign cannot be confined to a certain revenue, as sufficient to defray the publick charge. Yet the wisest States in the world have certainly defined a constant standing revenue for the publick use. For we read of the Dominion of *France*, which though the Kings could neither alienate, nor justly impare, yet *Henry* the fourth hath wofully mangled, and given occasion of those heavy oppressions of the people of that State; and also we are not ignorant of the Crown lands, and revenue of *England*. And this is but agreeable to Scripture, where we read that God commanded, in the division of the holy Land, that the Prince should have his portion, that he may no more oppress, *Ezek.* 45. 7, 8. For the Land must be divided into three parts; The first must be for God to maintain the Priests and Levites: The second for the Prince, the third for the people: and thus some say the Land in *England* was divided in the time of the pious *Saxon* Kings. Yet it must be confessed, that sometimes the publick charge may be so great, as that a standing revenue cannot defray it, and then the subjects for the general good and safety, are bound and may be commanded to contribute. But if this in a time of peace and safety be embezelled and mispent by a prodigal Prince, and his favourites and followers, this will no waies warrant him to fly upon the spoyl, and plunder his subjects. What *William* the Conqueror here in *England* did, it matters not much. For if he did derive his title from *Edward* the Confessor, as some Histories say he did pretend, then he was no Soveraign. If he did act as Conqueror, then all compact and right upon covenant is void, as his successors, who insist upon that title of conquest, give full liberty to the English to fight against them, and depose them if they can, and deal with them as enemies.

As for making Laws for the regulation of Traffick, Trade, Exchange, the value, stamp and coining of moneys, the sending out of Colonies for new Plantations, as also to make them as Provinces, or exempt them from subjection, because they will not allow protection, I grant all these are prerogatives of the Soveraign.

CAP. IX.

Of the Second Part. The 25. of the Book Of Counsel.

The heads of this Chapter are,
1. The difference between command, counsel, exhortation, dehortation.
2. The difference between counsel and command, made evident out of Scripture.
3. The qualifications of good Counsellors.
4. To advise with Counsellors apart, is better then to advise with them openly and in assemblies.

1. The difference between counsel, command, exhortation, dehortation, is easily known. For Counsel given, is a declaration of the means which tend unto some certain end, and also of the order and manner how they should be used to attain that end. Command is the will of a Superior made known, whereby the inferiour is bound to obey, or otherwise to suffer. Exhortation presseth the practise of some good to be done; as dehortation is the contrary. Counsel directs, command binds, exhortation endeavours to stir up or incite the will; dehortation keeps it back. Command is of a Superiour; Counsel, exhortation, dehortation are of a superiour, inferiour, equal. For any

of these may counsel, exhort, dehort, as any of them may be counselled, exhorted, dehorted. Its true, that these words are not alwaies taken strictly.

That command should be for the benefit of the party commanding, and counsel for the good of the party counselled, is meerly accidental in waies essential to them. And though sometimes both the intention and the event of both may be such as he determines, yet we know it is many times otherwise. For command may sometimes, nay often, be beneficial to the party commanded, and intended to be so; as counsel may be intended, not only for the good of the party counselled, but also counselling; and also prove so to be. The nature of exhortation, and dehortation, is as falsly, loosely and impertinently defined, as the former.

2. Upon the former supposed difference between counsel and command, he determines, *Thou shalt have none other Gods; Thou shalt not make any graven image*, &c. to be commands. Yet these are not for the benefit of God, but man keeping them. For in keeping them there is great reward. But, *Go and sell all thou hast*, &c. is only a counsel with him, because the party shall have benefit, even treasure in heaven if he do so. Yet even this is so a counsel, as it is a command. For man is bound to love God more then the world; and to preferr treasure in heaven, before treasure on earth, and this by command. As it directs, its counsel; as it binds, its command.

For one and the same sentence may be a command, a counsel and an exhortation too, yet in different respects; as it binds a command, as it directs a counsel, as it incites an exhortation. And very many exhortations include, or at least presuppose a command, and a counsel. But I wonder why Mr. *Hobbs* should make these words of *Peter, Repent and be baptized*, *Acts* 2. 38 a counsel only. Are not all men, especially which hear the Gospel, bound to repent? For doth not Saint *Paul* say, *And the time of this ignorance God winked at, but now commandeth all men everywhere to repent*, *Acts* 17. 30. And what will he contradict the Apostle, and in express terms? It seems he is but a Divine of the lowest rank, as he is a States-man far under the highest form. His presumption and boldness is very great, but his knowledge and judgement very defective. For if he had known, that repentance had been a principal duty, according to a principal command of the Gospel, and that it was nothing else but a return to obedience, after disobedience, he might have corrected himself, and avoided this errour.

3. In the next place, he undertakes to determine the qualifications of a good Counsellor of State; which hath been done to his hand, and far better then here we read. He is a good Counsellor, who gives good counsel; and that is only good counsel, which is agreeable to the wisdom and justice of God, and tends to the publick good of the State; therefore his first Condition is either imperfect, or else directly false. For the interest and ends of the Counsellor in his counsel, to be consistent with the ends and interest of a Prince counselled, is no waies absolutely good, but may be very wicked and unjust.

The rest of the conditions prescribed by him are good, yet none of the chiefest mentioned by others, omitted by him.

4. In the last part of this Chapter he endeavours to prove, but yet upon very weak, and also very false grounds, That its better to hear Counsellors apart, then in an Assembly. What he means by these words prefixed [supposing the number of them equal] I know not. For he argues against counsel given in Assemblies, without any mention of the equality of their number. Yet this is evident by this rule of God, that the privy Council and Parliaments of *England* are made useless, unprofitable, at least not so good as a secret pact Juncto. This is very unworthy and base, and hath been the ruine of many Princes. The Constitution of *England* required a Parliament, as the great Council of the Kingdom, *in arduis regni negotiis*; and a standing Privy-Counsel (as it was called) in other matters of lesser moment. That both these may be ill constituted, abused and turned into factions, there is no doubt, we have had too woful experience of this. Yet all these inconveniences, with others mentioned by the Author, may be prevented, and the Counsels rectified. The way to our good, and the welfare of *England*, is not to take them away and destroy them, but reduce them, if possibly it may be done, to their prime institution. Otherwise we may fear a military Government, or an absolute Monarch, or a Tyrannie, or an Anarchy. A wise council of Lords standing, and the great Council of the Parliament have been the best supports under God, of the peace and happiness of this Nation. In this I am brief, because here is little that is material, and it more properly belongs to that head of Ministers of State and Officers.

CAP. X.

Of the Second Part. The 26. of the Book. Of civil Laws.

The principal heads and parts of this Chapter are,
1. The definition of a Law civil, with certain conclusions thence deduced.
2. The interpretation of Laws.
3. The distribution of Laws in general.

In the administration of a Common-wealth once constituted; the first thing is Legislation; the second is the Execution. In the execution, 1. Officers are made. 2. Jurisdiction exercised according to those Laws. Therefore the proper place of treating concerning Laws civil in general, is in the first part of administration, which requires first that Laws be made. For God himself did avouch himself to be *Israels* Lord and King, and they avouch themselves his subjects and people, and this was the constitution of that State. This being done, in the next place he proceedeth to make Laws. And this is the order of all such as will imitate God, and proceed orderly to govern a State, as appears, *Exodus* 19. and the 20. Chapters, and so forward. This also was *Jethroes* counsel unto *Moses*, and approved of God. Thou shalt teach them Ordinances and Laws, and shalt shew them the way wherein they must walk, and the work that they must do. Moreover, thou shalt provide thee of all the people, able men, *&c.* and place such over them. This was making of Officers, after he had given them Laws, and let them Judge the people. This is jurisdiction, *Exod.* 18. 20, 21, 22. From hence it appears how preposterously, this man and others are that treat, 1. Of Magistrates. 2. Of Laws. The difference between Laws Civil in general, and the Civil Law of the Roman Empire, is more easily known, and learned from the Civilians, who have clearly delivered it, then from him. For Politicks speaks of Civil or Political Laws (made for the Government of State) more generally; and if it mention any Laws of particular States, they are but examples to the general rules concerning Laws. But let us pass by this, and proceed to his definition, which is as followeth.

T. H.

Civil Law is to every subject, those rules which the Common-wealth hath commanded him by word, writing, or other sufficient sign of the will to make use of it, for the distinction of right and wrong, that is, of what is contrary, and what is not contrary to the rule.

G. L.

In this definition, the *Genus* is, its a rule; the efficient cause is the Common-wealth; the party bound is the subject; the end is the distinction of wrong which is contrary, and right which is not contrary to the rule. But 1. The *Genus* is not a rule, which is an act of the understanding; whereas Law is not only an act of the understanding, but the will, which is *facultas imperans*. Many may give rules by their wisdom, which can make no Laws by their wills. 2. The efficient cause is not the Common-wealth, but *pars imperans*, the Soveraign who is but one part of it. 3. The end is not only to declare a distinction between right and wrong, but to bind the subject to do that which is right, and to forbear that which is wrong. For *lex est regula obligativa*. 4. Not content to give the definition, he explains what is right, and that is that which is not contrary to the Law; and wrong, and its that which is contrary. But what he means by *rule* is hard to know. If he mean by rule, law it self, then its absurd; if he intends some antecedent rule of divine wisdom, manifesting what is just or unjust, before a civil power command it, he is obscure. Though he undervalue the Philosopher so much, as far below him, though he was far above him, he might with *Marsulis* of *Padua*, in his *Defensor Pacis, pars 1. cap. 10*, have observed out of him a better definition of a Law given, *Ethn. ad Nicho. lib. 10. cap. 9. Lex est sententia, doctrina seu judicium universale justorum & conferentium civilium & suorum oppositorum cum præcepto coactivo per pœnam aut præmium de ejus observatione in hoc sæculo destribuenda.* More briefly, its a coactive precept of the Soveraign binding the subject to obedience; and upon the same to be rewarded, or upon disobedience to be punished in this life; where many things are to be observed. 1. The matter of this Law is something in it self just, and conducing to the publik good, yet so that it reacheth to the contrary. 2. This must be known, and judged to be so, by the wisdom and understanding of the Soveraign; for all Laws arr made by wisdom Political. 3. This judgement of the Law-giver must be made known unto the subject; therefore the Philosopher saith its λόγος, a word. And he means not only λόγος ενδιαθετὸς, but προφορικὸς, a word not only inwardly conceived in the mind of the Law-giver, απὸ φρονήοεως χγ νε̃, as *Aristotle* saith, but it must be uttered and made known, as the ten Commandements are called the ten words; therefore its said, *Exodus* 20. *God spake all these words.* 4. It must be *præceptum*, which includes the will of the Soveraign intending to bind the subject, and so declaring himself. 5. It must be an universal precept binding the whole community of the subject. 6. It must be a coactive precept, and backt with the sword for to make the Obligation effectual. In this respect the Philosopher saith, νόμας ἔχει αναγφδκην συναμιν; the Law must have a coactive force. And the Apostle saith, he beareth not the sword in vain: which words imply, the Law-giver must have a sword. 7. This sword protects and rewards the obedient who observe this Law according to their obligation, and it punisheth the disobedient; and for these two ends, the Law must be coactive and armed with a sword. 8. These rewards and punishments are to be conferrd and inflicted in this life; for it cannot reach the soul and the life to come; and this doth difference the civil Laws of men from the Laws of God, which bind men to obedience upon the promise of spiritual and eternal rewards, and for defect of obedience, unto eternal and spiritual penalties. This hath far more of the definition of a Law then his, and more fully declares the nature of a Law civil. Yet if either he, or any other will improve it, I shall like it well, for I know mine own imperfections. From his definition he infers several conclusions, the first whereof is.

T. H.

The Legislator in all Common-wealths is the Soveraign: Again, the Common-wealth is the Legislator by the Representative.

G. L.

That *pars imperans*, is the Legislator in every State, must needs be granted: but that the Common-wealth should be the Legislator, either by or without (*pars imperans*) the Soveraign, I do not understand. For it consists of two parts, the Soveraign and the subject; and if the whole Common-wealth make Laws, then the subject as well as the Soveraign is Legislator. In a Republick or free-State, there is a difference between the

Soveraign and the subject, much more in other models and
forms. Therefore he must needs speak either improperly or
untruly, when he saith the State is Legislator.

T. H.

*Conclusion 2. The Soveraign is not subject to the civil Laws,
because he hath power to make and repeal them at pleasure.*

G. L.

That the Soveraign in divers respects, and especially as a
Soveraign, is not subject unto, but above the Laws, is a certain
truth. For Laws do bind the subject, not the Soveraign, to obey
or be punished; but the Soveraign doth command as Superiour,
not obey as inferiour; doth punish, is not punished. The power
to make a Law, when there is none, and to repeal after that its
made, is sufficient evidence of his superiority, as also
dispensations in judgements and pardons be. Yet this supreme
will Legislative over men, is subject to the superiour will of
God, and must neither make, nor repeal Laws, but according
to wisdom and justice.

T. H.

*Conclusion 3. Custom is not Law by long continuance of time,
but by consent of the Soveraign.*

G. L.

This follows from the first Conclusion. For if the Soveraign
only be the Legislator, then continuance of time and practise of
the people, though universal, cannot make a Law. The
Soveraign must give either an express, or tacit consent; and this
consent is then most evident, when he makes the custom a rule
in judgement, and observes it. And the Civilians well observe,
that besides continuance of time, and the Soveraigns consent, A
third thing is required, and that is, that the beginning of it be
reasonable, as the Author here doth note.

T. H.

*Conclusion 4. The Law of Nature, and the Civil Law, contain
each other, and are of equal extent. For the Laws of Nature,*

which consist in equity, justice, gratitude and other moral
vertues on these depending, in the condition of meer nature,
are not properly laws, but qualities, that dispose men to peace
and obedience; when a Common-wealth is once actually
settled, then are they Laws, &c.

G. L.

1. This is no Conclusion from the definition, except he mean
that the rule of right and wrong be the Law of Nature. 2. The
Laws of Nature are the Laws of God, and not of man; and not
only subjects, but Soveraigns are bound by them. 3. Therefore
they bind not as commanded by the civil Soveraign, but as
written by the hand of heaven in the heart of man. Neither is
that which afterwards he makes the difference between the Law
of Nature, and the Law of civil Governors, any difference at
all, that the one is written, the other not. For both are written,
one by the hand of man, though every Civil Law be not
written, and the other by the hand of God: the one in the heart,
the other upon some other material substance; and that which
is written in the heart, may be written out of it. 4. Equity,
justice gratitude, and other moral vertues, are not Laws of
nature, but either habitual or actual conformities unto the
Laws of Nature. 5. How the Laws of Nature, and Laws Civil
should be of equal extent, and yet contain one another, and be
parts one of another, I do not understand. 6. A Law of Nature
is only then a civil Law, when its declared to be so by the civil
Soveraign, yet its a Law before. 7. For the most part learned
men do understand by the Laws of Nature, certain divine
principles imprinted upon the heart of man; by the Laws of
Nations, more immediate; by the Laws civil, more remote
Conclusions of constitutive Laws civil.

T. H.

Seeing all Laws have their authority and force from the will
of the Soveraign, a man may wonder whence proceed such
opinion as are found in the Books of Lawyers of eminence in
several Common-wealths, directly or by consequence, mak-
ing the Legislative power depend on private men, or
subordinate Judges: as for example, That the Common-Law
hath no Controuler but the Parliament. Item, That the
Common-Law hath two arms, Force and Justice, the one

whereof is in the King, the other deposited in the hands of the Parliament.

G. L.

The former Conclusion, which is the fifth in order, That the Laws of Princes and Countries subdued, depend upon the Soveraign conquering is true. And it is wisdom in the Conquerors to grant them the Laws and Customs of God, and no waies prejudicial to their power. For many are willing to change their Governors, yet unwilling to change their Government. But as concerning the two maximes of Law, I might refer him to the Learned in that profession, who no doubt can make them good against any thing he hath said. They seem to him to be unreasonable, partly because he is ignorant of the Constitution, both of this, and also of other States; partly because they are inconsistent with his Utopian principles. For he presupposeth, 1. That the King of *England* is an absolute Monarch. 2. That the Parliament, as a Parliament, is meerly a subject. 3. That the King hath power at will and pleasure to call Parliaments, and dissolve them; yet these hath he not made good, neither can he. 1. That our Kings are not absolute Monarchs is well known, the Laws and practice have made it manifest. And whatsoever ignorant persons and parasites may say, yet wise men, both English and Forreign States-men, who have dealt with *England*, have been assured of the contrary; especially when in certain leagues they have required the consent of the Parliament. Again, the Kings of *England* never made or repealed a Law, nor levied a subsidie alone themselves, without a Parliament. And they are sworn [*corroborare leges, quas vulgus elegerit*] For let [*Elegerit*] be what tense it will, *vulgus*, which is *populus, non rex, eligit leges*; and the late King in his answer to the 19. Propositions, did confess that the Lords and Commons had a share in the Legislative power. And it were very much to be wondered at, if that King, who himself alone could never make or repeal a Law, nor levy or impose a subsidie, nor revoke the judgement of any Court, nor alter a word or clause in any Law agreed upon in Parliament, should be an absolute Monarch. Its far more probable he was only trusted with the force for the execution of justice, according to Law and Judgement, according to the second maxime. And if he was no absolute

Soveraign, then his second supposition, that the Parliament, as such, is only an Assembly of private men and subjects, and to be considered in no other capacity, is false: As likewise his third, That the King can call and dissolve Parliaments at will and pleasure. For by the Constitution, the Laws and practise, he was bound to call them once a year, and oftner as the necessity and exigency of affairs, either of peace or war should require. And in such cases to dissolve them before the [*ardua Regni*] were disaptched, was both dangerous and destructive; and did argue either a bad constitution, or a corruption of the same.

T. H.

Law cannot be against reason, neither is it the letter, but the intention of the Law-giver that is the Law. And this reason is not private of subordinate Judges, but of the supreme Lawgiver.

G. L.

All this is willingly granted, if he understand by Reason, not the meer conceit or will of the sovereign, but that reason which is a ray of divine wisdom shining in the mind of the Law-giver, regulating his judgement, and expressed in the words of the Law. And the sense of a Law given by a learned Judge subordinate, may be very true, yet not authentick: because he that makes the Law, can interpret Law in that manner, and none else. I pass by his discourse concerning promulgation and interpretation of Law, as also the qualification of Judges, which belongs to that Chapter of Officers formerly mentioned. He might have done well to have improved these excellent Treatises of other learned Authors, who have informed us both more accurately, and also more particularly of these things, then he himself hath done. But he conceits himself as far above them, as they surpass ordinary men. Neither is his distribution of Laws worth the examination, as being very crude and indigested, as also heterogeneous. I proceed therefore to his two questions, concerning what assurance may be had of, and obedience ought to be given unto divine positive Laws. The questions are,

80   Leviathan

T. H.

1. How can a man without supernatural revelation, be assured of the revelation received by the declarer of those Laws?

2. How can he be bound to obey them?

The answer to the first, by sanctity, miracles, wisdom, success, without particular revelation, its impossible for a man to have assurance of a revelation made to another. Therefore no man can infallibly know by natural reason, that another hath had a supernatural revelation of Gods will, but only a belief.

G. L.

This presupposeth, 1. That there is a positive Law of God. 2. This positive Law is declared and witnessed to be the Law of God. 3. That this testimony concerning this Law is divine and infallible. 4. That it is such, because its grounded on, and agreeable to an immediate revelation from God of that Law to him that doth declare it, as to *Moses*, the Prophets or Apostles. For God formerly spake unto the Fathers by the Prophets, in the latter times to their children by his Son first, and after by his Apostles. The question here is not how we shall attain a demonstrative, clear, or intuitive knowledge of the matter of the Law, nor of the manner of the revelation; but how we may be assured that the declaration or testimony of him to whom the revelation was made, is divine, that we may believe it as divine and from God. The means whereby the divinity of the testimony was made evident at the first, were extraordinary, as signs, wonders, and divers miracles and gifts of the Holy Ghost, according to his own will, *Heb.* 2. 4. But after that upon these divine attestations the Gospel was generally received in all Nations, and the prophesies of the Old Testament in this particular fulfilled, these ceased; yet one thing alwaies did, and ever will manifest the testimony and doctrine of the Gospel to be divine, and that is the Holy-Ghost, who (by his powerful working upon the hearts of men, seriously attending to this truth, whereby a great change both inwardly in their hearts, and outwardly in their lives is wrought) doth mightily confirm it. And those who find, and feel in themselves the effects of sanctification and heavenly comfort, can no waies doubt, but are assured that God was in the Prophets and Apostles, and did speak by them. Besides when we consider, 1. That the more we understand them, the more excellency of wisdom we find in them. 2. That these positives are agreeable and no waies contrary to pure morals. 3. That they conduce effectually to holiness and eternal life. 4. That they were approved, received by the best men in the world, and sealed with the blood of many Martyrs, we must needs be fully satisfied that they are not false, feigned, fantastick conceits of deluded men, and not only so, but all these things may perswade any rational man to try upon practise, whether they be divine or no. And this never any did, but found the Apostles Doctrine to be of God. If we had nothing but the universal and perpetual agreement and tradition of the Church of all places and times, affirming the Scripture to be the Word of God, it were sufficient to produce in a rational man a greater measure of belief, then any Book or History in the world can possibly require or deserve. For this universal testimony of the best in several parts of the world, at such a distance as that they in their time neither heard of, nor knew one another, makes it more credible then any humane History can be. But to return unto Mr. *Hobbs*, I say its possible, and not impossible to know the divinity of the testimony or declaration immediately, but not of the revelation or matter revealed. Yet that such a revelation, and such a thing revealed there was, is known in some measure by consequence. And the divine Authority of this testimony may be infallibly known, and that by natural reason, yet by it as elevated and more perfected by outward representation and inward sanctification. And the matter of the revelation to another, together with the manner, may be believed, though not known. For when we once know that God hath revealed it, we believe the thing revealed to be true, though by artificial and intrinsecal arguments we cannot prove it to be so. For the testimony of God may be evident, though the thing testified be hidden and above our reason. The Conclusion is, That we may have an infallible knowledge of the positive Laws of God, so far as to know that they are from him, and are his Laws, and that without particular revelation, that they were revealed to another.

T. H.

If the divine positive Law be not against the Law of nature, and he undertake to obey it, he is bound by his own act to obey it,

*but not bound to believe it. For mans belief, and interiour
cogitations, are not subject to the commands, but only to the
operations of God, ordinary or extraordinary. Faith of
supernatural Law, is not a fulfilling, but only an assenting to
the same: its not a duty but a gift, &c.*

G. L.

His second question was, how a man can be bound to obey
supernatural positive Laws, whereof he hath no particular
revelation, that they were revealed to others declaring them.
To this he answers, 1. It must not be against the Law of nature,
which is the Law of God. And its true, that the Law of nature is
the Law of God, and this is a good rule. For the positive Laws
of God are not contrary to his pure moral Laws, which have an
intrinsecal rectitude in them. 2. He further adds, that if he
undertake to obey a supernatural positive Law of God, he is
bound to obey it, but not believe it. This is very obscure, and
very absurd. For, 1. To undertake to obey it, seems to be a
promise to obey it: and this is a voluntary Obligation, whereby
a man may bind himself to obey it as a divine Law, or as no
Law, or if as a Law, yet not as a Law of God; and then he doth
not obey as he ought to do. 3. It is absurd, To obey it as a
positive Law of God, and not believe it to be a Law of God. For
if he neither know nor believe it to be a Law of God, he cannot
obey it as a Law of God. His obedience is no obedience unto
God. 4. Whereas its said, That faith is not subject to Gods
command, its not a duty, its a gift, this must needs be a gross
errour. For though the active power whereby a man is enabled
to believe a divine positive truth, be the gift of God, yet the
exercise of this power, and the acts thereof, are subject to the
Law of God. Otherwise positive unbelief of a supernatural
divine positive Law, sufficiently declared and proposed could
be no sin. Its true, that some affirm that the first and natural
acts of the soul are not subject to any Law: yet these do grant
that all practical operations (and such assent unto divine truths
is) be subject unto Law. That faith is a duty, is apparent,
because God commands it, approves it, rewards it, and
reproves and punisheth unbelief. That we may the better
understand the drift of this Author in this discourse, he
produceth the examples of *Abraham* and *Moses*, declaring
positive Laws of God upon revelation made of them, which the

posterity of *Abraham* were to obey upon their declaration; and thence concludes,

T. H.

That it is manifest, and sufficiently appeareth, that in a Common-wealth, a subject who hath no certain and assured revelation particularly unto himself, concerning the will of God, is to obey for such, the command of the Common-wealth.

G. L.

But, 1. It was formerly made manifest, that neither *Abraham* nor *Moses* were Soveraigns, much less Common-wealths. 2. A Soveraign civil may declare something to be a Law of God, and yet it may be no such thing; and declare against a Law, and yet it may be (and many times it so falls out to be) a Law of God; and in neither of these cases is the subject bound to obey his Soveraign. 3. If that which is declared for a positive Law divine be sufficiently attested, especially by Miracles and Gifts of the Holy Ghost, by undoubted history and universal tradition, the matter be agreeable to the Law of nature, tends to · practise of piety, being practised, is conducing to an higher degree of holiness and justice; and by experience constantly found to be accompanied with rare and excellent effects tending to mans inward and real happiness, it is to be believed and obeyed as a divine Law, though all the Soveraigns in the world declare against it. If a subject do accept the Religion established by the civil Laws of his Countrey, he is free from civil penalities of man, yet not from the judgement of God, if that Religion be against the Laws of God. No Laws of man can bind above, much less against the Laws of God; and this all rational men will confess. *Austine* denies the perfection, and according to *Tullies* definition, the very being of a Common-wealth to the Roman State, because it commanded subjection unto, and worship of Devils. By what this Author hath delivered, Christ and the Apostles are made guilty, because they required obedience to the positive Laws of the Gospel, seeing they were contrary to all civil Laws of the world: Upon this account the Rulers of the Jews, heathen Princes, and the Roman Emperours, who persecuted the Christians, are justifiable; as all such who received the

Christian Religion contrary to their own Laws, are condemnable; but of this you will hear more hereafter. For he makes it indifferent what Religion any man professeth, if it be agreeable to the Laws of the State where he lives.

T. H.

There is also another distinction of Laws, into fundamental and not fundamental; but I could never see in any Author, what a fundamental Law signifieth, &c. A fundamental Law is that by which the subjects are bound to uphold whatsoever power is given unto the Soveraign, &c.

G. L.

This doth argue his ignorance in Politicks. For fundamental Laws in every State are those which concern the constitution; not fundamental, such as are made immediately to regulate the administration. The former are such as cannot be altered without taking asunder and disjoynting the very frame and form of Government; the latter may be altered, and yet the essential frame may stand. The former are the foundation of a State; the latter are but superstructions. The former determine the Soveraign who he is, and what his power, and also define the bounds of the liberty and subjection of the subject. The golden *Bull* is said to contain the fundamental Laws of the German Empire; as the *Salick*, or as some call it [the *Gallick*] of excluding females from succession to the Crown, is said to be one of the fundamentals of *France*.

T. H.

I find lex civilis, & jus civile, *promiscuously used for the same thing, even in the most learned Authors, which nevertheless ought not to be. For* Jus *is Liberty,* Lex *is obligation.*

G. L.

That they are often taken for the same, and in learned Authors, is certain, and that without any errour. But yet *Jus* doth not properly signifie the liberty left unto us by the Law; but *id quod Justum est*, and ought to be the matter of the Law. And when the Civilians take *Jura* and *Leges* to be the same, they understand by *Jus*, not *Jus vagum*, but *Jus à lege determinatum.* For the Laws determine what is right, and what is wrong: and in this sense, *Jus* cannot be liberty, as he doth fondly imagine; but must either be, or at least imply an Obligation.

CAP. XI.

Of the Second Part. The 27. of the Book. Of crimes, excuses, and extenuations.

The Author in this Chapter is methodical, and cannot much be charted with errours or misprisions, as in the former. The proper place for crimes, excuses, extenuations and aggravations is next to that of Laws. For as the Apostle teacheth us, Where there is no Law, there is no transgression. And herein the Authors of Politicks, seem to be defective, because, though they treat of Laws and Jurisdiction, yet they say little or nothing of Crimes. Yet the Civilians in this particular have done their part. He doth distinguish betwixt sins and crimes, and his distinction may be allowed, though hardly in Politicks. Yet the word *Crime* in Learned Authors is not alwaies taken, as here it is, for an offence, as it is an object or matter of Judgement. And sometimes causes judicial are distinguished into civil, criminal, capital. In which distinction criminals are onely one sort of causes. That which we call [*Sin*] in Divinity is nothing but disobedience to a Law in general, though it be strictly taken for disobedience to divine Law. Disobedience being an anomy, presupposeth a Law, and a Law must have a Soveraign and a Law-giver: and there can be no violation of a Law without wrong unto the Law-giver: And those offences are most hainous, which directly oppose and wrong the power of the Soveraign lawfully constituted, because they tend to the rasing of the very foundation and constitution of the Government it self. Such are, denying of the supreme power, resisting it, and revolting from it, so as to be Soveraigns our selves, or independent, or subject to another. The first law God gave was for to secure his Soveraignty, *Thou shalt have no other Gods but me*; as the Septuagint do well and truly turn it. And this by *Philo* is said to be the Commandment [πεζι μοναρχίας] of the supreme power of one God. All other offences are against the

Laws of administration, which though they may be hainous, yet are not so hainous as those former against the institution. These offences of disobedience may be considered, either with reference to the Laws antecedent, as violated, or to Jurisdiction following, in which sense the Author handles them, and calls them crimes. And these may be reduced unto certain heads, as they have been by Civilians, and also by the Lawyers of particular States; yet this is most exactly done by the Common-Law of *England*, which was entire before the Conquest, and followed the order of the ten Commandments of the moral Law of God. Thus some Antiquaries in Law do inform us.

The Author acquits all motions of the soul antecedent to a deliberate consent, resolution, and intention, from being sins; yet this I cannot do. Its certain, that to understand, know and remember that which is evil and unjust, cannot be sin, because God doth so: and all this may be done with a detestation of it; yet to like, approve, incline unto, delight in evil thus known and remembered, though we never yield a deliberate or any formal consent, must needs argue some imperfection, if not corruption in the heart of man, which should never think of evil, but with hatred. The rest of the Chapter is rational, if rightly understood, the greatest part whereof is taken up in that of aggravations, wherein he hath done better then others, yet he is far short of some who have both more largely, and also accurately handled that point out of Scriptures. Its a common theme of Casuists and Civilians, and might have been much improved. The original of all crimes and offences, are either from the understanding or the will, not the passions, as he affirms. From the understanding, either not apprehending, or not judging aright, from the will averse, or enclined another way by reason of corruption. Ignorance and error are from defect, or negligence, or wilfulness, severally or joyntly. And here its to be observed, That the more of meer will there is in any offence, the more hainous it is. The highest degree of wilfulness is in obstinacy, resisting all means and motives used for to rectifie the heart.

CAP. XII.

Of the Second Part. The 28. of the Book. Concerning punishments and rewards.

Upon obedience or disobedience, follow punishments or rewards, determined by Judgement, which is an act of Jurisdiction, and considers the Law as violated or observed. And here comes in according to order, that head of Jurisdiction in general, which properly is handled in that part of Politicks we call Administration. And he that undertakes to deliver a model of Politicks, and yet saith nothing of Jurisdiction, but proceeds from crimes to punishments, *per saltum*, as Mr. *Hobbs* doth, is but a superficial Author. But let us hear his definition of punishment.

T. H.

A punishment is an evil inflicted by publick Authority, on him that hath done, or omitted that which is judged by the same Authority to be a transgression of the Law, to the end that the will of men may be thereby better disposed to obedience.

G. L.

This is a very imperfect definition, and one reason is, the Author presumes much of his own judgement, and desires to be singular; otherwise he had a better definition made to his hands. For *pœna est vindicta noxæ*. This punishment is defined in general, as it includes the penalities inflicted by Parents, Masters, or any one who have power to command another: & it reacheth the punishments executed by God. This definition may easily be made so, as fully to express the nature of civil punishment intended by this Author. But for the better understanding of the nature of punishment, we must observe, that it may be considered several waies. 1. As determined by the Law, which binds the party subject either to obedience or punishment. 2. As deserved by the party offending, who is bound to suffer it. 3. As defined by the Judge upon judicial evidence. 4. As inflicted by the Minister of execution. 5. As suffered by the party condemned. 6. As prevented by pardon out of meer mercy, or upon satisfaction made and accepted. The efficient cause of punishing in a Common-wealth, is the

Soveraign or higher powers bearing the Sword; and as exercising Jurisdiction either by himself or his Minister. For a Soveraign doth punish as a Judge. The immediate and formal object of this act is *noxa civilis*, some offence or crime judged upon evidence to be a violation of the Law. The general nature of it is, ἀπόδοσις, retribution. The thing retributed or rendred is something that brings hurt or dammage to the delinquent or party offending, who as judged guilty, is the proper subject of it. Its called by some *Malum triste, propter malum turpe*. The proper act complete and consummate, is the inflicting of this evil determined by just judgement, so as that the party condemned doth actually suffer it. All this for the general notion of it, may be observed out of the words of the Apostle, who saith, That God will render to them who are contentious, and do not obey the truth, but obey unrighteousness, indignation and wrath: tribulation and anguish upon every soul of man that doth evil, *Rom.* 2. 8, 9. For here we have the Judge, the crime Judged to be so, the retribution or rendering, the thing or evil rendred so as to be suffered, the cause why its rendred. In this respect the higher powers are said to bear the sword to take vengeance upon evil doers, *Rom.* 13. 4.

The ends of punishment are many. 1. Some of them are to correct and reform the party punished; 2. Some for example, that others may hear and fear. 3. The end of all punishments in general, is to vindicate the power of the Law-giver, and the honour and force of the Law, to manifest Justice and the hatred of evil, and to procure the peace and tranquillity of the Community. Before the Author proceed to draw conclusions from his definition, he enquires how the Soveraign acquired the power of punishing. And resolves,

T. H.

That the subject in the first constitution, laid aside his power of self-preservation, by hurting, subduing, killing others in his own defence; and so did not give it, but left it to the Soveraign.

G. L.

This is ridiculous, absurd, and grounded upon his false principles. For, 1. The Soveraign is the Minister of God, and is bound to do (so that he keep within the compass of his Commission) that which God would do, and that is to punish evil. And as all his power of making Laws, Judgement, Peace, War, *&c.* are from God, so is this amongst the rest. By whom he is made a Soveraign, from him he hath the sword to punish. Men may give their consent, that such a man, or such a company of men shall raign, but the power is from God, not them. 2. In the constitution of a supreme Governor, no man can Covenant to be protected or defended in doing evil. Neither can any, or all higher powers in the world justly promise to protect any in evil: neither hath any man any power unjustly to preserve himself. For that of the Author, that in the state of nature every man hath right to every thing, is absolutely false and abominable. When a man subjects himself unto a Soveraign ordained of God, not only to protect the good, but punish the evil, he cannot except himself from his punitive power, if he do ill; because he subjects according to the just Laws of God, and cannot lawfully do any other waies. So that power to punish is given by God, not left by man unto higher powers civil.

After his definition of punishment civil, and determination of the means how power punitive is acquired, he 1. Draws conclusions from his definition. 2. Declares the several kinds of punishment. 3. Distinguisheth of rewards. 1. The conclusions are either good and pertinent, or false, or not deducible from the definition, and I will not trouble the Reader with the examination of them.

2. His distribution of punishments is tolerable. And here we must observe, 1. That punishment civil can only reach the body, and this temporal life of man, for the sword cannot reach the soul. 2. That these punishments, as well as spiritual, are either of loss or pain; *pœna damni aut sensus*, privative or positive. The one takes away some good, the other inflicts some positive evil. 3. That some of them take away life, either civil, as banishment, or natural, as death: and some take away such things as make life comfortable, as goods; such are fines, and confiscations; or liberty, as imprisonment, bondage; or our honour, as all ignominious penalties. Those which infer some positive evil contrary to nature, are all kind of tortures whatsoever, which cause pain in the body of man: and all these positive punishments tend to the destruction of life, either in part or in whole. 4. These penalties are so to be inflicted, and in such a measure and proportion, as that no man may gain by doing evil. 5. That though an innocent person, as such, cannot

be justly punished, yet as he is made one person with the guilty, he may justly suffer. Some are one person with the guilty by nature; as children with parents, some by consent, as sureties with the principal guilty of non-payment, or by Laws civil, as the subjects with the Soveraign. 6. The just execution of judgement is a means to avert Gods wrath, to protect the just, to preserve the State, and procure Gods mercy.

Rewards are contrary to punishments, and are due to such as are loyal and obedient subjects doing well. These either are ordinary, and general, as protection of life, liberty, estate; or extraordinary and more special, and such as enrich or advance, or give priviledges, immunities, and exemptions. And these latter should never be disposed of but according to desert, and by this means they would encourage the subject, and breed gallant men. Thus far his constitution of the *Leviathan*, the great monstrous animal hath been examined and viewed: and is found to consist of an absolute power, and absolute slavery. The head is an absolute Soveraign, and body and members absolute slaves.

CAP. XIII.

Of the Second Part. And the twenty ninth of the Book. Of those things which weaken, and tend to the dissolution of a Common-wealth.

All bodies Politick are truly mortal, as the Author saith, though not so mortal as the individual persons whereof they are constituted be. For by reason of succession of these singular and several persons, they are of longer continuance: and therefore said to be immortal; the proper meaning whereof is, that they are not so mortal. Many States are constituted by degrees, not in a moment, or any short time: and in the like manner, they decay by little and little, until they utterly vanish in a total dissolution. And though both constitution and dissolution seem sometimes to be fortuitous, yet they are not so: for its God who in his mercy plants and builds: and in his just judgement plucks up, and pulls down. This is the place assigned by Authors to the head of Politicks, which delivers the causes of the alteration, corruption and subversion of States.

Alterations of the forms of Government are sometimes for the better, and so they are a blessing; sometimes for the worse, and so they are the same with corruption. Corruption is from man; subversion from God, as the supreme and universal Judge. Corruption goes before, subversion follows. And this corruption is from the sins and crimes of the Governors, or governed, or both. The crimes of Governors are either Personal or Political: Personal are many times the same with the offences of the people: sins of them as men: Political are such as make them guilty as they are Governors, as ignorance, imprudence, negligence, injustice Political; and these not only in assuming and acquiring power, but in the administration of the same. The sins of the people as subjects, are impatiency, when they will not endure the severity of just Governors, good Laws, and impartial Judgement, a desire of innovation and alteration of Government, without just and necessary causes, open rebellion, secret treachery and conspiracy, sedition and such like. The sins of both, which are personal, are impiety against God; injustice and unmercifulness towards man, the abuse of peace and plenty to bravery, drunkenness, gluttony, lewdness, and such like Vices. And when in these they become impudent, incorrigible, and universally delinquent, their ruine is fatal and unavoidable: the harvest is ripe, and the sickle of Gods vengeance will cut them off.

The Apostle in his Epistle to the *Romans, cap.* 13. gives a perfect model of the best and most lasting States. 1. The higher powers must so ascend the Throne, as that it may be truly said, they were ordained of God, and advanced not only and meerly by his permission, but Commission and Command. 2. They must have a sword, and a sufficient coactive power. 3. They must use the same according to just judgement and wholsom Laws, for the protection of the good, and the punishment of the bad. 4. The people must be subject not only out of fear, but conscience. 5. They must obey their good and wholsom Laws. 6. They must give them such allowance as shall be sufficient to maintain and make good their just power. 7. They must love one another. 8. They must not live in rioting and drunkenness, chambering and wantonness, nor in strife and envying. In a word, they must be sober in themselves, just towards man, devout towards God. But when Prince Priest and people refuse to follow these Laws, they draw Gods judgements from heaven upon the Common-wealth. Idle, filthy, and abominable *Sodom* must be destroyed: Gold-thirsty and blood-thirsty *Babylon* cannot stand: Idolatrous and Apostate *Israel* and *Judah* must be wasted with sword, famine, pestilence, their Countrey made desolate, and the remnant carried captives and dispersed in remote parts, and in the midst of their enemies. But let us examine the causes of the weakening and dissolution of States determined by the Author.

T. H.

The 1. is when a man to obtain a Kingdom, is content sometimes with a less power, then to the peace and defence of the Common-wealth is necessarily required.

G. L.

This may prove to be a cause, yet very rarely. Princes and Monarchs (for of them he speaks) offend usually on the other hand. If they can, they will assume and challenge far more power then either God will, or man can give them; for they desire to be absolute Lords. Few of them are of brave *Theopompus* his mind, who willingly made his power less, that it might be more lasting. To be Dukes of *Venice* can in no wise satisfie their vast ambitious desires: The *Lacedemian Ephori* are terrible to them: The *Justitia Arragoniæ* cannot be endured; Legislative and judicial Parliaments do too much restrain and limit their power: with them its treason to affirm that there be any lawful means to reduce them into order, when they apparently transgress the Laws of nature, which are the Laws of God. The people indeed must be kept in awe and order, and this cannot be without power. But, what is here understood by power? It is not *potestas*, but *potentia*, strength and force; which may be great in a *Leviathan*, yet without wisdom and justice can never long keep the people in subjection. His examples of the *Roman* and *Athenian* free-States, are not fully applyed, neither do the applyed come home unto the point. *Rome* was strong enough to subdue a great part of the world, before she became imperial: and *Athens* in that Law concerning *Salamis* had power enough, but wanted wisdom, and therefore were reformed by the wise folly of *Solon*. That which is here spoken of the power of Kings, is not to derogate the least from that power which is due unto them by the constitution of the State wherein they raign. Some have more, some have less. Yet none should have less then is sufficient for the full discharge of their place: And it is to wished every one of them would keep the bounds determined by God and Constitution.

T. H.

A second cause of weakning and dissolving a State, are certain Doctrines. The first, That every private man is Judge of good and evil actions.

G. L.

Judgement is publick or private; publick no private man can pass; private he may; and that both of his own actions, and others too. The acts of others are private or publick: of both these he may Judge. Publick acts of the Governors are Laws, Judgements, Execution. Even of Laws he may, he must within himself, so far as they are a rule and bind him, enquire, examine and determine, whether good or evil. Otherwise, he can perform but only a blind obedience to the best: and if he conform unto the unjust, he in obeying man, disobeys God, which no good man will do. In other acts which are apparently just, we may judge of them truly as they are, and no otherwise. Yet this must not be done to palliate our disobedience to that which is just, or raise sedition, or rebel; but we may complain to God, and by our humble prayers seek redress.

T. H.

A second Doctrine, That whatsoever a man doth against conscience is sin. The conscience may be erroneous; and he that is subject to no Civil Law, sins in all he acts against his conscience. Yet to him that is in a Common-wealth, the Law is the publick conscience, by which he hath undertaken to be guided.

G. L.

Conscience is a mans knowledge of his own acts, as agreeable or disagreeable to the Law of God. Its not a faculty, but an act of the soul: and an act, not of the will, but understanding, and the same as practical. The proper act is knowledge; the object is his own acts, and these acts not any way, but as agreeable or disagreeable to the Law of God. For as *Aquinas* saith, there must be *applicatio facti ad legem*: Otherwise a mans understanding cannot judge of it as conformable or not unto the Law of God. These acts may be considered as to be done, or done. In the former respect conscience binds as a Law, though it be not the Law, but presupposeth or includeth the knowledge of the Law. In the latter respect it judgeth, and is a kind of judge of himself in some sort as superiour to himself. But before the tribunal of God it is a witness, and doth accuse or excuse. The great Question so much vexed by the Casuists, is whether an erroneous conscience doth bind. But let them determine what they please; an erroneous conscience in proper sense is no conscience. For an errour is no knowledge, but a defect of knowledge, or rather a plain want of knowledge, and also an act contrary to knowledge. Conscience is a knowledge in proper sense, and knowledge is true and certain: and its a knowledge of a mans own act or acts as agreeable to the Law of God; this an erroneous conscience cannot be. That conscience is such a knowledge, is made evident by the Apostle, saying, That when the Gentiles not having the Law, do the things contained in the Law, they having not the Law, are a Law unto themselves, who shew the work of the Law written in their heart by their conscience witnessing, *&c. Rom.* 12. 14, 15. Where we may observe, 1. That the conscience could not witness, accuse or excuse, except there were something to be accused or excused. 2. The thing accused as evil, or excused as good, must be something conformable, or contrary to the Law of God. 3. The conscience could not accuse or excuse any thing as good or evil, without knowledge both of the Law, and of the act that was contrary or consentaneous to that Law. 4. Therefore the Apostle before he makes mention of the conscience, affirmeth, 1. That they did the things contained in the Law. 2. They were a Law unto themselves. 3. That they did by their conscience witnessing, prove or demonstrate the work of the Law, (that is the work which the Law did command) written in their heart. To have the work of the Law written in their heart, is to have a certain true knowledge of it, not an erroneous mistake. But to return to the Author, Conscience in proper sense doth bind, yet not as it is knowledge, nor as knowledge of a mans proper act, nor as knowledge of the Law in general, but by vertue of the Law known as a rule of his particular act. For man being subject unto God, and under his Laws, cannot bind himself, and be his own Law-giver: but the

Law of God, not an errour, truly understood by him doth bind
him. But let the erroneous judgement of the practical understanding be called conscience, as by a Trope it may, because
there may be something of conscience in it; yet whether can it
bind or no? I answer, it cannot bind: for an errour of the
understanding, cannot be a binding rule to command the will
of man; neither can it be a rule at all. Again, an erroneous
judgement, especially practical, is a sin, and against the Law of
God; therefore it can no waies bind; only thus far most
Casuists do grant, that by it a man is so far bound, as not to act
against it; yet this it doth only *per accidens*, (for *per se*, he is
bound to act otherwise then it doth dictate.) For because God
hath made a mans reason his guide, he must needs be much
depraved in his will, that will act contrary unto his reason. And
he that will not scruple to act against his erroneous judgement,
will be bold to act against his judgement rightly informed. But
the full debate of this, I refer to another occasion. And these
things premised, I return unto Mr. *Hobbs* that of the Apostle,
Whatsoever is not of faith, is sin: and therefore whosoever acts
against faith and conscience, properly so taken, sinneth: and
for him to affirm that the true Doctrine of God revealed in the
Scripture, should be either false, or destructive of civil States
and Governments, is no waies tolerable. Whereas he alledgeth,
that the Law of the Common-wealth is the publick conscience
by which the subject hath bound himself to be guided, its too
loose and fallacious, if examined. For, 1. The Law is not the
publick conscience, but the publick rule of conscience in
matters civil. 2. Its a rule of the subjects obedience, not as its a
Law of the Common-wealth, but as it is agreeable and not
contrary to an higher Law, the Law of God. For the Laws civil
do not immediately bind the conscience and immortal soul, as
the civil Soveraign hath no power to punish it, for his sword
cannot reach that spiritual substance; Secondarily and by
consequence they may oblige the soul. 3. No subject may or
ought to make the Law of the State his absolute guide. For the
Law may be against the Law of God; and then, how can the
subject undertake to obey it, and make it his rule, and not
offend God? 4. Every subject is first bound and subject unto
God, before he be subjected to civil powers: and is first bound
to obey God more then man: and as his subjection unto man is
but conditional and subordinate to his subjection to God, so
his obedience to man is limited, and only to be performed in

such things as his supreme and absolute Lord doth allow him. And though man may suffer for his disobedience to humane Laws, yet he had better suffer a temporal then an eternal penalty; and offend man rather then God. Neither doth this doctrine any waies prejudice the civil power, nor encourage any man to disobedience and violation of civil Laws, if they be just and good, as they ought to be: and the subject hath not only liberty, but a command to examine the Laws of his Soveraign, and judge within himself, and for himself, whether they be not contrary to the Laws of his God.

T. H.

The third Doctrine, That faith and sanctity are not to be attained by Study and Reason, but by supernatural inspiration and infusion.

G. L.

That divine faith wherby we believe on Jesus Christ, and obtain eternal life in him, and that sanctity of life whereby we please God, and are accepted of him, are no doubt both merited by Christ, and inspired and wrought in us supernaturally by the power of the Holy-Ghost. And there can be no doubt of this to such as believe the Scripture to be the Word of God written, wherein we read, *That except a man be born again of water and the spirit, he cannot enter into the Kingdom of God, John 3. 5. And no man can come unto me except the Father draw him, cap.* 6. 44. And to believe that Jesus was the Son of the living God, was not from flesh and blood, but by revelation of his heavenly Father, Christ himself teacheth us, *Mat.* 16. 17. This revelation was an inspiration or infusion, except we will quarrel with words; and it was not natural; for then it might have been by and from flesh and blood; but it was supernatural and from God revealing, not only outwardly, but inwardly too. It is also further taught us in Scripture, *That no man can say, that Jesus Christ is the Lord but by the Spirit, 1 Cor.* 12. 3, Yet this faith and sanctity are so wrought in us, as that ordinarily God makes use of the Scriptures taught, explained, applyed unto mans heart, of hearing, study and meditation, which are acts of reason, and such acts as man may naturally perform, and also so neglect them, as to give God just cause to deny the inspiration of his Spirit for to make the word taught, heard, meditated effectual upon his heart. This Doctrine hath been believed and professed in the most peaceable Common-wealths of the world, and did strengthen, not weaken, much less dissolve the same. If he understand by the professors of this Doctrine, the phanatick Enthusiasts of these times, who pretend so much that Spirit which God never gave them, and upon this pretence boast themselves to be spiritual men, judging all, and to be judged of none, as they use to abuse the Scripture, then its true that these are enemies to all Government, and their Doctrine tends to the dissolution of all order, Ecclesiastical and Civil, and is to be rooted out of all Common-wealths.

T. H.

A fourth opinion repugnant to the nature of a Common-wealth is this, That he that hath the Soveraign power, is subject to the Civil Laws.

G. L.

There is no doubt but this is destructive of Government, and contrary to the very nature and essence of a Common-wealth; the essential parts whereof are, *imperans & subditus*, the Soveraign and the subject: take this difference away, you confound all, and turn the Common-wealth into a Community; yet though Soveraigns are above their own Laws, (how otherwise could they dispense with them and repeal them?) wise men have given advice to Princes for to observe their own Laws, and that for example unto others, and good Princes have followed this advice. Soveraigns are to govern by Laws, not to be subject unto them, or as Subjects obey them, or be punished by them. But what this man means by Soveraign, in the *hypothesis*, is hard to know. For he presupposeth all Soveraigns absolute, and all Kings of *England* such Soveraigns; and so in general it may be granted, that all Soveraigns are above the Laws civil; yet the application of this rule to particular Princes of limited power, may be false and no waies tolerable. The question is not so much concerning the superiority of the Soveraign over the Laws; but whether a Soveraign by Law for Administration, who is not sole Legislator, is not in divers respects inferiour to the Law; or whether an absolute Soveraign may not cease to be such, and *ex obligatione criminis, ex superiore fieri inferior.*

T. H.

A fifth Doctrine which tendeth to the dissolution of a Common-wealth is, That every man hath an absolute propriety in his goods, such as excludeth the right of the Soveraign. Every man hath indeed a propriety, that excludes the right of the subject which is derived from the Soveraign, without whole protection every man should have equal right to the same.

G. L.

1. If the subject have propriety, as the Author grants, it must needs be absolute, and must needs exclude not only the right of the fellow-subject, but of the Soveraign too. For propriety in proper sense is an indepedent right of total alienation, without any license of a Superiour or any other. 2. This propriety is not derived from the Soveraign, except he be despotical; and such indeed the Author affirmeth all Soveraigns to be: and in that respect the subjects can neither have propriety nor liberty; therefore he contradicts himself, when he saith in many places, that the Soveraign is absolute, and here, that the subject hath propriety. 3. Its to be granted, that even in a free-State, the subjects propriety cannot free from the publick charges: for as a Member of the whole body, he is bound to contribute to the maintenance of the State, without the preservation whereof he cannot so well preserve his own private right. 4. Propriety is by the Law of Nature and Nations at least agreeable unto both. And when men agree to constitute a Common-wealth, they retain their proper right, which they had unto their goods before the Constitution, which doth not destroy, but preserve propriety, if well ordered. For men may advance a Soveraign without any alienation of their estates. No man hath any propriety from God, but so as to be bound to give unto the poor, relieve the distressed, and maintain the Soveraign in his just Government; yet this doth not take away, but prove propriety, because every one gives, even unto the Common-wealth, that which is his own, not another mans, nor his Soveraigns, who may justly in necessary cases, for the preservation of the State, impose a just rate upon the subject.

But if the Reader seriously consider the Authors discourse in other parts of his Book, he may easily know whereat he aims. For, 1. He makes all Soveraigns absolute. 2. The Kings of *England* to be Soveraigns. And 3. in that respect to have a power to raise subsidies, and moneys without a Parliament. And 4. hath made that a mortal disease of our State, which is a great preservative of our liberty. For the people alwaies bear the purse, and could not by the King be charged with the least, without their consent by their *Representative* in the Parliament. This did poise and limit the regal power, prevented much riot and excess in the Court, made the Prince frugal, and hindred unnecessary wars. Yet good Princes, and frugal, never wanted money, were freely supplyed by their subjects, whilest they required in their need any thing extraordinary above the publick revenue, in a right way by Parliament.

T. H.

There is a sixth Doctrine plainly and directly against the essence of a Common-wealth, and its this, That the Soveraign power may be divided.

G. L.

The supreme power, as supreme, must needs be one, and cannot be divided. For as in a Natural, so in a Political body, there must be of necessity one only principle of motion. One supreme will directed by one judgement, and strengthened with one force of the sword, must command, judge, execute: Otherwise there can be no order or regular motion. Yet this supreme power may be in many persons, several and distinct physically, but morally reduced to one by the major part agreeing in one suffrage. That some have made in this State of *England* three Co-ordinate powers, with their several Negatives, and their several distinct rights of Soveraign power, can very hardly be made good by any reason, as I have hinted before. Yet even these do place all the *jura Majestatis*, in all joyntly. Our form of Government is confounded by the different opinions of common Lawyers, Civilians and Divines, who neither agree one with another, nor amongst themselves. It hath been declared, That the fundamental Government of this Kingdom hath been by King, Peers and Commons; yet this can satisfie no man, because there is no certainty what the power of Commons, what the power of Lords, what the power of the King is: Neither whether the house of Commons and of Lords, be two distinct houses or no: Or if they be distinct, wherein they are so distinct. For some affirm, that in

Legislation they ought to be but one, though in Judicial acts two. Yet suppose the Lords to have the Judicial power alone, nevertheless its a question what kind of Lords and Barons these should be. We read first of the forty Lords of the forty Counties in the *Saxons* time: after the Conquest we find three sorts of Barons in the higher house: and they were *Feudarii, rescriptitii, diplomatici*; Barons by Tenure, by Writ, by Patent. Lords by tenure were the first; but afterwards when any were called by the Kings Writ to Parliament, they by that very Writ were made Barons with suffrage amongst the former; and last were Lords by Patent, and such were most, yea almost all our Lords in latter times. And to multiply the last, was a policy in the King. For by that means, after the supremacy of the Pope was cast off, the Bishops did wholly depend upon the King, and the Barons by Patent were his creatures, and by them he might carry any cause, or at least hinder and cross the desires of the Knights and Burgesses. And herein few of our ordinary Histories can help us; because they relate only unto us matter of fact, how sometimes the King, sometimes the Barons, sometimes the Commons were ascendant and predominant, as now they all seem to be descendant. Yet for all this, a free Parliament, of just, wise and good men, might rectifie all this, and unite the supreme power so miserably divided to the hazard of the State.

T. H.

And as false Doctrine, so also often-times the example of different Government in a neighbouring Nation, disposeth men to alteration of the form already setled.

G. L.

That this may be a cause of the alteration, and also of ruine too, its very possible: and there seems to be some colour of reason in it, because we are bound to follow the best examples. And this may be powerful and prevalent with such as are given to Change and affect novelty. Yet with wise and understanding men its of no force, because they know full well, that some form of Government, which may be good to one, may prove not to be so to another; and that changes in this kind are dangerous. For to unsettle that which is firm, for to introduce that whereof we have had no experience, may prove the ruine of a State.

T. H.

*And as to rebellion in particular against Monarchy; one of the
most frequent causes is the reading of the Books of Policy and
Histories of the antient* Greeks *and* Romans, *&c.*

G. L.

This hath been formerly examined. The reading of these Books
cannot do so much hurt, as this *Leviathan* may do: For it is far
more dangerous and destructive of good government, then any
of their Histories, which can do no hurt to any but such as are
ignorant and ill-disposed. In those Books they may read of
Kings and Emperours, and of Monarchies as well as free-
States; and few are so void of understanding, but that they well
know they are bound to their own form of Government, and
are not to covet every model they read of. Such men as he do
shamefully debase free-States, as forms unlawful in themselves,
and so flatter limited Princes, as though they were absolute
Lords, and advance Monarchy so high, as though it were the
only form of Government, so instituted by God and commanded; that all Nations were bound unto it, and whosoever
doth not bow unto it, is a rebel against God. Yet he never
instituted immediately any Common-wealth but one, and that
was a free-State; and when a King was desired, he was
offended, and under a regal government it came to ruine.
Whereas he thinks these Books do teach Regicide and killing of
Kings, he is much mistaken. For subjects to murther their
lawful Soveraigns, is an horrid crime, and so much the more to
be detested, if done under the name of Tyrannicide. To plead
for Tyrants really such as such, is to be abhorred. They pervert
the very end of all government, abuse their power, act contrary
to the Laws of God and men, to the ruine of the State, are
enemies of mankind, the chiefest agents for the Devil. The
Question is, Whether a people having power in their hands,
may not restrain, or remove, or put to death such men, as being
guilty of many crimes, which the Laws of God have made
universally capital, so that no man in the world can plead
exemption? Some think that they are to be left to God, and
subjects must seek deliverance by prayers and tears; and the
truth is, Christians as Christians, have no other remedy: others
conceive, they may be restrained, and that by force, and their
own subjects do it: Others give this power only unto

Magistrates, or to such as share with them in the supreme power: Others are of a mind, that seeing they cease to be Kings or Soveraigns, they may be lawfully tryed, and put to death, as well as private men; and that without any ordinary jurisdiction: Others determine this to be lawful in such States as that of *Lacedemon* in *Grece*, and *Arragon* in *Spain*. What the Doctrine of the Church of *Rome* is, cannot be unknown. For the Pope doth arrogate an universal Ecclesiastical Jurisdiction, whereby he may excommunicate any Christian King, that shall not obey his Canons and Edicts, and upon this sentence once given, he may depose him, free his subjects from their allegiance, and command them as Catholicks to rise in rebellion against him; & some of them have taught, that its a meritorious art to poyson, stab, or any other way murther Kings for the promotion of the Catholick cause. This question after the terms thereof clearly explicated, is of very great moment; and let men advise well how they do determine either in their own judgement privately, or before others.

T. H.

There be Doctors, that think, there may be more sorts (that is more Soveraigns) then one in a Common-wealth; and set up a Supremacy against the Soveraignty; Canons against Laws; and a Ghostly Authority, against the Civil, &c.

G.L.

There cannot be any Soveraign but one, in one and the same Common-wealth: and to set up Supremacy against Soveraignty; Canons against Laws; Ghostly authority against Civil, must needs be a cause of division, confusion, dissolution. Yet this will not prove any inconsistency of an Ecclesiastical independent power with the Civil Soveraignty, in one and the same Community. And the distinction of the power of the keyes given by Christ unto the Church; and the power of the sword, trusted in the hands of the higher powers civil, is real, and signifies some things truly different one from another, though he either cannot or will not understand it. With Mr. *Hobbs* indeed this distinction can signifie nothing, because he hath given unto the civil Soveraign an infallible judgement, and an absolute power in all causes Ecclesiastical and Spiritual. His discourse may be good against those Ecclesiastical persons who have usurped civil power; otherwise its impertinent and irrational. And he must know, that it is alike difficult to prove, That the State hath the power of the keyes, as for to evince that the Church hath the power the sword. Its as great an offence for the State to encroach upon the Church, as for the Church to encroach upon the State; The Bishops of *Rome* have been highly guilty of the one, and many protestant Princes and States of the other. And though men will not see it, yet its clear enough, that one and the same Community is capable both of a Civil and Ecclesiastical Government at one and the same time: and that the Church and State are two distinct Common-wealths, the one spiritual, and the other temporal, though they consist of the same persons. And these persons, as Christians, considered in a spiritual capacity, make up the Community and Common-wealth Christian, which is the Church: as they are men, having temporal estates, bodily life and liberty, they are members of the civil Community and Common-wealth. The Power, Form of Government, Administration, Laws, Jurisdiction, Officers of the Church are distinct and different from those of the State. The sentence of the Church is, Let him be an Heathen, or a Publican, and the execution is expected from heaven according to the promise, *Whatsoever you bind on earth, shall be bound in heaven*; and this sentence doth take away some spiritual, but no temporal or civil right of the person judged, though the judgement be passed and made valid, both *in foro interiore & exteriore*. The sentence of the civil State is, Let him be fined, imprisoned, stigmatized, banished, put to death; and its executed by the sword. The several members of a Church National, and the whole Church joyntly, is subject to the civil power; and the civil Soveraign, if a Christian, is subject to the Church, because as a Christian, he is subject to Christ, and bound by his Laws. And as a civil Soveraign, he is bound to protect the Church, and he may by civil Laws ratifie the Ecclesiastical Canons, and then they bind not only under a spiritual but a civil penalty too. If Church-assemblies give cause of jealousie to the Civil powers, they may regulate them, and order their proceedings; if they offend, they may punish them. Their persons, lives, estates, are under the sword; and if this be taken from them, because they will not obey them to disobey Christ, they ought to suffer it patiently for Christs sake. In this case the Church may pray and weep, resist and rebel they may not; for Christians as Christians, have no power of the sword against any man, not their own members, much less against the civil Soveraign; whom if they resist, they must do it under another notion, or else they transgress, and can have no excuse. And here it is to be observed, 1. That Christ gathered Disciples, instituted Church-discipline, made Laws, and the Apostles executed them in making Officers, *Acts* cap. 1. & 16. made Laws, cap. 15. passed sentence and executed the same, 1. *Cor.* 5. and all this without any Commission from any civil Soveraign. Therefore its not true which some learned Divines have affirmed, That the State and Church are one body, endued with two powers or faculties; for they are two distinct bodies Politick. Its true, that if, as some conceive, there were no power but coactive of the sword, then they must needs be one body. But there is another power, as you heard before. 2. If a King become Christian, by this he acquires no power, not the least, more then he had before: and if he be Heathen or Mahometan, and all his subjects become Christian, he loseth not one jot of his former civil power, which they are bound to submit unto by the very Laws of Christianity. If he command any thing contrary to the Laws of Christ they may and must disobey, but deny his power, they may not, they must not. In this case a Christian may be perplexed between the Devil and a Goaler, as some of *Scotland* were said to be, when if they obeyed the Parliament, and joyned with Duke *Hamilton* to invade *England*, the Kirk did excommunicate them, and deliver them up to Satan; if they obeyed the Church prohibiting them, they were cast in prison by the State. The cause of this perplexity is not from this, that the Church and State are two distinct Common-wealths, but because the commands of the one or both may be unjust.

T. H.

Some make the power of levying money depend upon a general assembly; of conduct and command upon one man; of making Laws upon the accidental consent of three. Such government is no government, but a division of the Common-wealth into three independent factions, &c.

G. L.

Here again he hath made the Parliament, which is the bulwark of, and best remedy for to preserve our liberty, a disease; and hath turned the King, Peers and Commons into three independent factions; and this Government, he saith, some call a mixt Monarchy. Whether there can be a mixt State, is a question in Politicks; yet if we understand what mixture is, and could determine, whether this mixture be in the supreme power as fixed in the Constitution, or exercised in the Administration, we might more easily satisfie our selves. But this hath not been exactly done. For its probable, that in the exercise of the supreme power, in the three acts of Legislation, Judgement, Execution, there might be a mixture, and these brought to a just and regular temperament. But a mixt Monarchy in proper sense there cannot be. Yet a limited and well-poised Monarch there may be. To place the power Legislative, which includes all the rest, in three co-ordinate parties, granting to every one of them severally a negative, to me seems irrational; for it may easily turn them who should be one, into three factions, as here it is affirmed: at least it will retard all businesses, which for dispatch, require secrecy and expedition. But to place the universal power originally in the general assembly without any negative; the judicial in the Lords, and the executive in the King, seems to be far more agreeable to the rules of reason. This some think was our antient Constitution, and the same excellent.

Difficulty of raising moneys necessary for the defence and preservation of the State, monopolies, popularity in a subject, are diseases which much weaken a State; there is no doubt of this. That one City should ingross the wealth and strength of a Nation, and be so rich and populous as to be able to set forth a potent Army, and maintain it, may be judged very dangerous to a Common-wealth, as Mr. *Hobbs* informs us. By this City in particular, he means *London*, which, as some tell us, furnished the Parliament with men and moneys, whereby the King was vanquished and over-thrown. Yet they seldom did assist the Parliament but upon high terms, and advantagious to themselves; in so much as their Petitions were Commands unto the Parliament, which did depend more upon the City, then the City upon them, by which means they might in time engross the whole power, and so rule the Nation. Yet an army of their own did break their strength, and reduce them unto their own terms: and its clear, that City depends much upon the River, both for fuel, merchandize and provision, and by a wise provident counsel may be easily kept in order. And this might the more easily be done, because the Citizens have so many several interests, and the same inconsistent amongst themselves, as that they can hardly be united.

After all these diseases from within, which weaken and may dissolve a Government, he informs of a destructive cause, and that is a forreign or intestine war, wherein the enemy obtains a final victory, so that the Soveraign cannot protect his subjects in their loyalty. This indeed may cut off a line, change the Governors, and alter the form of Government. Yet in all this, the Community may continue, and never be like a subject matter without any form, but the Government may be the same, and the Governors only altered; nay the Constitution may stand firm, and the Administration only varied: or if the form be changed, yet the privation of the former is an introduction of the latter. Here its confessed, that when the power of protection faileth in the Soveraign, obligation in the subject is taken away. But he starts a question, though with him no question, whether the right of a Soveraign Monarch can be extinguished by the act of another? He saith it cannot. Yet experience tells us, it may. For a conquered Monarch, fallen into the power of another, ceaseth to be a Soveraign, and this is by the act of another. And again, if God by another take away his sword, though his person escape, and be at liberty, he hath but the name, and not the thing or real title. If his subjects freed from obligation, because he can give no protection, do submit themselves unto another, his right is lost. If his life be taken away, and his line cut off, all right is extinct, and in all these cases by the act of another; yet he thinks, that if the power of an assembly be suppressed, their right is extinct. The assembly in an Aristocracy, or Democracy, for such he means, may be extraordinary, or ordinary; and the same the immediate subject of the supreme power, or only trusted for a time with the administration and exercise thereof: and the power of an assembly may be suppressed for a time, and so only suspended, the assembly remaining still. Except he let us know what kind of assembly he understands, and what kind of suppression of power he means, he doth nothing. An assembly whose power depends upon a certain place, time, number, may lose their right, if once they be scattered or defective in that circumstance.

CAP. XIV.

Of the 2. part, the 30. of the book. Of the Office of the Soveraign Representative.

Its very expedient for those, whom it concerns, to know what Majesty is, and what be the several rights thereof, as also that in every State it be fixed in a certain subject, person or persons, that every one may know whom to obey and subject himself unto; yet the principal thing is for Soveraigns to exercise their power in the administration of the Common-wealth according to the rules of Wisdom and Justice, without which the best constitution in the world is in vain.

It might be worth the while to examine what the Author hath delivered concerning the office of a Soveraign Representative, if he had informed us in this point of any thing formerly unknown or more excellent, then we read in other Writers. But he is so far from having done any such thing, that he comes much short of others. The duties of all Civil Governors are most exactly taught in the Scriptures, which if this man had followed, he might have given Princes far more, and more excellent instructions.

In this Chapter we find little but what we heard before; for it consists chiefly in the repetition of his former rules, and his method is not exact. He presumes much of his own knowledge above others, and conceits he hath given us a better model of Government then ever any had before; and so much he admires his own rules, that he thinks them worthy to be taught in the Universities, and tacitly decries all former Politicks, and undertakes to prove his dictates out of Scripture, which he can never do.

Many of his Rules I confess are good, but most of them are such as are very ordinary and commonly known. But in those points wherein he is singular, he can hardly be excused from error. His first and chiefest care after the good of the people, is, to preserve the absolute power of Rulers, which he asserts to be their due; and lest they should lose any of them, he renews his Catalogue of them again. These must be taught the people, that they may know themselves to be absolute slaves. And Princes must take heed of transferring any of their Soveraign Rights unto another. But this was needless; for they have a desire of power before they do obtain it: and after they are once possessed of it, they not only keep that which is due, but also usurp far more then either God or man hath given them. Kings, who are but trusted with a limited power, endeavour to make themselves absolute Lords; and Despotical Soveraigns must be petty Dieties. The best Princes had always a greater care to exercise their power well, then to enlarge it. And by their Wisdom and Justice have governed more happily then any of these absolute Soveraigns, who desire rather to be great then good, and themselves more honourable then the people happy.

The Errours of this Author, vented in this part, as that Soveraign power Civil is absolute; A civil Law against Rebellion is no Obligation; A good Law is not a just Law, because no Law can be unjust. All his Rules of Government may be proved out of Scripture, and other such like, I will not here examine, because some of them are ridiculous; some of them have been formerly answered: and his proof of these in his next part shall be discussed.

CAP. XV.

Of the 2. part, the 31. of the Book. Of the Kingdom of God by nature.

This Chapter is the conclusion of the second part, the Leviathan, and makes way for the third following. The principal subject hereof is the Laws of nature as distinct to laws supernatural. For he truly and wisely makes God the King and Law-giver both in the Kingdom of God by nature, and above nature. That God is the universal King by nature, he seems to prove out of the Scripture.

T. H.

God is King, let the earth rejoyce, saith the Psalmist, *Psal* 96, 1. And again, *God is King, though the nations be angry, and he that sitteth upon the Cherubins, though the earth be moved, Psal.* 98. 1. Whether men will or not, they must be subject always to the Divine Power.

G.L.

In the Allegation of these two places he seems to follow the vulgar Latine and the Septuagint both for the number of the Psalms and the Translation. For with us they are the words of the first verses of the 97. and 99. *Psalms*, and are turned in another manner. The translations though seemingly different may agree in the substance. And its agreed on all hands, that the Psalmist speaks of the Kingdom of God; yet seeing there is a kingdom of God as Creator, and a kingdom of God as Redeemer; it may be a question whether his kingdom in general be here meant, or one of the former particular kingdoms. Both ancient and Modern Divines for the most part understand both the Psalms of the kingdom of Christ, and which is more, the Apostle, *Heb.* 1. 6. so expounds the former Psalm, which agrees with *Psal.* 2. which speaks to the same purpose, and undoubtedly intends the Kingdom of Christ. The Kingdom and Government of God is most properly so called in respect of Angels and men, as onely capable of Laws, Punishments and Rewards, no rational man will deny, yet he by his wisdom doth direct and order all creatures.

T. H.

God declareth his Laws three ways: By natural reason, Revelation, and Prophecy. From the difference of the natural and Prophetick Word of God, there may be attributed to God a two-fold Kingdom, Natural and Prophetick, &c.

G. L.

In the rest of this Chapter we may observe three things. 1. The manner how God declares his Laws. 2. The distinction of his Kingdom. 3. The ground of his Dominion. 1. God doth manifest himself both to Angels and men two wayes; by his Works and his Word. By his works in the Creation and Providence. By his word immediately by Revelation, mediately by Prophecie. In the latter he maketh use of man to speak to man, the same thing he hath spoken to man by Revelation: and the word of prophesie to man is the word of Revelation from God: and the matter of both is the same. The word of Creation and Providence is received by natural reason; the word of Revelation seems to be apprehended by reason supernaturally elevated and illuminated.

The Kingdom of God is natural, or supernatural, according to the natural or supernatural Laws. The first Kingdom by the rules and dictates of natural reason directs man unto a temporal peace and prosperity on Earth: The second by the Laws of Revelation orders him to a supernatural and eternal peace and felicity to be enjoyed fully in Heaven. For the former end all civil Policies were instituted: For the second the polity spiritual of the Church. The declaration of the Laws of Gods Kingdom by nature were universally always declared even to all nations; the Laws of his supernatural Kingdom were revealed universally at the first in the times of *Adam*, and after in the dayes of *Noah*. But after a general Apostacy, *Israel* was trusted with the Oracles of life untill the exhibition of the *Messias*: and after his Resurrection the Apostles received a Commission to teach all Nations, and make these Laws known more generally. So that this Author doth bewray his ignorance in divinity; and pretending to the knowledge of the Scripture, he little understands them, and much abuseth those heavenly Writings. For the Kingdom of God by Prophesie was in all times, and confined in a more special manner for a time unto the people of *Israel* for a special reason. And at the first election of them after their deliverance from the Egyptian bondage, he immediately instituted not onely their spiritual but their civil Government. In which respect their civil government might be called in a peculiar manner the Kingdom and Common-wealth of God: and so the government of no Nation in the world could be accounted.

T. H.

The right of Gods soveraignty is not derived from Creation, but from his irresistible Power.

G. L.

This is his great ignorance to think that Gods Soveraignty should be derived from the executive power or force and strength of his Godhead. For Dominion in general is twofold: *Possessionis aut regiminis*, of possession or government. That of possession we call propriety: in which respect God is absolute Lord of all his creatures, because he createth and preserveth them, so that their very being is more his then theirs. But his soveraign power over man ariseth not onely from propriety in general, but from Gods propriety in him as a rational, intellectual creature, ordinable to an higher end then the inanimate and irrational creature is capable of. For God created and preserved him a rational creature; and both as a creature and as rational he is wholly his. As he is rational, he is capable of Laws, Rewards, Punishments, and hath a power to become Gods subject by voluntary submission and donation of himself, and also to obey his Lord and Maker. This no irrational being hath or can have. So that Gods Dominion over man ariseth from Gods propriety in man as a rational being, and from the voluntary submission of man as a rational creature unto his God who made him such. Gods propriety in man is derived from creation and preservation; and both these were not onely from Gods power, as Mr. *Hobs* imagineth, but also from his Understanding and Will. For God by his wisdom made the world as well as by his power, and worketh all things according to the Counsel of his Will. Dominion of government is not onely from power, nor by power alone; for understanding, will and power, must all concur to Government. Therefore how absurd is that assertion of his which followeth, If there had been any man of irresistible power, there had been no reason why by that power he should not have ruled. If this were true, a Leviathan, a Dragon, an Elephant hath more power then man; and why should not brutes being stronger rule over men who are weaker? By this rule the strongest man in a Kingdom should be King: and he that hath the strength of *Goliah* or *Sampson*, should rule over others, though they have strength without wisdom and integrity.

T. H.

The Kingdom over men, and the right of afflicting them at his pleasure, belongeth naturally to God Almighty; not as Creatour and gracious, but as omnipotent.

G. L.

Obedience is due to God not meerly as gratitude to a benefactor, but as a duty unto him as a Law-giver. For as a Creatour he may have a right to command, because by Creation he hath an absolute propriety in his being, which is such as he is capable of a Law. And Creation is not to be considered as any kind of benefit, but such a benefit as his rational being was wholly derived from it, and also wholly and perpetually depends upon his preservation, and his eternal happiness upon his legislation and judgement. And though he may afflict at pleasure as omnipotent, because as such he can do it, yet he never afflicted any but as a legislatour and Judge, according to his just Laws. Because God is omnipotent he can afflict, but it doth not hence follow that he will afflict. But he instanceth in *Job*, and the man born blind, both afflicted by God as omnipotent: yet *Job* was upright indeed, but not altogether innocent: and though God did manifest unto him his glorious Majesty and Almighty power in his great works, yet this was not done to shew him the cause why God did afflict *Job*, but to humble him. And being humbled, he did not plead his integrity, but repented of his infirmity in dust and ashes. For though he was no hypocrite, yet he was a sinner, *Job* 42. 6. And though the blind man, *John* 9. was born blind, as we might justly be, yet he was conceived and born in sin as we are. But neither he nor his parents were guilty of any such notorious crime, as God doth usually recompence with exemplary punishment even in this life.

T. H.

Honour consisteth in the inward thought and opinion of the power and goodness of another; and therefore to honour God is to think as highly of his power and goodness as is possible. And of that opinion, the external signs in words and actions of men are called worship.

G. L.

This is the first Law of Gods Kingdom by nature in respect of God, that he is to be worshipped. Worship is sometimes an act of the soul terminated upon his Divine excellency and dignity: its called Reverence, and sometimes Adoration. Sometimes its an act terminated upon his supreme and universal Power: And so it is submission to him as Surpeme Lord and Law-giver. Sometime for obedience: and in this respect even the performance of our duty to our neighbours, as done in obedience to him as our supreme Lord, is an act of worship. And all acts of the soul terminated upon the Deity immediately are called worship. The worship of Reverence and Adoration is given unto God as most glorious and excellent in himself, yet so manifested and apprehended. The worshop of submission and obedience is given and ascribed to him as Supreme Lord; and the object of worship is some excellency apprehended in the party worshipped: And because the excellency of the Deity is Infinite and Eternal, therefore the highest degree of worship is due unto him: even to the annihilation of our selves, the resigning of our very being wholly unto him, and the emptying of our selves into the Ocean of his most blessed Being. God deserves and is worthy of all honour, glory and worship as excellent in himself. They may justly be required of the creature as depending solely and wholly upon him as Lord Creator, Preserver. And the creature is bound to worship him by vertue of his Law and Covenant. By performance of this dutie we are capable of Eternal bliss in and from him: and by his promise we come to have a right unto Eternal life.

The Excellency of God is his most perfect and blessed Essence, which cannot be known by man as it is in it self; yet its manifested to us by several distinct attributes, whereof some may be known by the light of Reason in some measure, but more perfectly by the Revelation of the Scriptures. These Attributes are many and distinct, and so given to God by himself: because by one act of Reason we cannot conceive of or understand his Essence; which is but one in it self, but represented to us as different and many, and so apprehended. And by our faith we believe the Divine perfections to be far greater then our Reason can apprehend them to be. They are in himself one infinite being, manifested by his works, and more fully by his Word. And our worship must ascend above our Reason, and must be performed according to our faith, which is a divine and supernatural light. For the distinct knowledge of this worship, with the several acts thereof, and the several names, we must not follow the Schoolmen, but search into the Scripture, & diligently observe the use of the words, as they are there applied to signifie the same.

How far Mr. *Hobs* is from the true understanding of worhsip in general, and of the worship of God in particular, may easily appear from this, that he makes worship to be nothing else but the outward signification by words and actions of internal honour; which with him is nothing else but the inward thought and opinion of the power and goodness of another. But neither is worship nor honour any such thing as he hath defined them. And his discourse of worship with the distinctions will be found very poor upon examination, except we allow him a soveraign power over words to impose what signification upon them he pleaseth, and the same different from that wherein they are used in Classical Authors.

Thus he hath finished his Politicks, set forth under the name of Leviathan in the Frontispiece: And though many have in this kind of learning far excelled him: yet he thinks it clear and the best, and most rational, though it neither agree with reason or Religion. And though his hope is not much, yet some hope he hath some Soveraign may put it in practice. If they have no better directions, they may make use of his principles, as some have done to their ruine. Princes and Ministers of State have no need to be taught them: for they know them too well and follow them too much.

THE CATCHING
OF
LEVIATHAN,
OR THE
GREAT WHALE.

Demonstrating, out of Mr. Hobs his own Works,
That no man who is throughly an Hobbist,
can be a good Christian, or a good
Common-wealths man, or reconcile
himself to himself.

Because his Principles are not only destructive
to all Religion, but to all Societies; extinguishing
the Relation between Prince and Subject, Parent
and Child, Master and Servant, Husband and
Wife: and abound with palpable contradictions.

By *John Bramhall*, D.D. and Bishop of Derry.

Prov. 12. 19. *The lip of truth shall be established
for ever, but a lying tongue is but for a moment.*

London, Printed by *E. T.* for *John Crook*, at the
sign of the Ship in Pauls Church-yard, 1658.

[NB: Margin notes and references in original now set in square
brackets in text.]

CHAP. 1.

That the Hobbian Principles are destructive to Cristianity and all Religion.

[Nature dictates the existence and worship of God.]
The Image of God is not altogether defaced by the fall of man, but that there will remain some practical notions of God and goodnesse; which, when the mind is free from vagrant desires, and violent passions, do shine as clearly in the heart; as other speculative notions do in the head. Hence it is, That there never was any Nation so barbarous or savage throughout the whole World, which had not their God. They who did never wear cloaths upon their backs, who did never know Magistrate, but their father, yet have their God, and their religious rites and devotions to him. Hence it is, That the greatest Atheists in any sudain danger do unwittingly cast their eyes up to Heaven, as craving aide from thence, and in a thunder creep into some hole to hide themselves. And they who are conscious to themselves of any secret crimes, though they be secure enough from the justice of men, do yet feel the blind blows of a guilty conscience, and fear divine vengeance. This is acknowledged by *T. H.* himself in his lucid intervalles. [C. c. 15. s. 14.] *That we may know what worship of God natural reason doth assigne, let us begin with his attributes, where it is manifest in the first place; That existency is to be attributed to him.* To which he addeth *infinitenesse, incomprehensibility, unity, ubiquity.* Thus for attributes, next for actions. *Concerning external actions, wherewith God is to be worshipped, the most general precept of reason is, that they be signes of honour,* under which are contained *Prayers, Thanksgivings, Oblations,* and *Sacrifices.* [T. H. no friend to religion.] Yet to let us see how inconsistent and irreconciliable he is with himself; elsewhere reckoning up all the laws of nature at large, even twenty in number, he hath not one word that concerneth religion, or that hath the least relation in the World to God. As if a man were like the Colt of a wilde Asse in the wildernesse, without any owner or obligation. Thus in describing the laws of nature, this great Clerk forgetteth the God of nature, and the main and principal laws of nature, which contain a mans duty to his God, and the principal end of his creation. Perhaps he will say that he handleth the laws of nature there, onely so far as may serve to the constitution or settlement of a Common-

wealth. In good time, let it be so. He hath devised us a trimne Commonwealth, which is neither founded upon religion towards God, nor justice towards man, but meerly upon self interest, and self preservation. Those raies of heavenly light, those natural seeds of religion, which God himself hath imprinted in the heart of man, are more efficacious towards the preservation of a Society; whether we regard the nature of the thing, or the blessing of God, then all his *pacts*, and *surrenders*, and *translations of power*. He who unteacheth men their duty to God, may make them eye-servants, so long as their interest doth oblige them to obey, but is no fit master to teach men conscience and fidelity.

Without religion, Societies are but like soapy bubbles, quickly dissolved. It was the judgement of as wise a man as *T. H.* himself, (though perhaps he will hardly be perswaded to it) that Rome ought more of its grandeur to religion, than either to strength or stratagems. *We have not exceeded the Spaniards in number, nor the Galles in strength, nor the Carthaginians in craft, nor the Grecians in art,* &c. *but we have overcome all nations by our piety and religion.* [*Cit. Har. Respons. Orat. in P. Clod.*]

Among his laws he inserteth *gratitude* [C. c. 3. s. 8.] to man as the third precept of the law of nature, but of the gratitude of mankind to their Creatour, there is a deep silence. If men had sprung up from the earth in a night like mushromes or excrescences, without all sense of honour, justice, conscience, or gratitude he could not have vilified the human nature more than he doth.

From this shameful omission or preterition of the main duty of mankind, a man might easily take the height of *T. H.* his religion. But he himself putteth it past all conjectures. His principles are brim full of prodigious impiety. (Le. p. 54.] *In these four things, opinions of ghosts, ignorance of second causes, devotion to what men fear, and taking of things casuall, for prognosticks, consisteth the natural seed of religion*; the culture and improvement whereof, he refereth only to *Policy*. Humane and divine politicks, are but politicks. [Ci. c. 16. s. 1.] And again, *Mankind hath this from the conscience of their own weaknesse, and the admiration of natural events, that the most part of men believe that there is an invisible God, the maker of all visible things.* And a little after he telleth us, That *superstition proceedeth from fear without* right reason, and Atheisme from an opinion of reason without fear; making Atheism to be more reasonable than supersitition. What is now become of that divine worship which natural reason did assigne unto God, the honour of existence, infinitenesse, incomprehensibility, unity, ubiquity? What is now become of that dictate or precept of reason, concerning *prayers, thanksgivings*, oblations, sacrifices, if uncertain opinions, ignorance, fear, mistakes, the conscience of our own weaknesse, and the admiration of natural events be the onely seeds of religion?

He proceedeth further, [Excuseth Atheisme, Ci. c. 14. s. 19.] That *Atheisme it self, though it be an erroneous opinion, and therefore a sin, yet it ought to be numbred among the sins of imprudence or ignorance*. He addeth, that *an Atheist is punished not as a Subject is punished by his King, because he did not observe laws: but as an enemy by an enemy, because he would not accept laws*. His reasons is, because *the Atheist never submitted his will to the will of God, whom he never thought to be*. [Ci. c. 15. s. 7.] And he concludeth that mans obligation to obey God, proceedeth from his weaknesse. *Manifestum est obligationem ad prestandum ipsi (Deo) obedientiam, incumbere hominibus propter imbecilitatem*. First it is impossible that should be a sin of meer ignorance or imprudence, which is directly contrary to the light of natural reason. The laws of nature need no new promulgation, being imprinted naturally by God in the heart of man. *The law of nature was written in our hearts by the finger of God, without our assent*; or rather *the law of nature is the assent it self*. [Qn. p. 137.] Then if nature dictate to us that there is a God, and that this God is to be worshipped in such and such manner, it is not possible that Atheisme should be a sin of meer ignorance.

Secondly, a rebellious Subject is still a Subject, *de jure*, thought not, *de facto*, by right, though not by deed: And so the most cursed Atheist that is, ought by right to be the Subject of God, and ought to be punished not as a just enemy, but as a disloyal traytour. Which is confessed by himself, *This fourth sin* (that is, of those who do not by word and deed confesse one God the supreme King of Kings) [Ci. c. 15. s. 19.] *in the natural kingdom of God is the crime of high treason, for it is a denial of divine power, or Atheisme*. Then an Atheist is a traitour to God, and punishable as a disloial Subject, not as an enemy.

Lastly it is an absurd and dishonourable assertion, to make our obedience to God to depend upon our weaknesse, because we cannot help it, and not upon our gratitude, because we owe our being and preservation to him. [1. Cor. 9:7.] *Who planteth a vineyard, and eateth not of the fruit thereof? Or who feedeth a flock and eateth not of the milk of the flock?* And again, [Rev. 4. 11.] *Thou are worthy O Lord to receive glory, and honour, and power, for thou hast created all things, and for thy pleasure they are and were created.* But it were much better, or at least no so ill, to be a downright Atheist, than to make God to be such a thing as he doth, and at last thrust him into the devils office, to be the cause of all sinne.

[Destroyes Gods ubiquity.] For *T. H.* his god is not the God of Christians, nor of any rational men. Our God is every where, and seeing he hath no parts, he must be wholly here, and wholly there, and wholly every where. So nature it self dictateth. [Ci. c. 15. s. 14.] *It cannot be said honourably of God that he is in a place, for nothing is in a place; but that which hath proper bounds of its greatness.* But *T. H.* his God is not wholly every where. [Le. p. 11.] *No man can conceive that any thing is all in this place, and all in another place at the same time, for none of these things ever have or can be incident to sense.* So far well, if by conceiving he mean comprehending; But then follows, That *these are absurd speeches taken upon credit, without any signification at all, from deceived Philosophers, and deceived or deceiving School-men.* Thus he denyeth the ubiquity of God. A circumscriptive, a definitive, and a repletive being in a place, is some heathen language to him.

[His eternity.] Our God is immutable without any shadow of turning by change, to whom all things are present, nothing past, nothing to come. But *T. H.* his god is measured by time, losing something that is past, and acquiring something that doth come every minute. That is as much as to say, That our God is infinite, and his god is finite, for unto that which is actually infinite, nothing can be added, neither time nor parts. Hear himself, [Qu. p. 266.] *Nor do I understand what derogation it can be to the divine perfection, to attribute to it potentiality, that is in English power,* (so little doth he understand what potentiality is) *and successive duration.* And he chargeth it upon us as a fault; that will not have eternity to be [Le. p. 374.] *an endlesse succession of time.* How, *successive duration,* and *an endlesse succession of time in God?*

Then God is finite, then God is elder to day, than he was yesterday. Away with blasphemies. Before he destroyed the ubiquity of God, and now he destroyeth his eternity.

[His simple city.] Our God is a perfect, pure, simple, indivisible, infinite essence; free from all composition of matter and form, of substance and accidents. All matter is finite, and he who acteth by his infinite essence, needeth neither organs, nor faculties, nor accidents, to render him more compleat. But *T. H.* his god is a divisible god, a compounded god, that hath matter, and qualities, or accidents. Hear himself. I argue thus, *The divine substance is indivisible, but eternity is the divine substance. The Major is evident because God is* Actus simplicissimus; *The minor is confessed by all men, that whatsoever is attributed to God, is God.* Now listen to his answer, [Qu. p. 267.] *The Major is so far from being evident, that* Actus simplicissimus *signifieth nothing. The Minor is said by some men, thought by no man, whatsoever is thought is understood.* The Major was this, *The divine substance is indivisible.* Is this far from being evident? Either it is indivisible or divisible. It is be not indivisible, then it is divisible, then it is materiate, then it is corporeal, then it hath parts, then it is finite by his own confession. [Ci. c. 15. s. 14.] *Habere partes, aut esse totum aliquid, sunt uttributa finitorum.* Upon this silly conceit, he chargeth me for saying, That *God is not just, but justice it self, not eternal, but eternity it self,* which he calleth *unseemly words to be said of God.* [Qu. p. 266.] And he thinketh he doth me a great courtesie in not adding *blasphemous and atheistical.* But his bolts are so soon shot, and his reasons are such vain imaginations, and such drowsie phantasies, that no sad man doth much regard them. Thus he hath already destroyed the ubiquity, the eternity, and the simplicity of God. I wish he had considered better with himself, before he had desperately cast himself upon these rocks.

But *paulo maiora canamus,* my next charge is, [His existence.] That he destroyes the very being of God, and leaves nothing in his place but an empty name. For by taking away all incorporal substances, he taketh away God himself. The very name (saith he) of an incorporal substance, is *a contradition. And to say that an Angel or Spirit is an incorporeal substance, it to say in effect, that there is no Angel or Spirit at all.* [Le. p. 214.] By the same reason to say, That God is an incorporal substance, is to say there is no God at all. Either God is incorporal, or he is finite, and consists of parts, and consequently is no God. This, That there is no incorporal spirit, is the main root of Atheisme, from which so many lesser branches are daily sprouting up.

When they have taken away all incorporal spirits, what do they leave God himself to be? He who is the fountain of all being, from whom and in whom all creatures have their being, must needs have a real being of his own. And what real being can God have among bodies and accidents? for they have left nothing else in the universe. Then *T. H.* may move the same question of God, which he did of devils, [Qu. p. 160.] *I would gladly know in what classis of entities, the Bishop ranketh God?* Infinite being and participated being are not of the same nature. Yet to speak according to humane apprehension (apprehension and comprehension differ much, *T. H.* confesseth that natural reason doth dictate to us, that God is infinite, yet natural reason cannot comprehend the infinitenesse of God) I place him among incorporeal substances or spirits, because he hath been pleased to place himself in that rank, [Joh. 4. 24.] *God is a spirit.* Of which place *T. H.* giveth his opinion, that it is unintelligible, and all others of the same nature, *and fall not under humane understanding.* [Le. p. 208.]

They who deny all incorporeal substances, can understand nothing by God, but either nature, (not *naturam naturantem*, that is, a real authour of nature, but *naturam naturatam*, that is the orderly concourse of natural causes, (as *T. H.* seemeth to intimate) or a fiction of the brain without real being, cherished for advantage and politick ends, as a profitable error, howsoever dignified with the glorious title of *the eternal causes of all things.*

We have seen what his principles are concerning the Deity, they are full as bad or worse concerning the Trinity. [The Trinity.] Hear himself. [Le. p. 268.] *A person is he that is represented, as often as he is represented. And therefore God who has been represented, that is, personated thrice, may properly enough be said to be three Persons, though neither the word Person nor Trinity be ascribed to him in the Bible.* And a little after, *to conclude the doctrine of the Trinity as far as can be gathered directly from the Scripture, is in substance this, that the God who is always one and the same, was he person represented by Moses, the person represented by his Son incarnate, and the person represented by the Apostles. As represented by the Apostles, the holy spirit by which they spake is God. As represented by his son that was God and Man, the Son is that God. As represented by Moses, and the High Priests; the Father, that is to say, the Father of our Lord Jesus Christ is that God.* From whence we may gather the reason why those names; Father, Son, and Holy Ghost, in the signification of the Godhead, are never used in the Old Testament. For they are persons, that is, they have their names from representing, which could not be, till diverse men had represented Gods person, in ruling or in directing under him.

Who is so bold as blind Bayard? The emblime of a little boy attempting to lade all the water out of the sea with a Coccleshel, doth fit *T. H.* as exactly as if it had been shaped for him, who thinketh to measure the profound and inscrutable mysteries of religion, by his own silly, shallow conceits. What is now become of the great adorable mysterie of the blessed undivided Trinity? it is shrunk into nothing. Upon his grounds there was a time when there was no Trinity. And we must blot these words out of our Creed, *The Father eternal, the Son eternal, the Holy Ghost eternal.* And these other words out of our Bibles, *Let us make man after our image.* Unlesse we mean that this was a consultation of God with Moses and the Apostles. What is now become of the eternal generation of the Son of God, if this Sonship did not begin until about four thousand years after the creation were expired. Upon these grounds every King hath as many *persons* as there be Justices of Peace, and petty Constables in his kingdom. Upon this account God Almighty hath as many *persons* as there have been Soveraign Princes in the World since Adam. According to this reckoning each one of us like so many Gerions, may have as many *persons* as we please to make procurations. Such bold presumption requireth another manner of confutation.

Concerning God the Son, forgetting what he had said elsewhere, where he calleth him *God and man*, and *the Son of God incarnate*, he doubteth not to say that *the word, hypostatical, is canting.* [Le. p. 21.] As if the same person could be both God and man without a personal, that is, an hypostatical, union of the two natures of God and man. He alloweth every man who is commanded by his lawful Soveraign, *to deny Christ with his tongue before men.* [Le. p. 271.] He deposeth Christ from his true kingly office, making his *kingdom not to commence or begin before the day of judgement.* [Ci. c. 17. s. 5, 6.] And *the regiment wherewith Christ governeth his faithful in this life, is not properly a kingdom, but a pastoral office, or a right to teach.* And a little after, *Christ had not kingly authority committed to him by his Father in this World, but onely consiliary and doctrinall.*

He taketh away his Priestly or propitiatory office; [Le. p. 248.] *And although this act of our redemption be not always in Scripture called a Sacrifice and oblation, but sometimes a price, yet by price we are not to understand any thing, by the value whereof he could claim right to a pardon for us from his offended father, but that price which God the Father was pleased in mercy to demand.* And again, [Le. p. 261.] *Not that the death of one man, though without sin, can satisfie for the offences of all men in the rigour of justice, but in the mercy of God, that ordained such Sacrifices for sin, as he was pleased in mercy to accept.* He knoweth no difference between one who is meer man, and one who was both God and man; between a Levitical Sacrifice, and the all-sufficient Sacrifice of the Crosse; between the blood of a Calf, and the precious blood of the Son of God.

And touching the Prophetical Office of Christ, I do much doubt whether he do believe in earnest, that there is any such thing as prophecy in the World. He maketh very little difference between· *a Prophet* and *a madman*, and *a demoniack*, [Le. p. 36.] *And if there were nothing else* (saith he) *that bewrayed their madnesse, yet that very arrogating such inspiration to themselves, is argument enough.* He maketh the pretence of inspiration in any man to be, and alwayes to have been, [Le. p. 169.] *an opinion pernicious to peace, and tending to the dissolution of all civil government.* He subjecteth all Prophetical Revelations from God, to the sole pleasure and censure of the Soveraign Prince, either to authorize them, or to exauctorate them. So as two Prophets prophesying the same thing at the same time, in the dominions of two different Princes, the one shall be a true Prophet, the other a false. And Christ who had the approbation of no Soveraign Prince, upon his grounds, was to be reputed a false Prophet every where. [Le. p. 232.] *Every man therefore ought to consider who is the Soveraign Prophet, that is to say, who it is that is Gods Vicegerent upon earth, and hath next under God the authority of governing Christian men, and to observe for a rule that doctrine which is the name of God he hath commanded to be taught, and thereby to examine and try out the truth of those doctrines which pretended Prophets, with miracle or without, shall at any time advance*, &c. *And if he disavow them, then no more to obey their voice; or if he approve them, than to obey them as men to whom God hath given a part of the spirit of their Soveraign.* Upon his principles the case holdeth as well among Jews and Turks and Heathens, as Christians. Then he that teacheth transubstantiation in France, is a true Prophet, he that teacheth it in England, a false Prophet. He that blasphemeth Christ in Constantinople, a true Prophet, he that doth the same in Italy, a false Prophet. [1. Sam. 15.] Then Samuel was a false Prophet to contest with Saul a Soveraign Prophet: [1 King. 13.] So was the man of God who submitted not to the more divine and prophetick spirit of Jeroboam. [1. King. 18.] And Elijah for reproving Ahab. [2. Chr. 18.] Then Micaiah had but his deserts, to be clapt up in prison, and fed with bread of affliction, and water of affliction, for daring to contradict *Gods Vicegerent upon earth.* [Jer. 38.] And Jeremiah was justly thrown into a Dungeon, for prophesying against Zedekiah his Liege Lord. If his principles were true, it were strange indeed, that none of all these Princes, nor any other that ever was in the World, should understand their own priviledges. And yet more strange, that God Almighty should take the part of such rebellious Prophets, and justifie their prophesies by the event, if it were true that *none but the Soveraign in a Christian* [Le. p. 250.] (the reason is the same for Jewish) *Common-wealth can take notice what is or what is not the word of God.*

Neither doth he use God the holy Ghost more favourably than God the Son. Where S. Peter saith Holy men of God spake as they were moved by the holy Spirit; [Lev. p. 214.] He saith *By the Spirit, is meant the voice of God in a dream or vision supernatural*, which dreams or visions he maketh to be no more than *imaginations, which they had in their sleep,* [Lev. p. 227.] *or in an extasie, which in every true Prophet were supernatural, but in false Prophets were either natural or feined*, and more likely to be false than true. *To say God hath spoken to him in a dream, is no more than to say, He dreamed that God spake to him*, &c. [Lev. p. 196.] *To say he hath seen a vision, or heard a voice, is to say. That he hath dreamed between sleeping and waking.* So S. Peters holy Ghost is come to be their own imaginations, which might be either feined, or mistaken, or true. As if the holy Ghost did enter onely at their

eyes, and at their eares, not into their understandings, nor into
their minds; Or as if the holy Ghost did not seale unto their
hearts the truth and assurance of their Prophesies. Whether a
new light be infused into their understandings, or new graces
be inspired into their heart, they are wrought, or caused, or
created immediately by the holy Ghost, And so are his
imaginations, if they be supernatural.

But he must needs fall into these absurdities, who maketh
but a jest of inspiration. *They who pretend Divine inspiration
to be a supernatural entering of the holy Ghost into a man, are
(as he thinks) in a very dangerous dilemma*; [Lev. p. 361.] *for if
they worship not the men whom they conceive to be inspired,
they fall into impiety: And if they worship them, they commit
idolatry.* So mistaking the holy Ghost to be corporeal,
something that is blown into a man, and the graces of the holy
Ghost to be corporeal graces. And *the words, impowered or
infused virtue, and, inblown or inspired virtue, are as absurd
and insignificant, as a round quadrangle.* [Lev. p. 17.] He
reckons it as a common errour, That *faith and sanctity are not
attained by study and reason, but by supernatural inspiration
or infusion.* And laieth this for a firm ground: [Lev. p. 169.]
*Faith and sanctity are indeed not very frequent, but yet they are
not miracles, but brought to passe by education, discipline,
correction, and other natural wayes.* I would see the greatest
Pelagian of them all flie higher.

Why should he trouble himself about the holy Spirit, who
acknowledgeth no spirit but either a subtile fluide invisible
body, or a ghost, or other idol or phantasme of the
imagination; who knoweth no inward grace or intrinsecal
holinesse. [Lev. p. 220.] *Holy is a word which in Gods
kingdome answereth to that which men in their kingdoms use
to call publick, or the kings.* And again, *wheresoever the word
holy is taken properly, there is still something signified of
propriety gotten by consent.* His holinesse is a relation, not a
quality; but for inward sanctification, or reall infused holinesse, in respect whereof the third person is called the holy
Ghost, because he is not onely holy in himself, but also maketh
us holy, he is so great a stranger to it, that he doth altogether
deny it, and disclaim it.

We are taught in our Creed to believe the Catholick or
Universal Church. But *T. H.* teacheth us the contrary, [De
Cive, c. 17. s. 22.] That *if there be more Christian Churches*

than one, all of them together are not one Church personally.
And more plainly, *Now if the whole number of Christians be
not contained in one Common-wealth,* [Le. p. 206.] *they are
not one person, nor is there an Universal Church, that hath any
authority over them.* And again, *The Universal Church is not
one person, of which it can be said, that it hath done, or
decreed, or ordained, or excommunicated, or absolved.* [Ci. c.
17. s. 26.] This doth quite overthrow all the authority of
general Councils.

All other men distinguish between the Church and the
Common-wealth: Onely *T. H.* maketh them to be one and the
same thing. *The Common-wealth of Christian men and the
Church of the same, are altogether the same thing, called by
two names, for two reasons. For the matter of the Church and
of the Common-wealth is the same, namely the same Christian
men; And the form is the same, which consisteth in the lawful
power of convocating them.* [Ci. c. 17. s. 21.] And hence he
concludeth, [Ci. c. 18. s. 1.] That *every Christian Common-
wealth is a Church endowed with all spiritual authority.* And
yet more fully, *The Church if it be one person, is the same thing
with the Common-wealth of Christians, called a Common-
wealth, because it consisteth of men united in one person their
Soveraign;* [Le. p. 205.] *And a Church because it consisteth in
Christian men united in one Christian Soveraign.* Upon which
account there was no Christian Church in these parts of the
World, for some hundreds of years after Christ, because there
was no Christian Soveraign.

Neither is he more orthodox concerning the Holy Scriptures,
Hitherto, that is, for the books of Moses, [Le. p. 283.] *the
power of making the Scripture canonical, was in the civil
Soveraign.* The like he saith of the Old Testament, made
canonical by Esdras. And of the New Testament, That *it was
not the Apostles which made their own writings canonical, but
every convert made them so to himself.* Yet with this
restriction, That [Le. p. 284.] *until the Soveraign ruler had
prescribed them, they were but counsel and advice, which
whether good or bad, he that was counselled might without
injustice refuse to observe, and being contrary to the Laws
established, could not without injustice observe.* He maketh
the Primitive Christians to have been in a pretty condition.
Certainly the Gospel was contrary to the Laws then
established. But most plainly, *The word of the Interpreter of*

the Scripture is the word of God. And the *same is the interpreter of the Scripture, and the Soveraign Judge of all Doctrines,* that is, the Soveraign Magistrate, [Ci. c. 17. s. 18.] *to whose authority we must stand no lesse, than to Theirs, who at first did commend the Scripture to us for the canon of faith.* Thus if Christian Soveraigns, of different communions, do clash one with another, in their interpretations, or misinterpretation of Scripture, (as they do daily) then the word of God is contradictory to it self; or that is the word of God in one Common-wealth, which is the word of the devil in another Common-wealth: and the same thing may be true, and not true, at the same time: which is the peculiar priviledge of *T. H.* to make contradictories to be true together.

All the power, virtue, use, and efficacy, which he ascribeth to the holy Sacraments, is to be *signes or commemorations.* [Le. p. 22.] As for any sealing, or confirming, or conferring of grace, he acknowledgeth nothing. [Ci. c. 17. s. 7.] The same he saith particularly of Baptisme: upon which grounds a Cardinals red hat, or a Serjeant at arms his mace, may be called Sacraments as well as Baptisme, or the holy Eucharist, if they be only signes or commemorations of a benefit. If he except, that Baptisme and the Eucharist, are of divine institution: but a Cardinals red hat, or a Serjeant at arms his mace are not: he saith truely, but nothing to his advantage or purpose, seeing he deriveth all the authority of the Word and Sacraments, in respect of Subjects, and all our obligation to them, from the authority of the Soveraign Magistrate, without which [Le. p. 133.] *these words repent and be baptized in the Name of Jesus, are but counsel, no command.* And to a Serjeant at arms his mace, and baptisme, proceed both from the same authority. And this he saith upon this silly ground, That *nothing is a command, the performance whereof tendeth to our own benefit.* He might as well deny the Ten Commandments to be commands, because they have an advantagious promise annexed to them, *Do this and thou shalt live*; And *cursed is every one that continueth not in all the words of this Law to doe them.*

Sometimes he is for holy orders, and giveth to the Pastors of the Church the right of ordination and absolution, and infallibility, too much for a particular Pastor, or the Pastours of one particular Church. [Ci. c. 17. s. 24.] *It is manifest, that the consecration of the chiefest Doctours in every Church, and imposition of hands, doth pertein to the Doctours of the same Church.* And *it cannot be doubted of, but the power of binding and loosing was given by Christ to the future Pastours, after the same manner as to his present Apostles.* [Ibid. l. 28.] And *our Saviour hath promised this infallibility in those things which are necessary to salvation, to his Apostles, until the day of judgement, that is to say, to the Apostles and Pastours, to be consecrated by the Apostles successively, by the imposition of hands.*

But at other times he casteth all this meale down with his foot. [Le. p. 323.] *Christian Soveraignes are the supreme Pastors, and the only persons whom Christians now hear speak from God, except such as God speaketh to in these daies supernaturally,* What is now become of the promised infallibility?

[Le. p. 296.] And *it is from the civil Soveraign, that all other Pastours derive their right of teaching, preaching, and all other functions pertaining to that office, and they are but his Ministers in the same manner as the Magistrates of Towns, or Judges in Courts of Justice, and Commanders of Armies.* What is now become of their Ordination? Magistrates, Judges, and Generals, need no precedent qualifications. He maketh *the Pastoral authority of Soveraigns to be* jure divino, *of all other Pastors* jure civili. He addeth, *neither is there any Judge of Heresie among Subjects, but their own civil Soveraign.*

Lastly, *The Church excommunicateth no man but whom she excommunicateth by the authority of the Prince.* [Ci. c. 17. s. 26.] And *the effect of excommunication hath nothing in it, neither of dammage in this World, nor terrour upon an Apostate, if the civil power did persecute or not assist the Church.* [Le. p. 277.] *And in the World to come, leaves them in no worse estate, than those who never believed. The damage rather redoundeth to the Church.* [Le. p. 288.] *Neither is the excommunication of a Christian Subject, that obeyeth the laws of his own Soveraign, of any effect.* Where is now their power of binding and loosing?

It may be some of *T. H.* his disciples desire to know what hopes of heavenly joies they have upon their masters principles. They may hear them without any great contentment, [Le. p. 240.] *There is no mention in Scripture, nor ground in reason, of the* cœlum empyreum, *that is, the Heaven of the blessed, where the Saints shall live eternally with God.* And again, [Le.

p. 241.] *I have not found any text that can probably be drawn to prove any ascension of the Saints into Heaven, that is to say, into any cœlum empyreum.* But he concludeth positively, that *salvation shall be upon earth, when God shall reign at the coming of Christ in Jerusalem.* And again, *In short, the Kingdom of God is a civil Kingdom,* &c. *called also the Kingdom of Heaven, and the Kingdom of Glory.* All the Hobbians can hope for, is, to be restored to the same condition which Adam was in before his fall. So saith *T. H.* himself, [Le p. 345. p. 30.] *From whence may be inferred, that the Elect, after the resurrection, shall be restored to the estate wherein Adam was before he had sinned. As for the beatifical vision he defineth to be a word unintelligible.*

But considering his other principles, I do not marvel much at his extravagance in this point. To what purpose should a *cœlum empyreum*, or Heaven of the blessed, serve in his judgement, who maketh the blessed Angels that are the inhabitants of that happy mansion, to be either idols of the brain, that it is in plain English, nothing, or thin, subtile, fluid bodies, destroying the Angelical nature. [Le. p. 207.] *The universe being the aggregate of all bodies, there is no real part thereof that is not also body.* And elsewhere, [Le. p. 371.] *Every part of the universe is body, and that which is not body, is no part of the universe. And because the universe is all, that which is no part of it, is nothing, and consequently no where.* How? by this doctrine he maketh not onely the Angels, but God himself to be nothing. Neither doth he salve it at all, by supposing erroneously Angles to be corporeal spirits, and by attributing the name of incorporeal spirit to God, *as being a name of more honour, in whom we consider not what attribute best expresseth his nature, which is incomprehensible, but what best expresseth our desire to honour him.* Though we be not able to comprehend perfectly what God is, yet we are able to comprehend perfectly what God is not, that is, he is not imperfect, and therefore he is not finite, and consequently he is not corporeal. This were a trim way to honour God indeed, to honour him with a lie. If this that he say here be true, That *every part of the universe is a body, and whatsoever is not a body, is nothing.* Then by this doctrine, if God be not a body, God is nothing; not an incorporeal spirit, but *one of the idols of the brain,* a meer nothing, though they think they dance under a net, and have the blind of Gods incomprehensibility, between them and discovery.

To what purpose should a *cœlum empyreum* serve in his judgement, who denieth the immortality of the soul? *The doctrin is now, and hath been a long time far otherwise; namely, that every man hath eternity of life by nature, in as much as his soul is immortal.* [Le. p. 339.] Who supposeth that *when a man dieth, there remaineth nothing of him but his carkase;* Who maketh *the word soul in holy Scripture to signifie always either the life, or the living creature?* And expoundeth the casting of body and soul into hell-fire, to be *the casting of body and life into hell-fire.* [Le. p. 340.] Who maketh this Orthodox truth, That the soules of men are substances distinct from their bodies, to be *an errour contracted by the contagion of the demonology of the Greeks, and a window that gives entrance to the dark doctrine of eternal torments.* Who expoundeth these words of Solomon, [Eccl. 12. 7.] [*Then shall the dust return to the earth as it was, and the spirit shall return unto God that gave it.*] Thus, *God onely knows what becomes of a mans spirit, when he expireth.* [Le. p. 344.] He will not acknowledge that there is a spirit, or any substance distinct from the body. I wonder what they think doth keep their bodies from stinking.

But they that in one case are grieved, in another must be relieved. If perchance *T. H.* hath given his disciples any discontent in his doctrine of *Heaven*, and *the holy* Angels, and *the glorified souls of the Saints*, he will make them amends in his doctrine of *hell*, and the *devils*, and the *damned spirits*. First of the devils; He fancieth that all those devils which our Saviour did cast out, were phrensies, and all *dæmoniacks*, [Le. p. 38, 39.] (or persons possessed,) *no other than mad-men*. And to justifie *our Saviours speaking to a disease as to a person*, produceth the example of inchanters. But he declareth himself most clearly upon this subject, in his Animadversions upon my reply to his defence of fatal destiny. [Qu. p. 160.] *There are in the Scripture two sorts of things which are in English translated devils. One is that which is called Satan, Diabolus, Abaddon, which signifieth in English an enemy, an accuser, and a destroyer of the Church of God, in which sense the devils are but wicked men. The other sort of devils are called in the Scripture dæmonia, which are the feigned gods of the heathen, and are neither bodies nor spiritual substances, but meer phansies and fictions of terrifed hearts, which St. Paul calleth nothings.* So *T. H.* hath killed the great infernal devil, and all his black Angels, and left no devils to be feared, but devils incarnate, that is wicked men.

And for *hell* he describeth the *kingdom of Satan,* or the *kingdom of darknesse,* to be *a confederacy of deceivers.* [Le. p. 333.] He telleth us that the places which set forth the torments of hell in holy Scripture, *do designe metaphorically a grief and discontent of mind, from the sight of that eternal felicity in others,* [Le. p. 244.] *which they themselves, through their own incredulity and disobedience have lost.* As if metaphorical descriptions did not bear sad truths in them, as well as literal, as if final desperations were no more than a little fit of grief or discontent; and a guilty conscience were no more than a transitory passion, as if it were a losse so easily to be borne, to be deprived for evermore of the beatifical vision: And lastly, as if the damned, besides that unspeakable losse, did not likewise suffer actual torments, proportionable in some measure to their own sins, and Gods justice.

Lastly for the damned spirits, he declareth himself every where, that their sufferings are not eternal, *The fire shall be unquenchable, and the torments everlasting: but it cannot be thence inferred, that he who shall be cast into that fire, or be formented with those torments,* [Le. p. 245.] *shall endure and resist them, so as to be eternally burnt and tortured, and yet never be destroyed nor dye. And though there may be many places that affirm everlasting fire, into which men may be cast successively one after another for ever: yet I find none that affirm that there shall be an everlasting life therein, of any individual person.* If he had said, and said only, that the pains of the damned may be lessened, as to the degree of them, or that they endure not for ever, but that after they are purged by long torments from their drosse and corruptions, as gold in the fire, both the damned spirits and the Devils themselves should be restored to a better condition, he might have found some Ancients (who are therefore called *the merciful Doctours*) to have joyned with him, though still he should have wanted the suffrage of the Catholick Church.

But his shooting is not at rovers, but altogether at randome, without either president or partner. All that *eternal fire,* all those torments which he acknowledgeth, is but this, That *after the resurrection, the reprobate shall be in the estate that Adam and his posterity were in, after the sinne committed, saving that God promised a Redeemer to Adam and not to them:* adding, [Le. p. 345, 346.] *that they shall live as they did* formerly, *marry, and give in marriage; and consequently engender* children *perpetually after the resurrection, as they did before,* which he calleth *an immortality of the kind, but not of the persons of men.* It is to be presumed, that in those their second lifes, knowing certainly from *T. H.* that there is no hope of redemption for them from corporal death upon their well doing, nor fear of any torments after death for their ill doing, they will passe their times here as pleasantly as they can. This is all the damnation which *T. H.* fancieth.

In summe I leave it to the free judgement of the understanding Reader, by these few instances which follow, to judge what the Hobbian principles are in point of religion. *Ex ungue leonem.*

First, that no man needs to put himself to any hazard for his faith, but may safely comply with the times. [Le. p. 231.] *And for their faith it is internal and invisible. They have the licence that Naaman had, and need not put themselves into danger for it.*

[2.] Secondly, he alloweth Subjects, being commanded by their Soveraign, to deny Christ. *Profession with the tongue is but an external thing, and no more than any other gesture, whereby we signifie our obedience. And wherein a Christian, holding firmly in his heart the faith of Christ, hath the same liberty which the Prophet Elisha allowed to Naaman,* &c. [Le. p. 271.] *Who by bowing before the idol Rimmon, denied the true God as much in effect, as if he had done it with his lips.* Alas why did St. Peter weep so bitterly for denying his Master, out of fear of his life or members? It seemeth he was not acquainted with these Hobbian principles. And in the same place he layeth down this general conclusion. *This we may say, that whatsoever a Subject is compelled to, in obedience to his Soveraign, and doth it not in order to his own mind, but in order to the laws of his Country, that action is not his, but his Soveraigns; nor is it he that in this case denieth Christ before men, but his Governour and the law of his Country.* His instance in *a mahumetan* commanded by a Christian Prince to be present at divine service, is a weak mistake, springing from his grosse ignorance in case-divinity, not knowing to distinguish between an erroneous conscience, as the Mahumetans is, and a conscience rightly informed.

[3.] Thirdly, if this be not enough, he giveth license to a Christian to commit idolatry, or at least to do an idolatrous act, for fear of death or corporeal danger. [Le. p. 360.] *To pray unto a King voluntarily for fair weather, or for any thing which God onely can do for us, is divine worship, and idolatry. On the other side, if a King compel a man to it by the terrour of death, or other great corporeal punishment, it is not idolatry.* His reason is, because *it is not a sign that he doth inwardly honour him as a god, but that he is desirous to save himself from death, or from a miserable life.* It seemeth T. H. thinketh there is no divine worshop, but internal. And that it is lawful for a man to value his own life or his limbs more than his God. How much is he wiser than the three Children, or Daniel himself? who were thrown, the first into a fiery furnace, the last into the Lyons denne, because they refused to comply with the idolatrous decree of their Soveraign Prince.

[4.] A fourth aphorisme may be this, [Lev. p. 193.] *That which is said in the scripture, it is better to obey God, than men, hath place in the Kingdome of God by pact, and not by nature.* Why? nature it self doth teach us that it is better to obey God, then men. Neither can he say that he intended this only of obedience, in the use of indifferent actions and gestures, in the service of God, commanded by the commonwealth, for that is to obey God and man. But if divine law and humane law clash one with another, without doubt it is evermore better to obey God than man.

His fifth conclusion may be that the sharpest and most successfull sword, in any war whatsoever, doth give soveraign power and authority to him that hath it, to approve or reject all sorts of Theologicall doctrines, concerning the Kingdome of God, not according to their truth or falsehood, but according to that influence which they have upon political affaires. Hear him, [Le. p. 241.] *But because this doctrine will appear to most men a novelty, I do but propound it, maintaining nothing in this or any other paradox of religion, but attending the end of that dispute of the sword, concerning the authority (not yet amongst my Countrymen decided) by which all sorts of doctrine are to be approved or rejected, &c. For the points of doctrine concerning the Kingdome of God, have so great influence upon the Kingdome of man, as not to be determined, but by them that under God have the soveraign power. Careat successibus opto, Quisquis ab eventu facta notanda putat.* Let him evermore want successe who thinketh actions are to be judged by their events. This doctrine may be plausible to those who desire to fish in troubled waters. But it is justly hated by those which are in Authority, and all those who are lovers of peace and tranquillity.

The last part of this conclusion smelleth ranckly of Jeroboam, [1. King. 12. 26.] *Now shall the Kindgome return to the house of David, if this people go up to do sacrifice in the house of the Lord at Jerusalem, whereupon the King took councell, and made two calves of gold, and said unto them, It is too much for you to go up to Jerusalem, behold thy Gods O Israel, which brought thee out of the land of Egypt.* But by the just disposition of Almighty God, this policy turned to a sin, and was the utter destruction of Jeroboam and his family. It is not good jesting with edg-tooles, nor playing with holy things: where men make their greatest fastnesse, many times they find most danger.

His sixth paradox is a rapper, [Ci. c. 12. s. 1.] *The civill lawes are the rules of good and evill, just and unjust, honest and dishonest, and therefore what the lawgiver commands that is to be accounted good, what he forbids bad.* And a little after, *before empires were, just and unjust were not, as whose nature is relative to a command, every action in its own nature is indifferent. That it is just or unjust proceedeth from the right of him that commandeth. Therefore lawfull Kings make those things which they command, just by commanding them, and those things which they forbid unjust by forbidding them.* To this adde his definition of a sin, *that which one doth, or omitteth, saith or willeth contrary to the reason of the commonwealth, that is the [civil] lawes.* [Ci. c. 14. s. 17.] Where by the lawes he doth not understand the written lawes, elected and aproved by the whole commonwealth, but the verball commands or mandates, of him that hath the soveraign power, as we find in many places of his writings. *The civil lawes are nothing else but the commands of him that is endowed with soveraign power in the commonwealth, concerning the future actions of his subjects.* [Ci. c. 6. s. 9.] *And the civil lawes are fastned to the lips of that man who hath the soveraigne power.* [Le. p. 109.]

Where are we? in Europe or in Asia? Where they ascribed a divinity to their Kings, and, to use his own phrase, made them *mortall gods. O King live for ever.* Flatterers are the common moaths of great pallaces, where Alexanders friends are more numerous than the Kings friends. But such grosse palpable pernicious flattery as this is, I did never meet with, so derogatory both to piety and policy. What deserved he who should do his uttermost endeavour to poison a common fountain, whereof all the commonwealth must drinke? He doth the same who poisoneth the mind of a soveraign prince.

Are *the civil lawes the rules of good and bad, just and unjust, honest and dishonest?* And what I pray you are the rules of the civil law it self? even the law of God and nature. If the civil lawes swerve from these more authentick lawes, they are Lesbian rules. *What the law-giver commands is to be accounted good, what he forbids bad.* This was just the garb of the Athenian Sophisters, as they are described by Plato. Whatsoever pleased the great beast [the multitude] they called holy, and just, and good. And whatsoever the great beast disliked, they called evill, unjust, prophane. But he is not yet arrived at the height of his flattery. *Lawfull Kings make those things which they command just by commanding them, And those things which they forbid unjust by forbidding them.* At other times when he is in his right wits he talketh of suffering, and *expecting their reward in heaven. And going to Christ by martydome. And if he had the fortitude to suffer death he should do better.* But I fear all this was but said in jest. How should they expect their reward in heaven, if his doctrine be true, that there is no reward in heaven? Or how should they be martyrs, if his doctrine be true, that *none can be Martyrs but those who conversed with Christ upon earth?* He addeth, [Le. p. 272.] *Before Empires were, just and unjust were not.* Nothing could be written more false in his sense, more dishonourable to God, more inglorious to the humane nature. That God should create man and leave him presently without any rules, to his own ordering of himself, as the Ostridg leaveth her egges in the sand. But in truth there have been empires in the world ever since Adam. And Adam had a law written in his heart by the finger of God, before there was any civil law. Thus they do endeavour to make goodnesse, and justice, and honesty, and conscience, and God himself, to be empty names without any reality, which signifie nothing, further than they conduce to a mans interest. Otherwise he would not, he could not say, That *every action as it is invested with its circumstances, is indifferent in its own nature.*

Something there is which he hath a confused glimmering of, as the blind man sees *men walking like trees*, which he is not able to apprehend and expresse clearly. We acknowledge, that though the laws or commands of a Soveraign prince be erroneous, or unjust, or injurius, such as a subject can not approve for good in themselves; yet he is bound to acquiesce, and may not oppose or resist, otherwise than by prayers and tears, and at the most by flight. We acknowledge that the civil laws have power to bind the conscience of a Christian, in themselves, but not from themselves, but from him who hath said, *Let every soul be subject to the higher powers.* Either they bind Christian subjects to do their Soveraigns commands, or to suffer for the testimony of a good conscience. We acknowledge that in doubtful cases *semper præfumitur pro Rege & lege*, the Soveraign and the law are always presumed to be in the right. But in plain evident cases which admit no doubt, it is alwayes better to obey God than man. Blunderers whilst they think to mend one imaginary hole, make two or three reall ones. They who derive the authority of the Scriptures or Gods Law from the civil laws of men, are like those who seek to underprop the heavens from falling with a bullrush. Nay, they derive not onely the authority of the Scripture, but even of the law of nature it self from the civil law. *The laws of nature* (which need no promulgation) [Le. p. 138.] *in the condition of nature are not properly laws, but qualities which dispose men to peace and to obedience. When a Common-wealth is one setled, then are they actually laws, and not before.* God help us into what times are we fallen, when the immutable laws of God and nature are made to depend upon the mutable laws of mortal men, just as if one should go about to controle the Sun by the authority of the clock.

But it is not worthy of my labour, nor any part of my intention, to pursue every shadow of a question which he springeth. It shall suffice to gather a posie of flowers (or rather a bundle of weeds) out of his writings, and present them to the Reader, who will easily distinguish them from healthful plants by the rankness of their smell. Such are these which follow.

[Le. p. 151.] 1. *To be delighted in the imagination onely, of being possessed of another mans goods, servants, or wife, without any intention to take them from him by force or fraud, is no breach of the law which saith, Thou shalt not covet.*

2. *If a man by the terrour of present death be compelled to do a fact against the law, he is totally excused, because no law can oblige a man to abandon his own preservation. Nature compelleth him to the fact.* [Le. p. 157.] The like doctrine he hath elsewhere. *When the Actor doth any thing against the Law of nature by command of the Author,* [Le. p. 81.] *if he be obliged by former covenants to obey him, not he, but the Author breaketh the law of nature.*

3. *It is a doctrine repugnant to civil Society, that whatsoever a man does against his conscience is sin.* [Le. p. 168.]

4. *The kimgdom of God is not shut, but to them that sin; that is to them who have not performed due obedience to the Laws of God;* [Ci. c. 18. s. 2.] *nor to them if they believe the necessary Articles of the Christian Faith.*

5. *We must know that the true acknowledging of sin is repentance it self.* [Ci. c. 17. s. 25.]

6. *An opinion publickly appointed to be taught cannot be heresie, nor the Soveraign Princes that authorise the same hereticks.* [Le. p. 318.]

7. *Temporal and spiritual government, are but two words to make men see double, and mistake their lawful Soveraign,* &c. [Le. p. 248.] *There is no other government in this life, neither of State nor Religion, but temporal.*

8. *It is manifest that they who permit* (or tolerate) [Ci. c. 13. s. 5.] *a contrary doctrine to that which themselves believe, and think necessary, do against their conscience and will, as much as in them lieth, the eternal destruction of their subjects.*

9. *Subjects sin if they do not worship God according to the laws of the Common-wealth.* [Ci. c. 15. s. 19.]

10. *To believe in Jesus* [in Jesum] *is the same as to believe that Jesus is Christ.* [Ci. c. 18. s. 10.]

11. *There can be no contradiction between the Laws of God, and the laws of a Christian Common-wealth.* [Le. p. 330.] Yet we see Christian Common-wealths daily contradict one another.

12. *No man giveth but with intention of good to himself, of all voluntary acts the object is to every man his own good.* [Le. p. 75.] Moses, St. Paul, and the Decii were out of his mind.

[Le. p. 74.] 13. *There is no natural knowledge of mans estate after death, much lesse of the reward which is then to be given to breach of faith, but onely a belief grounded upon other mens saying, that they know it supernaturally, or that they know those, that knew them, that knew others, that knew it supernaturally.*

[Le. p. 109.] 14. *Davids killing of Uriah, was no injury to Uriah, because the right to do what he pleased was given him by Uriah himself.*

[Ci. c. 18. s. 14.] 15. *To whom it belongeth to determine controversies which may arise from the divers interpretation of Scripture, he hath an imperial power over all men which acknowledge the Scriptures to be the word of God.*

[Ci. c. 6. s. 16.] 16. *What is theft, what is murder, what is adultry, and universally what is an injury, is known by the civil law; that is, the commands of the Soveraign.*

17. He admitteth the incestuous *copulations* of the Heathens *according to their heathenish lawes, to have been lawful marriages.* [Ci. c. 14. s. 10.] Though the Scripture teach us expressely, that for those abominations the land of Canaan spewed out her inhabitants, *Exod.* 18. 28.

18. *I say that no other Article of faith besides this that Jesus is Christ, is necessary to a Christian man for salvation.* [Ci. c. 18. s. 6.]

19. *Because Christs kingdom is not of this world, therefore neither can his Ministers, unless they be Kings, require obedience in his name. They had no right of commanding, no power to make lawes.* [Le. p. 269, 270.]

20. I passe by his errours about oathes, about vows, about the resurrections, about the kingdom of Christ, about the power of the keyes, binding, loosing, excommunication &c. His ignorant mistakes of *meritum congrui*, and *condigni*, active and passive obedience, and many more, for fear of being tedious to the Reader. His whole works are an heape of mishapen errours, and absurd paradoxes, vented with the confidence of a Jugler, the brags of a Mountebanck, and the authority of some Pythagoras, or third Cato, lately dropped down from heaven.

Thus we have seen how the Hobbian principles do destroy the existence, the simplicity, the ubiquity, the eternity, and infinitenesse of God, the doctrine of the blessed Trinity, the Hypostatical union, the Kingly Sacerdotal and Prophetical Offices of Christ; the being and operation of the Holy Ghost, Heaven, Hell, Angels, Devils, the immortality of the Soul, the Catholick, and all National Churches; the holy Scriptures, holy Orders, the holy Sacraments, the whole frame of Religion, and the Worship of God; the laws of Nature, the reality of Goodnesse, Justice, Piety, Honesty, Conscience, and all that is Sacred. If his disciples have such an implicite faith, that they can digest all these things, they may feed with Oestriches.

CHAP. 2.

That the Hobbian Principles do destroy all relations between man and man, and the whole frame of a Common-wealth.

The first Harping-iron is thrown at the heart of this great Whale; that is, his Religion; for *with the heart a man believeth unto righteousnesse*. Now let him look to his chine; that is, his Compage or Common-wealth. My next task is to shew that he destroyeth all relations between man and man, Prince and subject, Parent and child, Husband and wife, Master and servant, and generally all Society.

It is enough to dash the whole frame of his Leviathan or common-wealth in pieces, That he confesseth it is without example; as if the molding of a Common-wealth were no more than the making of gun-powder, which was not found out by long experience, but by meer accident. *The greatest objection* (faith *T. H.*) [Le. p. 107.] *is that of practice, when men ask when and where such power has by subjects been acknowledged.* It is a great objection indeed. Experience the Mistrisse of fooles, is the best, and almost the onely proof of the goodnesse or badnesse of any form of government. No man knoweth where a shooe wringeth, so well as he that weareth it. A new Physitian must have a new Church-yard, wherein to bury those whom he killeth. And a new unexperienced Politician, commonly putteth all into a combustion. Men rise by degrees from common souldiers to be decurions, from decurions to be Centurions, from Centurions to be Tribunes, and from Tribunes to be Generals, by experience, not by speculation. Alexander did but laugh at that Oratour who discoursed to him of Military affairs. The Locrian law was well grounded, that whosoever moved for any alteration in the tried policy of their Common-wealth, should make the proposition at his own perill with an halter about his neck.

New Statesmen promise golden mountains, but like fresh flies they bite deeper than those which were chased away before them. It were a strange thing to hear a man discourse of the Philosophers Stone, who never bestowed a groatsworth of charcole in the inquiry. It is as strange to hear a man dictate so magisterially in Politicks, who was never Officer nor Counsellor in his life, nor had any opportunity to know the intrigues of any one state. If his form of government had had any true worth or weight in it, among so many Nations, and so many succeeding Generations from the Creation to this day, some one or other would have light upon it. His Leviathan is but an idol of his own brain.

Neither is it sufficient to say, That *in long-lived Common-wealths the subjects never did dispute of the Soveraigns power.* [Ibid.] Power may be moderated, where it is not disputed of. And even in those kingdomes where it was least disputed of, as in Persia, they had their fundamental laws, which were not alterable at the pleasure of the present Prince. Whreof one was as we find in the story of Esther, and the book of Daniel, that the law of the Medes and Persians altered not: much lesse was it alterable by the onely breath of the Princes mouth, according to *T. H.* his Principles.

He urgeth, That *though in all places of the World men should lay the foundations of their houses on the sand, it could not thence be inferred, that so it ought to be.* [Ibid.] He was ashamed to make the application. So suppose all the world should be out of their wits and he onely have his right understanding. His supposition is a supposition of an impossibility, which maketh an affirmative proposition to turn negative, much like this other supposition, *If the skie fall we shall have larkes*; that is in plain English, We shall have no larkes. His argument had held much more strongly thus, *All the world lay the foundation of their houses upon firm ground, and not upon the sand*; Therefore he who crosseth the practice of the whole world, out of an over-weening opinion that he seeth further into a mill-stone than they all, is he that builds upon the sand, and deserveth well to be laught out of his humour.

But he persisteth still, like one that knows better how to hold a Paradox, than a Fort, *The skill of making and maintaining Common-wealths consisteth in certain rules, as doth Arethmatick and Geometry, and not as Tennis-play, on practice onely;*

which rules neither poor men had the leisure, nor men that have had the leisure, have hitherto had the curiosity or the method to find out. O excellent, how fortunate are we if we knew our own happinesse, to have this great discovery made in our dayes? What pity it is that this new Mercury did not live in the dayes of the old Mercury, *Qui feros cultus hominum recentum voce formavit catus.* That the art of preserving the world in perpetual tranquility, should not be discovered until the evening of the world. May we not hope (since he pleased to tell us that after the Resurrection, mankind shall be eternally propagated) [Le. p. 346.] that these monuments of his may escape the last fire, as well as some others are supposed to have escaped the generall Deluge, for the good of those successive generations, they being his own invention, as well as this frame of government.

Yet his argument is most improper, and most untrue. State-policy, which is wholly involved in matter, and circumstances of time, and place, and persons, is not at all like *Arithmetick and Geometry*, which are altogether abstracted from matter, but much more like *Tennis-play*. There is no place for liberty in Arithmetick and Geometry, but in policy there is, and so there is in Tennis-play. A game at Tennis hath its vicissitudes, and so have States. A Tennis plaier must change his play at every stroke, according to the occasion and accidents: so must a States-man move his rudder differently, according to the various faces of heaven. He who manageth a Common-wealth by general rules, will quickly ruine both himself, and those who are committed to his government. One mans meat is another mans poison; and those which are healthful Rules for one Society at one time, may be pernicious to another Society, or to the same society at another time. Some Nations are like Horses, more patient of their riders than others; And the same Nations more patient at one time than at another. In summe, general rules are easie, and signifie not much in policy. The quintessence of policy doth consist in the dexterous and skilful application of those rules to the subject matter.

But I will not rest in presumptions. Concerning forreign States, and first such as are not onely Neighbours but Allies, of a Common-wealth, such as have contracted friendship and confederated themselves together by solemne oaths, with invocation of the holy name of the great God of Heaven and earth: He teacheth, That [Ci. c. 2. s. 22.] *such an oath doth bind no more than* nudum pactum, *a naked Covenant.* It is true, that every Covenant is either lawful or unlawful. If it be unlawful, an oath cannot be the bond of iniquity: If it be lawful, it bindeth in conscience, though it were never confirmed by oath. It is true further, That he who can release a naked promise, can release the same promise confirmed by an oath, because it was not made or intended as a vow to God, but as a promise to man. But yet to say that *a naked Covenant bindeth no lesse than an oath*, or that *an oath addeth nothing to the obligation*, or that the meer violation of a Covenant is as great a sinne, as perjury and covenant-breaking twisted together, is absurd, and openeth a large gap to forreign war.

Secondly he teacheth, That [Le p. 63.] *in all times Kings and persons of Soveraign Authority, because of their indepency, are in continual jealousies, and in the state and posture of gladiatours, having their weapons pointing, and their eies fixed on one another.* It is good for a Soveraign Prince to have his sword alwaies by his side, to be ready to protect his Subjects, and offend those who dare invade him: but to put Princes in the posture of gladiators, watching continually where they may hit one another, or do one another a mischief, is dangerous. There can be no firm amity, where there is no mutual confidence. *T. H.* his perpetual diffidence and causelesse jealousies, which have no ground, but an universal suspicion of the humane nature, (much like the good womans fear, that the log would leap out of the fire, and knock out the brains of her child) do beget perpetual vexations to them that cherish them, argue a self-guiltinesse, teach them who are suspected, often to do worse than they imagined, and ordinarily produce hostility and war. [Ci. c. 15. s. 7.] *The state of Common-wealths among themselves is natural, that is, hostile. Neither if they cease to fight, is it peace, but a breathing space; wherein the one enemy observing the motion or countenance of the other, doth esteem his security not from pacts, but from the forces and counsels of his adversary.* He maketh confederacies to be but empty shews without any realty.

But for all other neighbour Common-wealths, which are not confederates, but exercise commerce one with another, by the Law of Nations; he reckons them all as enemies, and in a state of nature, (the Hobbian nature of man, is worse than the nature of Bears, or Wolves, or the most savage wild beasts) and maketh it lawful to destroy them, nocent or innocent, indifferently. [Le. p. 165.] *All men that are not Subjects, are either enemies, or else they have ceased from being so, by some precedent Covenants. But against enemies, whom the Common-wealth judgeth capable to do them hurt, it is lawful, by the original right of nature, to make war wherein the sword judgeth not, nor doth the victor make distinction of nocent and innocent.* Here is no precedent injury supposed, no refusal to do right, *omnia dat qui justa negat*, nor the least suspicion of any will to wrong them, but only that *the Commonwealth* (that is, the Prince) *judge them capable* to do them hurt.

Neither doth he hold it needful to denounce war in such cases, but maketh it lawful to suppresse them, and cut their throats without any warning. [Le. p. 61.] *From this* [natural] *diffidence of one another, there is no way for any man to secure himself so reasonable as anticipation, that is, by force or wiles to master the persons of all men he can, so long till he see no other power great enough to endanger him. And this is no more than this own conservation requireth, and is generally allowed.* [Ci. c. 5. s. 2, 1.] For *in the state of meer nature, the laws of nature are silent,* as to the actual exercise of them. And this he may do, *vel palam vell ex insidiis,* either by force or treachery. What is now become of the law of Nations? How much were the old Romans better neighbours than these new Hobbians? They did not so easily fall to the shedding of humane bloud, but sent their Legate first to demand justice, and after three and thirty dayes expectation in vain, to proclaim aloud upon the confines of the enemies Country, [Liv.] *Hear O Jupiter, and thou Juno Quirinus thou, and all ye hods, that this people is unjust,* &c. And then the Herald or Fæcial lanced his Javeline into the enemies Country, as a defiance, and beginning of war.

Thus destructive are his principles to the publick peace and tranquility of the World, but much more pernicious to the Common-wealth it self. He did prudently to deny that virtue did consist in a mean, for he himself doth never observe a mean. All his bolts fly over or under, but at the right mark it is in vain to expect him. Sometimes he fancieth an omnipotence in Kings, sometimes he strippeth them of their just rights. Perhaps he thinketh that it may fall out in politicks, as it doth sometimes in physick, *Bina venena invant.* Two contrary poysons may become a Cordial to the Common-wealth. I will begin with his defects, where he attributeth too little to Regal power.

Fist he teacheth, that no man is bound to go to warfare in person, except he do voluntarily undertake it. *A man that is commanded as a Souldier to fight against the enemy, may neverthelesse in many cases refuse without injustice.* [Le. p. 112.] Of these many cases, he setteth down onely two. First, *when he substituteth a sufficient souldier in his place, for in this case he deserteth not the service of the Common-wealth.* Secondly, *there is allowance to be made for natural timor-ousnesse, or men of feminine courage.* This might passe as a municipal law, to exempt some persons at some time in some places. But to extend it to all persons, places and times, is absurd, and repugnant to his own grounds, who teacheth that *justice and injustice do depend upon the command of the Soveraign,* that *whatsoever he commandeth, he maketh lawful and just by commanding it.* His two cases are two great impertinencies, and belong to the Soveraign to do, or not to do as Graces, [Judg. 7. 3.] *whoso is timerous or fearful, let him depart,* not to the Subjects as right. He forgetteth how often he hath denied all knowledge of good and evill to Subjects, and subjected their will absolutely to the will of the Soveraign, [Ci. c. 6. s. 13.] *The Soveraign may use every mans strength and wealth at his pleasure.* His acknowledgement that the Sover-aign hath *right enough to punish his refusal with death,* is to no purpose. The question is not whether his refusal be punishable or not, but whether it be just or not. Upon his principles a Soveraign may *justly enough* put the most innocent Subject in the World to death, as we shall see presently. And his exception *when the defence of the Common-wealth requireth at once the help of all that are able to bear armes,* is no answer to the other case, and it self a case never like to happen. He must be *a mortall god* indeed, that can bring all the hands in a Kingdome to fight at one battle.

Another of his principles is this, [Ci. c. 6. s. 3.] *Security is the end for which men make themselves subjects to others, which if it be not enjoyed no man is understood to have subjected himself to others, or to have lost his right to defend himself, at his own discretion. Neither is any man understood to have bound himself to any thing, or to have relinquished his right over all things, before his own security be provided for.* What ugly consequences do flow from this paradox, and what a large window it openeth to sedition and rebellion, I leave to the readers judgement. Either it must be left to the sovereign determination, whether the subjects security be sufficiently provided for, And then in vain is any mans sentence expected against himself, or to the discretion of the subject, (as the words themselves do seem to import,) and then there need no other bellowes to kindle the fire of a civill war, and put a whole commonwealth into a combustion, but this seditious Article.

We see the present condition of Europe what it is, that most soveraignes have subjects of a different communion from themselves, and are necessitated to tolerate different rites, for fear least whilst they are plucking up the tares, they should eradicate the wheat. And he that should advise them to do otherwise, did advise them to put all into fire and flame. Now hear this mercifull and peaceable Author, *It is manifest that they do against conscience, and wish, as much as is in them, the eternall destruction their subjects, who do not cause such doctrine and such worship, to be taught and exhibited to their subjects, as they themselves do believe to conduce to their eternall salvation, or tolerate the contrary to be taught and exhibited.* [Ci. c. 13. s. 5.] Did this man write waking or dreaming.

And howsoever in words he denie all resistance to the soveraign, yet indeed he admitteth it. [Ci. c. 2. s. 18.] *No man is bound by his pacts whatsoever they be, not to resist him, who bringeth upon him death or wounds, or other bodily dammage.* (by this learning the Scholler if he be able, may take the rod out of his masters hand, and whip him) It followeth, *Seeing therefore no man is bound to that which is impossible, they who are to suffer death or wounds or rather corporall dammage, and are not constant enough to endure them, are not obliged to suffer them. And more fully.* [Le. p. 112.] *In case a great many men together have already resisted the soveraign power unjustly, or committed some capitall crime, for which every one of them expecteth death, whether have they not the liberty to join together, and assist and defend one another? certainly they have, for they do but defend their lives, which the guilty man may as well do, as the innocent. There was indeed injustice in the first breach of their duty. Their bearing of armes subsequent to it, though it be to maintain what they have done, is no new unjust act.* Why should we not change the name of *Leviathan* into the *Rebells catechism?* Observe the difference beteen the primitive spirit, and the Hobbian spirit. The Thebæn Legion of known valour in a good cause, when they were able to resist, did chuse rather to be cut in pieces to a man, than defend themselves against their Emperour by armes, because they would rather die innocent, then live nocent. But T. H. alloweth Rebells and conspirators to make good their unlawfull attempts by armes: was there ever such a trumpetter of rebellion heard of before? perhaps he may say that he alloweth them not to justifie their unlawfull acts, but to defend themselves. First this is contrary to himself, for he alloweth them *to maintain what they had unjustly done.* This is too much and too intolerable, but this is not all. Secondly, If they chance to win the field who must suffer for their faults? or who dare thenceforward call their Acts unlawfull?

Will you hear what a casuist he is? *And for the other instance of attaining soveraignty by rebellion,* [Le. p. 73.] *it is manifest that though the event follow, yet because it cannot reasonably be expected; but rather the contrary, and because by gaining it so, others are taught to gain the same in like manner, the attempt thereof is against reason.* And had he no other reasons indeed against horrid Rebellion but these two? It seemeth he accounteth conscience or the bird in the breast to be but an Idoll of the brain. And the Kingdome of heaven (as he hath made it not valuable enough to be ballanced against an earthly Kingdome. And as for hell he hath expounded it and all the infernall fiends out of the nature of things, otherwise he could not have wanted better arguments against such a crying sin.

Another of this theorems is, that *no man is obliged by any pacts, to accuse himself.* [Ci. c. 2. s. 19.] Which in some cases is true, but in his sense, and in his latitude, and upon his grounds it is most untrue. When publick fame hath accused a man before hand, he may be called upon to purge himself or suffer. When the case is of publick concernment, and the circumstances pregnant, all nations do take the liberty to examine a man upon oath in his own cause, and where the safety and welfare of the commonwealth is concerned, as in cases of high treason, and for the more full discovery of conspiracies, upon the rack. Which they could not do lawfully if no man was bound in any case to discover himself. His reason is silly, *For in vain do we make him promise, who when he hath performed we know not whether he have performed or not.* And makes as much against all examination of witnesses as delinquents. *In vain do we make them give testimony, who when they have testified, we know not whether they have given right testimony or not.*

But his next conclusion will uncase him fully, and shew us what manner of man he is, *If the commonwealth come into the power of its enemies, so that they cannot be resisted, he who had the soveraignty before, is understood to have lost it.* [Ci. c. 7. s. 18.] What enemies he meaneth, such as have the just power of the sword, or such as have not, what he meaneth by the commonwealth the whole Kingdome, or any part of it, what he intendeth by *cannot by resisted*, whether a prevalence for want of forces to resist them, or a victory in a set battle, or a finall conquest. And what he meaneth by *losing the soveraignty*, loosing it *de facto*, or *de jure*, losing the possession only, or losing the right also, he is silent. It may be because he knoweth not the difference, *Qui pauca considerat facile pronuntiat*, He that considers little, giveth sentence more easily then truly, we must search out his sence some where else. *The obligation of subjects to the soveraign is understood to last as long, and no longer, than the power lasteth by which he is able to protect them, &c.* [Le. p. 114.] *Wheresoever a man seeth protection either in his own or in anothers sword, nature applieth his obedience to it, and his endeavour to maintain it.* By his leave this is right dogs play, which alwaies take part with the stronger side. But yet this is generall.

The next is more particular, *when in a war forreign or intestine the enemies get a final victory so as the forces of the commonwealth keeping the field no longer, there is no farther protection of subjects in their loyalty, then is the commonwealth dissolved, and every man at liberty to protect himself, by such courses as his own discretion shall suggest unto him.* Yet these words *final victory* are doubtfull. When Davids forces were chased out of the Kingdome, so that he was not able to protect his subjects in their loyalty, could this be called a final victory?

The next place is home, *He who hath no obligation to his former soveraign, but that of an ordinary subject hath liberty to submit to a Conquerour, when the meanes of his life is within the guards and garrisons of the enemy, for it is then that he hath no longer protection from him,* [Le. p. 190.] [his soveraign] *but is protected by the adverse party for his contribution.* And he concludeth that *a totall submission is as lawfull as a contribution.* Which is contrary to the sense of all

the world. If a lawful soveraign did give a generall release to his
subject, as well as he giveth him licence to contribute, he said
something. And to top up all these disloyall paradoxes he
addeth, That *they who live under the protection of a
Conquerour openly, are understood to submit themselves to
the government.* And that *in the very act of receiving protection
openly, and not renouncing it openly, they do oblige themselves to obey the Lawes of their protector, to which in
receiving protection they have assented.* [Q. p. 157.]

Where these Principles prevaile, adieu honour, and honesty,
and fidelity, and loyalty: all must give place to self-interest.
What for a man to deserte his Soveraign upon the first
prevalence of an enemy, or the first payment of a petty
contribution, or the first apparence of a sword, that is more
able to protect us for the present? Is this his great law of nature,
pactis standum, to stand to what we have obliged our selves?
Then Kings from whom all mens right and property is derived,
should not have so much right themselves in their own
inheritance as the meanest subject. It seemeth *T. H.* did take
his Soveraign for better, but not for worse. Faire fall those old
Roman spirits who gave thanks to Terentius Varro, after he
had lost the great battle of Cannæ by his own default, because
he did not despair of the Common-wealth. And would not sell
the ground that Hannibal was encamped upon, one farthing
cheaper than if it had been in time of peace, which was one
thing that discouraged that great Captain from continuing the
siege of Rome.

His former discourse hath as many faults as lines. First all
Soveraignty is not from the people. He himself acknowledgeth,
That *fatherly Empire or Power was instituted by God in the
Creation, and was Monarchical.* [Ci. c. 10. s. 3.] Secondly,
where the application of Soveraign power to the person is from
the people, yet there are other ends besides protection. Thirdly,
protection is not a condition, though it be a duty. A failing in
duty doth not cancel a right. Fourthly, protection ought to be
mutual. The subject ought to defend his King, as well as the
King his subject. If the King be disabled to protect his subject,
by the subjects own fault, because he did not assist him as he
ought, this doth not warrant the subject to seek protection
elsewhere. Fifthly, he doth not distinguish between a just
Conqueror who hath the power of the sword, though he abuse
it, and him that hath no power at all. I will try if he can

remember whose words these are; *They that have already instituted a Common-wealth, being thereby bound by covenant to own the actions and judgements of one,* [Le. p. 88.] *cannot lawfully make a new covenant among themselves to be obedient to any other, in any thing whatsoever without his permission. And therefore they that are subjects to a Monarch, cannot without his leave cast off Monarchy, nor transfer their person from him that beareth it, to another man.* This is home both for right and obligation.

Sixthly, there are other requisites to the extinction of the right of a Prince, and the obligation of a subject, than the present prevalence or conquest of an enemy. Seventhly, nature doth not dictate to a subject to violate his oaths and allegiance, by using his endeavours to maintain protection whersoeve he seeth it, either in his own sword or another mans. Eightly, total submission is not as lawful as contribution. Ninthly, actual submission doth not take away the Soveraigns right, or the subjects obligation. Tenthly, to live under the command or protection of a Conquerour doth not necessarily imply allegiance. Lastly, much lesse doth it imply an assent to all his laws, and an obligation to obey them.

These are part of T. H. his faults, on the one hand against Monarchs, opposite enough to peace and tranquillity, which none can approve who either have a settlement, or wish one. But his faults are ten times greater and grosser for Monarchs, on the other hand, in so much as I have thought sometimes that he observed the method of some old cunning Parliament men, who when they had a mind to crosse a bill, were alwaies the highest for it in the House, and would insert so many and so great inconveniences into the act, that they were sure it could never passe.

Tuta frequensq; via est per amici fallere nomen.

So he maketh the power of Kings to be so exorbitant, that no subject who hath either conscience or discretion, ever did or can endure, so to render Monarchy odious to mankind.

I passe by his accommodating of the four first Commandments of the Decalogue to Soveraign Princes, which concern our duty to Almighty God. Let his first Paradox of this kind be this. [Le. p. 177.] *A Monarch doth not bind himself to any man by any pacts, for the Empire which he receiveth.* [Ci. c. 7. s. 11.] And *it is vain to grant Soveraignty by way of precedent covenants. The opinion that any Monarch receiveth his power by covenant; that is to say, on condition,* (learnedly expounded) [Le. p. 89.] *proceedeth from want of understanding this easie truth, that covenants being but words and break* (marke that) *have no force to oblige,* &c. *but from the public sword.* What is now become of all our Coronation-oathes, and all our Liberties and great Charters?

Another Paradox is this. [Ci. c. 15. s. 19.] *Every Monarch may make his Successour by his last will, and that which one may transfer to another by testament, that he may by the same right give or sell whilest he is living. Therefore to whomsoever he disposeth it either for love or money, it is lawfully disposed.* And [Le. p. 99.] *there is no perfect form of government where the disposing of the succession is not in the present Soveraign.* The whole body of the kingdom of England were of another mind in King Johns case, and if he had disposed the Soveraignty to a Turke, as some of our Historiographers relate that he made an overture, it is not likely that they would have turned Turkish slaves.

Hear a third Paradox. [Ci. c. 6. s. 18.] *The Soveraign hath so much power over every subject by law, as every one who is not subject to another hath over himself; that is, absolute, to be limitted by the power of the Common-wealth, and by no other thing.* What neither by the Laws of God, nor Nature, nor Nations, nor by the laws of the Land, neither co-actively nor directively? Would not this man have made an excellent guide for Princes? But more of this anon.

I proceed. *When the Soveraign commandeth any thing to be done against his own former law, the command as to that particular fact, is an abrogation of the law.* [Le. p. 157.] Parliaments may shut up their shops, there is no need of them to repeale former laws.

His fifth excesse is a grievous one, That [Le. p. 161.] *before the institution of a Common-wealth, every man had a right to do whatsoever he thought necessary to his own preservation, subduing, hurting, or killing any man, in order thereunto. And this is the foundation of that right of punishing which is exercised in every Common-wealth.* And his sentence in brief is this; That if the Magistrate do examine and condemn the Delinquent, then it is properly punishment, if not, it is an *hostile act,* but both are justifiable. Judge Reader, whether thou wilt trust St. Paul or *T. H.* St. Paul telleth us, that the

Magistrate is *the ordinance of God, the Minister of God, the Revenger of God,* [Ro. 13. 2, 4.] the Sword-bearer of God *to execute wrath upon him that doth evil.*

No saith *T. H.* punishment is not an act of the Magistrate as he is a Magistrate, or as he is an Officer of God to do justice, or a revenger of evil deeds; but as he is the onely private man who hath not laid down his natural right to kill any man at his own discretion, if he do but suspect that he may prove noisome to him, or conceive it necessary for his own preservation. Who ever heard of such a right before, so repugnant to the Laws of God and Nature? But observe Reader what is the result of it, that the Soveraign may lawfully kill any of his subjects, or as many of them as he pleaseth, without any fault of theirs, without any examination on his part, meerly upon suspicion, or without any suspicion of the least crime, if he do but judge him to be hurtful or noisome, as freely as a man may pluck up a weed, because it hinders the nourishment of better plants. *Before the institution of a Common-wealth every one may lawfully be spoiled and killed by every one, but in a Common-wealth onely by one,* [Ci. c. 10. s. 1.] that is the Soveraign. And *by the right of nature we destroy without being unjust, all that is noxious, both beasts and men.* He makes no difference between a Christian and a wolfe. Would you know what is noxious with him, even *whatsoever he thinketh can annoy him.* [Qu. p. 116 & 140.] Who would not desire to live in his Common-wealth, where the Soveraign may lawfully kill a thousand innocents every morning to his breakfast? Surely this is a Common-wealth of fishes, where the great ones eat the lesser.

It were strange if his Subjects should be in a better condition for their fortunes, than they are for their lifes, no I warrant you: do but hear him. *Thy dominion and thy property is so great, and lasteth so long, as the Common-wealth* (that is, the Soveraign) *will.* [Ci. c. 12. s. 7.] Perhaps he meaneth in some extraordinary cases? Tush, in all cases, and at all times. When thou didst chuse a Soveraign, even in chusing him thou madestt him a deed of gift of all thou hast. *Et tu ergo tuum jus civitate concessisti, and therefore thou hast granted all thy right to the Common-wealth.* [Ibid.]

Yet some may imagine that his meaning is only that property may be transferred by Laws or Acts of Parliament from one to another. *As the Lacedemonians, when they permitted children to steal other mens goods, they transferred the right from the owners to the children.* [Ci. c. 14. s. 10.] No, no, *T. H.* is not for general laws, but particular verbal mandates. *The Kings word is sufficient to take any thing from any subject, if there be need, and the King is judge of that need.* [Le. p. 106.] If by need he did understand extream necessity, for the preservation of the Common-wealth, it might alter the case. But his need is like Ahabs need of Naboths vineyard. There is neither necessity, nor Common-wealth in the case. The Lacedemonian thefts were warranted by a general law, not only consented to universally, but sworn unto. And if it had been otherwise, the value was so small, and the advantage apprehended, to be so great to the Common-wealth, that no honest Subject would contradict it.

Right and Title may be transferred by Law, and there can be no wrong, where consent is explicate and universal; such consent taketh away all errour. But if the consent be onely implicite, to the making or admitting of just laws, and unjust laws be obtruded in the place of just: the Subject suffers justly by his own Act: but he or they that were trusted sinne. And if he be a Soveraign, oweth an account to God, if subordinate, both to God and man. But he justifieth the taking away of mens estates, either in part, or in whole, without president Law, or president necessity, or subsequent satisfaction. And maintaineth, that not only the Subject is bound to submit, but that the Soveraign is just in doing it.

I cannot passe by his good affection to the Nobility of Europe: [Le. p. 184.] *In these parts of Europe, it hath been taken for a right of certain persons, to have place in the highest Councel of State by inheritance, but good councel comes not by inheritance. And the politicks is an harder study than Geometry.* I think he mistakes the Councel of State for the Parliament. And who more fit to concur in the choice of Laws, than they who are most concerned in the Laws, than they who must contribute most, if there be occasion, to the maintenance of the Laws. No art is hereditary more than politicks. A Musitian doth not beget a Musitian. Yet we see the fathers eminence in any Art, begets a propension in his posterity to the same. And where two or three successive generations do happilly insist in the steps one of another, they raise an Art to great perfection. I do easily acknowledge that Politicks are an harder study than Geometry, and the practise more than the

Theorye, gained more by experience than by study. Therefore our Parliaments did prudently permit the eldest sons of Barons, to be present at their consultations, to fit them by degrees, for that person which they must one day sustein. But he had a mind to shew the States men his teeth, as he had done to all other professions.

There are many other errours and mistakes in his Politicks, as this, [Ci. c. 7. s. 4.] *That Soveraignty cannot be divided,* or that *there cannot be a mixed form of government,* [Le. p. 170. &c.] which is a meer mistaking of the question. For though it be sometimes stiled a mixed monarchy, because it doth partake of all the advantages of Aristocracy and Democracy, without partaking of their inconveniences: yet to speak properly, it is more aptly called a temperated or moderated Soveraignty, rather than divided or mixed. Neither did any English Monarch communicate any essential of Soveraignty to any Subject or Subjects whatsoever. All civil power, legislative, judiciary, military, was ever exercised in the name of the King, and by his authority. The three Estates of the Kingdom assembled in Parliament, were but suppliants to the King, to have such or such Laws enacted. What is it then that hath occasioned this mistake? though the King hath not granted away any part of his Soveraign power: yet he hath restrained himself by his Coronation-oath, and by his great Charters, from the exercise of some part of it in some cases, without such and such requisite conditions, (except where the evident necessity of the Common-wealth, is a dispensation from Heaven for the contrary). So he hath restrained himself in the exercise of his legislative power, that he will governe his Subjects by no new Laws, other than such as they should assent unto. It is not then any legislative power, which the two Houses of Parliament have either exclusively without the King, or inclusively with the King, but a receptive, or rather a preparative power, *sine qua non,* without which no new laws ought to be imposed upon them: and as no new laws, so no new taxes or imposition, which are granted in England by a Statute Law.

But this it is evident how much his discourse of *three souls animating one body,* is wide from the purpose, and his supposition of *setting up a supremacy against the Soveraignty, Canons against Laws, and a ghostly authority against the civil,* weigheth lesse than nothing, seeing we acknowledge, That the civil Soveraign hath an Architectonicall power, to see that all Subjects within his domiinions do their duties in their several callings, for the safety and tranquility of their Common-wealth, and to punish those that are exorbitant with the civil sword, as well those who derive their habitual power immediately from Christ, as those who derive it from the Soveraign himself. Then the constitution of our English policy was not to be blamed, the exercise of the power of the keys, by authority from Christ, was not to be blamed; but *T. H.* deserveth to be blamed, who presumeth to censure before he understand.

Another of his whimsies is: [Le. p. 182.] *That no law can be unjust; by a good Law I mean, not a just law, for no law can be unjust, &c. It is in the Laws of the Common-wealth, as in the laws of gaming. Whatsoever the Gamsters all agree on, is injustice to none of them.* An opinion absurd in itself, and contradictory to his own ground. There may be laws tending to the contumely of God, to Atheisme, to denial of Gods providence, to Idolatry, all which he confesseth to be crimes of high treason against God. There may be Laws against the Law of nature, which he acknowledgeth to be the [Ci. c. 14. s. 4.] *divine Law, eternally, immutable, which God hath made known to all men, by his eternal word born in themselves, that is to say, natural reason.* But this question, whether any law can be unjust, hath been debated more fully between him and me, in my answer to his Animadversions. [Nu. 14.] The true ground of this and many other of his mistakes, is this, That he fancieth no reality of any natural justice or honesty, nor any relation to the Law of God or nature, but only to the Laws of the Common-wealth. So from one absurdity being admitted, many others are apt to follow.

His Oeconomicks are no better than his Politicks. He teacheth parents [Ci. c. 9. s. 7.] *that they cannot be injurious to their children, so long as they are in their power.* Yes, too many wayes, both by omission and commission. He teacheth mothers [Ci. c. 9. s. 2.] *that they may cast away their infants, or expose them at their own discretion lawfully.* He teacheth parents indifferently, that [Qu. p. 137.] *where they are free from all subjection, they may take away the lifes of their children,* or kill them, and this justly.

What horrid doctrines are these? It may be he will tell us, that he speaketh only of the state of meer nature, but he doth not; for he speaketh expresely of Common-wealths, and paralleth Fathers with Kings and Lords, to whom he ascribeth absolute dominion, who have no place in his state of meer nature. Neither can be speak of the state of meer nature, for therein, according to his grounds, the children have as much priviledge to kill their Parents, as the Parents to kill their children, seeing he supposeth it to be a state of war of all men against all men.

And if he did speak of the state of meer nature, it were all one. For first his state of meer nature is a drowsie dream of his own feigning, which looketh upon *men as if they were suddenly grown out of the ground like mushrooms*. [Ci. c. 8. s. 1.] The primigenious and most natural state of mankind, was in Adam before his fall, that is, the state of innocence. Or suppose we should give way to him to expound himself of the state of corrupted nature, that was in Adam and his family after his fall. But there was no such state of meer nature as he imagineth. There was Religion, there were Laws, Government, Society: and if there ever were any such barbarous savage rabble of men, as he supposeth, in the World, it is both untrue and dishonourable to the God of nature, to call it the state of meer nature, which is the state of degenerated nature. He might as well call an hydropical distemper, contracted by intemperance, or any other disease of that nature, the natural state of men. But there never was any such degenerate rabble of men in the World, that were without all Religion, all Government, all Laws, natural and Civil, no, not amongst the most barbarous Americans, (who except some few criminal habits, which those poor degenerate people, deceived by national custom, do hold for noble) have more principles of naturall piety, and honesty, and morality, then are readily to be found in his writings. As for the times of civill war, they areso far from being without all pacts and governours, that they abound overmuch with pacts and governours making policy not only to seem, but to be double.

This evident truth may be demonstrated from his own grounds. [Ci. c. s. 4.] *All those places of holy Scripture by which we are forbidden to invade that which is another mans, as, thou shalt not kill, thou shalt not steale, thou shalt not commit adultery, do confirm the last of distinction of mine and thine. For they suppose the right of all men, to all things to be taken away.* How can that be, when he confesseth every where that there are the eternal lawes of God and nature. But that which is much more true, they both suppose and demonstrate that there never was any such *right of all men to all things*. Let him call them lawes or theorems, or what he please, they confute that state of meer nature which he maketh the foundation of his commonwealth.

Hitherto he hath been too high for the parents. Now they must expect a cooling card. *The question who is the better man hath no place in the condition of meer nature, where all men are equall.* Are the parent and child equall? *Yes, they are equall who can do equall things one against another, But they who can do the greatest things, that is to kill, can do equall things. Therefore all men by nature are equall among themselves.* If the son have as strong an arme, and as good a cudgell as his father, he is as good a man as his father.

Another of his aphorismes is, [Le. p. 102.] *paternall dominion is not so derived from generation, as if therefore the parent had dominion over his child, because he begat him, but by the childs consent, either expresse, or by other sufficient arguments declared.* And will you see how this consent is gained? *The attaining to soveraign power is by two waies, one by naturall force, as when a man maketh his children submit themselves and their children to his government, as being able to destroy them if they refuse.* [Le. p. 88.] These principles are so false that the very evidence of truth doth extort the contrary from him at other times. *The Bishop saw there was paternall government in Adam, which he might do easily, as being no deep consideration.* [Qu. p. 139.] And again, *To kill ones parent, is a greater crime than to kill another, For the parent ought to have the honour of a soveraign, though he have surrendred his power to the civil law because he had it originally by nature.* [Le. p. 160.] Great is truth, and prevaileth.

If this were *no deep consideration*, the more he deserveth to be blamed, who at sometimes robbeth both parents of their honour, some other times the man only, as *by the right of nature the dominion over an infant doth belong first to him who hath him first in his power. And it is manifest that he that is born is sooner in the power of his mother than of any other, so that she might either bring him up, or cast him out, at her pleasure, and by right.* [Ci. c. 9. s. 2.] Never without the fathers licence, again, *in the state of nature it cannot be known who is father of an infant, but by the relation of the mother. Therefore he is his, whom the mother would have him to be, and therefore the mothers.* [Ibid. s. 3.] Doth this man believe in earnest that marriage was instituted by God in Paradice, and hath continued ever since the creation, He might as well tell us in plain termes, that all the obligation which a child hath to his parent, is because he did not take him by the heeles and knock out his braines against the walls, so soon as he was born. Though this be intolerable, yet there is something of gratitude in it, and in that respect it is not altogether so ill as his forced pacts.

How repugnant is this which he saith of the mothers dominion over her children, to the law of nations? By the law of the twelve tables a father might sell his child twice, *bis vanum dicat*. The mother had no hand in it. Neither doth the judiciall law of the Jewes, dissent from this, [Exod. 21. 7.] *If a man sell his daughter to be a maid servant.* [Num. 30. 4.] So likewise a childs vow might be invalidated by the authority of a father, but not of a mother.

He aboundeth every where with such destructive conclusions as these, as *to generation God hath ordained to man an helper, and there be alwaies two that are equally parents, The dominion therefore over the child should belong equally to both, and he be equally subject to both, which is impossible, for no man can obey two masters.* [Le. p. 102.] Whether had he forgotten the commandement, Honour thy father and thy mother, or thinketh he that obedience is not a branch of honour?

In the next place his principles destroy the subordination of a wife to her husband. *The inequality of naturall strength is lesse than that a man can acquire dominion over a woman without war?* [Ci. c. 9. s. 3.] And he giveth this reason why the contrary custome prevaileth, because [Ibid. s. 6.] *commonwealths were constituted by fathers of families, not by mothers of families, and from hence it is that the domesticall dominion belongs to the man.* The scriptures assign another reason of the subjection of the woman, and the rule of the man, namely the ordinance of Almighty God. *Gen.* 3. 16. And St. Paul secondeth it, *Women are commanded to be under obedience, as also saith the law.* 1. *Cor.* 14. 34. I trow that law was not made by fathers of families. *Wives submit yourselves unto your own husbands, as unto the Lord. Eph.* 5. 22. Why, because of the civill law? No such thing *for the husband is the head of the wife, even as Christ is the head of the Church, v. 23. And the man is the image and glory of God, but the woman is the glory of the man, for the man is not of the woman, but the woman of the man, neither was the man created for the woman, but the woman, for the man.* 1. Cor. 11. 7. 8. 9. He would not *suffer a woman to usurp authority over a man.* 1. *Tim.* 2. 12. much lesse over her own husband. I might cite St. Peter to the same purpose, but I am afraid lest he should accuse both S. Peter and St. Paul of partiality, as well as the first founders of commonwealths.

Upon his principles no man is sure of his own wife, if the soveraign please to dispose her to another. *For although the law of nature do prohibit theft, or adultery. &c. Yet if the civill law commend a man to invade any thing, that is not theft or adultery.* And what is the civill law in his sense? [Ci. c. 14. s. 10.] *the command of the lawgiver. And his command is the declaration of his will.* [Ibid. s. 13.] So if the lawgiver do but declare his pleasure that any one shall enjoy such a mans wife, or that she shall no longer be his wife, according to his grounds, husband and wife must both obey. *What is theft? what is murder? what is adultery? is known by the civill law, that is by the commands of him that is Soveraign in the commonwealth.* [Ci. c. 6. s. 16.] And without the Soveraignes command, if either party do but suspect one another, the party suspected is disobliged, *for there is no pact, where credit is not given to him that maketh the pact, neither can faith be violated where it is not had.*

The next politicall relation is between the Master and the servant, [Ci. c. 8. s. 9.] which the Hobbian principles do overthrow as well as the rest. One of these principles is, that *a Master cannot do any wrong to his servant, because the servant hath subjected his will to the will of his Master.* In all such submissions there is evermore either expressed or implied a *salvo*, [Ci. c. 8. s. 7.] or a saving of his duty to God, and his allegiance to his Prince. If his master shall punish him for not doing contrary to these, or by menaces compell him to do contrary to these, he doth him wrong. No man can transfer that right to another, which he had not himself. The servant before his submission to his master, had no right to denie due obedience to god, or due allegiance to his Prince.

Another is his Paradoxes is, that *whosoever is obliged to obey the commands of any other, before he know what he will command, is bound to all his commands simply, and without restriction. Now he that is obliged, is called a servant, he to* whom he is bound, a Master. [Ci. c. 8. s. 1.] What if the masters command be contrary to the lawes of God or nature? Or the lawes of the common-wealth. In the presence of a greater authority, a lesser authority ceaseth. Such implicite obligations are ever to be understood, *quantum jus fasque fuerit*, according to law and equity.

Hitherto servants have been grieved, but now they shall be relieved, if T. H. his authority can do it. [Ci. c. 8. s. 4.] *Servants who are holden in bonds are not comprehended in the definition of servants, because they serve not by pact, but to avoid beating, And therefore if they fly away, or kill their master, they do nothing contrary to the lawes of nature. For to bind them is a sign that the binder did suppose them not sufficiently bound by any other obligation.* His consequence is infirm, because the Master binds his servant therefore he distrusts him, therefore there were no pacts. A man may give his parole for true imprisonment, and having given it to a just enemy, is obliged to hold it, what if his conquerour or master did spare his life, upon condition that he should be true prisoner, untill he could find out a fit exchange for him. This was a lawfull pact. Then doth not T. H. instruct the prisoner well, to cut his Conquerours throat, who spared his life, upon a lawfull condition.

But to dispell these umbrages, he teacheth that [Ibid. s. 9.] *a servant who is cast into bonds, or any way deprived of his corporall liberty, is freed from that other obligation which did arise from his pact.* So as according to his principle, If a servant, (that is more than a captive,) having not only had his life spared by a just Conquerour, but also contracted and engaged himself to by a loyall servant, as firmly as may be, shall neverthelesse be cast into any bonds by his master, or be restrained of his corporall liberty, upon delinquency, or just suspicion, he is acquitted of all his pacts and obligations, and as free to run away, or cut his masters throat, as if he had never pacted or ingaged at all.

His defaults come so thick, I am weary of observing them. Take an hotchpotch together.

1. *In the state of nature profit is the measure of right.* [Ci. c 1. s. 10.]

2. *Every one is an enemy to every one whom he neither commandeth nor obeyeth.* [Ci. c. 9. s. 3.]

3. *Not onely to contend against one, but even this very thing*

not to consent, is odious; for not to consent with one in some thing, is tacitely to accuse him of errour in that thing, as to dissent in many things, is to hold him for a foole. [Ci. c. 1. s. 5.] In the name of God what doth he hold the whole World to be? I am sure he dissenteth from them all in many things.

4. *It is not reasonable that one perform first, if it be likely that the other will not perform afterwards, which whether it be likely or no, he that feareth shall judge.* [Ci. c. 2. s. 11.] It is true he addeth, That *in the civil state, where both parties may be compelled, he who is to perform first by the contract, ought to perform first.* But what if the civil power be not able to compel him? What is there be no witnesses to prove the contract? then the civil power can do nothing. May a man violate his faith in such cases upon general suspicions of the fraud and unfaithfulnesse of mankind?

5. *If a people have elected a Soveraign for term of life, and he die, neither the people before election, nor he before his death, having ordained any thing about a place of meeting for a new election, it is lawful for every one, by equal, that is natural right, to snatch the Soveraign to himself if he can.* [Ci. c. 7. s. 16.] His opinion of the state of nature is a very bundle of absurdities.

6. *When a Master commandeth his servant to give money to a stranger, if it be not done, the injury is done to the Master, whom he had before covenanted to obey, but the dammage redoundeth to the stranger, to whom he had no obligation, and therefore could not injure him.* [Le. p. 74.] True according to his Principles, who maketh neither conscience nor honesty nor obligation from any one to any one, but openly by pacts or promises. All just men are of another mind.

7. *Those men which are so remisly governed, that they dare take up arms to defend or introduce a new opinion, are still in war, and their condition not peace, but onely a cessation of arms, for fear of one another.* [Le. p. 91.] Why is the fault rather imputed to the remisnesse of the Governour, than to the sedition of the people, and a state of war feigned, where none is? The reason is evident, because he had no hand in the government, but had a hand in the introduction of new opinions.

8. *In a Soveraign assembly, the liberty to protest is taken away, both because he that protesteth there, denieth their Soveraignty, and also whatsoever is commanded by the*

Soveraign power, is as to the subject, justified by the command,
though not so alwayes in the sight of God. [Le. p. 117.] That is
not taken away which all Soveraigns do allow, even in the
competition for a Crown, as was verified in the case of the King
of Spain and the House of Braganza, about the kingdom of
Portugal. It is no denial of Soveraignty, to appeal humbly from
a Soveraign misinformed, to himself better informed. The
commands of a Soveraign person or assembly are so far
justified by the command, that they may not be resisted; but
they are not so far justified, but that a loyal subject may
lawfully seek with all due submission, to have them rectified.

9. *If he whose private interest is to be debated and judged in*
a Soveraign Assembly, make as may friends as he can, it is no
injustice in him. And though he hire such friends with money,
unlesse there be an expresse law against it, yet it is no injustice.
[Le. p. 122.] It is to be feared that such provocations as this,
are not very needful in these times. Is it not unlawful to blind
the eyes of the wise with bribes, and make them pervert
judgement? Others pretend expedition, or an equal hearing;
but he who knoweth no obligation but pacts, is for downright
hiring of his Judges, as a man should hire an hackney-coach for
an hour. There is no gratitude in hiring, which is unlawful in
the buyer, though not so unlawful as in the seller of Justice. If
any man digged a pit, and did not cover it, so that an oxe or an
asse fell into it, he who digged it was to make satisfaction.
[Exod. 21, 33.] He that hireth his Judges with money to be for
him right or wrong, diggeth a pit for them, and by the equity of
his Mosaical-Law, will appear not to be innocent.

Thus after the view of his Religion, we have likewise
surveighed his Politicks, as full of black ugly dismal rocks as
the former, dictated with the same magisteral authority; A
man may judge them to be twins upon the first cast of his eye.
It was Solomons advice, *Remove not the ancient land marks*
which thy fathers have set. [Pov. 22. 28.] But *T. H.* taketh a
pride in removeing all ancient land-marks, between Prince
and subject, Father and child, Husband and Wife, Master
and servant, Man and Man. Nilus after a great overflowing,
doth not leave such a confusion after it as he doth, nor an hog
in a garden of herbs. I wish he would have turned
probationer a while, and made trial of his new form of
government first in his own house, before he had gone about
to obtrude it upon the Common-wealth. And that before his

attempts and bold endeavours, to reform and to renew the policy of his native Country, he had thought more seriously and more sadly of his own application of the fable of *Peleus his foolish daughters, who desiring to renew the youth of their decripit father, did by the counsel of Medea cut him in pieces, and boyle him together with strange herbs; but made not of him a new man.* [Le. p. 177.]

CHAP. 3.

That the Hobbian Principles are inconsistent one with another.

My third Harping-Iron is aimed at the head of his Leviathan, or the rational part of his discourse, to shew that his Principles are contradictory one to another, and consequently destructive one of another. It is his own observation. [Le. p. 58.] *That which taketh away the reputation of wisdom in him that formeth a Religion, or addeth to it when it is already formed, is an enjoyning a belief of contradictories, for both parts of a contradiction cannot possibly be true. And therefore to enjoyn the belief of them, is an argument of ignorance.* How he will free himself from his own censure, I do not understand; let the Reader judge.

He affirmeth that an hereditary kingdom is the best form of government; [Ci. c. 10. s. 18.] *We are made subjects to him upon the best condition, whose interest it is that we should be safe and sound. And this cometh to passe when we are the Soveraigns inheritance,* (that is in an hereditary Kingdom) *for every one doth of his own accord study to preserve his own inheritance.* Now let us hear him retract all this. [Le. p. 99.] *There is no perfect form of government where the disposing of the succession is not in the present Soveraign.* [Ci. c. 9. s. 13.] And whether he *transfer it by testament, or give it, or sell it, it is rightly disposed.* [Le. p. 193.]

He affirmeth, *That which is said in the Scripture, it is better to obey God than man, hath place in the kingdom of God by pact, and not by nature.* One can scarcely meet with a more absurd senslesse Paradox, That in Gods own kingdom of Nature, (where he supposeth all men equal, and no Governour but God,) it should not be better to obey God than man, the

Creatour than the creatour, the Soveraign rather than a fellow-subject. Of the two it had been the lesse absurdity to have said, that it had place in the kingdom of God by nature, and not by pact, because in the kingdom of God by pact, Soveraigns are as *mortal gods.*

Now let us see him Penelope like, unweave in the night what he had woven in the day, or rather unweave in the day, what he had woven in the night. [Le. p. 321.] *It is manifest enough, that when man receiveth two contrary commands, and knows that one of them is Gods, he ought to obey that, and not the other, though it be the command even of his lawful Soveraign.* Take another place more expresse, speaking of the first kingdom of God by pact with Abraham, &c. He hath these words, [Le. p. 249.] *Nor was there any contract which could adde to, or strengthen the obligation, by which both they and all man else were bound naturally to obey God Almighty.* [Ibid.] And before any such Kingdom of God by pact, *As the moral law they were already obliged, and needed not have been contracted withall.* [Ci. c. 16. s. 2. s. 1.] He fancieth that God reigneth by pact over Adam and Eve, but *this pact became presently voide.* And if it had stood firm, what Kingdom of God by nature could have been before it? But he reckons his Kingdom of God by pact from Abraham, *from him the Kingdom of God by pact takes its beginning.* But in Abrahams time, and before his time, the World was full of Kings: every City had a King, was it not better for their subjects to obey God than them? yet that was the Kingdom of God by nature, or no Kingdom of God at all.

Sometimes he saith the Laws of nature are Laws, [Le. p. 185.] *whose Laws (such of them as oblige all mankind) and in respect of God, as he is the god of Nature, are natural, in respect of the same God, as he is King of Kings, are laws;* [Ci. c. 2. s. 1.] and *right reason is a Law.* And he defines the Law of nature, to be *the deictate of right reason.* Where by the way observe, what he makes to be the end of the Laws of nature, *The long conservation of our lives and members, so much as is in our power.* By this the Reader may see what he believes of honesty, or the life to come. At other times he saith that they are no laws. *Those which we call the Laws of nature, being nothing else but certain conclusions understood by reason of things to be done; or to be left undone. And a law, if we speak properly and accurately, is the speech of him that commandeth something by right to others, to be done, or not to be done, speaking properly, they are not laws, as they proceed from nature.* [Ci. c. 3. s. 33.]

It is true, he addeth in the same place, That *as they are given by God in holy Scripture, they are most properly called Laws, for the holy Scripture is the voice of God ruling all things by the greatest right.* But this will not salve the contradiction, for so the Laws of nature shall be no Laws to any but those who have read the Scripture, contrary to the sense of all the World. And even in this he contradicteth himself also. *The Bible is a Law? to whom? to all the World; he knoweth it is not: How came it then to be a Law to us?* [Q. p . 136.] *Did God speak it* viva voce *to us? Have we any other warrant for it than the word of the Prophets? Have we seen the miracles? Have we any other assurance of their certainty, than the authority of the Church?* And so he concludeth, That the authority of the Church is the authority of the Common-wealth, the authority of the Common-wealth, the authority of the Sovereign, and his authority was given him by us. And so [Ibid.] *the Bible was made Law by the assent of the Subjects.* And *the Bible is their only Law, where the civil Soveraign hath made it so.* [Le. p. 332.] Thus in seeking to prove one contradiction we have met with two.

He teacheth [Ci. c. 3. s. 29.] *that the Laws of nature are eternal and immutable, that which they forbid can never be lawful, that which they command never unlawful.* [Ci. c. 5. s. 2.] At other times he teacheth, that *in war, and especially in a war of all men against all men, the Laws of nature are silent.* And that they do not oblige as Laws, before there be a Common-wealth constituted. *When a Common-wealth is once setled, then are they actually Laws, and not before.* [Le. p. 138.]

He saith *true religion consisteth in obedience to Christs Lieutenants, and in giving God such honour, both in attributes and actions, as they in their severall Lieutenancies, shall ordein.* [Qu. p. 334. p. 341.] Which Lieutenant upon earth is the *supreme civill magistrate.* And yet contrary to this he excepteth from the obedience due to soveraign Princes, *all things that are contrary to the lawes of God, who ruleth over rulers.* [Ci. c. 6. s. 13.] Adding that *we cannot rightly transfer the obedience due to him upon men.* And more plainly, [Ci. c. 15. s. 18.] *If a soveraign shall command himself to be*

*worshipped with divine attributes and actions, as such as imply
an independance upon God, or immortality, or infinite power,
to pray unto them being absent, or to ask those things of them
which only God can give, to offer sacrifice, or the like.
Although Kings command us we must abstein.* He confesseth
*that the subjects of Abraham had sinned, if they had denied the
existence or providence of God, or done any thing that was
expressely against the honour of God, in obedience to his
commands.* [Ci. c. 16. s. 7.] And [Le. p. 192.] *actions that are
naturally signes of contumely, cannot be made by humane
power a part of divine worship, cannot be parts of divine
worhsip,* and yet religion may consist in such worship, is a
contradiction.

He confesseth, [Ci. c. 15. s. 18.] *That if the Common-wealth
should command a Subject to say or do something that is
contumelious unto God, or should forbid him to worship God,
he ought not to obey.* And yet maintaineth *that a Christian
holding firmly the faith of Christ in his heart, if he be
commanded by his lawful Soveraign, may deny Christ with his
tongue,* alledging, *That profession with the tongue is but an
external thing.* And *that it is not he in that case, who denieth
Christ before men, but his Governour, and the law of his
Country.* [Le. p. 271.] Hath he so soon forgot himself? Is not
the denial of Christ contumelious to God?

He affirmeth that *if a Soveraign shall grant to a Subject any
liberty inconsistent with Soveraign power, if the Subject refuse
to obey the Soveraigns command, being contrary to the liberty
granted, it is a sin, and contrary to his duty, for he ought to
take notice of what is inconsistent with Soveraignty, &c.* [Le.
p. 157.] *And that such liberty was granted through ignorance
of the evil consequence thereof.* Then a Subject may judge not
only what is fit for his own preservation, but also what are the
essentiall rights of Soveraignty, which is contrary to his
doctrine elsewhere. [Ci. c. 12. s. 1.] *It belongs to Kings to
discern what is good and evil; and private men, who take to
themselves the knowledge of good and evil, do covet to be as
Kings, which consisteth not with the safety of the Common-
wealth*; which he calleth *a seditious doctrine,* and one of the
diseases of a Commonwealth. [Le. p. 168.] Yet such is his
forgetfulnesse, that he himself licenseth his own book *for the
Presse,* and to *be taught in the Universities,* as conteining
nothing contrary to the *word of God or good manners,* or to

the disturbance of publick tranquility. [Le. p. 395.] Is not this to take to himself the knowledge of good and evil?

In one place he saith that *the just power of Soveraigns is absolute, and to be limited by the strength of the Commonwealth, and nothing else.* [Ci. c. 6. s. 18.] In other places he saith his power is to be limited by the Laws of God and nature. As [Le. p. 167.] *there is that in Heaven, though not on earth, which he should stand in fear of, and whose Laws he ought to obey.* And *though it be not determined in Scripture, what Laws every King shall constitute in his dominions, yet it is determined, what Law he shall not constitute.* And [Le. p. 199. p. 169.] *it is true, that Soveraigns are all subject to the laws of nature, because such laws be divine, and cannot by any man or Common-wealth be abrogated.* In one place he maintaineth that *all men by nature are equal among themselvs.* [Ci. c. 1. s. 3.] In another place, that *the father of every man was originally his Soveraign Lord, with power over him of life & death.* [Le. p. 178.]

He acknowledgeth that God is not onely *good,* and *just,* and *merciful,* but the best. That nature doth dictate to us that *God is to be honoured;* and that *to honour, is to think as highly of his power and goodnesse as is possible,* [Ci. c. 15. s. 9.] and that *nothing ought to be attributed to him, but what is honourable.* [Le. p. 188.] Nothing can be more contrary to this goodnesse, or more dishonourable to God, than to make him to be the cause of all the sinne in the World. [Qu. p. 175.] *Perhaps he will say that this opinion maketh God the cause of sin: But doth not the Bishop think him the cause of all actions? And are not sins of commission actions? Is murder no action? And doth not God Himself say,* Non est malum in civitate quod ego non feci? *And was not murder one of those evils?* The like doctrine he hath. Qu. p. 108 and 234.

I chanced to say, that if a child, before he have the use of reason, shall kill a man in his passion; yet because he had no malice to incite him to it, nor reason to restrein him from it, he shall not die for it in the strict rules of particular justice, unless there be some mixture of publick justice in the case, shewing onely what was the law, not what was my opinion. An innocent child for terrour to others, in some cases may be deprived of those honours and inheritances, which were to have discended upon him from his father, but not of his life. Amazia slew the murderers of the King his father, [2. Chro. 25.

4.] *but he slew not their children, but did as it is written in the Law, in the book of Moses, The fathers shall not dye for the children, not the children for the fathers*, [Deut. 24. 16.] And he presently taxed me for it, *The Bishop would make but an ill Judge of innocent children.* [Qu. p. 277.] And the same merciful opinion he maintaineth elsewhere. [Le. p. 165.] *All punishments of innocent Subjects, be they great or little, are against the law of nature. For punishment is only for transgression of the law, and therefore there can be no punishment of the innocent.* Yet within few lines after he changeth his note. *In Subjects who deliberately deny the authority of the Common-wealth established, the vengeance is lawfully extended, not onely to the fathers, but also to the third and fourth generation.* [Ibid.] His reason is, because *this offence consisteth in renouncing of subjection: so they suffer not as Subjects, but as enemies.* Well, but the children were born subjects as well as the father, and they never renounced their subjection, how come they to lose their birth-right, and their lives for their fathers fault, if *there can* be no punishment of the innocent, so the contradiction stands still.

But all this is but a copy of his countenance, I have shewed formerly expressely out of his principles, *That the foundation of the right of punishing, exercised in every Common-wealth*, is not the just right of the Soveraign for crimes committed, but *that right which every man by nature had to kill every man.* Which right he saith every Subject hath renounced, but the Soveraign, by whose authority punishment is inflicted, hath not. So if he do examine the crime in justice, and condemn the delinquent, then is properly punishment. If he do not, then it is an hostile act, but both waies just and allowable. Reader, if thou please to see what a slippery memory he hath: for thine own satisfaction, read over the beginning of the eight and twentieth Chapter of his Leviathan. Innocents cannot be justly punished, but justly killed upon his principles.

But this very man, who would seem so zealous sometimes for humane justice, that there can be no just punishment of innocents, no just punishment, but for crimes committed, how standeth he affected to divine justice? He reguardeth it not at all, grounding every where Gods right to afflict the Creatures upon his omnipotence: and maintaining that God may as justly afflict with eternal torments without sin, as for sin. *Though God have power to afflict a man, and not for sinne, without injustice: Shall we think God so cruel, as to afflict a man, and not for sinne, with extream and endlesse torments? Is it not cruelty? No more than to do the same for sinne, when he that afflicteth might without trouble have kept him from sinning.* [Q. p. 13.] Whether God do afflict eternally, or punish eternally; whether the Soveraign proceed judically, or in a hostile way, so it be not for any crime committed; it is all one as to the justice of God and the Soveraign, and all one as to the sufferings of the innocent. But [Le. p. 105.] *it may and doth often happen in Common-wealths, that a Subject may be put to death by the command of the Soveraign power, and yet neither do the other wrong*; that is to say, both be innocent, for that is the whole scope of the place. It is against the law of nature to punish innocent Subjects, saith one place, but innocent Subjects may lawfully be killed or put to death, saith another.

Sometimes he maketh the institution of Soveraignty to be only the laying down the right of Subjects, which they had by nature. *For he who renounceth or passeth away his right, giveth not to any other man, a right which he had not before, because there is nothing to which every man had not right by nature, but onely standeth out of his way, that he may enjoy his own original right, without hinderance from him, not without hinderance from another.* [Le. p. 65.] And elsewhere, *The Subjects did not give the Soveraign that right, but onely in laying down theirs, strengthened him to use his own, &c.* [Le. p. 162.] *So it was not given, but left to him, and to him only.* And *the translation of right doth consist onely in not resisting.* [Ci. c. 2. s. 4.] He might as well have said, and with as much sense, *the transferring of right doth consist in not transferring of right.* At other times he maketh it to be a surrender, [Le. p. 87.] *or giving up of the subjects right to govern himself to this man. A conferring of all their power and strength upon one man, that may reduce all their wills by plurality of voices to one wil. An appointing of one man to bear their person, and acknowledging themselves to be the authours of whatsoever the Soveraign shall act, or cause to be acted in those things which concerne the common safety; a submission of their wills to his will, their judgements to his judgement.* [Le p. 109.] And *David did no injury to Uriah, because the right to do what he pleased, was given him by Uriah himself.* Before we had a transferring without transferring, now we have a giving up without giving up, an appointing or constituting, without appointing or constituting, a subjection without subjection, an authorising without authorising. What is this?

He saith that *it cannot be said honourably of God, that he hath parts or totality, which are the attributes of finite things.* [Ci. c. 15. s. 14.] If it cannot be said honourably of God, that he hath parts or totality, then it cannot be said honourably of God that he is a body; for everybody hath parts and totality. Now hear what he saith, [Le. p. 371.] *Every part of the Universe is body; And that which is no body, is no part of the Universe. And because the Universe is all, that which is no part of it, is nothing.* Then if God have no parts and totality, God is nothing. Let him judge how honourable this is for God.

He saith, *We honour not God but dishonour him by any value lesse than infinite.* [Le. p. 357.] And how doth he set an infinite value upon God, [Qu. p. 266.] who every where maketh him to subsist by *successive duration.* Infinite is that to which nothing can be added, but to that which subsisteth by successive duration, something is added every minute.

He saith, *Christ had not a Kingly authority committed to him by his Father in the World, but onely consiliary and doctrinal.* [Ci. c. 17. s. 6.] He saith on the contrary, *That the kingdom of Judea was his hereditary right from King David, &c.* And when it pleased him to play the King, he required entire obedience, Math. 21. 2. *Go into the village over against you, and streightway ye shall find an asse tied, and a colt with her, loose them and bring them unto me. And if any man say ought unto you, ye shall say, The Lord hath need of them.* [Ci. c. 11. s. 6.]

He saith, *The institution of eternal punishment was before sin.* [Ci. c. 4. s. 9.] And [Le. p. 321.] *if the command be such as cannot be obeyed without being damned to eternal death, then it were madnesse to obey it.* And *what evil hath excommunication in it, but the consequent, eternal punishment?* [Ci. c. 17. s. 25.] At other times he saith there is no eternal punishment. *It is evident that there shall be a second death of every one that shall be condemned at the day of Judgement, after which he shall die no more.* [Le. p. 245.] He who knoweth no soul nor spirit, may well be ignorant of a spiritual death.

He saith, *It is a doctrine repugnant to civil society, that whatsoever a man does against his conscience is sin.* [Le. p. 168.] Yet he himself saith, *It is a sin whatsoever one doth against his conscience, for they that do that, despise the Law.* [Ci. c. 12. s. 2.]

He saith, *That all power secular and spiritual under Christ, is united in the Christian Common-wealth*; [Ci. c. 18. s. 1.] that is, the Christian Soveraign: Yet he himself saith on the contrary, *It cannot be doubted of, that the power of binding and loosing; that is, of remitting and retaining sins,* (which we call the power of the keyes) *was given by Christ to future Pastours in the same manner as to the present Apostles. And all power of remitting sin which Christ himself had, was given to the Apostles.* [Ci. c. 17. s. 25.] All spiritual power is in the Christian Magistrate. Some spiritual power (that is the power of the keyes) is in the successours of the Apostles, that is not in the Christian Magistrate, is a contradiction.

He confesseth, That *it is manifest that from the ascension of Christ until the conversion of Kings, the power Ecclesiastical was in the Apostles, and so delivered unto their successours by imposition of hands.* [Le. p. 267.] And yet straight, forgetting himself, he taketh away all power from them, even in that time when there were no Christian Kings in the World. He alloweth them no power to make any Ecclesiastical laws or constitutions, or to impose any manner of commands upon Christians. *The office of the Apostles was not to command, but teach.* [Ci. c. 17. s. 24.] As Schoole-Masters, not as Commanders. [Le. p. 269.] Yet Schoole-Masters have some power to command. He suffereth not the Apostles to ordain, but those whom the Church appointeth, nor to excommunicate, or absolve, but whom the Church pleaseth. He maketh the determination of all controversies to rest in the Church, not in the Apostles. And resolveth all questions into the authority of the Church. *The election of Doctours and prophets did rest upon the authority of the Church of Antioch.* And [Ci. c. 17. s. 24.] *if it be inquired by what authority it came to passe that it was received for the command of the Holy Ghost, which those Prophets and Doctors said proceeded from the Holy Ghost, we must necessarily answer, By the authority of the Church of Antioch.* Thus every where he ascribeth all authority to the Church, none at all to the Apostles, even in those times before there were Christian Kings. *He saith not, tell it to the Apostles; but tell it to the Church, that we may know the definitive sentence, whether sin, or no sin, is not left to them, but to the Church.* [Ci. c. 17. s. 25.] And *it is manifest, that all authority in spiritual things, doth depend upon the authority of the Church.* [Ci. c. 18. s. 1.]

Thus not contented with single contradictions, he twisteth them together; for according to his definition of a Church, there was no Christian Church at Antioch, or in those parts of the World, either then or long after. Hear him. [Le. p. 248.] *A Church is a company of men professing Christian Religion, united in the person of one Soveraign, at whose command they ought to assemble, and without whose authority they ought not to assemble.* Yet there was no Christian Soveraign in those parts of the World then, or for two hundred years after, and by consequence, according to his definition, no Church.

He teacheth, That *when the civil Soveraign is an infidel, every one of his own subjects that resisteth him, sinneth against the Laws of God, and rejecteth the counsel of the Apostles, that admonisheth all Christians to obey their Princes, and all children and servants to obey their Parents and Masters in all things.* [Le. p. 330.] As for not resisting, he is in the right, but for obeying in all things, in his sense, it is an abominable errour. Upon this ground, he alloweth Christians to deny Christ, to sacrifice to idols, so they preserve faith in their hearts. He telleth them, *They have the license that Naaman had, and need not put themselves into danger for their faith.* That is, they have liberty to do any external acts, which their infidel Soveraigns shall command them. Now hear the contrary from himself. *When Soveraigns are not Christians, in spiritual things; that is, in those things which pertain to the manner of worshipping God, some Church of Christians is to be followed;* [Ci. c. 18. s. 13.] Adding, that when we may not obey them, yet we may not resist them, but *eundum est ad Christum per martyrium,* we ought to suffer for it.

He confesseth, That *matter and power are indifferent to contrary forms and contrary acts.* [Qu. p. 292.] And yet maintaineth every where that all matter is necessitated by the outward causes to one individual form; that is it is not indifferent. And all power by his Principles is limited and determined to one particular act. Thus he scoffeth at me for the contrary, *very learnedly, as if there were a power that were not a power to do some particular act, or a power to kill, and yet to kill no body in particular.* [Qu. p. 108.] *Nor doth power signifie any thing actually, but those motions and present acts, from which the act that is not now, but shall be hereafter, necessarily proceedeth.* If every act be necessary, and all power determined to one particular act, as he saith here, how is power indifferent to contrary Acts, as he saith there?

He acknowledgeth, That [Le. p. 4.] *though at some certain distance the reall and very object seem invested with the phansie it begets in us, yet still the object is one thing, the image or phansie is another.* [Qu. p. 245.] And yet affirmeth the contrary, That *the Preachers voice is the same thing with hearing, and a phansie in the hearer.* Even so he might say, that the colour or the sight, is the same thing with seeing. Men utter their voice many times, when no man heareth them.

He saith, *Inspiration implies a gift supernatural, and the immediate hand of God.* [Le. p. 324.] On the contrary he saith, [Le. p. 196.] *To say a man speakes by supernatural inspiration, is to say he finds an ardent desire to speak, or some strong opinion of himself, for which he can alledge no natural and sufficient reason.* [Le. p. 169.] He reckoneth this opinion, *that faith and sanctity are not to be attained by study and reason, but by supernatural inspiration, among the diseases of a Common-wealth.* [Le. p. 214.] And lastly he acknowledgeth *no proper inspiration, but blowing of one thing into another,* not metaphorical, *but inclining the spirit.*

He saith, [Qu. p. 307.] *Ordinary men understand the word body and empty, as well as learned men; And when they hear named an empty vessel, the learned as well as the unlearned, mean and understand the same thing, namely, that there is nothing in it that can be seen, and whether it be truly empty, the plow-man and the Schoole-man know alike.* Now hear him confesse the contrary. *In the sense of common people not all the Universe is called body, but onely such parts thereof as they can discern by the sense of feeling to resist the force, or by the of their eyes to hinder them from a farther prospect, therefore in the common language of men, air and aeriall substances, use not to be taken for bodies.* [Le. p. 207.]

He holdeth that no law may be made to command the will. [Qu. p. 138.] *The stile of law is, Do this, or do not this; or if thou do this thou shalt suffer this. But no law runs thus. Will this, or will not this; or if thou have a will to this, thou shalt suffer this.* And yet he definith sin to be *that which is done, or left undone, or spoken, or willed contrary to the reason of the Common-wealth* [De Ci. c. 14. s. 17.] Then the laws of men are made to bind the will if that which is willed contrary to the laws be a sin.

He saith, *Necessary is that which is impossible to be otherwise, or that which cannot possibly be, and possible and impossible have no signification in reference to the time past, or time present, but onely time to come.* [Qu. p. 26 & p. 36.] Yet in the very same paragraph he asserteth *a necessity from eternity, or an antecedent necessity, derived from the very beginning of time.*

He saith, *There is no doubt a man can will one thing or other, or forbear to will it* [Qu. p. 310.] If a man can both will and forbear to will the same thing, then a man is as free to will as to do. But he teacheth the contrary every where, That *a man is free to do if he will, but he is not free to will.*

He saith, *Though God gave Solomon his choise, that is, the thing which he should chuse, it doth not follow that he did not also give him the act of election*; [Qu. p. 75.] that is, determine him to that which he should chuse. To give a man choice of two things, and determine him to one of them, is contradictory.

He confesseth, That *it is an absurd speech to say the will is compelled.* [Qu. p. 208.] And yet with the same breath he affirmeth, That *a man may be compelled to will.* The reason why the will cannot be compelled is, because it implyeth a contradiction. Compulsion is evermore against a mans will; How can a man will that which is against his will? Yet faith *T. H. Many things may compel a man to do an action in producing his will.* [Ibid.] That a man may be compelled to do an action, there is no doubt, but to say he is compelled to do that action which he is willing to do, that is when a new will is produced, or that a will to do the action is produced then when the man is compelled, is a contradiction.

He maketh the soveraign Prince to be [Ci. c. 17. s. 27.] *the onely authentick interpreter of Scripture,* [Le. p. 296.] and *to have Pastor all authority jure divino, which all other Pastors hath but jure civili*, yet in all questions of faith, and interpretation of the word of God, he obligeth the soveraign to make use of Ecclesiastical Doctours, rightly ordained by imposition of hands, to whom he saith *Christ hath promised an infallibility,* His glasse that *this infallibility is not such an infallibility, that they cannot be deceived themselves, but that a subject cannot be deceived in obeying them,* [Ci. c. 17. s. 24.] is absurd, for such an infallibility (upon his grounds) the Soveraign had without their advice. [Qu. p. 214.] To passe by

his confused and party coloured discourse, how doth this agree
with his former objection? which I shall insert here *mutatis
mutandis*. *That the right interpretation of scripture should
depend upon the infallibility of Ecclesiasticall Doctors, many
incommodities and absurdities which must follow from thence,
do prohibit, the chiefest whereof is this, that only all civill
obedience would be taken away, contrary to the precept of
Christ, but also all society, and humane peace would be
dissolved, contrary to the lawes of nature. For whilst they
make the Ecclesiasticall Doctors the infallible Judges; what
pleaseth God, and what displeaseth him, the subjects cannot
obey their Soveraigns, before the Doctors have judged of their
commands whether they be conformable to Scripture or not.
And so either they do not obey, or they obey for the judgment
of their Doctors, that is they obey their Doctors, not their
Soveraign, Thus civill obedience is taken away.* These are his
own words with a little variation, onely putting in the Doctors
for the subjects. I consider not what is true or false in them for
the present, but only shew the inconsistency of his grounds, how
he buildeth with one hand, and pulleth down with the other.

He saith *it is determined in Scripture what lawes every
christian King shall not consitute in his dominions*. [Le. p.
199.] And in the next words, *Soveraigns in their own
dominions are the sole Legislators.* And that [Le. p. 169.] *those
books only are canonicall in every nation, which are
established for such by the soveraign authority.* Then the
determinations of Scripture upon his grounds are but civill
lawes, and do not tie the hands of Soveraignes. He teacheth us
every where that *the subsequent commands of a Sovereign
contrary to his former lawes is an abrogation of them.* And that
*it is an opinion repugnant to the nature of a commonwealth,
that he that hath the soveraign power is subject to the civill
lawes.* The determinations of Scripture upon his grounds do
bind the hands of Kings, when they themselves please to be
bound, no longer.

To conclude sometimes he doth admit the soul to be a
distinct substance from the body, sometimes he denieth it.
Sometimes he maketh reason to be a naturall faculty,
sometimes he maketh it to be an acquired habit. In some places
he alloweth the will to be a rationall appetite, in other places he
disallowes it. Sometimes he will have it to be a law of nature,
that man must stand to their pacts, Sometimes he maketh

covenants of mutuall trust in the state of nature to be void. Sometimes he will have no punishment but for crimes that might have been left undone, At other times he maketh all crimes to be inevitable. Sometimes he will have the dependence of actions upon the will to be truly liberty, At other times he ascribeth liberty to rivers, which have no will. Sometimes he teacheth that though an action be necessitated, yet the will to break the law maketh the action to be unjust, at other times he maketh the will to be much more necessitated than the action. He telleth us that civill law-makers may erre and sin in making of a law, And yet the law so made is an infallible rule. Yes to lead a man infallibly into a ditch. What should a man say to this man? How shall one know when he is in earnest, and when he is in jest. He setteth down his opinion just as Gipsies tell fortunes, both waies, that if the one misse the other may be sure to hit, that when they are accused of falsehood by one, they may appeale to another. *But what did I write* in such a place.

It was the praise of John Baptist, that he was *not like a reed shaken with the wind*, bending or inclining, hither and thither, this way and that way, now to old truths, then to new errours. And it is the honour of every good Christian. St. Paul doth excellently describe such fluctuating Christians by two comparisons, the one of little children, the other of a ship lying at Hull, *Eph.* 4. 14. *That we henceforth be no more children tossed too and fro, and carried about with every wind of doctrine,* as a child wavers between his love and duty, to his parent or nurse on the one hand, and some apple or other toy which is held forth to him on the other hand, or as a ship lying at anchor changeth its positure with every wave, and every puffe of wind. As the last company leaves them, or the present occasion makes them, so they vary their discourses.

When the time was T. H. was very kind to me, to let me see the causes and grounds of my errours. *Arguments seldome work on men of wit and learning, when they have once ingaged themselves in a contrary opinion. If any thing will do it, it is the shewing of them the causes of their errours.* One good turn requireth another. [Q. p. 334.] Now I will do as much for him. If it do not work upon himself: Yet there is hope it may undeceive some of his disciples. A principall cause of his errours is a fancying to himself a generall state of nature, which is so far from being generall, that there is not an instance to be found of it in the nature of things, where mankind was altogether without laws & without governours, guided only by self interest, without any sense of conscience, justice, honesty, or honour. He may search all the corners of America with a candle and lanthorn at noon day, and after his fruitlesse paines, return a *non est inventus*.

Yet all plants and living creatures are subject to degenerate and grow wild by degrees. Suppose it should so happen that some remnant of men, either chased by war, or persecution, or forced out of the habitable world for some crimes by themselves committed, or being cast by shipwrack upon some deserts, by long conversing with savage beasts, lions, beares, wolves and tygers, should in time become more bruitish (it is his own epithite,) than the bruites themselves, would any man in his right wits make that to be the universall condition of mankind, which was onely the condition of an odd handfull of men, or that to be the state of nature, which was not the state of nature, but an accidentall degeneration?

He that will behold the state of nature rightly, must look upon the family of Adam, and his posterity in their successive generations from the creation to the deluge, and from the deluge, untill Abrahams time, when the first Kingdome of God by pact is supposed by *T. H.* to begin. All this while (which was a great part of that time the world hath stood) from the creation lasted the Kingdom of God by nature, as he phraseth it, And yet in those daies there were lawes and government, and more Kings in the world, then there are at this present, [Gen. 14.] we find nine Kings engaged in one war, and yet all their dominions but a narrow circuit of land. And so it continued for divers hundreds of years after, as we see by all those Kings which Joshua discomfited in the land of Canaan. Every City had its own King. The reason is evident, The originall right of fathers of families was not then extinguished.

Indeed *T. H.* supposeth that men did spring out of the earth like Mushromes or Mandrakes. [Ci. c. 8. s. 1.] *That we may return again to the state of nature, and consider men as if they were even now suddenly sprouted and grown out of the earth, after the manner of Mushroms, without any obligation of one to another.* But this supposition is both false and Atheistical, howsoever it dropt from his pen. Mankind did not spring out of the earth, but was created by God, not many suddenly, but one to whom all his posterity were obliged as to their father and ruler.

A second ground of his errours is his grosse mistake of the laws of nature, which he relateth most imperfectly, and most untruely. A moral Heathen would blush for shame, to see such a catalogue of the laws of nature.

First he maketh the laws of nature to be laws and no laws: Just as *a man and no man, hit a bird and no bird, with a stone and no stone, on a tree and no tree:* not *laws* but *theorems*, laws which required not *performance* but *endeavours*, laws which were silent, and could not be put in execution in the state of nature. [Ci. c. 14. s. 9.] *Where nothing was another mans, and therefore a man could not steal, where all things were common, and therefore no adultery, where there was a state of war, and therefore it was lawfull to kill, where all things were defined by a mans own judgement, and therefore what honours he pleased to give unto his father: and lastly, where there were no publick judgements, and therefore no use of witnesses.* As for the first table he doth not trouble himself much with it, except it be to accommodate it unto Kings. Every one of these grounds here alledged, are most false, without any verisimilitude in them, and so his superstructure must needs fall flat to the ground.

Secondly he relateth the laws of nature most imperfectly, smothering and concealing all those principall laws, which concern either piety, and our duty towards God, or justice, and our duties towards man.

Thirdly, sundry of those laws which he is pleased to take notice of, are either misrelated, or misinterpreted by him. He maketh the only end of all the laws of nature to be *the long conservation of a mans life and members*, most untruely. He maketh every man by nature *the only judge of the means of his own conservation*, most untruely. His father and Soveraign in the weightiest cases, is more judge than himself. He saith that *by the law of nature every man hath right to all things, and over all persons*, most untruely. He saith the natural condition of mankind is *a war of all men against all men*, most untruely. And that *nature dictateth to us to relinquish this feigned right of all men to all things*, most untruely. And that *nature dictateth to a man to retein his right of preserving his life and limbs, though against a lawfull magistrate*, lawfully proceeding, most untruely. I omit his uncouth doctrine about pacts made in the state of nature: and that he knoweth no gratitude, but where there is a trust, *fiducia*. These things are unsound, and the rest of his laws, for the most part, poor triviall things, in comparison of those weightier dictates of nature, which he hath omitted.

All other Writers of Politicks do derive Common-wealths from the sociability of nature, which is in mankind, most truely. But he will have the beginning of all humane society to be from mutual fear: as much contrary to reason as to authority. We see some kind of Creatures delight altogether in solitude, rarely, or never in company. We see others, (among which is mankind) delight altogether in company, rarely, or never in solitude. Let him tell me what mutuall fear of danger did draw the silly Bees into swarms; or the Sheep and doves into flocks; and what protection they can hope for, one from another? and I shall conceive it possible, that the beginning of humane society might be from fear also.

And thus having invented a fit foundation for his intended building, ycleped *the state of meer nature*, which he himself first devised for that purpose, he hath been long moduling and framing to himself a new form of policy, to be builded upon it: but the best is, it hath onely been in paper. All this while he hath never had a finger in morter. This is the new frame of *absolute Soveraignty*, which *T. H.* knew right well would never stand, nor he should be ever permitted to reer it up in our Europæn Climates or in any other part of the habitable World, which had ever seen any other form of civil government. Therefore he hath sought out for a fit place in America, among the Savages, to try if perhaps they might be perswaded, that the Laws of God and nature, the names of good and evil, just and unjust, did signifie nothing but at the pleasure of the Soveraign Prince.

And because there hath been much clashing in these Quarters about Religion, through the distempered zeal of some, the seditious orations of others, and some pernicious principles, well meant at first, but ill understood, and worse pursued: to prevent all such garboiles in his Common-wealth, he hath taken an order to make his Soveraign to be *Christs Lieutenant upon earth, in obedience to whose commands true religion doth consist.* Thus making policy to be the building, and religion the hangings, which must be fashioned just according to the proportion of the policy; and (not as Mr. *Cartwright* would have had it) making religion to the building, and policy the hangings, which must be conformed to religion.

Well the law is costly, and I am for an accommodation, that *T. H.* should have the sole privilege of setting up his form of government in America, as being calculated and fitted for that Meridian. And if it prosper there, then to have the liberty to transplant it hither: who knoweth (if there could but be some means devised to make them understand his language) whether the Americans might not chuse him to be their Soveraign? But all the fear is, that if he should put his principles in practise, as magistrally as he doth dictate them, his supposed subjects might chance to tear their *mortal God* in pieces with their teeth, and entomb his Soveraignty their bowels.

FINIS

An Advertisement to the Reader.

Because I know but of one Edition of Mr. Hobs *his Leviathan and of his Questions concerning Liberty; therefore I have cited them two by the page. Le. standing for Leviathan, and Qu. for Questions. But because there are sundry editions of his book* De Cive, *I have cited that by the Chapter and Section, according to his Paris Edition.*

A SURVEY OF MR HOBBES *HIS* LEVIATHAN
[Edward, Earl of Clarendon]

THE INTRODUCTION

I have alwaies thought it a great excess in those who take upon them to answer other Mens Writings, to hold themselves oblig'd to find fault with every thing that they say, and to answer every clause, period, and proposition which he, to whom they have made themselves an adversary, hath laid down; by which, besides the voluminousness that it produces, which in it self is grievous to any Reader, they cannot but be guilty of many impertinences, and expose themselves to the just censures of others, and to the advantage of their Antagonists; since there are few Books which do not contain many things which are true, and cannot, or need not be contradicted. And considering withall, that those Books have in all times don most mischief, and scatter'd abroad the most pernicious errors, in which the Authors, by the Ornament of their Style, and the pleasantness of their method, and subtlety of their Wit, have from specious premises, drawn their unskilful and unwary Readers into unwarrantable opinions and conclusions, being intoxicated with terms and Allegorical expressions, which puzzel their understandings, and lead them into perplexities, from whence they cannot disentangle themselves; I have proposed to my self, to make some Animadversions upon such particulars, as may in my judgment produce much mischief in the World, in a Book of great Name, and which is entertain'd and celebrated (at least enough) in the World; a Book which contains in it good learning of all kinds, politely extracted, and very wittily and cunningly disgested, in a very commendable method, and in a vigorous and pleasant Style: which hath prevailed over too many, to swallow many new tenets as maximes without chewing; which manner of diet for the indigestion Mr *Hobbes* himself doth much dislike. The thorough novelty (to which the present age, if ever any, is too much inclin'd) of the work receives great credit and authority from the known Name of the Author, a Man of excellent parts, of great wit, some reading, and somewhat more thinking; One who has spent many years in foreign parts and observation, understands the Learned as well as modern Languages, hath long had the reputation of a great Philosopher and Mathematician, and in his age hath had conversation with very many worthy and extraordinary Men to which, it may be, if he had bin more indulgent in the more vigorous part of his life, it might have had a greater influence upon the temper of his mind, whereas age seldom submits to those questions, enquiries, and contradictions, which the Laws and liberty of conversation require: and it hath bin alwaies a lamentation amongst Mr *Hobbes* his Friends, that he spent too much time in thinking, and too little in exercising those thoughts in the company of other Men of the same, or of as good faculties; for want whereof his natural constitution, with age, contracted such a morosity, that doubting and contradicting Men were never grateful to him. In a word, Mr *Hobbes* is one of the most antient acquaintance I have in the World, and of whom I have alwaies had a great esteem, as a Man who besides his eminent parts of Learning and knowledg, hath bin alwaies looked upon as a Man of Probity, and a life free from scandal; and it may be there are few Men now alive, who have bin longer known to him then I have bin in a fair and friendly conversation and sociableness; and I had the honor to introduce those, in whose perfections he seemed to take much delight, and whose memory he seems most to extol, first into his acquaintance. In all which respects, both of the Author and the work, it cannot reasonably be imagined, that any vanity hath transported me, who know my self so incompetent for the full disquisition of this whole work, which contains in it many parts of knowledg and Learning in which I am not conversant; and also the disadvantage, that so many years have passed since the publication of this Book, without any thing like an answer to the most mischievous parts of it as to Civil Government; at least I had seen none such, till after I had finished this discourse, what was at *Montpelier* in the moneth of April One thousand six hundred and seventy, where I wanted many of those Books which had bin necessary to have bin carefully consulted and perused, if I had propos'd to my self to have answer'd many of those Scholastic points, which seem to me enough expos'd to just censure and reproch, and which I did suppose some University Men would have taken occasion from, to have vindicated those venerable Nurseries from that vice and ignorance, his superciliousness hath thought fit to asperse them with. I do confess since that time I have read several answers and reflexions, made by Learned Men of both the Universities, in English and in Latine upon his *Leviathan*, or his other works published before and after; which several answers (though they have very pregnantly discover'd many gross errors, and grosser oversights in those parts of Science in which Mr *Hobbes* would be thought to excel, which are like to put him more out of countenance then any thing I can urge against him, by how much he values himself more upon being thought a good Philosopher, and a good Geometrician, then a modest Man, or a good Christian) have not so far discouraged me, as to cause me, either to beleive what I had thought of and prepared before, to be the less pertinent to be communicated, or at all to inlarge, or contract my former conceptions (though probably many things which I offer are more vigorously urg'd, and expressed in some of the other answers.) Notwithstanding all which, his Person is by many received with respect, and his Books continue still to be esteem'd, as well abroad as at home: which might very well have prevail'd, with those before mention'd arguments, to have diverted me from pretending to see farther into them then other Men had don, and to discover a malignity undiscerned that should make them odious. But then how prevalent soever these motives were with me; when I reflected upon the most mischievous Principles, and most destructive to the Peace both of Church and State, which are scatter'd throughout that Book of his *Leviathan*, (which I only take upon me to discover) and the unhappy impression they have made in the minds of too many; I thought my self the more oblig'd, and not the less competent for those animadversions, by the part I had acted for many years in the public administration of Justice, and in the Policy of the Kingdom. And the leasure to which God hath condemn'd me, seems an invitation, and obligation upon me, to give a testimony to the World, that my duty and affection for my King and Country, is not less then it hath ever bin, when it was better interpreted, by giving warning to both, of the danger they are in by the seditious Principles of this Book, that they may in time provide for their Security by their abolishing and extirpating those, and the like excesses. And as it could not reasonably be expected, that such a Book would be answer'd in the time when it was publish'd, which had bin to have disputed with a Man that commanded thirty Legions, (for *Cromwel* had bin oblig'd to have supported him, who defended his Usurpation;) so afterwards Men thought it would be too much ill nature to call Men in question for what they had said in ill times, and for saying which they had a plenary Indulgence and Absolution. And I am still of opinion, that even of those who have read his Book, and not frequented his Company, there are many, who being delighted with some new notions, and the pleasant and clear Style throughout the Book, have not taken notice of those down-right Conclusions, which overthrow or undermine all those Principles of Government, which have preserv'd the Peace of this Kingdom through so many ages, even from the time of its first Institution; or restor'd it to Peace, when it had at some times bin interrupted: and much less of those odious insinuations, and perverting some texts of Scripture, which do dishonour, and would destroy the very Essence of the Religion of Christ. And when I called to mind the good acquaintance that had bin between us, and what I had said to many who I knew had inform'd him of it, and which indeed I had sent to himself upon the first publishing of his *Leviathan*, I thought my self even bound to give him some satisfaction why I had entertained so evil an opinion of his Book.

When the Prince went first to *Paris* from *Jersey*, and My Lords *Capel* and *Hopton* stayed in *Jersey* together with my self, I heard shortly after, that Mr *Hobbes* who was then at *Paris*, had Printed his Book *De Cive* there. I writ to Dr *Earles*, who was then the Princes Chaplain, and his Tutor, to remember me kindly to Mr *Hobbes* with whom I was well acquainted, and to desire him to send me his Book *De Cive*, by the same token that *Sid. Godolphin* (who had bin kill'd in the late Warr) had left him a Legacy of two hundred pounds. The Book was immediately sent to me by Mr *Hobbes*, with a desire that I would tell him, whether I was sure that there was such a Legacy, and how he might take notice of it to receive it. I sent him word that he might depend upon it for a truth, and that I believed that if he found some way secretly (to the end there might be no public notice of it in regard of the Parliament) to demand it of his Brother *Francis Godolphin*, (who in truth had told me of it) he would pay it. This information was the ground of the Dedication of this Book to him, whom Mr *Hobbes* had never seen.

When I went some years after from *Holland* with the King (after the Murther of his Father) to *Paris*, from whence I went shortly his Majesties Ambassador into *Spaine*, Mr *Hobbes* visited me, and told me that Mr *Godolphin* confessed the Legacy, and had paid him one hundred pounds, and promised to pay the other in a short time; for all which he thankt me, and said he owed it to me, for he had never otherwise known of it. When I return'd from *Spaine* by *Paris* he frequently came to me, and told me his Book (which he would call *Leviathan*) was then Printing in *England*, and that he receiv'd every week a Sheet to correct, of which he shewed me one or two Sheets, and thought it would be finished within little more then a Moneth; and shewed me the Epistle to Mr *Godolphin* which he meant to set before it, and read it to me, and concluded, that he knew when I read his Book I would not like it, and thereupon mention'd some of his Conclusions; upon which I asked him, why he would publish such doctrine: to which, after a discourse between jest and earnest upon the Subject, he said, *The truth is, I have a mind to go home.*

Within a very short time after I came into *Flanders*, which was not much more then a Moneth from the time that Mr *Hobbes* had conferred with me, *Leviathan* was sent to me from *London*; which I read with much appetite and impatience. Yet I had scarce finish'd it, when Sr *Charles Cavendish* (the noble Brother of the Duke of *Newcastle* who was then at *Antwerp*, and a Gentleman of all the accomplishments of mind that he wanted of body, being in all other respects a wonderful person) shewed me a Letter he had then receiv'd from Mr *Hobbes*, in which he desir'd he would let him know freely what my opinion was of his Book. Upon which I wished he would tell him, that I could not enough wonder, that a Man, who had so great a reverence for Civil Government, that he resolv'd all Wisdom and Religion it self into a simple obedience and submission to it, should publish a Book, for which, by the constitution of any Government now establish'd in Europe, whether Monarchical or Democratical, the Author must be punish'd in the highest degree, and with the most severe penalties. With which answer (which Sr *Charles* sent to him) he was not pleased; and found afterwards when I return'd to the King to *Paris*, that I very much censur'd his Book, which he had presented, engross'd in *Vellam* in a marvellous fair hand, to the King; and likewise found my judgment so far confirmed, that few daies before I came thither, he was compell'd secretly to fly out of *Paris*, the Justice having endeavour'd to apprehend him, and soon after escap'd into *England*, where he never receiv'd any disturbance. After the Kings return he came frequently to the Court, where he had too many Disciples; and once visited me. I receiv'd him very kindly, and invited him to see me often, but he heard from so many hands that I had no good opinion of his Book, that he came to me only that one time: and methinks I am in a degree indebted to him, to let him know some reason why I look with so much prejudice upon his Book, which hath gotten him so much credit and estimation with some other men.

I am not without some doubt, that I shall in this discourse, which I am now ingaged in, trangress in a way I do very heartily dislike, and frequently censure in others, which is Sharpness of Language, and too much reproching the Person against whom I write; which is by no means warrantable, when it can be possibly avoided without wronging the truth in debate. Yet I hope nothing hath fallen from my Pen, which implies the least undervaluing of Mr. *Hobbes* his Person, or his Parts. But if he, to advance his opinion in Policy, too imperiously reproches all men who do not consent to his Doctrine, it can hardly be avoided, to reprehend so great presumption, and to make his Doctrines appear as odious, as they ought to be esteemed: and when he shakes the Principles of Christian Religion, by his new and bold Interpretations of Scripture, a man can hardly avoid saying, He hath no Religion, or that He is no good Christian; and escape endeavouring to manifest, and expose the poison that lies hid and conceled. Yet I have chosen, rather to pass by many of his enormous sayings with light expressions, to make his Assertions ridiculous, then to make his Person odious, for infusing such destructive Doctrine into the minds of men, who are already too licentious in judging the Precepts, or observing the Practice of Christianity.

The Survey of Mr. Hobbes's Introduction

It is no wonder that Mr *Hobbes* runs into so many mistakes and errors throughout his whole discourse of the nature of

Government from the nature of Mankind, when he laies so wrong a foundation in the very entrance and Introduction of his Book, as to make a judgment of the Passions, and Nature of all other Men by his own observations of Himself, and believes, (Pag. 2^d.) *that by looking into himself, and considering what he doth when he do's think, opine, reason, hope, fear, &c. and upon what grounds*, he shall thereby read, and know what are the thoughts and passions of all other men upon the like occasions. And indeed by his distinction in the very subsequent words (Pag. 2.) between *the similitude of passions, and the similitude of the object of the passions*, and his confession, that *the constitution individual and particular education*, do make so great a difference and disparity, he reduces that general Proposition to signify so very little, that he leaves very little to be observed, and very few Persons competent to observe. We have too much cause to believe, that much the major part of mankind do not think at all, are not endued with reason enough too opine, or think of what they did last, or what they are to do next, have no reflexion, without which there can be no thinking to this purpose: and the number is much greater of those who know not how to comprehend *the dissimilitude of the objects from the passions*, nor enough understand the nature of fear, as it is distinguish'd from the object that is fear'd: so that none of these Persons (which constitute a vast number,) are capable to make that observation, which must produce that knowledg which may enable them to judg of all the World. And how many there are left, who are fit from their *individual constitutions or particular educations*, and not withstanding the corruption introduced *by dissembling, lying, counterfeiting, and erroneous Doctrine*, to make that judgement, I leave to Mr. *Hobbes* to determine. And tis probable, that those very few may conclude, that what they do *when they think, opine, reason, hope, fear*, contributes very little to their knowing *what the thoughts and passions of other men are*. And they may the rather be induced to make that conclusion, since there are so very few who think and opine as Mr. *Hobbes* doth, and whose hopes and fears are like his, with reference to the objects, or the nature it self of those passions; and that the dissimilitude is greater between the passions themselves, then between the objects; and that men are not more unlike each other in their faces, or in their clothes, then in their thinking, hoping, and fearing. Since then Mr. *Hobbes* founds so much of his whole Discourse upon the Verity and Evidence of this first Proposition, that we shall very often have occasion to resort to it as we keep him company; and since the same seems to me to be very far from being *the true Key to open the cipher of other mens thoughts*: it will not be amiss to examine, and insist a little longer on this Conclusion, that we may discern whether all, or any of us are endued with such an infallible Faculty, that we can conclude what the thoughts and passions of other men are, by a strict observation and consideration of our own thoughts and passions; which would very much enable us to countermine and disappoint each others thoughts and passions, and would be a high point of wisdom. In the disquisition whereof, that we may not intangle the passion and the object together, for want of skill to sever them, it may not be amiss to suppose the same passion to be in two several men whose passions have the same object, and then consider whether they are like to discover each others thoughts and passions, their hopes and their fears, by each mans looking into himself, and considering what he do's when he thinks, hopes, or fears. If Mr. *Hobbes* loved, to as great a height as his passion can rise to, the same object that is likewise loved by another, he would hardly be able to make any judgment of the others love by his own; but upon a mutual confession and communication, their passions would be found not to be the same. If Mr. *Hobbes*, and some other man were both condemn'd to death, (which is the most formidable thing Mr. *Hobbes* can conceive) the other could no more by looking into himself know Mr. *Hobbes*'s present thoughts, and the extent of his fear, then he could, by looking in his face, know what he hath in his Pocket. Not only the several complexions, and constitutions of the body, the different educations, and climates dispose the affections and passions of men to different objects, but have a great influence upon the passions themselves. As the fears, so the hopes of Men are as unlike as their gate, and meen. If a Sanguine, and a Melancholic man hope the same thing, their hopes are no more alike each others, then their clompexions are; the hope of the one retaining still somewhat like despair, whilst the hope of the other looks like fruition: so little similitude there is in the passions themselves without any relation to their objects. That a man of great courage, and a very cowardly man have not the same countenance, and presence of mind in an approch of danger, proceeds not from the ones liking to be killed more then the others, but rather from the difference of their natural Courage. But let us suppose a man of courage, and a coward equally guilty, or equally innocent (that there may be no difference from the operation of conscience) to be brought to die together by a judgment which they cannot avoid and so to be equally without hope of life (and death in Mr. *Hobbes* judgment is equally terrible to all, and with equal care to be avoided, or resisted,) How comes it to pass, that one of these undergo's death with no other concernment then as if he were going any other Journy, and the other with such confusion and trembling, that he is even without life before he dies; if it were true that all Men fear alike upon the like occasion? There will be the same uncertainty in concluding what others do, by observing what we our selves do, when we think, opine, or reason. How shall that man, who thinks deliberately, opines modestly, and reasons dispassion-ately, and by this excellent temper satisfies his own judgement in a conclusion, in which at the same time he discerns others may differ from him: I say, How shall such a man by his own way of reasoning judg another mans, who usually thinks precipitately, opines arrogantly, and reasons superciliously, and concludes imperiously that man to be mistaken, who determines othewise then he do's? To conclude, Mr. *Hobbes* might as naturally have introduced his unreasonable Doctrine of the similitude of the passions, from the wisdom that he saies is acquired by the reading of men, as from his method of reading ones self. That saying of *Nosce teipsum*, in the sense of *Solon* who prescribed it, was a sober truth, but was never intended as an expedient to discover the similitude of the thoughts of other men by what he found in himself, but as the best means to suppress and destroy that pride and self-conceit, which might temt him to undervalue other men, and to plant that modesty and humility in himself, as would preserve him from such presumtion.

The Survey of Chapters 1, 2, 3.

Having resolved not to enter into the Lists with Mr. *Hobbes* upon the Signification of words, or Propriety of expressions, in which he exercises an absolute Dictatorship; and indeed not to enlarge upon any particular that to me seems erroneous, except it be an Error of that kind and consequence, as carries with it, or in it, somwhat that is hurtful to the Peace and Policy of the Kingdom, or prejudicial to the sincerity of Religion; I should have passed over the first, second, and third Chapters without any Animadversion, not troubling my self whether the *imagination and memory are but one thing, which for divers considerations hath divers names*, (p. 5.) if I had not some apprehension, that by an unnecessary reflexion upon the Scholes in the close of his second Chapter, and finding fault with the using some words in the sense they ought not be used, he hopes to dispose his Readers to such a prejudice and contemt towards them, that they may more easily undervalue them in more serious instances: the principal foundation that he laies for the support of all his Novelties, being to lessen and vilifie all the Principles, and all the Persons, which he well foresees most like to be applied to the demolishing his new Structure.

Amongst the many excellent parts and faculties with which Mr. *Hobbes* is plentifully endowed, his order and method in Writing, and his clear expressing his conceptions in weighty, proper, and significant words, are very remarkable and commendable; and it is some part of his Art to introduce, upon the suddain, instances and remarques, which are the more grateful, and make the more impression upon his Reader, by the unexpectedness of meeting them where somewhat else is talk'd of: for thereby he prepares and disposes the fancy to be pleased with them in a more proper and important place. No man would have imagin'd, that in a Philosophical Discourse of Dreams, and Fayries, and Ghosts, and Goblins, Exorcisms, Crosses, and Holy-water, he would have taken occasion to have reproved *Job* for saying, that *the inspiration of the Almighty giveth men understanding*, Job. 32. 8. which can be no good expression, if it be incongruity to say, *that good thoughts are inspired into a man by God*: and 'tis pity that St. *Paul* did not better weigh his words, when he said, that *we are not sufficient of our selves to think any thing of our selves, but our sufficiency is of God*, 2. Cor. 3. 5. or when he said to the *Philippians, that it is God which worketh in you both to will, and to do of his good pleasure*, Phil. 2. 13. and that St. *John* had not bin better advised, when he said, *He that committeth sin, is of the Devil*, 1. John 3. 8. Upon any of which Texts a

man can hardly enlarge in discourse, without saying, that good
thoughts *are inspir'd, or infus'd* (which he thinks he hath made
the more ridiculous, by turning into other words of the like
signification) *by God, and evil thoughts by the devil*, which in
his understanding, are *amongst the many words making
nothing understood*; whereas there are few expressions in
which the sense of the speaker is better understood, or by
which the sense of the Apostles can be made more clear then by
those expressions. But this Comical mention of the power and
goodness of God, and of the Devils activity and malignity, in a
place so improper and unnatural for those reflexions, will the
more incline his Disciples to undervalue those common notions
of the goodness and assistance of God, and of the malice and
vigilance of the Devil; and by making themselves merry with
that proper and devout custom of speaking, and the natural
results from thence, by degrees to undervalue those other
conceptions of Religion and Piety, which would restrain and
controul the licentious imagination of the excellency of their
own understandings; and prepare them to believe, that all the
Discourses of Sanctity, and the obligations of Christianity, and
the essentials of a Church, Faith, and Obedience to the dictates
of Gods Spirit, are but the artifice and invention of Churchmen, to advance their own pomp and worldly interest, and that
Heaven and Hell are but words to flatter or terrifie men; at
least, that the places of either are so situated, and have no other
extent or degree of pain and pleasure, then he hath thought fit
to assign to them towards the end of his *Leviathan*.

Nor in this instance of the train of imaginations, in his third
Chapter, less wonderful. And indeed, Mr. *Hobbes* had the
more reason for his opinion of the similitude of thoughts, and
that by looking into himself when he thinks, and upon what
grounds, he can thereby know the thoughts of other men, when
he was with the velocity of a thought, in a moment of time,
able to decipher that impertinent Question, What was the value
of a Roman penny; and to discover a succession of thoughts in
the Enquirer, the last of which determined in the resolution of
delivering up the King: which was so rare a faculty, that such a
similitude of thoughts cannot be concluded to be in other men.
And since erroneous Doctrines have so great an influence upon
the minds of men, as to corrupt the natural motives, he knows
best whether he had not before this formed his new Scheme of
Loyalty, and digested all those imaginations towards the

dissolution of Allegiance, and eluding the obligation of all Oaths; which if he had don, he had the Key ready to decipher by, and might easily discover that which no man in *England* could discover who had not the same Key.

The Survey of Chapters 4, 5, 6, 7, 8, 9.

We shall with less reflexion pass over his fourth Chapter of Speech, which he saies, was the noblest and most profitable *Invention* of all other, whether properly or improperly, he shall do well to consider; together with his fifth and sixth Chapters, which with those which precede, and two or three which follow, he intends as a Dictionary, for the better understanding and defining very many terms and words, which he is to make use of throughout the rest of his Work; and which whoever can carry with him in his memory, as he expects every man shall do, shall be often more confounded in the understanding many parts of his Book, then if he forgets them all. In which yet many things are said very wittily and pleasantly; tho it may be many critical men, whom he hath provoked, may believe many of his Expressions to be incongruous, and his Definitions not so exact as might have bin expected from so great an Artist; and that all those Chapters are rather for delight, in the novelty and boldness of the expression, then for any real information in the substantial part of knowledg: since few men, upon the most exact reading them over, find themselves wiser then they were before but rather think that they better understood before what *Contemt* signifies, then by being now told, (*pag.* 24) *that it is nothing else but an immobility or contumacy of the heart, in resisting the action of certain things, and proceeding from that the heart is already moved otherwise, by other more potent objects, or from want of experience of them*; or that they do better understand the nature and original of Laughter, by being informed (*pag.* 27) *that suddain glory is the passion which maketh those grimaces called Laughter, and is caused either by some suddain act of their own that pleaseth them, or by the apprehension of some deformed thing in another, by comparison whereof they suddainly applaud themselves.* In which kind of Illustrations those Chapters, and in truth his whole Book abounds, and discovers a master faculty in making easie things hard to be understood: and men will probably with the more impatience and curiosity, tho with the less reverence, enter upon the third part of his Book, which is to define Christian Politics, after he hath so well defin'd and describ'd Religion to be *Fear of Power invisible, feigned by the mind, or imagined from tales publicly allowed* (p. 26.) all which I leave to his Friends of the Universities. Nor shall I spend more time upon the seventh, eighth, and ninth Chapters, leaving them to the Schole-men to examine, who are in his debt for much mirth which he hath made out of them, I for my part being very indifferent between them, as believing that the Schole-men have contributed very little more to the advancement of any noble or substantial part of Learning, then Mr. *Hobbes* hath don to the reformation or improvement of Philosophy and Policy. Yet I may reasonably say so much on their behalf, that if Mr. *Hobbes* may take upon him to translate all those terms of Art (the proper signification whereof is unanimously understood, and agreed between all who use them, and which in truth are a cipher to which all men of moderate Learning have the key) into the vulgar Language by the assistance of *Ryders Dictionary*, he hath found a way to render and expose the worthiest Professors of any Science, and all Science it self to the cheap laughter of all illiterate men, which is contrary to Mr. *Hobbes*'s own rule and determination, (*pag.* 17) where he saies, *That when a man upon the hearing any Speech, hath those thoughts which the words of that Speech, and their connexion, were ordained and constituted to signifie, then he is said to understand it.* And surely the signification of words and terms, is no less ordain'd and constituted by custom and acceptation, then by Grammar and Etymologies. If it were otherwise, Mr. *Hobbes* himself would be as much exposed to ignorant Auditors, when he reads a Lecture upon the Optics, or even in his ador'd Geometry, if a pleasant Translator should render all his terms as literally, as he hath don the Title of the sixth Chapter of *Suarez*: for every Age, as new things happen, find new words in all Languages to signifie them. The Civilians, who are amongst the best Judges of Latine, can hardly tell how *investitura* came into their Books, to signifie that which it hath ever signified since the Quarrel begun between the Emperor and the Pope upon that subject, which is now as well understood in Latine, as any word in *Tully*. And if *Bombarda* had no original but from the sound, as *Petavius* (a very good Grammarian, besides his other great Learning) saies it had not, we have no reason to be offended with the Schole-men for finding words to discover their own Conceptions, which equally serve our own turn.

The Survey of Chapters 10, 11, 12.

I do acknowledg, that in the tenth, eleventh, and twelfth Chapters, many things are very well said: and tho some things as ill, with reference to Religion, and to the Clergy, as if there were a combination between the Priests of the Gentiles, *Aristotle*, the Schole-men, and the Clergy of all Professions, to defame, pervert, and corrupt Religion; yet he resumes that Argument so frequently, that I shall chuse to examine the reason and justice of all his Allegations rather in another place, then upon either of these three Chapters; to which I shall only add, that according to his natural delight in Novelties of all kinds, in Religion as well as Policy, he hath supplied the Gentiles with a new God, which was never before found in any of their Catalogues, *The God Chaos*, (pag. 55.) to which he might as warrantably have made them an additional present of his own Idol, *Confusion*. And he will as hardly find a good authority for the aspersion with which he traduces the Policy of the *Roman* Common-wealth in all its greatness and lustre, (*pag. 57.*) *That it made no scruple of tolerating any Religion whatsoever in the City of* Rome *it self, unless it had something in it that could not consist with their civil Government.* Which how untrue soever, was a very seasonable intimation of the wisdom of *Oliver*'s Politics, at that time when he published his *Leviathan*: whereas in truth, that great People were not more solicitous in any thing, then in preserving the unity and integrity of their Religion from any mixtures; and the Institution of the Office of *Pontifex Maximus* was principally out of that jealousie, and that he might carefully watch that no alteration or innovation might be made in their Religion. And tho they had that general awe for Religion, that they would not suffer the Gods of their Enemies, whom they did not acknowledg for Gods, to be rudely treated and violated; and therefore they both punished their Consul for having robb'd the Temple of *Proserpine*, and caused the full damages to be restored to the injur'd Goddess: yet they neither acknowledg'd her Divinity, nor suffer'd her to have a Temple, or to have any Devotion paid to her within their Dominions; nor indeed any other God or Goddess to be ador'd, and those to whom

Sacrifices were made by the Authority of the State. Nor will Mr. *Hobbes* be able to name one Christian Kingdom in the World, where it is believed, that the King hath not his Authority from Christ, unless a Bishop Crown him; tho all Christian Kingdoms have had that reverence for Bishops, as to assign the highest Ecclesiastical Functions to be alwaies perform'd by them: but they well know the King to have the same Authority in all respects before he is crown'd, as after. And what extravagant Power soever the Court of *Rome* hath in some evil Conjunctures heretofore usurp'd, and would be as glad of the like opportunities again; yet in those Kingdoms where that Authority is own'd and acknowledg'd, there want not those who loudly protest against that Doctrine, That a King may be depos'd by a Pope, or that the Clergy and Regulars shall be exemt from the Jurisdiction of their King. And yet upon these unwarrantable suggestions, he presumes to declare, That all the changes of Religion may be attributed to one and the same Cause, and that is, *unpleasing Priests; and those not only amongst Papists, but even in that Church that hath presumed most of Reformation*, by which he intends the Church of *England*, at that time under the most severe and barbarous Persecution; and therefore it was the more enviously and maliciously, as well as dis-honestly alledged.

The Survey of Chapters 13, 14, 15, 16.

The thirteenth, fourteenth, fifteenth, and sixteenth Chapters, will require a little more disquisition, since under the pretence of examining, or rather (according to his Prerogative) of determining what the natural condition of mankind is, he takes many things for granted which are not true; as (*pag.* 60.) that *Nature hath made all men equal in the faculties of body and mind*, and imputes that to the Nature of Man in general, which is but the infirmity of some particular Men; and by a mist of words, under the notion of explaining common terms (the meaning whereof is understood by all Men, and which his explanation leaves less intelligible then they were before) he dazles Mens eies from discerning those Fallacies upon which he raises his Structure, and which he reserves for his second part. And whosoever looks narrowly to his preparatory Assertions, shall find such contradictions, as must destroy the foundation of all his new Doctrine in Government, of which some particulars shall be mentioned anon. So that if his Maxims of one kind were marshailed together, collected out of these four Chapters, and applied to his other Maxims which are to support his whole *Leviathan*, the one would be a sufficient answer to the other; and so many inconsistencies and absurdities would appear between them, that they could never be thought links of one chain; whereas he desires men should believe all the Propositions in his Book to be a chain of Consequences, without being in any degree wary to avoid palpable contradictions, upon the presumtion of his Readers total resignation to his judgment. If it were not so, would any man imagine that a man of Mr. *Hobbes*'s sagacity and provoking humor, should in his fourth Page so imperiously reproch the Scholes for absurdity, in saying, That *heavy Bodies fall downwards out of an appetite to rest, thereby ascribing knowledg to things inanimate*; and himself should in his sixty second Page, describing the nature of foul weather, say, *That it lieth not in a shower or two of rain, but in an inclination thereto of many daies together*: as if foul weather were not as inanimate a thing as heavy Bodies, and inclination did not imply as much of knowledg as appetite doth. In truth, neither the one or the other word signifies in the before-mention'd instances, more then a natural tendency to motion and alteration.

When God vouchsafed to make man after his own Image, and in his own Likeness, and took so much delight in him, as to give him the command and dominion over all the Inhabitants of the Earth, the Air, and the Sea, it cannot be imagin'd but that at the same time he endued him with Reason, and all the other noble Faculties which were necessary for the administration of that Empire, and the preservation of the several Species which were to succeed the Creation: and therefore to uncreate him to such a baseness and villany in his nature, as to make Man such a Rascal, and more a Beast in his frame and constitution then those he is appointed to govern, is a power that God never gave to the Devil; nor hath any body assum'd it, till Mr. *Hobbes* took it upon him. Nor can any thing be said more contrary to the Honor and Dignity of God Almighty, then that he should leave his master workmanship, Man, in a condition of War of every man against every man, in such a condition of confusion, (*pag.* 64.) *That every man hath a right to every thing, even to one anothers body*; inclin'd to all the malice, force and fraud that may promote his profit or his pleasure, and without any notions of, or instinct towards justice, honor, or good nature, which only makes man-kind superior to the Beasts of the Wilderness. Nor had Mr. *Hobbes* any other reason to degrade him to this degree of Bestiality, but that he may be fit to wear those Chains and Fetters which he hath provided for him. He deprives man of the greatest happiness and glory that can be attributed to him, who devests him of that gentleness and benevolence towards other men, by which he delights in the good fortune and tranquillity that they enjoy, and makes him so far prefer himself before all others, as to make the rest a prey to advance any commodity or conveniency of his own; which is a barbarity superior to what the most savage Beasts are guilty of,

> – *Quando leoni,*
> *Fortior eripuit vitam leo? quo nemore unquam*
> *Expiravit aper majoris dentibus apri?*

Man only, created in the likeness of God himself, is the only creature in the World, that out of the malignity of his own nature, and the base fear that is inseparable from it, is oblig'd for his own benefit, and for the defence of his own right, to worry and destroy all of his own kind, until they all become yoaked by a Covenant and Contract that Mr. *Hobbes* hath provided for them, and which was never yet entred into by any one man, and is in nature impossible to be entred into.

After such positive and magisterial Assertions against the dignity and probity of man-kind, and the honor and providence of God Almighty, the instances and arguments given by him are very unweighty and trivial to conclude the nature of man to be so full of jealousie and malignity, as he would have it believed to be, from that common practice of circumspection and providence, which custom and discretion hath introduced into human life. For men shut their Chests in which their mony is, as well that their servants or children may not know what they have, as that it may be preserved from Thieves; and they lock their doors that their Houses may not be common; and rude armd, and in company, because they know that there are ill men, who may be inclined to do injuries if they find an opportunity. Nor is a wariness to prevent the damage and injury that Thieves and Robbers may do to any man, an argument that Mankind is in that mans opinion inclin'd and disposed to commit those out-rages. If it be known that there is one Thief in a City, all men have reason to shut their doors and lock their chests; and if there be two or three Drunkards in a Town, all men have reason to go arm'd in the streets, to controul the violence or indignity they might receive from them. Princes are attended by their Guards in progress, and all their servants arm'd when they hunt, without any apprehension of being assaulted; custom having made it so necessary, that many men are not longer without their Swords then they are without their Doublets, who never were jealous that any man desir'd to hurt them. Nor will the instance he gives of the inhabitants in *America*, be more to his purpose then the rest, since as far as we have any knowledg of them, the savage People there live under a most intire subjection and slavery to their several Princes; who indeed for the most part live in hostility towards each other, upon those contentions which engage all other Princes in War, and which Mr. *Hobbes* allows to be a just cause of War, jealousie of each others Power to do them harm. And these are the notable instances by which Mr. *Hobbes* hath by his painful disquisition and investigation, in the hidden and deep secrets of Nature, discover'd that unworthy fear and jealousie to be inherent in mankind, (*pag.* 63.). *That the notions of right and wrong have no place, but Force and Fraud are the two cardinal Virtues; that there is no propriety, no dominion, no mine or thine distinct, but only that to be every mans that he can get, and for so long as he can keep it*, and this struggle to continue, till he submits to the servitude to which he hath design'd him for his comfort and security.

Mr. *Hobbes* would do very much honour to *Aristotle*, and repair much of the injury he hath don to him, if he can perswade men to believe, (*pag.* 59) that the *bringing in his Philosophy and Doctrine, hath bin a cause to take away the reputation of the Clergy*, and to incline the People to the reformation of Religion; and yet he hath more authority for that, then for most of his Opinions, tho it may be he doth not know it. For in the year a thousand two hundred and nine, *Aristotles* Metaphysics, which had bin lately brought from *Constantinople*, were condemn'd, and forbidden to be read by a Council in *Paris*, upon a supposition or apprehension, that that Book had contributed very much to the new Heretical Opinions of the *Albigenses*. So far the French Clergy of that age concurred in opinion with Mr. *Hobbes*: but we may much more reasonably conceive, That it hath bin illiteratness, stupid ignorance, and having never heard of *Aristotle*, that may at any time have brought contemt upon the Clergy: and tho men may too unreasonably, it may be, adhere to *Aristotle* in some particulars, and so may be reasonably contradicted, yet no man of the Clergy or Laity was ever contemned for being thought to understand *Aristotle*. Indeed Mr. *Hobbes* may easily refute *Aristotle*, and all who have writ before or since him, if he be the Soveraign Magistrate, not only to enact what Laws he pleases, and to interpret all that were made before according to his pleasure, and to adopt them to be the Laws of Nature, which he declares (*pag.* 79) to me *immutable and eternal*. And we have great reason to watch him very narrowly, when his Legislative fit is upon him, least he cast such a net over us, knit by what he calls the Law of Nature, or by his Definitions, that we be deprived of both the use of our liberty, and our reason to oppose him. He is very much offended with *Aristotle*, for saying in the first Book of his Politics, That by Nature some are fit to command, and others to serve; which he saies, (*pag.* 77.) is not only against reason, but also against experience, for *there are very few so foolish that had not rather govern themselves, then be governed by others*. Which Proposition doth not contradict any thing said by *Aristotle*, the Question being, Whether Nature hath made some men worthier, not whether it hath made all others so modest as to confess it; and would have required a more serious Disquisition, since it is no more then is imputed to Horses, and other Beasts, whereof men find by experience, that some by nature are fitter for nobler uses, and others for vile, and to be only Beasts of burden. But, indeed, he had the less need of reason to refute him, when he had a Law at hand to controul him, which he saies, is the Law of Nature, (*pag.* 77.) *That every man must acknowledg every other man for his equal by nature*; which may be true as to the essentials of human Nature, and yet there may be inequality enough as to a capacity of Government. But whatever his opinion is, we have *Solomons* judgment against him. *Insipiens erit servus sapientis*, Prov. 11. 29. And many Learned Men are of opinion, That the *Gibeonites*, who by the help of an impudent lie found the means to save their lives, were a People by nature of low and abject spirits, fit only to do the low and mean services for which they were prepared. And some of the Fathers believe, That when the Patriarch *Jacob*, in his dying

Prophesie of *Issachar*, declar'd *Issachar is a strong ass, couching down between two burdens. And he saw that rest was good, and the land that it was pleasant, and bowed his shoulder to bear, and became a servant unto tribute*, Gen. 49. 14, 15. *Jacob* for-saw that in that Tribe there would be *depressio intellectus*, and that they would be only fit to be servants. And 'tis very true, that *Aristotle* did believe, that Divine Providence doth shew and demonstrate who are fit and proper for low and vile offices, not only by very notable defects in their understandings, incapable of any cultivation, but by some eminent deformity of the body (tho that doth not always hold) which makes them unfit to bear rule. And without doubt, the observation of all Ages since that time hath contributed very much to that Conclusion which Mr. *Hobbes* so much derides, of Inequality by nature, and that Nature it self hath a bounty which she extends to some men in a much superior degree then she doth to others. Which is not contradicted by seeing many great defects and indigencies of Nature in some men, wonderfully corrected and repair'd by industry, education, and above all, by conversation; nor by seeing some early blossoms in others, which raise a great expectation of rare perfection, that suddainly decay, and insensibly wither away by not being cherished and improved by diligence, or rather by being blasted by vice or supine laziness: those accidents may somtimes happen, do not very often, and are necessary to awaken men out of the Lethargy of depending wholly upon the Wealth of Natures store, without administring any supply to it, out of their industry and observation. And every mans experience will afford him abundance of examples in the number of his own acquaintance, in which, of those who have alwaies had equal advantages of Education, Conversation, Industry, and it may be of virtuous Inclinations, it is easie to observe very different parts and faculties; some of quick apprehension, and as steady comprehension, wit, judgment, and such a sagacity as discerns at distance as well as at hand, concluding from what they see will fall out, what is presently to be don; when others born, and bred with the same care, wariness, and attention, and with all the visible advantages and benefits which the other enjoied, remain still of a heavier and a duller alloy, less discerning to contrive and fore-see, less vigorous to execute, and in a word, of a very different Classis to all purposes; which can proceed from no other cause, but the distinction that Nature her self made between them, in the distribution of those Faculties to the one with a more liberal hand then to the other.

Did not all the World at that time, and hath it not ever since believed, that *Julius Cesar* had from nature a more exalted Spirit and Genius, then any of those who were overcome by him; tho some of them appear'd, or were generally believ'd to be superior in the conduct of great Affairs? There is judgment gotten by experience very necessary, but the first attemt and direction of the mind, the first daring proceeds purely from Nature and its influence. When we see a *Marius* from a common Soldier, baffle the Nobility of *Rome*, and in despight of opposition, make himself seven times Consul: or a *Dioclesian*, from a mean and low birth, and no other advantage of Education then every other common Soldier had with him, nor countenance or assistance from any Superior, but what his own Virtue purchased, to raise himself to the full state and power of the greatest Emperor, and to govern as great, or a greater part of the World, then ever *Cesar* did, and after having enjoied that Empire above eighteen years in the highest glory, to give it over, and divest himself of it, merely for the ease and pleasure of retirement to his private House and Garden, and to die in that repose after he had enjoied it some years; must we believe such a Man to have no advantages by nature, above all other men of the same time? When *Marmurius*, or *Vecturius* (for he went by both names) one of the thirty Tyrants, from a common Blacksmith who made arms (for the man who killed him having bin before his servant, and wrought under him, told him, *Hic est gladius quem ipse fecisti*) raised him self, not by a suddain mutiny and insurrection, but by passing all the degrees of a Soldier, during many years in a regular and disciplin'd Army, to be Emperor by a common voice and election, as a Man the fittest for the Command; is it possible for us to believe, that this Man received no other talent from Nature, then she afforded to every other Blacksmith. Besides many particular Examples of this kind in every particular Kingdom, in most of which the visible advantages of Friends, Patrons, and other accidental Concurrences have not at all contributed to the preferment of them before other men, the World hath yielded us an example near our own time (for it is little more then two hundred years since) of such a prodigious progress and success in the power of one Man, that there is nothing of Story ancient or modern that is parallel to it,

The great *Tamberlane*, who (tho not so mean a Person in his original, as he is vulgarly conceived to have bin) was born a poor Prince over a contemn'd and barbarous Country and People, whose manners he first cultivated by his own native justice and goodness, and by the strength of his own Genius, improved his own Faculties and Understanding to a marvellous Lustre and Perfection, towards which neither his Climate nor his conversation could contribute. Upon this stock he rais'd and led an Army of his Subjects, into the better Dominions of their Neighbors who contemned them. With these he fought, and won many Battels, subdued and conquer'd many Kingdoms; and after the total defeat of the greatest Army that was then in the World, he took the greatest Emperor of the World Prisoner, and for the contemt that he had shew'd towards him, treated him as his vilest Slave. And it hath bin as notorious, that after the death of these, and the like such extraordinary Persons, the Forces by which they wrought those wonders, and the Counsellors and Officers whose administration co-operated with them, suddainly degenerated; and as if the Soul were departed from the Body, became a Carcass without any use or beauty. And can we believe, that those stupendous men had no talent by nature above others? And are we bound to believe, (*pag.* 77.) *that by the Law of Nature every man is bound to acknowledg other for his equal by nature?*

But where are those Maxims to be found which Mr. *Hobbes* declares, and publishes to be the Laws of Nature, in any other Author before him? That is only properly call'd the Law of Nature, that is dictated to the whole Species: as, to defend a mans self from violence, and to repel force by force; not all that results upon prudential motives unto the mind of such as have bin cultivated by Learning and Education, which no doubt can compile such a Body of Laws, as would make all other useless, except such as should provide for the execution of, and obedience to those. For under what other notion can that reasonable Conclusion, which is a necessary part of the Law of Nations, be call'd the Law of Nature, which is his fifteenth Law, (*pag.* 78.) *That all men that mediate Peace be allowed safe conduct?* And of this kind much of the Body of his Law of Nautre is compil'd; which I should not dislike, the Style being in some sense not improper, but that I observe that from some of these Conclusions which he pronounces to be (*pag.* 79.) *immutable and eternal as the Laws of Nature*, he makes

deductions and inferences to controul Opinions he dislikes, and
to obtain Concessions which are not right, by amuzing men
with his method, and confounding rather then informing their
understandings, by a chime of words in definitions and
pleasant instances, which seem not easie to be contradicted,
and yet infer much more then upon a review can be deduc'd
from them. And it is an unanswerable evidence of the
irresistible force and strength of Truth and Reason, that whil'st
men are making war against it with all their power and
stratagems, somwhat doth still start up out of the dictates and
confessions of the Adversary that determines the Controversie,
and vindicates the Truth from the malice that would oppress it.
How should it else come to pass, that Mr. *Hobbes*, whil'st he is
demolishing the whole frame of Nature for want of order to
support it, and makes it unavoidably necessary for every man
to cut his neighbors throat, to kill him who is weaker then
himself, and to circumvent, and by any fraud destroy him who
is stronger, in all which there is no injustice, because Nature
hath not otherwise provided for every particular mans security;
I say, how comes it to pass, that at the same time when he is
possessed of this frenzy, he would in the same, and the next
Chapter, set down such a Body of Laws prescribed by Nature it
self, as are *immutable and eternal*? that there appears, by his
own shewing, a full remedy against all that confusion, for
avoiding whereof he hath devis'd all that unnatural and
impossible Contract and Covenant? If the Law of the Gospel,
*Whatsoever you require that others should do to you, that do
ye to them*, be the Law of all men, as he saies it is (*pag.* 65.)
that is, the Law of Nature, *Naturâ, íd est jure gentium*, saies
Tully, it being nothing else but *quod naturalis ratio inter omnes
homines constituit*; If it be the Law of Nature that every man
strive to accommodate himself to the rest, as he saies it is (*pag.*
76.) and *that no man by deed, word, countenance or gestures,
declare hatred or contemt of another*; If all men are bound by
the Law of Nature, (*pag.* 78.) *That they that are at
controversie, submit their right to the judgment of an
arbitrator*, as he saies they are: If Nature hath thus providently
provided for the Peace and Tranquillity of her Chldren, by
Laws immutable & eternal, that are written in their hearts:
how come they to fall into that condition of war, as to be every
one against every one, and to be without any other cardinal
Vritues, but of force and fraud? It is a wonderful thing, that a

man should be so sharp-sighted, as to discern mankind so well inclosed and fortified by the wisdom of Nature, and so blind as to think him in a more secure estate by his transferring of right to another man, which yet he confesses is impossible intirely to transfer; and by Covenants and Contracts of his own devising, and which he acknowledges to be void in part, and in other parts impossible to be perform'd.

But I say, if in truth Nature hath dictated all those excellent Conclusions to every man, without which they cannot be called the Laws of Nature; and if it hath farther instituted all those Duties which are contain'd in the Second Table, all which he saies were the Laws of Nature: I know not what temtation or authority he could have, to pronounce mankind to be left by Nature in that distracted condition of war, except he prefer the authority of *Ovids Metamorphosis*, of the sowing of *Cadmus*'s teeth, before any other Scripture, Divine or Humane. And it is as strange, that by his Covenants and Contracts which he is so wary in wording (as if he were the Secertary of Nature) that they may bind that man fast enough whom he pleases to assign to those Bonds; and as if he were the Plenipotentiary of Nature too, to bind and to loose all he thinks fit: he hath so ill provided for the Peace he would establish, that he hath left a door open for all the Confusion he would avoid, when, notwithstanding that he hath made them divest themselves of the liberty they have by Nature, and transfer all this into the hands of a single Person, who thereby is so absolute Soveraign, that he may take their Lives and their Estates from them without any act of Injustice, yet after all this transferring and devesting, every man reserves a right (as inalienable) to defend his own life, even against the sentence of Justice. What greater contradiction can there be to the Peace, which he would establish upon those unreasonable conditions, then this Liberty, which he saies can never be abandoned, and which yet may dissolve that peace every day? and yet he saies, *(pag. 70.) This is granted to be true by all men, in that they lead Criminals to execution and prison with armed men, notwithstanding such Criminals have consented to the Law by which they are condemned.* Which indeed is an argument, that men had rather escape then be hanged; but no more an argument that they have a right to rescue themselves, then the fashion of wearing Swords is an argument that men are afraid of having their throats cut by the malice of their neighbors: both which are arguments no man would urge to men, whose understandings he did not much undervalue. But upon many of these Particulars there is a more proper occasion hereafter for enlargement. And so we pass through his prospect of the Laws of Nature, and many other Definitions and Descriptions, with liberty to take review of them upon occasion, that we may make hast to his Second Part, for, which he thinks he hath made a good preparation to impose upon us in this First; and he will often tell us when he should prove what he affirms, that he hath evinc'd that Point, and made it evident in such a Chapter in his First part, where in truth he hath said very much, and proved very little, I shall only conclude this, with an observation which the place seems to require, of the defect in Mr. *Hobbes*'s Logic, which is a great presumption, that from very true Propositions he deduces very erroneous and absurd Conclusions. That no man hath power to transfer the right over his own life to the disposal of another man, is a very true Proposition, from whence he infers, that he hath reserved the power and disposal of it to himself, and therefore that he may defend it by force even against the judgment of Law and Justice; whereas the natural consequence of that Proposition is, That therefore such transferring and covenanting (being void) cannot provide for the peace and security of a Commonwealth. Without doubt, no man is *Dominus vitæ suæ*, and therefore cannot give that to another, which he hath not in himself. God only hath reserv'd that absolute Dominion and Power of life and death to Himself, and by his putting the Sword into the hand of the Supreme Magistrat, hath qualified and enabled him to execute that Justice which is necessary for the peace and preservation of his People, which may seem in a manner to be provided for by Mr. *Hobbes* Law of Nature, if what he saies be true, (*pag. 68.*) *That right to the end containeth right to the means.* And this sole Proposition, that men cannot dispose of their own lives, hath bin alwaies held as a manifest and undeniable Argument, that Soveraigns never had, nor can have their Power from the People.

Second Part.

The Survey of Chapters 17, 18.

Mr. *Hobbes* having taken upon him to imitate God, and created Man after his own likeness, given him all the passions and affections which he finds in himself, and no other, he prescribes him to judg of all things and words, according to the definitions he sets down, with the Autority of a Creator. After he hath delighted himself in a commendable method, and very witty and pleasant description of the nature and humor of the World, as far as he is acquainted with it, (upon many particulars whereof, which he calls Definitions, there will be frequent occasion of reflexions in this discourse, without breaking the thred of it by entring upon impertinent exceptions to matters positively averred without any apparent reason, when it is no great matter whether they be true or no.) He comes at last to institute such a Common-wealth as never was in nature, or ever heard of from the beginning of the World till this structure of his, and like a bountifull Creator, gives the Man he hath made, the Soveraign command and Government of it, with such an extent of power and autority, as the Great *Turk* hath not yet appear'd to affect. In which it is probable he hath follow'd his first method, and for the Man after his own likeness hath created a Government, that he would him self like to be trusted with, having determined Liberty, and Propriety, and Religion to be only emty words, and to have no other existence then in the Will and Breast of this Soveraign Governor; and all this in order to make his People happy, and to enjoy the blessing of Peace. And yet with all this, his Governor would quickly find his power little enough, that is, of little continuance, if his Government be founded upon no other security then is provided in his institution: and the justice he assign's will be as weak a support to his Governor, as he supposes a Covenant would be to the peoples benefit; the imagination whereof he conceives to be so ridiculous, that it can only proceed from want of understanding, that Covenants being but words and breath, have no force to oblige, contain, constrain, or protect any man, but what they have from the Public Sword, that is from the untied hands of his Soveraign Man: as if Justice, which is the support of his Governor when he breaks and violates all the Elements of Justice, because all men are in justice bound to observe contracts, were more then a word, or a more valiant word and stronger breath to constrain, and protect any man, when that Sword is wrested from his Soveraign Man, or his hand is bound by the many hands which should be govern'd by him. But the People need not be offended with him, for giving so extravagant a power to a Person they never intended should have such an Empire over them: if they will have patience till he hath finished his Scheme of Soveraignty, he will infeeble it again for them to that degree, that no ambitious man would take it up, if he could have it for asking. But to prosecute the argument in his own order.

As he hath made a worse Man by much, by making him too like himself; so he hath made a much worse Common-wealth then ever was yet known in the World, by making it such as he would have: and nothing can be more wonderful, then that a man of Mr. *Hobbes* his Sagacity, should raise so many conclusions of a very pernicious influence upon the Peace and Government of every Kingdom and Common-wealth in Europe, upon a mere supposition and figment of a Common-wealth instituted by himself, and without any example. He will not find any one Government in the world, of what kind soever, so instituted, as he dogmatically declares all Government to be; nor was mankind in any nation since the Creation upon such a level, as to institute their Government by such an assembly and election, and covenant, and consent, as he very unwarrantably more then supposes. And it was an undertaking of the more impertinence, since by his own rule, (pag. 95.) *where there is already erected a soveraign power*, which was then, and still is in every Kingdom and State in Europe, and for ought we know in the whole world, *there can be no other representative of the same People, but only to certain particular ends limited by the Soveraign*. So that he could have no other design, but to shake what was erected, and the Government was not at that time in any suspence but in his own Country, by the effect of an odious and detestable Rebellion; which yet could not prevail with an effective Army of above one hundred thousand men, with which the Usurper had subdued three Nations, to submit to the Usurper in such a new model, and to transfer their right by such Covenants, as he conceives mankind to be even oblig'd to do by the Law's of Nature; and to induce them to do which, I do heartily wish that Mr. *Hobbes* could truly vindicate himself from designing, when he published his *Leviathan*; upon which disquisition we cannot avoid enlarging hereafter upon further provocation.

It had bin kindly don of Mr. *Hobbes*, if according to his laudable custom of illustrating his definitions by instances, as he often doth with great pregnancy, he had to this his positive determination added one instance of a Government so instituted. There is no doubt there are in all Governments many things don by, and with the consent of the People; nay all Government so much depends upon the consent of the People, that without their consent and submission it must be dissolved, since where no body will obey, there can be no command, nor can one man compel a million to do what they have no mind to do: but that any Government was originally instituted by an assembly of men equally free, and that they ever elected the Person who should have the Soveraign power over them, is yet to be proved; and till it be proved, must not be supposed, to raise new doctrines, upon which shake all Government. How Soveraign power was originally instituted, and how it came to condescend to put restraints upon it self, and even to strip it self of some parts of its Soveraignty for its own benefit and advantage, and how far it is bound to observe the contracts and covenants it hath submitted to, I shall deliver my opinion before this Discourse is finish'd, and shall refer the approbation of it to Mr. *Hobbes*, supposing he will never think all the reason in the world to be strong enough to prove, that what all men see is, cannot be. But by the way, he had dealt more like the Magistrate he affects to be, if he had founded his Government upon his own imperious averment, and left every man to question it that dares; then to take notice, and foresee an objection which he saies is the strongest he can make, and make no better an answer to it, then to answer one question with an other. He sees men will ask (and it is not possible they can avoid it) Where, and When such power hath by subjects bin acknowledg'd? which he would have us believe is substantially answered by his other question, When, or Where has there bin a Kingdom long free from Sedition and Civil War? which might receive a very full answer, by assigning many Governments under which the Subjects have enjoyed very long Peace, Quiet, and Plenty, which never was, nor ever can be enjoied one hour under his (as shall be proved when we examine it.) But it will serve his turn, if it hath once bin disquieted by a Sedition or Civil War; and so all Goverment that is known and established, must be laid aside and overthrown, to erect an other that he supposes will cure all defects. If Mr. *Hobbes* had thought fit to write problematically, and to have examin'd, as many have don, the nature of Government, and the nature of Mankind that is to be govern'd, and from the consideration of both, had modestly proposed such a form, as to his judgment might better provide for the security, peace, and happiness of a People, (which is the end of Government,) then any form that is yet practic'd and submitted to; he might well have answered one objection of an inconvenience in his new form, with an other of a greater inconveniecne in all other forms. But when he will introduce a Government of his own devising, as founded and instituted already, and that not as somewhat new, but submitted to by the Covenants, and Obligations, and Election our selves have made, and so that we are bound by the rules of Justice founded upon our own consent, to pretend neither to liberty, or property, other then our Governor thinks fit to indulge to us; he must be contented not to be beleived, or must vouchsafe to tell us when, and where that consent of ours was given, and we submitted to those obligations: and it will be no kind of answer or satisfaction, to say magisterially, that if it be not so, it should be so for our good, which we cleerly find will turn to our irreparable damage and destruction. And it is a very confident thing, that he should hope to support his Soveraign right in so unlimited an extent upon the Law of Nature, because (p. 176.) *that forbids the violation of Faith*, without being pressed to tell us, when, and where that faith was given, that is so obligatory, and the violation whereof must be so penal. But it is more prodigiously bold, to confess upon the matter, that there hath not hitherto bin any Common-wealth, where those rights have bin acknowledged, or challeng'd, and to undervalue the argument, by making it as ridiculous, as if the Savage People of *America* should deny there were any grounds or principles of reason so to build, as their Architecture is not yet arrived at: So he thinks, that tho his Savage Country-men, and Neighbors, have yet only bin accustomed to Governments imperfect, & apt to relapse into disorders, he hath found out principles by *industrious meditation*, to make their constitution everlasting. And truly he hath some reason to be confident of his Principles, if tho they cannot be proved by reason, he be sure they are Principles from autority of

Scripture, as he professes them to be, and which must be examin'd in its course. In the mean time he may be thought to be too indulgent to his Soveraign Governor, and very neer to contradict himself, that after he hath made the keeping and observation of promises to be a part of the Law of Nature, which is *unalterable and eternal*, and so the ground and foundation of that obedience which the Subject must render, how tyrannically soever exacted, yet *all Covenants entred into by the Soveraign to be void; and that to imagine that he is or can be bound to perform any promise or covenant, proceeds only from want of understanding*. And it would be worth his pains to consider, whether the assigning such a power to his Governor, or the absolving him from all Covenants and promises, be a rational way to establish such a Peace as is the end of Government: and since he confesses the justest Government may be overthrown by force, it ought prudently to be considered, what is like to prevent that force, as well as what the subject is bound to consent to; and whether people may not be very naturally dispos'd to use that force against him that declares himself to be absolv'd from all Oaths, Covenants, and Promises, and whether any obligation of reason or justice can establish the Government in him, who founds it upon so unrighteous a determination.

If Mr. *Hobbes* did not affect to be of the humor of those unreasonable Gamesters, which he saies (Pag. 19.) *is intolerable in the society of men, who will after trump is turned, use for trump, upon every occasion, that suit whereof they have most in their hand*, whom he likens to those men who clamor and demand right reason for Judg, yet seek no more, but that things should be determined by no other mens reason then their own; I say, if Mr. *Hobbes* were not possessed by this supercilious spirit which he condemns, since this his institution of Soveraignty is a mere imagination, he might with as much reason, if he would have bin pleased to have called it so, because it would have carried with it more equality and consequently more security, have supposed a Covenant to be on the Soveraigns part: which that he may not do, he will not admit that they who are his Subjects make any Covenant with their Soveraign to obey him; which if he did, he could as well covenant again with them to govern righteously, without making them the Judges of his justice, or himself liable to their controul and jurisdiction. So that the Soveraign hath no security for the obedience of his People, but the promise they have made to each other; and consequently if they rebell against him, he cannot complain of any injustice don to him, because they have broke no promise they made to him. And truly, by his own Logic, they may release to one another when they think it convenient: whereas if the promises be mutual, I do not say conditional, the Soveraign must not be at the mercy of his Subjects; but as they put themselves under his power, so he promises them not to use that power wantonly or tyrannically (which will be a proper and significant word against all his interpretation;) by which they have as much obligation upon him to be just, as he hath upon them to be obedient, which is no other, then that they swarve from justice, if they withdraw their obedience from him. This had bin a more natural and equitable institution, and more like to have lasted, having in it the true essential form of contracts, in which it will never be found that one party covenants, and the other not; which is the reason Mr. *Hobbes* himself gives, why no Covenant can be made with God, and that (Pag. 89.) *the pretence of Covenant with God, is so evident a lye, even in the pretenders own consciences, that it is not only an act of an unjust, but also of a vile and unmanly disposition*, which assertion is destructive of our Religion, and against the express sense of Scripture.

The impossibility alledg'd for such a Covenant, because it could not be don before he was Soveraign, for that the Subjects who submit to him were not yet one person, and after he is Soveraign what he doth is void, is but a fancy of words which have no solid signification. Nor is the instance which he gives of the popular Government, by which he would make the imagination of such a Covenant ridiculous, of any importance; for he saies (Pag. 90.) *No man is so dull as to say, that the People of Rome made a Covenant with the Romans to hold the Soveraignty on such or such conditions, which not perform'd the Romans might lawfully depose the Roman People*; which is, according to his usual practice, to put an objection into the mouth of a foolish adversary to make his Readers merry. And yet he laies so much weight upon it, that he saies it is only over inclination to a popular Government, that men do not see that there is the same reason with reference to Monarchy. And so there is, and the reason good to either. For doth not every man know, that knows any thing of the Government of Rome, that when the Soveraignty was intirely vested in the Senate, and had long bin so, the People of Rome made a great alteration in the Soveraignty by making Tribunes (by which *Machiavel* saies their Government was the more firm and secure) and afterwards by introducing other Magistrates into the Soveraignty? Nor were the Admissions and Covenants the Senate made in those cases ever declared void, but observed with all punctuallity: which is argument enough, that the Soveraign power may admit limitations without any danger to it self or the People, which is all that is contended for.

As there never was any such Person (Pag. 88.) *of whose acts a great multitude by mutual Covenant one with an other have made themselves every one the author, to the end he may use the strength and means of them all, as he shall think expedient for their peace, and common defence*, which is the definition he gives of his Common-wealth; So if it can be supposed, that any Nation can concur in such a designation, and devesting themselves of all their right and liberty, it could only be in reason obligatory to the present contractors, nor do's it appear to us, that their posterity must be bound by so unthrifty a concession of their Parents. For tho *Adam* by his Rebellion against God forfeited all the privileges which his unborn posterity might have clamed if he had preserved his innocence, and tho Parents may alienate their Estates from their Children, and thereby leave them Beggars; yet we have not the draught of any Contract, nor is that which Mr. *Hobbes* hath put himself to the trouble to prepare, valid enough to that purpose, by which they have left impositions and penalties upon the Persons of their posterity: nor is it probable that they would think themselves bound to submit thereunto. And then the Soveraign would neither find himself the more powerful, or the more secure, for his contractors having covenanted one with an other, and made themselves every one the author of all his actions: and it is to be doubted, that the People would rather look upon him as the *Visier Basha* instituted by their Fathers, then as Gods Lieutenant appointed to govern them under him.

It is to no purpose to examine the Prerogatives he grants to his Soveraign, because he founds them all upon a supposition of a contract and covenant that never was in nature, nor ever can reasonably be supposed to be; yet he confesses it to be *the generation* (Pag. 87.) *of the great Leviathan*, and which falling to the ground all his Prerogatives must likewise fall too; and so much to the damage of the Soveraign power, (to which most of the Prerogatives are due) that men will be apt to suppose, that they proceed from a ground which is not true, and so be the more inclined to dispute them. Whereas those Prerogatives are indeed vested in the Soveraign by his being Soveraign, but he do's not become Soveraign by vertue of such a contract and covenant, but are of the essence of his Soveraignty, founded upon a better title then such an accidental convention, and their designing a Soveraign by their Covenants with one another, and none with or to him, who is so absolutely to command them. And here he supposes again, that whatsoever a Soveraign is possessed of, is of his Soveraignty; and therefore he will by no means admit, that he shall part with any of his power which he calls *essential and inseparable rights*, and that whatever grant he makes of such power, the same is void: and he do's believe that this Soveraign right was at the time when he published his Book so well understood (that is *Cromwel* liked his Doctrine so well) that it would be generally acknowledged in *England* at the next return of peace. Yet he sees himself deceived: it hath pleased God to restore a blessed and a general peace, and neither King nor People believe his Doctrine to be true, or consistent with peace. How, and why the most absolute Soveraigns may, as they find occasion, part with, and deprive themselves of many branches of their power, will be more at large discovered in another place: yet we may observe in this the very complaisant humor of Mr. *Hobbes*, and how great a Courtier he desir'd to appear to the Soveraign power that then govern'd, by how odious and horrible a usurpation soever, in that he found a way to excuse and justify what they had already don in the lessening and diminution of their own Soveraign power, which it concern'd them to have believ'd was very lawfully and securely don. For, they having, as the most popular and obliging act they could perform, taken away *Wardships* and Tenures, he confesses after his enumeration of twelve Prerogatives, which he saies (Pag. 92.) *are the rights which make the essence of Soveraignty*, for these, he saies, *are incommunicable, and inseparable*, I say, he confesses, *the power to coin mony, to dispose of the estates and persons of infant heirs, and all other statute prerogatives may be transferred by the Soveraign*; whereas he might have bin informed, if he had bin so modest as to think he had need of any information, that those are no Statute Prerogatives, but as inherent and inseparable from the Crown, as many of those which he declares to be of the Essence of the Soveraignty. But both those were already entred upon, and he was to support all their actions which were past, as well as to provide for their future proceedings.

If Mr. *Hobbes* had known any thing of the constitution of the Monarchy of *England*, supported by as firm principles of Government as any Monarchy in *Europe*, and which enjoied a series of as long prosperity, he could never have thought that the late troubles there proceeded from an opinion receiv'd of the greatest part of England, *that the power was divided between the King, and the Lords, and the House of Commons*, which was an opinion never heard of in *England* till the Rebellion was begun, and against which all the Laws of *England* were most cleer, and known to be most positive. But as he cannot but acknowledg, that his own Soveraignty is obnoxious to the Lusts, and other irregular passions of the People; so the late execrable Rebellion proceeded not from the defect of the Laws, nor from the defect of the just and ample power of the King, but from the power ill men rebelliously possessed themselves of, by which they suppressed the strength of the Laws, and wrested the power out of the hands of the King: against which violence his Soveraign is no otherwise secure, then by declaring that his Subjects proceed injustly; of which no body doubts but that all they who took up arms against the King, were guilty in the highest degree. And there is too much cause to fear, that the unhappy publication of this doctrine against the Liberty and propriety of the Subject (which others had the honor to declare before Mr. *Hobbes*, tho they had not the good fortune to escape punishment as he hath don, I mean Dr. *Manwaring*, and Dr. *Sibthorpe*) contributed too much thereunto. For let him take what pains he will to render those precious words unvaluable, and of no signification; a better Philosopher then he, and one who understood the rules of Government better, having lived under just such a Soveraign as Mr. *Hobbes* would set up (I mean *Seneca*,) will be believed before him, who pronounces, *Errat siquis existimat tutum esse ibi Regem, ubi nihil a Rege tutum est; Securitas securitate mutua paciscenda est.* And he go's very far himself towards the confessing this truth, when he is forced to acknowledg, (Pag. 96.) *That the riches, power, and honor of a Monarch, arise only from the riches, strength and reputation of his subjects;*

for no King can be rich, nor glorious, nor secure, whose subjects are either poor or contemptible: which assertion will never be supported, by saying, that that condition shall be made good, and preserv'd to them by the justice and bounty of the Soveraign. For riches, and strength, and reputation are not aery words, without a real and substantial signification, nor do consist so much in the present enjoying, especially if it shall depend upon the casual pleasure of any man, as in the security for the future, that being a mans properly, that cannot be taken from him, but in that manner, and by those Rules, as are generally looked upon as the fundamentals of Government. And when he is transported by his passion and his appetite, and for making good his institution, to cancel and tread under foot all those known obligations, and make the precious terms of Property and Liberty absurd and insignificant words, to be blown away by the least breath of his monstrous Soveraign, without any violation of justice, or doing injury to those he afflicts; I say, when he is thus warmed by the flame of his passions, which he confesses (Pag. 96.) *alwaies dazzles, never enlightens the understanding*, he is so puzled by his own notions, that he makes himself a way out by distinctions of his own modelling and devising: and so he is compell'd to acknowledg, that tho his illimited Soveraign, whatsoever he doth, can do no injury to his subjects, nor be by any of them accused of injustice, yet that he (p. 90.) *may commit iniquity, tho not injustice or injury in the proper signification*, which is far more unintelligible then the Beatifical vision, for the obscurity and absurdity whereof he is so merry with the Schole-men.

As Mr. *Hobbes* his extraordinary and notorious ignorance in the Laws and constitution of the Government of *England* makes him a very incompetent Judg or informer of the cause or original of the late woful calamities in *England*, of which he knows no more then every other man of *Malmesbury* doth, and upon which there will be other occasion hereafter to inlarge; so his high arrogance and presumption that he doth understand them, makes him triumph in the observation, and wonder that so manifest a truth should of late be so little observed, That in a Monarchy, he that had the Soveraignty from a descent of six hundred years, was alone called Soveraign, had the title of Majesty from every one of his Subjects, and was unquestionably taken by them for their King, was notwithstanding never

considered as their Representative, that name without contradiction, passing for the title of those men, which at his
command were sent up by the People to carry their Petitions,
and give him, if he permitted it, their advice; which he saies
(Pag. 95.) *may serve as an admonition for those that are the
true and absolute Representative of a People* (which he hath
made his Soveraign to be) *to take heed how they admit of any
other general Representative upon any occasion whatsoever*:
all which is so unskilful and illiterate a suggestion, as could not
fall into the conception of any man who is moderately versed in
the principles of Soveraignty. And if Mr. *Hobbes* did not make
war against all modesty, he would rather have concluded, that
the title of the Representative of the People was not to be
affected by the King, then that for want of understanding his
Majesty should neglect to assume it, or that his faithful
Counsel, and his Learned Judges, who cannot be supposed to
be ignorant of the Regalities of the Crown, should fail to put
him in mind of so advantageous a Plea, when his fundamental
rights were so foully assaulted, and in danger. But tho the King
knew too well the original of his own power, to be contented to
be thought the Representative of the People, yet if Mr. *Hobbes*
were not strangely unconversant with the transactions of those
times, he would have known, which few men do not know,
that the King frequently, and upon all occasions reprehended
the two Houses, both for assuming the Style and appellation of
Parliament, which they were not, but in, and by his Majesties
conjuction with them, and for calling themselves the Representative of the People, which they neither were, or could be to
any other purpose then to present their Petitions, and humbly
to offer their advice, when and in what his Majesty required it;
and this was as generally understood by men of all conditions
in *England*, as it was that Rebellion was Treason. But they who
were able by false pretences, and under false protestations to
raise an Army, found it no difficult matter to perswade that
Army, and those who concurred with them, that they were not
in rebellion.

The Survey of Chapter 19.

I shall heartily concur with Mr. *Hobbes* in the preference of
Monarchy before all other kind of Government for the
happiness of the people, which is the end of Government: and

surely the people never enjoied (saving the delight they have in the word Equality, which in truth signifies nothing but keeping on their hats) Liberty or Property, or received the benefit of speedy and impartial Justice, but under a Monarch; but I must then advise that Monarch for his greatness and security, never so far to lessen himself as to be considered as the peoples Representative, which would make him a much less man then he is. His Majesty is inherent in his office, and neither one or other is conferred upon him by the people. Let those who are indeed the Deputies of the people, in those occasions upon which the Law allow's them to make Deputies, be called their Representatives which term can have no other legitimate interpretation then the Law gives it, which must have more autority then any Dictionary that is, or shall be made by Mr. *Hobbes*, whose animadversion or admonition will never prevail with any Prince to change his Soveraign Title, for Representative of the people; and much the less for the pains which he hath taken (pag. 95.) *to instruct men in the nature of that Office*, and how he comes to be their Representative.

I cannot leave this Chapter without observing Mr. *Hobbes* his very officious care that *Cromwell* should not fall from his greatness, and that his Country should remain still captive under the Tyranny of his vile Posterity, by his so solemn Declarations, that he who is in possession of the Soveraignty, tho by Election (Pag. 98.) *is obliged by the Law of nature to provide, by establishing his Successor, to keep those that had trusted him with the government, from relapsing into the miserable condition of Civil war; and consequently he was, when elected, a Soveraign absolute.* And then he declares positively, contrary to the opinion of all the World, that (Pag. 100.) *by the institution of Monarchy, the disposing of the Successor is alwaies left to the judgment and the will of the present possessor; and that if he declares expresly that such a man shall be his heir either by word or writing, then is that man immediately after the decease of his predecessor invested in the right of being Monarch.* Mr. *Hobbes* was too modest a man to hope that his *Leviathan* would have power to perswade those of *Poland* to change their form of Government; and what *Denmark* hath gotten by having don it since, cannot in so short a time be determin'd; or that the Emperor would dissolve and cancel the Golden Bull, and invest his Posterity in the Empire in spite of the Electors; or that the Papacy should be made

Hereditary, since *Cesar Borgia* was so long since dead, and he
had carried that spirit with him: and therefore I must appeal to
all dispassion'd men what Mr. *Hobbes* could have in his
purpose in the year One thousand six hundred fifty one, when
this Book was printed, but by this new Doctrine scarcely heard
of it till then, to induce *Cromwell* to break all the Laws of his
Country, and to perpetuate their slavery under his Progeny, in
which he follow'd his advice to the utmost of his power, tho his
Doctrine proved false and most detested. And tho Mr. *Hobbes*
by his presence of mind, and velocity of thought, which had
inabled him to forsee the purpose of rebelling, and taking the
King Prisoner, and delivering him up, from that question
proposed to him, concerning the value of a *Roman* penny,
might at that time discern so little possibility of his own
Soveraign's recovery, that it might appear to him a kind of
absurdity to wish it; yet methinks his own natural fear of
danger, which made him fly out of *France*, as soon as his
Leviathan was publish'd and brought into that Kingdom,
should have terrified him from invading the right of all
Hereditary Monarchies in the World, by declaring, that by the
Law of Nature which is immutable, it is in the power of the
present Soveraign to dispose of the succession, and to appoint
who shall succeed him in the Government; and that the word
Heir doth not of it self imply the Children or neerest Kindred of
a man, but whom soever a man shall any way declare he would
have succeed him; contrary to the known right and establishment throught the World, and which would shake if not
dissolve the Peace of all Kingdoms. Nor is there any danger of
the dissolution of a Common-wealth by the not nominating a
Successor; since it is a known maxime in all Hereditary
Monarchies, That the King never dies, because in the minute of
the exspiration of the present, his Heir succeeds him, and is in
the instant invested in all the dignities, and preheminences of
which the other had bin possessed: and if there were no other
error or false doctrine in the *Leviathan* (as there are very many
of a very pernicious nature) that would be cause enough to
suppress it in all Kingdoms.

The Survey of Chapter 20.

It is modestly don of Mr. *Hobbes* at last, after so many
Magisterial determinations of the institution of Soveraignty,

and the rights and autority of it, and what is not it, to confess that all these Discourses (*pag. 105.*) are only *what he finds by speculation, and deduction of Soveraign Rights from the nature, need, and designs of men in erecting of Commonwealths, and putting themselves under Monarchs, &c.* and therefore if he finds that all his speculation is positively contradicted by constant and uncontroverted practice, he will believe that his speculation is not, nor ought to be of autority enough to introduce new Laws and Rules of Government into the World. And it is high time for the Soveraign Power to declare, That it doth not approve those Doctrines, which may lessen the affections and tenderness of Princes towards their Subjects, and even their reverence to God himself, if they thought that they could change Religion, and suppress the Scripture it self; and that their power over their Subjects is so absolute, that they give them all that they do not take from them; and that Property is but a word of no signification, and lessens the duty and obedience of Subjects, and makes them less love the constitution of the Government they live under; which may prove so destructive to them, if they have temtation from their passions or their appetite to exercise the Autority they justly have. It is fit therefore that all men know, that these are only his speculations, and not the clame of Soveraign Power.

It had bin to be wished, that Mr. *Hobbes* had first taken the pains to have inform'd himself of the power and autority exercised by Elective Princes over their Subjects, and their submission rendred to them by their subjects, before he had so positively determin'd, that Elective Kings are not Soveraigns, at least that he had given a better reason for his assertion. He that hath supreme autority over all, and against whom there is no Appeal, may very justly and lawfully be called a Soveraign. And if he would enquire into the autority of the Emperor, in the proper Dominion of the Empire, he would find that he hath as Soveraign a power as any Prince in Christendom clames, and yet he is Elective. And it is a more extravagant speculation to conclude, That because the Electors have the absolute power to chuse the Emperor, that the Soveraignty is in them before they chuse him, and that they may keep it to themselves if they think good, because none have a right to give that which they have no right to possess; when it is known to all the World that the Electors have a right to chuse the Emperor, and yet that till they have chosen him, the Soveraignty is not in them, nor that they can possess it themselves, and chuse whether they will give it to another; and that when they have chosen him, he is a Soveraign Prince, and superior to all those who have chosen him, by all the marks of Soveraignty which are known in practice, tho not possibly in speculation. And he knows well there is another Soveraign Prince greater then the Emperor, and almost as great as he would have his Soveraign to be in the extent of his power, who is likewise Elective, and that is the Pope, and that the Conclave cannot retain that Soveraignty to themselves, but having by their Election conferr'd it upon him, he is thereby become as absolute a Monarch as Mr. *Hobbes* can wish. And truly, if he would rectifie his speculations, that is, his conceptions and imaginations, by examining those of other men (a fatal neglect he hath bin guilty of throughout his whole life) he could hardly have avoided the knowing, that on every *Michaelmas* day the whole common People of *London* chuse the Lord Major, and yet the Office is not in them till they do chuse him, tho his Predecessor were dead, nor can they keep it to themselves; and so they can give that which they cannot possess, which is diametrically contrary to his speculation; which would likewise have bin controuled by all Elections of the Kingdom.

He might have saved himself much labor (since he agrees that a Soveraign by acquisition, which is somwhat we understand, hath the same full Soveraignty with his other by institution) if he had spar'd all that which is mere speculation; and I will gratifie him, not by insisting upon the Paternal Dominion, otherwise then as it must be confessed to be the original of Monarchy, because we will do the Mother no wrong, who is so meet a help in the generation. And before I proceed further upon this Argument, to which I will presently return, I must lament in this place Mr. *Hobbes*'s so positive determining a point of Justice, in which he could have no experience, and against all the practice of the Christian World, (pag. 104.) *that he who hath Quarter granted him in War, hath not his life given, but deferred till farther deliberation*; which Doctrine, found only as he confesses by speculation, served to confirm that Tyrannical Power in a Judgment they had given, when three great and noble Persons, who were Prisoners of War, were contrary to all form and rule condemn'd to be murder'd; which Sentence was barbarously executed, and afterwards reiterated upon others, the rather probably upon his speculative determination.

And since we are now come to that Chapter of Dominion Paternal and Despotical, in which he discourses of his Government by acquisition, which he will have by force; or by institution, which he calls by consent, and confesses, that the rights and consequences of Soveraignty are the same in both; it may not (I conceive) be unseasonable to state, and lay down that Scheme of Government, which men reasonably believe was originally instituted, and the progress and alterations which were afterwards made, and all those Covenants, Promises, and Conditions which were annexed to it, and by the observation of which it hath alwaies acquired strength and lustre, and bin as much impair'd, when endeavors have bin used to extend it beyond its bounds and just limits, and to make it more absolute, then is consistent with the Peace and Happiness of the People, which was, and is the end of its Institution. And in the first place we must deny, as we have hitherto don, Mr. *Hobbes* his ground-work, upon which, with many ill-consequences even from thence, his foundation is supported, and that is, That War is founded in Nature, which gives the stronger a right to whatever the weaker is possessed of; so that there can be no peace, or security from oppression, till such Covenants are made, as may appoint a Soveraign to have all that power which is necessary to provide for that peace and security; and out of, and by this Institution, his Magistrate grows up to the greatness and size of his *Leviathan*. But we say, that Peace is founded in nature; and that when the God of nature gave his Creature, Man, the dominion over the rest of his Creation, he gave him likewise natural strength and power to govern the World with peace and order: and how much soever he lost by his own integrity, by falling from his obedience to his Creator, and how severe a punishment soever he under-went by that his disobedience, it do's not appear that his dominion over Man-kind was in any degree lessened or abated. So that we cannot but look upon him, during his life, as the sole Monarch of the World: and that lasted so long, as we may reasonably compute, that a very considerable part of the World, that was peopled before the Flood, was peopled in his life, *since it lasted upon the point of two parts of that term*: so that his Dominion was over a very numerous People. And during all that time, we have no reason to imagine that there was any such Instrument of Government by Covenants and Contracts, as is contain'd in this Institution. And yet we do acknowledg, that he was by nature fully possessed of all that *plentitudo potestatis*, which doth of right belong to a Magistrate; and we may very reasonably believe, having no color to think the contrary, that his Son *Seth*, who was born a hundred and thirty years after him, and lived above a hundred years after he was dead, govern'd his descendants with the same absolute Dominion, which might well be continued under his Successor to the very time of the Flood: for we may very reasonably believe that *Noah* conversed with *Seth*, since it is evident they lived one hundred years together in the same Age. Nor have we the least color to believe, that there was either Sedition or Civil War before the Flood; their rebellion against God in a universal exercise of Idolatry, which implies a general consent amongst themselves, being in the opinion of most Learned Men, the crying Sin that provoked God to drown the World.

After the Flood, we cannot but think that *Noah* remain'd the sole Monarch of the World during his life, according to that model with which he had bin very well acquainted for the space of five hundred years; and he lived long enough after to see a very numerous increase of his Children and Subjects; who after his death, when the multiplication was very great, came from the East into the Land of *Shinar*, the pleasant vally of *Shinar*, where God, in the beginning, had plac'd the Father of Man-kind, *Adam*; and Learned men are of opinion, that the great and principal end of the building of *Babel*, over and above the high Tower for their fame and renown to posterity, was, that they intended it for the Metropolis of an Universal Monarchy; so little doubt there was yet made of an entire subjection and obedience. Sure we are, that the Generations of *Noah*, when Man-kind was exceedingly increas'd, did divide the Nations in the Earth; and Mr. *Mead* assures us, that the word which we translated *divided* signifies not *a scattering*, or any thing of confusion, but a *most distinct partition*. So that this great division of the Earth being perform'd in this method and order, there is no room for the imagination and dream of such an irregular and confus'd dispersion, that every man went whither he listed, and setled himself where he liked best, from whence that Institution of Government might arise which Mr. *Hobbes* fancies. Under this Division, we of the Western World have reason to believe our selves of the posterity of *Japheth*, and that our Progenitors did as well know under what Government they were to live, as what portion they were to possess: and we have that blessing of *Japheth*, that God would inlarge him into the Tents of *Shem*, and that *Cham* should be his servant, to assure and confirm us, that the Inundation, which almost cover'd us, of the *Goths* and *Vandals* from *Scythia*, and other Northern Nations (whose original habitations we cannot to this day find) were not of the Children of *Cham*, which we might otherwise have suspected.

As Man-kind encreas'd, and the age of man grew less, so that they did not live to see so great a Progeny issue out of their own loins as formerly, and their subjects growing less, their kindred also grew at so great distance, that the account of their relations was not so easily or so carefully preserv'd; hereby they who had the Soveraign Powers exercis'd less of the Paternal Affection in their Government, and look'd upon those they govern'd as their mere subjects, not as their Allies; and by degrees, according to the custom of exorbitant Power, considering only the extent of their own Jurisdiction, and what they might do, they treated those who were under them not as Subjects, but as slaves, who having no right to any thing but what they gave them, would allow them to possess nothing but what they had no mind to have themselves. Estates they had none that they could call their own, because when their Soveraign call'd for them, they were his; their persons were at his command, when he had either occasion or appetite to use them, and their Children inherited nothing but the subjection of their Parents: so that they were happy or miserable, as he who had the power and command over them exercised that power with more or less rigor or indulgence, they submitting to both, acknowledging the dominion to be naturally absolute, and their subjection and obedience to be as natural. Kings had not long delighted themselves with this exorbitant exercise of their power (for tho the power had bin still the same, the exercise of it had bin very moderate, whil'st there remain'd the tenderness or memory of any relation) but they begun to discern (according to their faculties of discerning, as their parts were better or worse) that the great strength they seem'd to be possess'd of, must in a short time end in absolute weakness, and the plenty they seem'd to enjoy, would become exceeding want and beggary; that no man would build a House that his Children should not inherit, nor cultivate Land with good husbandry and expence, the fruit and profit whereof might be taken by another man; that whil'st their subjects did not enjoy the convenience and delight of life, they could not be sure of the affection and help of them, when they should enter into a difference with one who is as absolute as themselves, but they would rather chuse to be subject to him, whose Subjects liv'd with more satisfaction under him: in a word, that whil'st they engross'd all power, and all wealth into their own hands, they should find none who would defend them in the possession of it; and that there is great difference between the subjection that love and discretion paies, and that which results only from fear and force, and that despair puts an end to that duty, which nature, and it may be Conscience too, would still perswade them to pay, and to continue; and therefore that it was necessary that the subjects should find profit and comfort in obeying, as well as Kings pleasure in commanding. These wise and wholsom Reflexions prevail'd with Princes for their own benefit to restrain themselves, to make their Power less absolute, that it might be more useful; to give their Subjects a property that should not be invaded but in such cases, and with such and such circumstances, and a liberty that should not be restrain'd, but upon such terms as they could not but think reasonable. And as they found the benefit to grow from those condescentions in the improvement of Civility, and those additions of delight which makes Life and Government the more pleasant, they inlarg'd the Graces and Concessions to their Subjects, reserving all in themselves which they did not part with by their voluntary Grants and Promises. And if we take a view of the several Kingdoms of the World, we shall see another manner of beauty, glory and lustre in those Governments, where those condescentions, concessions, and contracts have bin most or best observ'd, then in those Dominions where the Soveraigns retain to themselves all the Rights and Prerogatives which are invested in them by the original nature of Government; upon which we shall inlarge hereafter.

This is the original and pedigree of Government, equally different from that which the levelling fancy of some men would reduce their Soveraign to, upon an imagination that Princes have no autority or power but what was originally given them by the People, and that it cannot be presumed that they would give them so much as might be applied to their own destruction, and from that which Mr. *Hobbes* hath instituted, by framing formal Instruments by which an assembly of mankind (which was never heard of, nor can be conceiv'd practicable) hath devolv'd from themselves into one Man of their own choice, an absolute Power by their own consent, to exercise it in such a manner as to his pleasure is agreeable, without the observation of the common rules of Justice or Sobreity; whereas it cannot be imagin'd possible in nature, that ever such an assembly of men of equal autority in themselves, will ever agree to make one Man their Soveraign with such an absolute Jurisdiction over the rest, as must devest them of all property as well as power for the future; and whereas in truth all power was by God and Nature invested into one Man, where still as much of it remains as he hath not parted with, and shar'd with others, for the good and benefit of those (and the mutual security of both) for whose benefit it was first intrusted to him; the rest, which is enough, remains still in him, and may be applied to the preservation of the whole, against the fancies of those who think he hath nothing but what they have given him; and likewise against those who believe that so much is given him, that he hath power to leave no body else any thing to enjoy; the last of which are no less enemies to Monarchy then the former.

I am very unwilling to enter into the lists with Mr. *Hobbes* upon the interpretation of Scriptures, which he handles as imperiously as he doth a Text of *Aristotle*, putting such unnatural interpretation on the words, as hath not before fallen into the thoughts of any other man, and drawing very unnatural inferences from them; insomuch as no man can think he is really in earnest, when, to prove that the Kings word is sufficient to take any thing from any Subject when there is need, and that the King is Judge of that need, he alledges the example of our Saviour, who, he saies, as King of the Jews (p. 106) *commanded his Disciples to take the Asses Colt to carry him to Jerusalem*, which he saies the owner permitted, *and did not ask whether his necessity was a sufficient title, nor whether he was Judg of that necessity, but did acquiesce in the will of the Lord*: which is a very bold and ungrave wresting of Scripture to purposes it could not intend; since our Saviour did not profess to do one act as King of the Jews, but declar'd *that his kingdom was not of this world*. And at that time he told the Messengers who were sent for the Ass, that if they were ask'd what they meant by it, they should answer, that the Lord had need of him, upon which he knew, and he said, that they would let him go, and upon that he grounded their Commission. If the owner would not permit them to take it, the Messengers had no autority to have brought them to him. And his inference from, and the gloss he makes upon the question that God asked of Adam, (p. 106.) *Hast thou eaten?* hath as little warrant from that text, as the other improper instance of our Saviour. And sure when Mr. *Hobbes* thought fit by this example of our Saviour in this place to wrest all property from the Subject, he did not intend in any other place so far to devest him of any autority, that men were not *bound to believe any thing he said, or to do any thing he commanded, because he had no Commission which required obedience, his Kingdom being not yet of this world.* So unwary he is in the contradicting himself; as all men are, who first resolve what they are to prove, before they consider what it is that is true.

We are not obliged, nor indeed have any reason to believe, that God was offended with the Children of Israel for desiring a King, which was a Government himself had instituted over them, and to which they had bin long accustomed, and had undergon much misery, and confusion whilst there was no King in Israel; but for their mutinous manner of asking it, and the reason they gave for it, that they might be like other nations, which God had taken all possible care that they should not be, and enjoined them to learn nothing of them. And the description, which *Samuel* made of the exorbitant power of Kings, which indeed the Kings of the Nations did exercise, by whose example they desir'd to be govern'd, was rather to terrify them from pursuing their foolish demand, then to constitute such a Prerogative as the King should use whom God would appoint to go in and out before them; which methinks is very manifest, in that the worst Kings that ever reign'd over them, never challeng'd, or assum'd those Prerogatives. Nor did the people conceive themselves liable to those impositions; as appears by the application they made to *Rehoboam* upon the death of *Solomon*, that he would abate some of that rigor his Father had exercised towards them; the rough rejection of which, contrary to the advice of his wisest Counsellors, cost him the greater part of his Dominions: and when *Rehoboam* would by Arms have reduc'd them to obedience, God would not suffer him, because he had bin in the fault himself.

I am willing to take an occasion in this place to wish, that no better Divines then Mr. *Hobbes* had, from this place in *Samuel*, presum'd very unwarrantably to draw inferences, to lessen the Subjects reverence and obedience to Kings, and to raise a prejudice and disesteem in Kings towards their Subjects, as people whose affections and good Will are of no use to them, since they can present nothing to them that is their own, nor have any thing to give, but what they make take from them; which two very different rather then contrary conclusions, too many Divines (and some of parts) according to their several inclinations and appetites, have presumed to wrest from that place of Scripture; the one party of them, as is said before, endeavouring maliciously to render Monarchy odious and insupportable, by the unlimited affections, and humors, and pretences, and power of a single uncontroulable person; the other believing as unreasonably, that the dispositions, natures, and hearts of the people, cannot be appli'd to the necessary obedience towards their Princes, nor their reverence and duty be so well fix'd and devoted to them, as by thinking that they have nothing of their own, but whatsoever they enjoy they have only by the bounty of the King, who can take it from them when he pleases: and to this last party Mr. *Hobbes* his speculation hath for the present disposed him to adhere, tho in any other particular opinion he doth not concur with any Divine of any Church in Christendom. For the first, whoever doth well consider the wonderful confused Government that was exercised over the Children of Israel from the death of *Joshua*, when the Monarchy was interrupted, under the Judges for the space of above three hundred years, the barbarous negligence in the instruction of the people in the knowledg of God, and of their duty to him, insomuch that the very next generation after the death of *Joshuah* had lost, or was without the whole History of what God had don for them, and of what he expected from them; so unfaithful a guide, or rembrancer is Tradition, when the Scripture it self is not to be found: I say, whoever considers likewise the quality, and talent, and humor of many of the very Judges who had bin over them, as the repeted Acts of indiscretion and folly in *Sampson*, which could not but make his judgment to be in the less reverence, & the strength of his arms to be more admir'd then that of his head; with the present state they were then in under the Sons of *Samuel*, who were no better than the Sons of *Ely* had bin, will not perhaps so very much blame them for desiring a King: and tho the manner of their asking it might, as hath bin said, offend

Samuel, and in some degree displease God, yet he might not be offended absolutely with the thing it self, since it was no more then God himself had in a manner prescrib'd to them, as well as foretold, without any kind of disapprobation. *When thou art come into the Land which the Lord thy God giveth thee, &c, and shalt say, I will set a King over me, like as all the Nations which are about me, Thou shalt in any wise set him a King over thee, whom the Lord thy God shall chuse.* Deut. 17. 14, 15, 16, 17. God was well content that they should have a King, but reserv'd the election of him to himself: he would have no transferring of rights, or covenanting for one another, he would chuse his own Representative. Nor amongst all the customes of the Nations, which he forbid them to follow, did God ever shew the least dislike of their Government by Kings, which had bin instituted originally by himself, and probably bin continued by them even from the time of the institution, however their manners were degenerated, and the knowledg of him totally forgotten. And in what degree of grace and favor that high calling hath bin ever since with him, appears by the mention of them throughout the whole current of Scripture, by the Prerogatives he hath granted to them, and by his imparting to them even his own appellation.

They who will in the next place, deduce the extent of that absolute and illimited power of Kings from that declaration by *Samuel*, which indeed seems to leave neither Property, or Liberty in their subjects, and could be only intended by *Samuel* to terrify them from that mutinous and seditious clamor, since it hath no foundation from any other part of Scripture, nor was ever practic'd or exercis'd by any good King who succeeded over them, and was blessed, and approv'd by God. And therefore when those State Empirics, of what degree or quality soever, will take upon them to prescribe a new diet and exercise to Soveraign Princes, and invite them to assume new powers and prerogatives over the people, by the Precepts, Warrants, and Prescriptions of the Scripture, they should not presume to make the sacred writ subject to their own private fancies. And if according to the more authentic method of interpreting doubtful places, they had recourse to that place, where the same matter is first handled, they would then have found, by resorting to the before mention'd place in Deuteronomy, another kind of Scheme for the power, and government of Kings. There, when God intended that they should be governed by a King whom he would himself chuse, he prescrib'd what he should not do, and what he should do. *He should not multiply Horses to himself*, &c. which only concern'd that people, that they might have no temtation to return to Egypt, *Ye shall henceforth no more return that way* &c. *Nor shall he multiply Wives*, &c. Tho multiplying of Wives seem'd to be permitted, yet he was to have a care that the number of them did not turn his heart away. *Nor should he greatly multply unto himself Silver, and Gold* &c. not so affect, and set his heart upon being rich, as to be temted to oppress his Subjects, or to injure his Neighbors; and so far the negative directed. Then for the affirmative, *That he should write a copy of the Law in a Book*, &c. Deut. 17, 18, 19, 20. *that it should be with him, and he should read therein all the daies of his life, that he might learn to fear the Lord his God, and to keep all the words of the Law, and these Statutes to do them; that his heart be not lifted up, and that he turn not aside from the Commandment to the right hand, or to the left*; and from this Text the *Rabinns* concluded, that he was to write a Book of the Law for himself, and if he had none before he was King, he was obliged assoon as he was King to have two, one whereof he was to have alwaies with him, *sive cum vadit ad prælium, sive cum sedet in judicio, aut in mensa, &c.* Those were the injunctions which God prescrib'd to his King, and were observ'd by all those who were bless'd and approv'd by him; for *David* seems by the words of *Nathan* to have some particular allowance for the great number of his Wives; and his multiplying gold, and silver, was for the building of the Temple, and no private use of his own; and *Solomons* excessive greatness, was from the immediate bounty of God himself; but he no sooner violated those Precepts, and exceeded that moderation that was prescrib'd to him towards his Subjects, and with reference to the multiplying Wives, then his heart turn'd away from God, and God turn'd away from him.

This pleasant suggestion by which he would discountenance that importunate and impertinent demand of an example of such a Government as he would institute, that tho *in all places of the world men should lay the foundation of their houses in sand, it could not thence be infer'd that so it ought to be*, will never perswade men to change a Government they have bin for many hundred years happy under (tho with some vicissitudes of fortune) for an imaginary Government by his Rules of

Arithmetic and Geometry, of which no Nation hath ever yet
had the experiment: and if there by any Country where is a
Sand of that nature, that hath supported the greatest edifices
for hundreds of years, against all the storms of wind, and rage
of tempests, he shall be much too nice and scrupulous a person,
who will by any Rules of Architecture forbear to build his
House there, because he will not lay his foundation upon Sand,
which by experience is found to be of equal firmness with a
Rock.

The Survey of Chapter 21.

Mr. *Hobbes* is so great an enemy to freedom, that he will not
allow Man that which God hath given him, the Freedom of his
Will; but he shall not entangle me in that Argument, which he
hath enough exercis'd himself in with a more equal Adversary,
who I think hath bin much too hard for him at his own
weapon, Reason, the Learned Bishop of *Derry*, who was
afterwards Arch-Bishop of *Armagh*, and by which he hath put
him into greater choler then a Philosopher ought to subject
himself to, the terrible strokes whereof I am not willing to
undergo, and therefore shall keep my self close to that freedom
and liberty only that is due to Subjects, and of which, his
business in this Chapter, is to deprive them totally.

A man would have expected from Mr. *Hobbes*'s Inventory of
the several Rights and powers of his Soveraign in his eighteenth
Chapter, of which one was to prescribe Rules (*pag.* 91.)
*whereby every man might know what goods he may enjoy, and
what actions he might do, without being molested by any of his
fellow Subjects*, which he saies, *Men call Propriety*, that some
such Rule should be established as might secure that Propriety,
how little soever: but he hath now better explain'd himself, and
finds, that Liberty and Property are only fences against the
Invasion or force of fellow Subjects, but towards the Soveraign
of no use or signification at all. No man hath a Propriety in any
thing, that can restrain the King from taking it from him, and
the liberty of a Subject (*pag.* 109.) *lieth only in those things,
which in regulating their actions, the Soveraign hath pretermitted, such as is the liberty to buy and sell, and otherwise
contract with one another; to chuse their own abode, their own
diet, their own trade of life, and to institute their children as
they think fit, and the like.* I wonder he did not insert the

liberty to wear his Clothes of that fashion which he likes best, which is as important as most of his other Concessions. And yet he seems to be jealous, that even this liberty should make men imagine, that the Soveraign power should be in any degree limited, or that any thing he can do to a Subject, and upon what pretence soever, may be called injustice or injury, the contrary whereof he saies he hath shewed already; for he takes it as granted, that all that he hath said he hath proved: and if he hath not, he hath don it now substantially by the example of *Jepthah*, in causing his daughter to be sacrific'd (of which he is not sure) and by *Davids* killing *Uriah*, which he saies, tho it was against equity, yet it was not an injury to *Uriah*, because the right was given him by *Uriah*, which I dare swear *Uriah* never knew he had don. And by such unnatural Arguments he would perswade men to be willing to be undon; very like those which the *Stoics* as obstinately maintain'd, That a wise man could not be injur'd, because he was not capable nor sensible of it. But I wonder more, that he doth not discern what every other man cannot but discern, that by his so liberal taking away, he hath not left the Subject any thing to enjoy even of those narrow concessions which he hath made to him. For how can any man believe that he hath liberty to buy and sell, when the Soveraign power can presently take away what he hath sold, from him who hath bought it, and consequently no man can sell or buy to any purpose? Who can say that he can chuse his own abode, or his own trade of life, or any thing, when assoon as he hath chosen either, he shall be requir'd to go to a place where he hath no mind to go, and to do somwhat he would not chuse to do? for his person is no more at his own disposal then his goods are; so that he may as graciously retain of himself all that he hath granted.

Whether the Soveraign Power or the Liberty of the Subject receive the greater injury and prejudice by this brief state and description he makes of the no liberty, that is, the portion he leaves to the Subject, would be a great question, if he had not bin pleas'd himself to determine, that his Subject (for God forbid that any other Prince should have such a Subject) is not capable of any injury; by which the whole mischief is like to fall upon the Soveraign. And what greater mischief and ruine can threaten the greatest Prince, then that their Subjects should believe, that all the liberty they have, consists only in those things which the Soveraign hath hitherto pretermitted, that is, which he hath not yet taken from them, but when he pleases in regulating their actions to determine the contrary, they shall then have neither liberty to buy or sell, nor to contract with each other, to chuse their own abode, their own diet, their own trade of life, or to breed their own children; and to make their misery compleat, and their life as little their own as the rest, that nothing the Soveraign can do to his subject, on what pretence soever, as well in order to the taking away his Life as his Estate, can be called injustice or injury; I say, what greater insecurity can any Prince be in or under, then to depend upon such Subjects? And alas! what security to himself or them can the Sword in his hand be, if no other hand be lift up on his behalf, or the Swords in all other hands be directed against him, that he may not cut off their heads when he hath a mind to it? And it is not Mr. *Hobbes*'s autority that will make it believ'd, that he who desires more liberty, demands an exemption from all Laws, by which all other men may be masters of their lives; and that every Subject is author of every act the Soveraign doth, upon the extravagant supposition of a consent that never was given; and if it were possible to have bin given, must have bin void at the instant it was given, by Mr. *Hobbes*'s own rules, as shall be made out in its place. He himself confesses, (*pag. 295.*) and saies it is evident to the meanest capacities, that *mens actions are deriv'd from the opinions they have of the good and evil which from those actions redound unto themselves, and consequently men that are once possessed of an opinion that their obedience to the Soveraign power will be more hurtful to them then their disobedience, will disobey the Laws, and thereby over throw the Common-wealth, and introduce confusion and civil War, for the avoiding whereof, all civil Government was ordained.* If this be true, (as there is no reason to believe it to be) is it possible that any man can believe, that the People, for we speak not of convincing the Philosophers and the Mathematicians, but of the general affections of the People, which must dispose them to obedience, that they can be perswaded by a long train of Consequences, from the nature of man, and the end of Government, and the institution thereof by Contracts and Covenants, of which they never heard, to believe that it is best for them to continue in the same nakedness in which they were created, for fear their clothes may be stoln from them, and that they have parted with their liberty to save their lives?

There is no question, but of all calamities the calamity of War is greatest, and the rage and uncharitableness of civil War most formidable of all War. Indeed forreign War seldom destroies a Nation, without domestic Combinations and Conspiracies, which makes a complication with civil War; and sure nothing can more inevitably produce that, then an universal opinion in the People, that their Soveraign can take from them all they have whenever he hath a mind to it, and their lives too, without any injustice, and consequently that their obedience to him will be more hurtful to them then their disobedience; so well hath he provided for the security of his Soveraign, if his doctrine were believ'd.

Mr. *Hobbes* is too much conversant in both those learned Languages, to wish that the Western World were depriv'd of the Greek and Latine Tongues, for any mischief they have don; and upon my conscience, whatever errors may have bin brought into Philosophy by the autority of *Aristotle*, no man ever grew a Rebel by reading him; and if the greatest Monarch that hath ever bin in the World, except the Monarch of the World, had thought his Tutor *Aristotle* had bin so great an enemy to Monarchy (yet he knew he was born and bred in a Republic) and that his Works contribute so much to sedition, as Mr. *Hobbes* supposes, he would not have valued his Person so much, nor read his Works with such diligence as he did. And if Mr. *Hobbes* would take a view of the Insurrections, and the civil Wars which have at any time bin stirr'd up in the Western parts, he will not find that they have bin contriv'd or fomented by men who had spent much time in the reading Greek and Latin Authors, or that they have bin carried on upon the Maxims and Principles which they found there. *Jack Straw* and *Wat Tyler*, whose Insurrection, in respect of the numbers and the progress it made, was as dangerous as hath happened in any Age or Climate, had never read *Aristotle* or *Cicero*; and I believe, had Mr. *Hobbes* bin of this opinion when he taught *Thucydides* to speak English, which Book contains more of the Science of Mutiny and Sedition, and teaches more of that Oratory that contributes thereunto, then all that *Aristotle* and *Cicero* have publish'd in all their Writings, he would not have communicated such materials to his Country-men. But if this new Philosophy, and Doctrine of Policy and Religion should be introduc'd, taught, and believ'd, where *Aristotle* and *Cicero* have don no harm, it would undermind Monarchy more in two months, then those two great men have don since their deaths; and men would reasonably wish, that the Author of it had never bin born in the English Climate, nor bin taught to write and read.

It is a very hard matter for an Architect in State and Policy, who doth despise all Precedents, and will not observe any Rules of practice, to make such a model of Government as will be in any degree pleasant to the Governor, or governed, or secure for either; which Mr. *Hobbes* finds; and tho he takes a liberty to raise his Model upon a supposition of a very formal Contract, that never was, or ever can be in nature, and hath the drawing and preparing his own form of Contract, is forc'd to allow such a latitude in obedience to his subject, as shakes the very pillars of his Government. And therefore, tho he be contented that by the words of his Contract, (*pag.* 112.) *Kill me, and my fellow if you please*, the absolute power of all mens lives shall be submitted to the disposal of the Governors will and pleasure, without being oblig'd to observe any rules of Justice and Equity; yet he will not admit into his Contract the other words, (*pag.* 112.) *I will kill my self, or my fellow*, and therefore that he is not bound by the command of his Soveraign to execute any dangerous or dishonorable office; but in such cases, men are not to resort so much to the words of the submission, as to the intention: which Distinction surely may be as applicable to all that monstrous autority which he gives his Governor to take away the Lives and Estates of his Subjects, without any cause or reason, upon an imaginary Contract, which if never so real, can never be supposed to be with the intention of the Contractor in such cases. And the subtle Distinctions he finds out to excuse Subjects from yielding obedience to their Soveraigns, and the Prerogative he grants to fear, for a whole Army to run away from the Enemy without the guilt of treachery or injustice, leaves us some hope, that he will at last allow such a liberty to Subjects, that they may not in an instant be swallowed up by the prodigious power which he pleases to grant to his Soveraign. And truly, he degrades him very dis-honorably, when he obliges him to be the Hang man himself, of all those Malefactors, which by the Law are condemn'd to die; for he gives every man autority, without the violation of his duty, or swerving from the rules of Justice, absolutely to refuse to perform that office. Nor hath he provided much better for his security, then he hath for his honor, when he allows it lawful for any number of men, (*pag.* 112) *who have rebelled against the Soveraign, or committed some capital crime, for which every one of them expects death, then to join together, and defend each other, because they do but defend their lives, which the guilty man,* he saies, *may do as well as the innocent.* And surely, no man can legally take his life from him who may lawfully defend it; and then the murderer, or any other person guilty of a capital Crime, is more innocent, and in a better condition then the Executioner of Justice, who may be justly murdered in the just execution of his office. And it is a very childish security that he provides for his Soveraign against this Rebellion, and defence of themselves against the power of the Law, (*pag.* 113.) that he declares *it to be lawful only for the defence of their lives, and that upon the offer of pardon for themselves, that self-defence is unlawful*: as if a body that is lawfully drawn together, with strength enough to defend their lives against the power of the Law, are like to disband and lay down their Arms, without other benefit and advantage then only of the saving of their lives. But tho he be so cruel as to devest his Subjects of all that liberty, which the best and most peaceable men desire to possess, yet he liberally and bountifully confers upon them such a liberty as no honest man can pretend to, and which is utterly inconsistent with the security of Prince and People; which unreasonable Indulgence of his, cannot but be thought to proceed from an unlawful affection to those who he saw had power enough to defend the transcendent wickedness they had committed, tho they were without an Advocate to make it lawful for them to do so, till he took that office upon him in his *Leviathan*, as is evident by the instance he gives in the next Paragraph, that he thinks it lawful for every man to have as many wives as he pleases, if the King will break the silence of the Law, and declare that he may do so; which is a Prerogative he vouchsafes to grant to the Soveraign, to balance that liberty he gave to the Subject to defend himself and his companion against him, and is the only power that may inable him to be too hard for the other.

If Mr. *Hobbes* did not believe that the autority of his Name, and the pleasantness of his style, would lull men asleep from enquiring into the Logic of his Discourse, he could not but very well discern himself, that this very liberty which he allows the Subject to have, and which he doth without scruple enjoy, to sue the Soveraign, and to demand the hearing of his Cause, and that Sentence be given according to the Law, results only from that condescention and contract which the Soveraign hath made with his Subject, and which can as well secure many other Liberties to them, as their power to sue the King; for there could be no Law precedent to that resignation of themselves and all they had, at the institution of their supreme Governor; and if there had bin, it had bin void and invalid, it being not possible that any man who hath right to nothing, and from whom any thing that he hath may be taken away, can sue his Soveraign for a debt which he might take, if it were due from any other man but can by no means be due from him to whom all belongs, and who hath power to forbid any Judg to proceed upon that complaint, or any other person to presume to make that complaint, were it not for the subsequent contract which he calls a precedent Law, by which the Soveraign promises, and obliges himself to appoint Judges to exercise Justice even where himself is party, and that he will be sued before those Judges, if he doth not pay what he ow's to his Subjects. This is the Contract which gives that capacity of suing, and which by his own consent and condescention lessens his Soveraignty, that his Subjects may require Justice from him. And yet all these promises, and lessenings, he pronounces as void, and to amount to contradictions, that must dissolve the whole Soveraign power, and leave the people in confusion and war. Whereas the truth is, these condescentions, and voluntary abatements of some of that original power that was in them, have drawn a cheerful submission, and bin attended by a ready obedience to Soveraignty, from the time that Subjects have bin at so great a distance from being consider'd as Children, and that Soveraigns have bin without those natural tendernesses in the exercise of their power, and which in the rigor of it could never have bin supported. And where these obligations are best observ'd, Soveraignty flourishes with the most lustre, and security; Kings having still all the power remaining in them, that they have not themselves parted with, and releas'd to their Subjects, and their Subjects having no pretence to more liberty or power then the King hath granted and given to them: and both their happiness, and security consists in containing themselves within their own limits, that is, Kings not to affect the recovery of that exorbitant power, which their Ancestors wisely parted with, as well for their own as the peoples benefit; and Subjects to rejoice in those liberties which have bin granted to them, and not to wish to lessen the power of the King, which is not greater then is necessary for their own preservation. And to such a wholsom division, and communication of power as this is, that place of Scripture (with which Mr. *Hobbes* is still too bold) *a Kingdom divided in it self cannot stand*, cannot be appli'd.

But that this Supreme Soveraign, whom he hath invested with the whole property and liberty of all his Subjects, and so invested him in it, that he hath not power to part with any of it by promise, or donation, or release, may not be too much exalted with his own greatness, he hath humbled him sufficiently by giving his Subjects leave to withdraw their obedience from him when he hath most need of their assistance, for *the* (pag. 114.) *obligation of Subjects to the Soveraign is understood (he saies) to last as long, and no longer, then the power lasts to protect them.* So that assoon as any Town, City, or Province of any Princes Dominions, is invaded by a Forreign Enemy, or possessed by a Rebellious Subject, that the Prince for the present cannot suppress the power of the one, or the other, the people may lawfully resort to those who are over them, and for their Protection perform all the Offices and duties of good Subjects to them, (pag. 114.) *For the right men have by nature to protect themselves when none else can protect them, can by no covenant be relinquish'd, and the end of obedience is protection, which wherever a man seeth it either in his own, or in an others sword, nature applieth his obedience to it, and his endeavours to maintain it.* And truly it is no wonder if they do so, and that Subjects take the first opportunity to free themselves from such a Soveraign as he hath given them, and chuse a better for themselves. Whereas the duty of Subjects is, and all good Subjects believe they owe, another kind of duty and obedience to their Soveraign, then to withdraw their subjection because he is oppress'd; and will prefer poverty, and death it self, before they will renounce their obedience to their natural Prince, or do any thing that may advance the service of his Enemies. And since Mr. *Hobbes* gives so ill a testimony of his government (which, by the severe conditions he would oblige mankind to submit to for the support of it, ought to be firm, and not to be shaken) (pag. 114.) *that it is in its own nature not only subject to violent death by forreign war, but also from the ignorance, and passion of men, that it hath in it from the very institution many seeds of natural mortality by internal discord*, worse then which he cannot say of any Government, we may very reasonably prefer the Government we have, and under which we have enjoi'd much happiness, before his which we do not know, nor any body hath had experience of, and which by his own confession is liable to all the accidents of mortality which any others have bin; and reject his that promises so ill, and exercises all the action of War in Peace, and when War comes, is liable to all the misfortunes which can possibly attend or invade it.

Whether the relation of Subjects be extinguisht in all those cases, which Mr. *Hobbes* takes upon him to prescribe, as Imprisonment, Banishment, and the like, I leave to those who can instruct him better in the Law of Nations, by which they must be judged, notwithstanding all his Appeals to the Law of Nature; and I presume if a banish'd Person (p. 114.) *during which*, he saies, *he is not subject*, shall join in an action under a Forreign power against his Country, wherein he shall with others be taken prisoner, the others shall be proceeded against as Prisoners of War, when he shall be judg'd as a Traitor and Rebel, which he could not be, if he were not a Subject: and this not only in the case of an hostile action, and open attemt, but of the most secret conspiracy that comes to be discover'd. And if this be true, we may conclude it would be very unsafe to conduct our selves by what Mr. *Hobbes* (p. 105.) *finds by speculation, and deduction of Soveraign rights from the nature, need, and designs of men*. Surely this woful desertion, and defection in the cases above mention'd, which hath bin alwaies held criminal by all Law that hath bin current in any part of the World, receiv'd so much countenance and justification by Mr. *Hobbes* his Book, and more by his conversation, that *Cromwel* found the submission to those principles produc'd a submission to him, and the imaginary relation between Protection and Allegiance so positively proclam'd by him, prevail'd for many years to extinguish all visible fidelity to the King, whilst he perswaded many to take the Engagement as a thing lawful, and to become Subjects to the Usurper, as to their legitimate Soveraign; of which great service he could not abstain from bragging in a Pamphlet he set forth in that time, that he alone, and his doctrine, had prevail'd with many to submit to the Government, who would otherwise have disturb'd the public Peace, that is, to renounce their fidelity to their true Soveraign, and to be faithful to the Usurper.

It appears at last, why by his institution he would have the power, and security of his Soveraign, wholy and only to depend upon the Contracts, and Covenants which the people make one with another, to transfer all their rights to a third person (who shall be Soveraign) without entring into any Covenant with the Soveraign himself, which would have devested them of that liberty to disobey him, which they have reserv'd to themselves; or receiving any Covenant from him, which might have obliged him to have kept his promise to them; by which they might have had somewhat left to them which they might have called their own, which his institution will not bear, all such promises being void. But if he be so tender hearted, as to think himself oblig'd to observe all the promises, and make good all the Grants he hath made, by which he may be disabled to provide for their safety, which is the ground that hath made all those Grants and promises to be void, he hath granted him power to remedy all this, by (p. 114.) *directly renouncing, or transferring the Soveraignty to another: and that he might openly, and in plain terms renounce, or transfer it, he makes no doubt*; and then he saies, *if a Monarch shall relinquish the Soveraignty both for himself, and his heirs, his subjects return to the absolute liberty of nature. Because tho nature may declare who are his sons, and who are the neerest of his kin, yet it dependeth on his own will who shall be his Heir: and if he will have no Heir, There is no Soveraignty, or Subjection.* This seems the hardest condition for the poor Subject that he can be liable unto, that when he hath devested himself of all the right he had, only for his Soveraigns protection, that he may be redeem'd from the state of War and confusion that nature hath left him in, and hath paid so dear for that protection, it is left still in his Soveraigns power to withdraw that protection from him, to renounce his subjection, and without his consent to transfer the Soveraignty to another, to whom he hath no mind to be subject. One might have imagin'd that this new trick of transferring, and covenanting, had bin an universal remedy, that being once applied would for ever prevent the ill condition and confusion that nature had left us in, and that such a right would have bin constituted by it, that Soveraignty would never have fail'd to the Worlds end: and that when the subject can never retract, or avoid the bargain he hath made, how ill soever he likes it, or improve it by acquiring any better conditions in it, it shall notwithstanding be in the Soveraigns power without his consent, and it may be without his privity, in an instant to leave him without any protection, without any security, and as a prey to all who are to strong for him. This indeed is the greatest Prerogative that he hath conferr'd upon his Soveraign, when he had given him all that belongs to his Subjects, that when he is weary of Governing, he can destroy them, by leaving them to destroy one another. For Kings and Princes to resign and relinquish their Crown and Soveraignty, is no new transaction, nor it may be the better for being old. Some have left them out of Melancholy, and devotion, and when they have ceased to be Kings made themselves Monks, and repented the change of their conditions afterwards. Some out of weakness and bodily infirmities, have not bin able to sustain the fatigue that the well exercising the Government required, and therefore have desir'd to see those in the quiet possession of it, to whom it would of right belong when they were dead; and the more reasonably, if they forsaw any difficulties like to arise about their admission in those seasons; as *Charles* the fifth apprehended with reference to some of his dominions in *Italy*, if his Son *Philip* was not in possession of them, before his Brother *Ferdinando* came to be Emperor. Some Princes have bin so humorous, as upon the frowardness and refractoriness of their Subjects, and because they could not govern in that manner they had a mind to do, to abdicate the Government, and would have bin glad afterwards to have resumed it. And others have bin so wanton, as to relinquish their Crown because they did not like the Climate in which their Dominions lay, and only that they might live in a better Air, and enjoy the delights and pleasures of a more happy Situation. But all these generally never attemted it, or imagin'd they could do it, without the approbation and consent of their Subjects, which was allwaies desir'd, and yielded to, with great formality. And it is very strange that in those seasons of Abdication, which supposes a suspension of Soveraignty, especially in Elective Kingdoms, for in Hereditary the immortality of the King, who never dies, may make a difference, this invention of Mr. *Hobbes*, of transferring one anothers right, and covenanting with one another, hath never bin heard of; and tho the

Soveraignty is invested by election, the people have very little share in that election.

If Mr. *Hobbes* would have exercis'd his Talent in that spacious feild, as he might have don with more innocence, and, it may be, more success, and have undertaken *by his speculation and deduction of Soveraign rights, from the nature, need, and designs of men*, to prove that it is not in the just power of a Monarch to relinquish and renounce his Soveraignty, with what formality and consent soever; nor more in the autority and power of the King to abdicate and relinquish his Soveraignty over his people, then it is in the autority of the people to withdraw their submission and obedience from him; and that the practice of such renunciations, tho never very frequent, hath bin the original and introduction of that mischeivous doctrine sow'd amongst the people, of their having a co-ordinate power with the Soveraign, which will be much cherished by his new institution, since men are easily perswaded to believe, that they can mar what they can make, and may lawfully destroy what they create, that is, the work of their own hands; I say, if he would have laid out his reason upon that argument, he could have made it shine very plausibly, and might have made many Proselytes to his opinion; since many Learned men are so much in their judgment against that right of relinquishing and transferring in Princes, that they believe it to be the only cause wherein Subjects may lawfully take up defensive Arms, that they may continue Subjects, and to preserve their Subjection and obedience from being alien'd from him to whom it is due; and that no consent or concurrence can more make such an alienation lawful, then it can dissolve the bonds of Wedlock, and qualify both parties to make a new choice for themselves, that may be more grateful to them. But he thinks it to be more glory, to discover that to be right reason, which all other men find to be destructive to it, and (*pag.* 91.) *that the suddain and rough bustling in of a new truth*, will raise his fame, as it hath done that of many other Heretics before, and which he saies, *doth never break the peace, but only sometimes awake the War*; which, to use his own commendable expression, is (*pag.* 8.) *like handing of things from one to another, with many words making nothing understood.*

The Survey of Chapter 22.

I should pass over his two and twentieth Chapter of Systemes, Subject, Political, and Private, which is a title as difficult to be understood by a literal translation as most of those to any Chapter in *Suarez*; as few Congregations, when they meet in a Church to pay their devotions to God Almighty, do know that they are an irregular systeme: in which, besides vulgar notions well worded, every man will discover much of that which he calls signs of error, and misreckoning, to which (he saies) (pag. 116.) *all mankind is too prone*, and with which that Chapter abounds, and will require no confutation, but that I find, and wonder to find mention of Laws, and Letters Patents, Bodies Politic, and Corporations, as necessary institutions for the carrying on and advancement of Trade, which are so many limitations and restraints of the Soveraign power, and so many entanglements under Covenants and Promises, which as they are all declar'd to be void, it is in vain to mention. I did not think Mr. *Hobbes* had desir'd to establish trade, or any industry for the private accumulation of riches in his Common-wealth. For it is possible to imagine, that any Merchant will send out Ships to Sea, or make such a discovery of his Estate, if it may be either seized upon before it go's out, or together with the benefit of the return when it comes home? If trade be necessary to the good of a Nation, it must be founded upon the known right of Propriety, not as against other Subjects only, but against the Soveraign himself; otherwise trade is but a trap to take the collected wealth of particular men in a heap, and when it is brought into less room, to have it seized on, and confiscated by the omnipotent word of the King with less trouble, and more profit. And if any Laws, Letters Patents, Charters, or any other obligations or promises, can oblige the Soveraign power in these cases which refer to trade and forreign adventures, why should they not be equally valid for the securing all the other parts and relations of Propriety? However, whatsoever rigor Mr. *Hobbes* thinks fit to exercise upon the Nobility and Gentry of the Nation, he must give over all thoughts of trade, if he doth not better provide to secure his Merchants both of their liberty, and propriety.

It is a good observation, and an argument for the preference of Monarchy before any other form of Government, in that where the Government is popular, and the depressing the

interest and reputation of particular Subjects is an essential
policy of that Government, yet in the managing the affairs of
their Colonies and Provinces at a distance from them, they
chuse to commit the same to a single person, as they do the
Government and conduct of their Armies, which are to defend
their Government; which is a tacite implication, if not
confession, that in their own judgment they think the
Monarchical the best form of Government. But he might have
observ'd likewise, that in all those Monarchical Commissions,
at what distance soever, there are limits and bounds set, by
referring to instructions for the punctual observation and
performance of what that State or Government hath bin bound
by promise and contract to perform; which hath the same force
to evince, that the performance of promises and conditions, is
very consistent with Monarchical Government: for the hazards
that may arrive from thence may be as dangerous to that
Government if it be at a great distance, as upon any
supposition whatsoever, yet is never left to the discretion of a
Governor.

If is a wonderful latitude that Mr. *Hobbes* leaves to all his
Subjects, and contradictory to all the moral precepts given to
the World, and to all the notions of Justice, that he who hath
his private interest depending, and to be debated and judg'd
before any Judicatory, may make as many Friends as he can
amongst those Judges, even by giving them Mony; as if, tho it
be a crime in a Judg to be corrupt, the person who corrupts him
may be innocent, because he thinks his own cause just, and
desires to buy justice for Mony which cannot be got without it;
and so the grossest and most powerful Bribery shall be
introduc'd, to work upon the weakness and poverty, and
corruption of a Judg, because the party thinks his cause to be
just, and chuses rather to depend upon the affection of his Judg
whom he hath corrupted, then upon the integrity of his cause,
and the justice of the Law. But he doth not profess to be a strict
Casuist; nor can be a good observer of the Rules of moral
honesty, who believes that he may induce another to commit a
great Sin, and remain innocent himself. Nor is he in truth a
competent Judg of the most enormous crimes, when he reckons
(pag. *56.*) *Theft, Adultery, Sodomy, and any other vice that
may be taken for an effect of power, or a cause of pleasure,* to
be of such a Nature, as amongst men are taken to be against
Law, rather then against Honor.

The Survey of Chapter 23.

I should with as little trouble have passed by his twenty third Chapter of his Public Ministers, and the fanciful Similes contin'd therein, not thinking it of much importance what public or private Ministers he makes for such a Soveraignty as he hath instituted; but that I observe him in this place (as most luxurious Fancies use to do) demolishing and pulling down, what he had with great care and vigilance erected and establish'd as undeniable truth before. And whereas he hath in his eighteenth Chapter, (*pag.* 91) pronounced *the right of Judicatory, of hearing and deciding all Controversies which concern Law, either Civil or Natural, or concerning Fact*, to be inseparably annexed to the Soveraignty, and incapable of being aliened and transferred by him; and afterwards declares, *That the Judgments given by Judges qualified, and commission'd by him to that purpose, are his own proper Judgments, and to be regarded as such*, which is a truth generally confess'd; in this Chapter, against all practice and all reason, he degrades him from at least half that Power, and fancies a Judg to be such a party, that if the Litigant be not pleased with the opinion of his Judg in matter of Law, or matter of Fact, he may therefore (*pag.* 125.) (*because they are both subjects to the Soveraign*) appeal from his Judg, and ought to be tried before an other: for tho the Soveraign may hear and determine the Cause himself if he please, yet if he will appoint another to be Judg, it must be such a one as they shall both agree upon: for as the Complainant hath already made choice of his own Judg, so the Defendant must be allow'd to except against such of his Judges, whose interest maketh him suspect them; which was never heard of before this Institution, and the consequence of it will best appear by an instance to be very ridiculous. Let us suppose that an Information were preferr'd in the Kings Bench (as it may well be) against Mr. *Hobbes*, for writing and publishing such a seditious Book against the establish'd Government of Church and State, as his *Leviathan* is; because the Soveraign Judg will not hear and determine this himself, but refers it those Judges who are appointed and commission'd by him to examine and punish Crimes of such a nature, would it be reasonable that Mr. *Hobbes* should except against his Judges, because by their knowing the Law he may suspect them, and refuse to be tri'd before any but those whom he shall agree upon? and (*pag.* 125.) *can those be the properties of just and rational Judicature?* He hath forgotten, that before he erected his Soveraignty, when there could be no Judicature, he saies, (*pag.* 78.) *it is of the Law of Nature, That they who are at Controversie, submit their right to the judgment of an Arbitrator*; there indeed for want of Judicature, there was a necessity of a mutual consent, without which no man could take upon him to be an arbitrator. If a man hath a Suit upon matter of Title or Interest with a Judg, notwithstanding that he is sworn to do right, he is so far from being bound to bring his Action before that Judg, that he may chuse whether it shall depend in that Court of which that Judg is a Member, tho the major part be unconcern'd, but may have his Right tried in another Court: but if he should have any part in the choice of his own Judg, especially if he be criminal, Justice would be well administred. Himself acknowledges, that the judgement of such Judges, is the judgment of the Soveraign; and a greater Person then the Soveraign hath given a fair warning to those Judges; *Take heed what ye do, for ye judg not for man, but for the Lord, who is with you in the judgment* 2. Chron. As it is the Kings judgment, he will punish it severely if it be corrupt; and if he cannot discover it to be corrupt, for want of complaint, or want of evidence, God will punish it because it was his judgment: a corrupt Judg, of all guilty persons, can never escape punishment.

I am very glad that Mr. *Hobbes* is pleas'd with any part of the administration of Justice in his own Country (which he would hardly like if he were exposed to it:) and he might have observ'd that great Priviledg of the Lords in *England*, of being tried in all capital Crimes by their Peers, by Men of their own quality and condition, to be a greater Priviledg then the Nobility of any Nation in *Europe* enjoy. The Grandees of *Spain*, and the Dukes, and Peers, and Mareschals of *France*, in those Transgressions undergo the same forms of Justice, and are tried before the same Judges, as the meanest Peasant is for the like or the same Crime: and tho he calls it, and saies it hath bin ever acknowledg'd as a Priviledg of Favor, yet they look upon it as a Priviledg of Right, of which they cannot be deprived by the Word and Autority of the King. And it may be he would be hardly able to bring this Priviledg under his original Institution of Government; since probably men being then all equal, they would never have consented to such a difference, rather then equality, in the form of Justice that was to be exercis'd towards them; and he values it too lightly, who thinks it can be taken from them by any Arbitrary Power. I cannot comprehend what Mr. *Hobbes*'s meaning is, in making an Embassador sent from his Prince, to congratulate, or condole, or to assist at a Solemnity, to be but a private Person, because he saies, (*pag.* 126.) *the business is private, and belonging to him in his natural capacity*: whereas, his being sent Embassador, and having in the performance of his Office of congratulating or condoling, or in his assistance at the Solemnity, the respect shew'd to him, and the priviledg and precedence of the Person of his Master, he cannot but be a public Person. Nor can an Embassador come to be but a private Person any other way, then by presuming to negotiate some unlawful thing, which he is not warranted by his Commission to do; and even in that case he expects to be treated as a public Person, as well by the security that Prince gave him by his Reception, as by the autority of the Prince who sent him, and expects to be sent to, and tried before his own Master: which depends much upon the nature and circumstances of the Transgression. But I wonder how Mr. *Hobbes* could bring the Rights and Priviledges of Embassadors under his disquisition, since they cannot depend upon his Institution: for they neither do nor can proceed from the Covenants, or Contracts, or transferring of Rights between private persons; but he must make a new Institution for Soveraigns, in which he will hardly be able to preserve them without some Covenants, which he hitherto so much abhors.

The Survey of Chapter 24.

It is the custom and delight that Mr. *Hobbes* takes in the frequent repeting, almost in every Chapter, the lewd principles in his Institution, with some variety of pleasant expressions and instances, which he would have understood to add new vigor to his former Arguments, that obliges me by Tautologies to put the Reader in mind of what I have said before, and to repete the same that hath bin said; and so I must say again upon this Chapter of the nutrition and procreation of a Common-wealth, that he hath propos'd a very ungracious method to himself in forming his Government, by assigning a greater power and autority to his Soveraign, then any honest Magistrate desires, or will ever exercise, or can think himself secure in; and such a liberty and property to the Subject, as they can take no delight in, and consequently can never wish well to that Government, under which they shall enjoy no more. Nor will they ever believe themselves to be in possession of liberty or plenty, when it is in the power of any one man to dispossess them of both, or either, at his good will and pleasure, without any violation of any Justice that they can resort to, or complain of. It is a very uncomfortable Propriety that any man can have in his Lands and Goods, because his Neighbour cannot take them from him, if his Prince can justly take them from him, and give them to his Neighbour. Princes have their particular Affections and Inclinations which sway them as much as other men, and are prevail'd upon by the same strong motives and impulsions; and if they may take away all from those they do not like, and as much as they think fit from those they like less, to give to those they love, and to such as they like better, there can be no valuable propriety in any body but the Soveraign alone: and when it is once found to be in him alone, he will not be long able to defend his own Propriety, or his own Soveraignty. It is *Machiavels* exception against the entertaining of forreign Forces, that they are only mercenary, and therefore indifferent in their affections which party wins or loses; and no doubt those Soldiers fight most resolutely, who fight to defend their own. And surely they who have nothing of their own to lose but their lives, are as apt to throw those away where they should not, as where they should be exposed; and it is the usual Artifice in all Seditions, for the Leaders and Promoters of them, to perswade the People, that the tendency and consequence of such and such actions don by the Magistrate, extends to the depriving them of all their propriety, the jealousie of which hurries them into all those acts of rage and despair, which prove so fatal to Kingdoms. And there was never yet a wise and fortunate Prince, who hath not enervated those Machinations, by all the professions, and all the vindications of that Propriety, which they are so vigilant to preserve and defend. And therefore it is a wonderful preposterous foundation to support a Government, to declare that the Subject hath no propriety in any thing that excludes the Soveraign from a right of disposing it; and it may be easily believ'd, that there is not one Prince in *Europe*, I mean that is civilz'd (for of the absolute power of the Great Turk, from whence Mr. *Hobbes* hath borrowed his

Model, we shall have occasion to discourse in another place) would be able to retain his Soveraignty one whole year, after he should declare, as Mr. *Hobbes* doth, that his Subjects have no propriety in any thing they possess, but that he may dispose of all they have. For tho they do too often invade that propriety, and take somewhat from them that is not their own, they bear it better under the notion of oppression and rapine, and as they look upon it as the effect of some powerful Subjects evil advice (which will in time be discover'd, and reform'd by the justice of the Prince, as hath often fallen out) then they would ever do under a claim of right, that could justly take away all they have, because it is not the subjects but their own. And if Mr. *Hobbes* had taken the pains, and known where to have bin inform'd of the Proceedings and Transactions of *William the Conqueror*, he would have found cause to believe, that that great King did very dexterously endeavor, from the time that he was assured that his Possession would not be disturb'd, to devest himself of the Title of a Conqueror, and made his Legal Claim to what he had got by the Will of *Edward the Confessor*, whose Name was pretious to the Nation, and who was known to have a great Friendship for that Prince, who had now recover'd what had bin his. And he knew so well the ill consequence which must attend the very imagination that the Nation had lost its Propriety, that he made hast to grant them an assurance, that they should still enjoy all the benefits and priviledges which were due to them by their own Laws and Customs, by which they should be still govern'd, as they were during that Kings whole Reign, who had enough of the unquestionable Demesnes and Lands belonging to the Crown, of which he was then possessed without a Rival, and belonging to those great Men who had perish'd with their Posterity in the Battel with *Harold*, to distribute to those who had born such shares, and run such hazards in his prosperous adventure. And those Laws and Customs which were before the Conquest, are the same which the Nation and Kingdom have been since govern'd by to this day, with the addition of those Statutes and Acts of Parliament, which are the Laws of the successive Kings, with which they have gratifi'd their Subjects, in providing such new security for them, and advantages to the public, as upon the experience and observation of the Ages and Times when they were made, contributed to the honor and glory of the King, as well as the happiness of the People; many of which are but the Copies and Transcripts of antient Land-marks, making the Characters more plain and legible of what had bin practic'd and understood in the preceding Ages, and the observation whereof are of the same profit and convenience to King and People.

Such were the Laws in *Tullies* time, which Mr. *Hobbes* wonderfully cites, to prove that which *Tully* never heard of, and which indeed is quite contrary to the end of his Discourse (*pag.* 127.) Is it possible that *Tully* could ever have said, *Let the Civil Law be once abandoned, or but negligently guarded (not to say oppressed) and there is nothing that any man can be sure to receive from his ancestor, or to leave to his children?* and again, *take away the Civil Law, and no man knows what is his own, and what another mans?* I say, he could never have mention'd and insisted upon this grand security of man-kind, if he had understood the Law to be nothing but the breath of the Soveraign, who could grant, and dissolve, or repeal this Law, with the speaking a word that his will or fancy dictates to him. How can any man receive from his Ancestor, or leave to his Children, if he be not sure that his Ancestor had, and that his Children shall have a propriety? It was the importance of, and delight in this propriety, that produc'd that happy and beneficial agreement between the Soveraign power and the naked Subject, which is mention'd before; that introduc'd the beauty of Building, and the cultivating the Earth by Art as well as Industry, by securing men, that they and their Children should dwell in the Houses they were at the charge to build, and that they should reap the harvest of those Lands which they had taken the pains to sow. Whatsoever is of Civility and good Manners, all that is of Art anbd Beauty, or of real and solid Wealth in the World, is the product of this paction, and the child of beloved Propriety; and they who would strangle this Issue, desire to demolish all Buildings, eradicate all Plantations, to make the Earth barren, and man-kind to live again in Tents, and nurish his Cattle by successive marches into those Fields where the grass grows. Nothing but the joy in Propriety reduc'd us from this barbarity; and nothing but security in the same, can preserve us from returning into it again. Nor will any man receive so great prejudice and damage by this return, as the Kings and Princes themselves, who had a very ample recompence which they still enjoy, by dividing their unprofitable propriety with their Subjects, having ever since receiv'd much more profit from the propriety in the hands of the Subjects, then they did when it was in their own, or then they do from that which they reserv'd to themselves; and they continue to have the more, or less upon a true account, as this paction is the more or less exactly observ'd and compli'd with.

Mr. *Hobbes* is much mistaken in his Historical conclusions, as for the most part he uses to be, when he saies, (*pag.* 129) that the *Conqueror, and his successors, have alwaies laid arbitrary Taxes on all Subjects Lands*; except he calls what hath bin don by the free consent of the Subject, which is according to the paction, to be the arbitrary Tax of the Soveraign, because the Law is the stamp of his own Royal Autority. And if such arbitrary Taxes have in truth at any time bin laid upon the Subjects, he might have observ'd (for somtimes it hath bin don) that the Soveraign hath receiv'd much more damage then profit by it, and the Kingdom bin in a worse state of security then it was before. Nor can any argument be made from the glory and prosperity of some Crowns, which have somtimes exercis'd that arbitrary Power, and reduc'd the Rules they ought to govern by, to the standard of their own Will; which yet they have don with such formality, as implies the consent of their Subjects, tho they dare not but consent. It hath bin too frequently seen too, that the hurt and wounded patience of the People, hath, when it may be it was least apprehended, redeem'd themselves (for *læsa patientia est furor*) by as unwarrantable Rebellion from unwarrantable Oppression, or out of contemt of their own ruin, because they have so little comfort in their preservation, have obstinately refused to give any assistance to their Soveraign when he hath real need of it, because he hath wantonly extorted it from them when he had no need. And then men pay too dear for their want of providence, and find too late, that the neglect of Justice is an infallible underminer, how undiscern'd soever, of that security which their Policy would raise for themselves, in the place of that which Wisdom and Justice had provided for them. I agree, that it being impossible to fore-see what the expences which a Soveraign may be put to will amount to, it is as impossible by land, or otherwise to set aside such a proportion as is necessary; but those extraordinary occasions must be supplied by such extraordinary waies, and with those formalities which the Soveraign obliges himself to observe; by observing whereof, much less inconvenience shall befall Him or the Public, then by cancelling those Laws which establish Propriety.

   If Mr. *Hobbes* had not bin a professed Enemy to Greek and Latine Sentences, as an Argument of indigestion, when they come up again unchewed and unchanged, he might have learn'd from *Seneca*, who understood, and felt the utmost extent of an absolute Soveraignty, and had a shrewd fore-sight what the end of it would be, how the propriety of the Subject might well consist with the power of the Prince: *Jure civili* (saiest he) *omnia Regis suns, & tamen illa quorum ad Regem pertinet universa possessio, in singulos dominos descripta sunt, & unaquæque res habet possessorem suum. Itaque dare Regi, & domum, & manicipium, & pecuniam possumus, neo donare illi de suo dicimur. Ad Reges enim potestas omnium pertinet, ad singulos proprietas.* And that Prince who thinks his power so great, that his Subjects have nothing to give him, will be very unhappy if he hath ever need of their hands, or their hearts.

The Survey of Chapter 25.

When Mr. *Hobbes* hath erected such a Soveraign, and instituted such a People, that the one may say and do whatsoever he finds convenient for his purpose, and the other must neither say or do any thing that may displease him; the consideration of what, and how counsel should be given under such a Government, can require very little deliberation. And the truth is, the discourse of this Chapter, with the differences between Command and Counsel, is more vulgar and pedantic then he is usually guilty of; and it is easie to be observ'd, that in his description of the office of a Counsellor, and of the ability of counselling, (*pag.* 134.) that it *proceeds from experience and long study, and that it requires great knowledg of the disposition of man-kind, of the rights of Government, and of the nature of Equity, Law, Justice, and Honor, not to be attain'd without study: and of the strengths, commodities, places both of their own Country and their Neighbors; and also of the inclinations and designs of all Nations that may any way annoy them: and this,* he saies, *is not attained without much Experience*; he makes so lively a representation of that universal understanding, which he would be thought to be possessed with, that he could not be without hope that

Cromwell would think him worthy to be a Counsellor, who had given him such an earnest that he would serve him with success, and without hesitation. Yet I see no reason (if to ask Counsel of another, is to permit him to give such Counsel as he shall think best; and if it be the Office of a Counsellor, when an Action comes into deliberation, to make manifest the consequence of it in such a manner, as he that is counselled may be truly and euidently inform'd) why he is so very angry with those two words, *exhort* and *dehort*, as to brand those who use either, with the style of corruption, and being brib'd by their own interest; since it is very agreeable to the faith and integrity of a Counsellor, to perswade him that asks his advice to do that which he thinks best to be don, and to disswade him from doing that which he thinks to be mischievous, which is to exhort and dehort; and the examples of Persons, and the autority of Books, may be pertinently applied to either: since few accidents fall out in States and Empires, which have not in former times happened in such conjunctures, and then if the same hath bin faithfully represented to posterity, with all the circumstances and successes, which is the natural end of all good Histories to transmit, nothing can more properly be reflected on, or bring clearer light to the present difficulties in debate, then the memory of what was upon those occasions don fortunatly, or unhappily left undon, which surely cannot but introduce useful and pertinent Reflexions into the consultation. And it is not easie to comprehend what that great ability is, which his Counsellor is to attain to by long study, and cannot be attain'd without, if that study be not to be conversant with Books, and if neither the examples in, or autority of Books be in any degree to be consider'd. Nor are such expressions which may move the affections or passions of him who asks Counsel, or of those who are to give it, repugnant to the office of a Counsellor, since the end of Counsel is to lead men to chuse that which is good, and avoid that which is worse; and he to whom the Counsel is given, will best judg whether it tends to others ends rather then his own, and will value it accordingly. And he is much a better Counsellor, who by his experience and observation of the nature and humor of the People who are to be govern'd, and by his knowledg of the Laws and Rules by which they ought to be govern'd, gives advice what ought to be don, then he who from his speculative knowledg of man-kind, and of the Rights of Government, and of the nature of Equity and Honor, attain'd with much study, would erect an Engine of Government by the rules of Geometry, more infallible then Experience can ever find out.

I am not willing now, or at any time, to accompany him in his sallies which he makes into the Scriptures, and which he alwaies handles, as if his Soveraign-power had not yet declared it to be the word of God; and to illustrate now his Distinctions, and the difference between Command and Counsel, he thinks fit to fetch instances from thence, *Have no other Gods but me, Make to thy self no graven Image*, &c he saies, (*pag. 133.*) *are commands, because the reason for which we are to obey them, is drawn from the will of God our King, whom we are obliged to obey:* but these words, *Repent, and be baptized in the name of Jesus, are Counsel, because the reason why we should do so, tendeth not to any benefit of God Almighty, who shall be still King in what manner soever we rebel, but of our selves, who have no other means of avoiding the punishment hanging over us for our sins*; as if the latter were not drawn from the will of God as much as the former, or as if the former tended more to the benefit of God then the latter. An ordinary Grammarian, without any insight in Geometry, would have thought them equally to be commands: But Mr. *Hobbes* will have his Readers of another talent in their understanding, and another subjection to his dictates.

The Survey of Chapter 26.

However Mr. *Hobbes* enjoines other Judges to retract the judgments they have given when contrary to reason, upon what autority or president soever they have pronounced them, yet he holds himself oblig'd still *tueri opus*, to justify all he hath said; therefore we have reason to expect, that to support his own notions of Liberty and Propriety, contrary to the notions of all other men, he must introduce a notion of Law, contrary to what the world hath ever yet had of it. And it would be answer enough, and it may be the fittest that can be given to this Chapter, to say, that he hath erected a Law, contrary and destructive to all the Law, that is acknowled'g and establish'd in any Monarchy or Republic that is Christian; and in this he hopes to secure himself by his accustomed method of definition, and defines, that Civil Law (which is a term we do not dislike) is to every Subject those Rules which the Common-wealth hath commanded him by word, writing, or other sufficient sign of the Will to make use of for the distinction of right, in which he saies there is nothing that is not at first sight evident, that is to say of what is contrary, and what is not contrary to the Rule. From which definition his first deduction is, that the Soveraign is the Sole Legislator, and that himself is not subject to Laws, because he can make, and repeal them: which in truth is no necessary deduction from his own definition; for it doth not follow from thence, tho he makes them Rules only for Subjects, that the Soveraign hath the sole power to repeal them; but the true definition of a Law is, that it is to every Subject the rule which the Common-wealth hath commanded him by word, writing, or other sufficient sign of the Will made, and publish'd in that form and manner, as is accustomed in that Common-wealth to make use of for the distinction of right, that is to say, of what is contrary, and what is not to the Rule? and from this definition, no such deduction can be made, since the form of making and repealing Laws is stated, and agreed upon in all Common-wealths.

The opinions and judgments which are found in the Books of eminent Lawyers, cannot be answer'd, and controuled by Mr. *Hobbes* his wonder, since the men who know least are apt to wonder most; and men will with more justice wonder, whether he comes by the Prerogative to controul the Laws and Government establish'd in this, and that Kingdom, without so much as considering what is Law here or there, but by the general notions he hath of Law; and what it is by his long study, and much cogitation. And it is a strange definition of Law, to make it like his propriety, to be of concernment only between Subject and Subject, without any relation of security as to the Soveraign, whom he exempts from any observation of them, and invests with autority by repealing those which trouble him, when he thinks fit, to free himself from the observation thereof, and by making new: and consequently he saies, he was free before, for he is free that can be free when he will. The instance he gives for his wonder, and displeasure against the Books of the Eminent Lawyers, is, that they say, that the Common Law hath no controuler but the Parliament, that is, that the Common Law cannot be chang'd or alter'd but by Act of Parliament, which is the Municipal Law of the

Kingdom. Now methinks if that be the judgment of Eminent Lawyers, Mr. *Hobbes* should be so modest as to believe it to be true, till he hears others as Eminent Lawyers declare the contrary: for by his instance, he hath brought it now only to relate to the Law of *England*, and then methinks he should be easily perswaded, that the Eminent Lawyers of *England* do know best whether the Law be so, or no. I do not wish that Mr. *Hobbes* should be convinc'd by a judgment of that Law upon himself, which would be very severe, if he should be accused for declaring, that the King alone hath power to alter the descents and inheritances of the Kingdom; and whereas the Common Law saies the Eldest shall inherit, the King by his own Edict may declare, and order, that the younger Son shall inherit: or for averring, and publishing, that the King by his own autority can repeal and dissolve all Laws, and justly take away all they have from his Subjects; I say, if the judgment of Law was pronounc'd upon him for this Seditious Discourse, he would hardly perswade the World, that he understood what the Law of *England* is, better then the Judges who condemn'd him, or that he was wary enough to set up a *jus vagum* and *incognitum* of his own, to controul the estblish'd Government of his own Country. He saies the Soveraign is the only Legislator: and I will not contradict him in that. It is the Soveraign stamp, and Royal consent, and that alone, that gives life, and being, and title of Laws, to that which was before but counsel and advice: and no such constitution of his can be repeal'd and made void, but in the same manner, and with his consent. But we say, that he may prescribe or consent to such a method in the form, and making these Laws, that being once made for him, he cannot but in the same form repeal, or alter them; and he is oblig'd by the Law of justice to observe and perform this contract, and he cannot break it, or absolve himself from the observation of it, without violation of justice: and any farther obligation upon him then of justice, I discourse not of. For the better cleering of this to that kind of reason by which Mr. *Hobbes* is swai'd, let us suppose this Soveraignty to reside, and be fix'd in an assembly of men; in which kind of Government it is possible to find more marks and foot-steps of such a deputing, and assigning of interests, as Mr. *Hobbes* is full of, then we can possibly imagine in the original institution of Monarchy. If the soveraign power be deputed into the hands of fifteen, and any vacant place to be suppli'd by the same

Autority that made choice of the first fifteen, may there not at that time of the election certain Rules be prescrib'd (I do not say conditions) for the better exercise of that Soveraign power: and by the accepting the power thus explain'd, doth not the Soveraign, tho there should be no Oath administered for the observation thereof, which is a circumstance admitted by most Monarchy, tacitly covenant that he will observe those Rules? and if he do's willfully decline those Rules, doth he not break the trust reposed in him? I do not say forfeit the trust, as if the Soveraignty were at an end, but break that trust, violate that justice he should observe? If the Soveraign power of fifteen, should raise an imposition for the defence of the Common-wealth, if they should appoint this whole imposition to be paid only by those whose names are *Thomas* (when *Thomas* was before in no more prejudice with the Common-wealth, then any other appellation in Baptism) may not this inequality be call'd a violation of Justice, and a breach of trust, since it cannot be suppos'd that such an irregular autority was ever committed to any man, or men by any deputation? Of the Prerogative of necessity to swerve from Rules prescrib'd, or to violate Laws tho sworn to, shall be spoken to in its due time.

It needs not be suppos'd, but must be confess'd, that the Laws of every Country, contain more in them concerning the rights of the Soveraign, and the common administration of Justice to the people, then can be known to, and understood by the person of the Soveraign, and he can as well fight all his Battels with his own hand and sword, as determine all causes of right by his own tongue and understanding. The consequence of any confusion which Mr. *Hobbes* can suppose, would not be more pernicious, then that which would follow the blowing away all these maximes of the Law, if the Kings breath were strong enough to do it. It is a maxime in the Law (as is said before) that the eldest Son shall inherit, and that if three or four Females are heirs, the inheritance shall be equally divided between them. Doth Mr. *Hobbes* believe that the word of the King hath power to change this course, and to appoint that all the Sons shall divide the Estate, and the Eldest Daughter inherit alone? and must not all the confusion imaginable attend such a mutation? All Governments subsist and are establish'd by firmness and constancy, by every mans knowing what is his right to enjoy, and what is his duty to do: and it is a wonderful method to make this Government more perfect, and more durable, by introducing such an incertainty, that no man shall know what he is to do, nor what he is to suffer, but that he who is Soveraign to morrow, may cancel, and dissolve all that was don or consented to by the Soveraign who was yesterday, or by himself as often as he changes his mind. It is the Kings Office to cause his Laws to be executed, and to compel his Subjects to yield obedience to them, and in order thereunto, to make choice of Learn'd Judges to interpret those Lawes, and to declare the intention of them, who (pag. 140.) *by an artificial perfection of reason gotten by long study, and experience in the Law*, must be understood to be more competent for that determination, then Mr. *Hobbes* can be for the alteration of Law and Government, by the artificial reason he hath attain'd to by long study of Arithmetic and Geometry.

No Eminent Lawyer hath ever said that the two Arms of a Common-wealth are Force and Justice, the first whereof is in the King, the other deposited in the hands of the Parliament; but all Lawyers know, that they are equally deposited in the hands of the King, and that all justice is administred by him, and in his name: and all men acknowledg that all the Laws are his Laws; his consent and autority only giving the power and name of a Law, what concurrence, or formality soever hath contributed towards it: the question only is, whether he can repeal, or vacate such a Law, without the same concurrence and formality. And methinks the instance he makes of a Princes (*pag.* 139.) *subduing an other people, and consenting that they shall live, and be govern'd according to those Laws under which they were born, and by which they were formerly govern'd*, should manifest to him the contrary. For tho it be confess'd, that those old Laws become new by this consent of his, the Laws of the Legislator, that is of that Soveraign who indulges the use of them; yet he cannot say that he can by his word vacate and repeal those Laws, and his own concession, without dissolving all the ligaments of Government, and without the violation of faith, which himself confesses to be against the Law of Nature.

Notwithstanding that *the Law is reason*, and (pag. 139.) *not the letter, but that which is according to the intention of the Legislator (that is of the Soveraign) is the law*, yet when there is any difficulty in the understanding the Law, the interpretation thereof may reasonably belong to Learn'd Judges, who by their education, and the testimony of their known abilities before they are made Judges, and by their Oaths to judg according to Right, are the most competent to explain those difficulties, which no Soveraign as Soveraign can be presum'd to understand or comprehend. And the judgments and decisions those Judges make, are the judgements of the Soveraigns, who have qualified them to be Judges, and who are to pronounce their sentence according to the reason of the Law, not the reason of the Soveraign. And therefore Mr. *Hobbes* would make a very ignorant Judg, when he would not have him versed in the study of the Laws, but only a man of good natural reason, and of a right understanding of the Law of Nature; and yet he saies, (pag. 154.) *that no man will pretend to the knowledg of right and wrong without much study.* And if that power of interpretation of Law be vested in the person of the Soveraign, he may in a moment overthrow all the Law; which is evident enough by his own instances, if, to use his own expressions, *his understanding were not dazled by the flame of his passions.* For to what purpose is all the distinction and division of Laws into human and divine, into natural and moral, into distributive and penal, when they may be all vacated, and made null by the word, or perverted by the interpretation of the Soveraign? To what purpose is a penalty of five shllings put upon such an action, if the Soveraign may make him who doth that action, by his interpretation, or omnipotence, to pay five hundred pounds? Nor by his rule, is his ador'd Law of Nature of any force, which he saies, (pag. 144.) *is the Law of God immutable and eternal, nay Heaven and Earth shall pass away, but not one title of the Law of Nature shall pass, for it is the eternal Law of God*; He, I say, hath as much subjected that to the arbitrary power and discretion of his Soveraign, as he hath don the Liberty and property of the Subject; for he saies, (pag. 138.) *the Law of Nature is a part of the Civil Law in all Common-wealths in the World,* and that tho *it be naturally reasonable, yet it is by the Soveraign power that it is Law,* and he saies likewise, *that all Laws written, and unwritten, and the Law of Nature it self, have need of interpretation*: and then he makes his supreme Soveraign the only legitimate interpreter. So that he hath the Law of Nature as much in his power, as under his jurisdiction, as any other part of the Civil Law: and yet he confesses his subject is not bound to pay obedience to any thing that his Soveraign enjoins against the Law of Nature. In such Labyrinths men entangle themselves, who obstinately engage in opinions relating to a science they do not understand; nor was it possible for him to extend the Prerogative of his Soveraign to such an illimited greatness, without making some invasion upon the Prerogative of God himself. I believe every man who reads Mr. *Hobbes*, observes that when he entangles himself in the Laws of *England*, and affects to be more learned in them then the Chief Justice *Cook*, the natural sharpness and vigor of his reason is more flat and insipid then upon other arguments, and he makes deductions which have no coherence, involves himself in the terms without comprehending the matter, concludes the Law saies that which it do's not say, and that the Law hath made no provision in cases which are amply provided for, and in a word loses himself in a mist of words that render him less intelligible then at other times. Nor hath he better luck, when out of Justinians Institutions, he would make a parallel between the Imperial Laws and the Laws of *England*, and resolves that the Decrees of the Common People, which were put to the question by the Tribune, and had the force of Laws, were like the Orders of the House of Commonns in *England*; whereas no Orders made by a House of Commons in *England*, are of any validity or force, or receive any submission longer then that House of Commons continues: and if any order made by them be against any Law or Statute, it is void when it is made, and receives no obedience. Indeed when Mr. *Hobbes* published his *Leviathan*, he might have said that it had the autority and power of the Emperor, or of the whole People of *Rome*, and which would have lasted till this time, if he had bin believ'd, and his doctrine could have bin supported by him, or them for whom it was provided.

Probably Mr. *Hobbes* did take delight in being thought to confute a great Lawyer in the Common Law of *England*: tis certain he hath bin transported to slight usage of him, by that delight or some like passion, more then by the defect of reason in that which he would contradict. He saies tis against the Law of Nature to punish the innocent; that he is innocent that acquits himself judicially, & is acknowledg'd for innocent by the Judg: and yet he saies, when a man is accus'd of a Capital crime, and seeing the power of the Enemy, and the frequent corruption of Judges, runs away for fear of the effect, yet being taken and brought to Tryal, maketh it appear that he was not guilty of the crime, and is acquitted thereof, however is condemn'd to lose his goods, this he saies, is a manifest condemnation of the innocent. He confesses afterwards, that the Law may forbid an innocent man to fly, and that he may be punished for flying; but he thinks it very unreasonable, that flying for fear of injury, should be taken for presumtion of guilt, whereas it is taken only for the guilt of flying, when he is declar'd innocent for the other. And methinks he confesseth, that a man, who must know his own innocence better then any body else, and knows that he must lose his Goods if he flies his trial, hath no reason to complain, if after he be cleer'd from the crime, he be condemned to lose his goods, which he knew he must lose when he fled; and therefore tho he be judicially acquitted for the crime, he is not innocent, but as judicially condemned to lose his goods for his guilt in flying, the Law and penalty of flying being known to him, whether written, or not written, as well as the Law against the crime was. To his other dictates of the Office of a Judg, that he needs not be learn'd in the Laws, because he shall be told by the Soveraign what judgment he shall give; and of the Laws of *England*, that the Jury is Judg of the Law, as well as of the fact, there needs no more be said, then that he is not inform'd, nor understands what he delivers, and whether his notions of the divine positive Law be more agreeable to truth, will be examin'd hereafter.

The Survey of Chapter 27.

(*Pag.* 151.) *That to be delighted in the imagination of being possessed of another mans Wife, or Goods, is no breach of the Law that saies, Thou shalt not covet: that the pleasure a man may have in imagining the death of him from whose life he expects nothing but damage and displeasure, is no sin: That to be pleas'd in the fiction of that which would please a man if it were real, is a passion so adherent to the nature of man, and every other living creature, as to make it a sin, were to make a sin of being a man,* is a Body of Mr. *Hobbes*'s Divinity, so contrary to that of our Savior and his Apostles, that I shall without any enlargement leave it to all men to consider, which of them they think most fit to believe and follow. Yet methinks he gives some encouragement to those who might expect Justice against him, by his own judgment (*pag.* 152.) upon the man that *comes from the* Indies *hither, and perswades men here to receive a new Religion, or teach them any thing that tends to disobedience to the Laws of this Country: tho he be*

*never so well perswaded of the truth of what he teacheth, he
commits a crime, and may be justly punished, not only because
his Doctrine is false, but because he do's that which he would
not approve in another, that coming from hence should
endeavor to alter Religion there.* And how far this Declaration
of his own judgment, may operate to his own condemnation,
and to the condemnation of most of his Doctrines in his
Leviathan, which are so contrary to all the Laws established in
his Country, he should have don well to have considered
before he committed the transgression; for he doth acknowledg, that in a Common-wealth, where by the negligence
or unskilfulness of Governors & Teachers, false Doctrines are
by time generally receiv'd, the contrary truths may be generally
offensive; and prudent men are seldom guilty of doing any
thing, or least when it is in their own election to do it or not to
do it, which they foresee will be offensive to the Government,
or Governors whom they are subject to and must live under;
especially when he confesses, *(pag. 91.) that tho the most
sudain and rough bustling in of a new truth that can be, do's
never break the peace, yet it doth sometimes wake the war;* and
if the secure and sound sleep of Peace be once broken, and that
fierce and brutish Tyger War is awakened, when, or how he
will be lulled into a new sleep, the wisest Magistrate cannot
fore-tell, and therefore will with the more vigilance discountenance and suppress such bustlers, who impudently make their
way with their elbows into modest company, to dispose them
to suspect, and then to censure the wisdom of their Fore-
fathers, for having bin swaied by their own illiterate experience, so as to prefer it before the cleer reason of thinking, and
Learned Men, who by cogitation have found a surer way for
their security: and there cannot be a more certain Expedient
found out for the dissolving the peace of any Nation, how
firmly soever establish'd, then by giving leave, or permitting
men of parts and unrestrained fancy, to examine the constitution of the Government both Ecclesiastical and Civil, and to
vent and publish what their wit and inventions may suggest to
them, upon or against the same, which would expose the
gravity and wisdom of all Government, the infallibility of
Scripture, and the Omnipotence of God himself, by their light
and scurrilous questions and instances, to the mirth and
contemt of all men, who are without an awful veneration for
either; of which there needs not be a more convincing evidence,

then the presumption of Mr. *Hobbes* throughout his *Leviathan*, of which it will not be possible not to give some in the progress we shall make.

He is over subtle in his Distinction, that every crime is a sin, but not every sin a crime; that from the relation of sin to the Law, and of crime to the Civil Law, may be inferr'd, that where the Law ceaseth, sin ceaseth, that the Civil Law ceasing, crimes cease; and yet that violation of Covenants, Ingratitude, Arrogance, can never cease to be sin, yet are no crimes, because there is no place for accusation, every man being his own Judg, and accused only by his own conscience, and cleer'd by the uprightness of his own intention; and when his intention is right, his fact is no sin, if otherwise, his fact is sin but not crime: that when the Soveraign power ceaseth, that is, when the King is so oppressed that he cannot exercise his power, crime also ceaseth, there being no protection where there is no power, which he is careful to repete, whether it be to the purpose, or, as sure it is not, very pertinent in the difference between sin and crime. And to all that huddle of words in that whole Paragraph, I shall say no more, but that it looks like the Discourse of some men, which himself saies (*pag.* 39.) *may be numbred amongst the sorts of madness, namely, when men speak such words, as put together, have in them no signification at all,* by their non-coherence and contradiction.

False Principles of right and wrong cannot but produce many crimes, and the greater the presumption of those is who publish them, the confusion that results thereby must be the greater: and yet notwithstanding this bundle of false Principles which are contain'd in this Book, the strength of the Laws, and the good constitution of the Government, hath hitherto, for ought appears, resisted the operation and malignity of the Institution of his Soveraignty, with how much confidence soever offered by him, and a true and lawful Soveraign could never be induc'd to affect that power which Mr. *Hobbes* so frankly assign'd to the Soveraign whom he intended to institute. And without doubt that unreasonable Proposition, That Justice is but a vain word, can never be established for Reason, so unanswerably as by the establishment of his Principles, which would make all Laws Cobwebs, to be blown away by the least breath of the Governor; nor by his ratiocination did *Marius*, or *Sylla*, or *Cesar*, ever commit any crime, since they were all Soveraigns by acquisition, and so in his own judgment possessed of all

those powers which arise from his Institution, whereby they
might do all those acts which they did, and no man could
complain of injury or injustice, every man being the Author of
whatever damage he sustain'd or complain'd of; nor will he be
able to lay any crime to any of their charges (tho he seems to
condemn them) and at the same time to support his Institution
of a Common-wealth. But it is the less wonder, since from his
own constitution, according to his first model, and knowing
from whence his own obedience proceeds, he concludes, that of
all passions, that which least inclines men to break the Laws, is
fear. He provides such terrible Laws as no body can love, and
must fear too much to be willing to be subject to them, which
want of willingness must make them glad of any alteration,
which can bring no security to the Soveraign. And I cannot
enough recommend to Mr. *Hobbes* that he will revolve his own
judgment and determination in this Chapter, (*pag. 158.*) *That
he, whose error proceedeth from a peremtory pursuit of his
own Principles and reasonings, is much more faulty then he
whose error proceeds from the autority of a Teacher, or an
Interpreter of the Law publicly autoriz'd; and that he that
groundeth his actions on his private judgment, ought, according to the rectitude or error thereof, to stand or fall.* And if his
fear be so predominant in him, as he conceives it to be in most
men, it will dispose him first to enquire what the opinion of the
Judges is, who are the autoriz'd Interpreters of Law, before he
publishes his seditious Principles against Law, least he be
obliged to stand or fall, according to the rectitude or error
thereof. Tho every Instance he gives of his Soveraigns absolute
power, makes it the more unreasonable, formidable, and
odious, yet he gives all the support to it he can devise. And
indeed, when he hath made his Soveraigns word, a full and
enacted Law, he hath reason to oblige his Subject to do
whatsoever he commands, be it right or wrong, and to provide
for his security when he hath don; and therefore he declares,
(*pag. 157.*) *That whosoever doth any thing that is contrary to a
former Law by the command of his Soveraign, he is not guilty
of any crime, and so cannot be punished, because when the
Soveraign commands any thing to be don against a former
Law, the command as to that particular Fact is an abrogation
of the Law*; which would introduce a licence to commit
Murder, or any other crime most odious, and against which
Laws are chiefly provided. But he hath in another place given

his Subject leave to refuse the Soveraigns command, when he requires him to do an act or office contrary to his honor: so that tho he will not suffer the Law to restrain him from doing what the Soveraign unlawfully commands, yet his honor, of which he shall be Judg himself, may make him refuse that command tho lawful: as if the Soveraign commands him to Prison, as no doubt he lawfully may for a crime that deserves death, he may in Mr. *Hobbes* opinion refuse to obey that command: whereas Government and Justice have not a greater security, then that he that executes a verbal command of the King against a known Law, shall be punished. And the Case which he puts in the following Paragraph, that the Kings Will being a Law, if he should not obey that, there would appear two contradictory Laws, which would totally excuse, is so contrary to the common Rule of Justice, that a man is obliged to believe, when the King requires any thing to be don contrary to any Law, that he did not know of that Law, and so to forbear executing his Command. And if this were otherwise, Kings of all men would be most miserable, and would reverse their most serious Counsels and Deliberations, by incogitancy, upon the suggestion and importunity of every presumptuous Intruder. Kings themselves can never be punished or reprehended publicly (that being a reproch not consistent with the reverence due to Majesty) for their casual or wilful errors and mistakes, let the ill consequence of them be what they will; but if they who maliciously lead, or advise, or obey them in unjust resolutions and commands, were to have the same indemnity, there must be a dissolution of all Kingdoms and Governments. But as Kings must be left to God, whose Vice-gerents they are, to judg of their breach of Trust; so they who offend against the Law, must be left to the punishment the Law hath provided for them, it being in the Kings power to pardon the execution of the Sentence the Law inflicts, except in those cases where the Offence is greater to others then to the King; as in the murder of a Husband or a Father, the offence is greater to the Wife and to the Son for their relation, then to the King for a Subject; and therefore, upon an Appeal by them, the Transgressor may suffer after the King hath pardon'd him.

It is a great prerogative which Mr. *Hobbes* doth in this Chapter indulge to his fear, his precious bodily fear of corporal hurt, that it shall not only extenuate an ill action, but totally excuse and annihilate the worst he can commit, that, if a man

by the terror of present death be compelled to do a Fact against
the Law, he is wholly excused, because no Law can oblige a
man to abandon his own preservation: and supposing such a
Law were obligatory, yet a man would reason, (pag. 157.) *If I
do it not I die presently, if I do it I die afterwards, therefore by
doing it there is time of life gain'd, Nature therefore compels
him to the Fact*: by which a man seems by the Law of Nature to
be compell'd, even for a short reprieve, and to live two or three
daies longer, to do the most infamous and wicked thing that is
imaginable: upon which fertile soil he doth hereafter so much
enlarge, according to his natural method, in which he usually
plants a stock, supposes a principle, the malignity whereof is
not presently discernable, in a precedent Chapter, upon which
in a subsequent one he grafts new and worse Doctrine, which
he looks should grow and prosper by such cultivation as he
applies to it in Discourse; and therefore I shall defer my
Considerations to the contrary, till I wait upon him in that
enlarged disquisition.

The Survey of Chapter 28.

The eight and twentieth Chapter being a Discourse of
Punishments and Rewards, it was not possible for him to forget
in how weak a condition he had left his Soveraign, for want of
power to punish; since want of power to punish, and want of
autority to cause his punishment to be inflicted, is the same
thing; especially when the guilty person is not only not oblig'd
to submit to the Sentence, how just soever, but hath a right to
resist it, and to defend himself by force against the Magistrate
and the Law: and therefore he thinks it of much importance, to
enquire, by what door the right and autority of punishing in
any case came in. He is a very ill Architect, that in building a
House, makes not doors to enter into every office of it; and it is
very strange, that he should make his doors large and big
enough in his institution, to let out all the liberty and propriety
of the Subject, and the very end of his Institution being to make
a Magistrate to compel men to do their duty (for he confesses,
they were before obliged by the Law of Nature to perform it
one towards another, but that there must be a Soveraign Sword
to compel men to do that which they ought to do) yet that he
should forget to leave a door wide enough for this compulsion
to enter in at by punishment, and bringing the Offender to

Justice; since the end of making the Soveraign is disappointed, and he cannot preserve the peace, if guilty persons have a right to preserve themselves from the punishment he inflicts for their guilt. It was very improvidently don, when he had the draught of the whole Contracts and Covenants, that he would not insert one, by which every man should transfer from himself the right he had to defend himself against public Justice, tho not against private violence. And surely reason and Self-preservation, that makes a man transfer all his Estate and Interest into the hands of the Soveraign, and to be disposed by him, that he make be secure against the robberey and rapine of his neighbors & companions, will as well dispose him to leave his life to his discretion, that it may be secure from the assault of every other man, who hath a right to take it from him. But he thinks life too precious to part with willingly, and therefore cares for no more then to invest his Soveraign with a just title to punish, how unable soever he leaves him to execute it. And truly his fancy is very extraordinary in bringing it to pass. He will not suffer his power to punish to be grounded upon the concession or gift of the Subjects, from which fountain all his other extravagant powers flow, which are as unnatural for them to give, but saies it was originally inherent in him by the right of Nature, by which every man might subdue or kill another man, as he thought best for his own preservation; which right still remain'd in him, when all other men transferred all their rights to him, because he never contracted with them to part with any thing, and so he comes (*pag.* 162.) *to a right to punish, which was not given but left to him, and to him only, as entire as in the condition of mere nature.* Is not this mere fancy without any reason? which he needed not have exercis'd to so little purpose, to erect a lawful Power, which any man may lawfully resist and oppose. Nor is the right much greater that is left in him, then what, it seems, is tacitly reserv'd to every man, who notwithstanding all transferring, hath still right to resist the Sword of Justice in his own defence, and for ought appears, to kill him that carries it. So that in truth, his Soveraign is vested in no other autority, then lawfully to fight so many Duels as the Law hath condemned men to suffer death, since he can command none of his Subjects to execute them, and they have all lawful power to defend their own lives. How this right and autority of punishing came into the hands of the Soveraign, we shall not follow his example in repeting, having before confessed, that it neither is nor can be grounded on any concession or gift of the Subject, but is indubitably inherent in the office of being Soveraign, and inseparably annexed to it by God himself.

Corporal, or Capital punishment, Ignominy, Imprisonment, or Exile, are not better understood then they were before his Definitions and Descriptions which he makes of them, and in which he doth not so much consider the nature of a Definition, as that he may insert somwhat into it, to which he may resort to prove somwhat, which men do not think of when they read those Definitions: and assuming to himself to declare what will serve his turn to be the Law of Nature, or the Law of Nations, he makes such Inferences and Consequences, as he thinks necessary to prove his desperate Conclusions. There cannot be a more pernicious Doctrine, and more destructive to Peace and Justice, then that all men who are not Subjects are enemies; & that against Enemies, whom the Common-wealth judges capable to do them hurt, it is lawful by the original right of Nature to make War; which would keep up a continual War between all Princes, since they are few who are not capable to do hurt to their Neighbors. Nor can this mischief be prevented by any Treaty or League; for whil'st they are capable of doing hurt, the lawfulness still remains, and being the original right of Nature, cannot be extinguished. But the Wisest and most Learned who have wrote of the Law of Nature and of Nations, abominate this Proposition; and the incomparible *Grotius* saies, (*De Jure B. & P. lib. 2. cap. 1. part. 17.*) *Illud minime ferendum est, quod quidam tradiderunt, jure gentium arma recte sumi ad imminuendam potentiam crescentem, quæ nimium aucta nocere potest.* It may be a motive when there is other just cause in prudence towards the War, but that it gives a title in Justice, *ab omni æquitatis ratione abhorret.* And he saies in another place (*cap 22. part. 5.*) that it must *constare, non tantum de potentia, sed & de animo; & quidem ita constare, ut certum id sit ea certitudine quæ in morali materia locum habet.* And yet from this erroneous Proposition, and because in (*pag. 165.*) *War the Sword judgeth not, nor doth the victor make distinction of nocent and innocent, nor has other respect of mercy, then as it conduceth to the good of his own People,* he makes no scruple to tell *Cromwell, That as to those who deliberately deny his Autority* (for the *Autority of the Commonwealth established,* could have no other signification) *the vengeance is lawfully extended, not only to the Fathers, but* *also to the third and fourth generations not yet in being, and* *consequently innocent of the fact for which they are afflicted,* *because they that so offend suffer not as Subjects but as* *Enemies*, towards whom the Victor may proceed as he thinks fit and best for himself. After the giving which advice, it was a marvellous confidence that introduc'd him into the Kings presence, and encourag'd him still to expect, that his Doctrine should be allow'd to be industriously taught and believed.

If Mr. *Hobbes* were condemn'd to depart out of the dominion of the Commonwealth, as many men believe he might with great Justice be, and so become an exil'd person, he would be a more competent Judg to determine whether Banishment be a punishment, or rather an escape, or a public command to avoid punishment by flight; and he would probably then be of opinion, that the mere change of air is a very great punishment. And if he remembers his own Definition, (*pag.* 108.) *That a free-man is he, that in those* *things which by his strength and wit he is able to do, is not* *hindred to do what he hath a will to*, he would believe that the taking that freedom from him, and the restraining that liberty, is a very severe punishment, whether justly or unjustly inflicted, and is in no degree mitigated by his declaring, (*pag.* 165.) that *a banish'd man is a lawful enemy of the Common-* *wealth that banished him, as being no more a member of the* *same*, and then he may be lawfully prosecuted as well in, and after he hath undergon the punishment of Banishment as he was before; but the duty that a banish'd Person still ow's to his Country, and to the Soveraign of it, is set down before. But the truth is, he hath very powerfully extinguish'd all those differences and priviledges, which all Writers of the *Jus* *gentium* have carefully preserv'd between a just and unjust War, between lawful Enemies and the worst Rebels and Traitors, and hath put the last into a better condition then the former, by making them liable only to those pains and forfeitures which the Law hath literally provided for them, and which in some cases preserves their Estates for their Families; whereas the lawful Enemy, even after quarter given, remains at the mercy of the Victor, who may take his life, and inflict any other punishment upon him arbitrarily, and according to his own discretion. In the last place, he hath very much obliged his Soveraign, in telling him so plainly why he hath compared him to *Leviathan*, because he hath raised him to the same greatness, and given him the same power which *Leviathan* is described to have in the 41 Chapter of *Job*, *There is nothing on earth to be compared with him, he is made so as not to be afraid, he seeth every high thing to be below him, and is King of all the children of pride*, Job 41. 33, 34. And if he had provided as well to secure his high station, as he hath for the abatement of the pride of the Subject, whom he hath sufficiently humbled, he might more glory in his work: but the truth is, he hath left him in so weak a posture to defend himself, that he hath reason to be afraid of every man; and the remedies he prescribes afterwards to keep his prodigious power from dissolution, are as false and irrational as any other advice in his Institution, as will appear hereafter.

The Survey of Chapter 29.

Mr. *Hobbes* takes so much delight in reiterating the many ill things he hath said, for fear they do not make impression deep enough in the minds of men, that I may be pardon'd if I repete again somtimes what hath bin formerly said; as this Chapter consisting most of the same pernicious doctrines which he declar'd before, tho in an other dress, obliges me to make new, or other reflexions upon what was I think sufficiently answer'd before, and it may be repete what I have said before. He is so jealous that the strength of a better composition of Soveraignty may be superior, and be preferr'd before that of his institution, that he devises all the way he can to render it more obnoxious to dissolution, and like a Mountebank Physician accuses it of diseases which it hath not, that he may apply Remedies which would be sure to bring those or worse diseases, and would weaken the strongest parts, and support of it, under the pretence of curing its defects. So in the first place he finds fault (pag. 167.) *that a man to obtain a Kingdom is sometimes content with less power, then to the peace and defence of the Common-wealth is necessarily required*, that is, that he will observe the Laws and Customs of the Kingdom, which by long experience have bin found necessary for the Peace and defence of it. And to this he imputes the insolence of *Thomas Beckett* Arch Bishop of *Canterbury* (page. 168.) *who was supported against* Harry *the Second by the Pope, the Subjection of Ecclesiastics to the Common-wealth having* he saies *bin*

dispensed with by William *the Conquerour at his reception, when to took an oath, not to infringe the liberty of the Church.*
And this extravagant power of the Pope he imputes to the Universities and the doctrine taught by them; which reproch to the Universities being in a Paragraph of his next Chapter, I chuse to join in the answer with the case of *Thomas Beckett* and *Henry* the Second.

Mr. *Hobbes* hath so great a prejudice to the reading Histories (as if they were all enemies to his Government) that he will not take the pains carefully to peruse those, from which he expects to draw some advantage to himself; presuming that men will not believe, that a man, who so warily weighs all he saies in the balance of reason, will ever venture to alledg any matter of fact that he is not very sure of. But if he had vouchsafed to look over the Records of his own Country before the time of King *Henry* the Eight, he would have found the Universities allwaies opposed the power of the Pope, and would have no dependance upon him, and that the Kings alone introduc'd his authority, and made it to be submitted to by their Laws. Nor did the Church of *England* owe their large priviledges to any donation of the Popes, whose jurisdiction they would never admit, but to the extreme devotion and superstition of the People, and the piety and bounty of the Kings, which gave greater donatives and exemptions to the Church and Clergy, then any other Kingdom enjoied, or then the Pope gave any where. Christianity in the infancy of it wrought such prodigious effects in this Island upon the barbarous affections of the Princes and People who then were the inhabitants of it, that assoon as they gave any belief to the History of our Saviour, they thought they could not do too much to the Persons of those who preached him, and knew best what would be most acceptable to him. From hence they built Churches, and endow'd them liberally, submitted so entirely to the Clergy, whom they look'd upon as Sacred persons, that they judged all differences, and he was not look'd upon as a good Christian who did not entirely resign himself to their disposal: they gave great exemtion to the Church and Church men, and annex'd such Priviledges to both, as testified the veneration they had for the Persons, as well as for the Faith. And when they suspected that the Licentiousness of succeeding ages might not pay the same devotion to both, they did the best they could to establish it, by making Laws to that purpose, and obliging the severall Princes to maintain and defend the rights and priviledges of the Church; rights and priviledges which themselves had granted, and of which the Pope knew nothing, nor indeed at the time did enjoy the like himself. It is true, that by this means the Clergy was grown to a wonderful power over the People, who look'd upon them as more then mortal men, and had surely a greater autority then any Clergy in Christendom assum'd in those ages, and yet it was generally greater then in other Kingdoms, then it had ever bin since. Nor could it be otherwise during the Heptarchy, when those little Soveraigns maintain'd their power by the autority their Clergy had with their people, when they had little dependance upon the Prince. But when by the courage and success of two or three couragious Princes, and the distraction that had bin brought upon them by strangers, the Government of the whole Island was reduced under one Soveraign, the Clergy, which had bin alwaies much better united then the Civil state had bin, were not willing to part with any autority they had enjoied, nor to be thought of less value then they had bin formerly esteemed, and so grew troublesom to the Soveraign power, somtimes by interrupting the progress of their Councils by delaies, and somtimes by direct and positive contradictions. The Princes had not the confidence then to resort to Mr. *Hobbes* original institution of their right, the manners of the Nation still remained fierce and barbarous, and whatsoever was pliant in them, was from the result of Religion, which was govern'd by the Clergy. They knew nothing yet of that primitive contract that introduced Soveraignty, nor of that Faith that introduced subjection; they thought it would not be safe for them to oppose the power of the Sacred Clergy, with a mere secular, profane force, and therefore thought how they might lessen and divide their own troublesome Clergy, by a conjunction with some religious and Ecclesiastical combination. The Bishops of *Rome* of that age had a very great name and autority in *France*, where there being many Soveraign Princes then reigning together, he exercis'd a notable Jurisdiction under the Style of Vicar of Christ. The Kings in *England* by degrees unwarily applied themselves to this Spiritual Magistrate; and that he might assist them to suppress a power that was inconvenient to them at home, they suffered him to exercise an autority that proved afterwards very mischeivous to themselves, and for which they had never made pretence before, and which was then heartily opposed by the Universities, and by the whole Clergy, till it was impos'd upon them by the King. So that it was not the Universities, and Clergy, that introduc'd the Popes autority to shake and weaken that of the King, but it was the King who introduc'd that power to strengthen, as he thought, his own, howsoever it fell out. And if the precedent Kings had not call'd upon the Pope, and given him autority to assist them against some of their own Bishops, *Alexander* the Third could never have pretended to exercise so wild a jurisdiction over *Henry* the Second, nor he ever have submitted to so infamous a subordination; nor could the Pope have undertaken to assist *Beckett* against the King, if the King had not first appeal'd to him for help against *Beckett*.

For the better manifestation of that point, which Mr. *Hobbes* his speculation and Geometry hath not yet made an enquiry into, it will not be amiss to take a short Survey of the Precedent times, by which it will be evident how little influence the Popes autority had upon the Crown, or Clergy, or Universities of *England*; and how little ground he hath for that fancy, from whence soever he took it, (pag. 168.) *that* William *the* Conquerour *at his reception had dispens'd with the subjection of the Ecclesiasticks by the Oath he took not to infringe the liberty of the Church*; whereas they who know any thing of that time, know that the Oath he took was the same, and without any alteration, that all the former Kings, since the crown rested upon a single head, had taken, which was at his Coronation, after the Bishops and the Barons had taken their Oaths to be his true and faithful Subjects. The Arch Bishop, who crown'd him, presented that Oath to him, which he was to take himself, which he willingly did, to defend the Holy Church of God, and the Rectors of the same, To Govern the universal people subject to him, justly, To establish equal Laws, and to see them justly executed. Nor was he more wary in any thing, then (as hath bin said before) that the people might imagine, that he pretended any other title to the Government, then by the Confessor: tho it is true, that he did by degrees introduce many of the *Norman* customes which were found very useful, or convenient, and agreeable enough, if not the same, with what had bin formerly practis'd. And the common reproch of the Laws being from time to time put into *French*, carries no weight with it: for there was before that time so rude a collection of the Laws, and in Languages as forreign to that of the Nation, British, Saxon, Danish, and Latine, almost as unintelligible as either of the other, that if they had bin all digested into the *English* that was then spoken, we should very little better have understood it, then we do the *French*, in which the Laws were afterwards render'd; and it is no wonder, since a reduction into Order was necessary, that the King who was to look to the execution, took care to have them in that Language which himself best understood, and from whence issued no inconvenience, the former remaining still in the Language in which they had bin written.

Before the time of *William* the First, there was no pretence of jurisdiction from *Rome* over the Clergy, and the Church of *England*; for tho the infant Christianity of some of the Kings and Princes had made some journies thither, upon the fame of the Sanctity of many of the Bishops who had bin the most eminent Martyrs for the Christian Faith, and when it may be they could with more ease and security make a journy thither, then they could have don to any other Bishop of great notoriety out of their own Country; for Christianity was not in those times come much neerer *England* then *Dauphiné*, *Provence*, and *Languedoc* in *France*, and those Provinces had left their bountiful testimonies of their devotion, which grew afterwards to be exercis'd with the same piety in Pilgrimages first, and then expeditions to the Holy Land, without any other purpose of transferring a Superiority over the *English* Nation, to *Rome*, then to *Jerusalem*. And after the arrival of *Austin* the Monk and his Companions, who were sent by Pope *Gregory*, and who never enjoy'd any thing in *England* but by the donation of the Kings, the *Brittish* Clergy grew so jealous of their pretences, that tho the Nation was exceedingly corrupted by the person and the doctrine of *Pelagius*, which had bin spred full two hundred years before *Austin* came, the reformation and suppression of that Heresy was much retarded by those mens extolling or mentioning the Popes autority, which the *Brittish* Bishops were so far from acknowledging, that they would neither meet with them, nor submit to any thing that was propos'd by them, and declar'd very much against the pride and insolence of *Austin*, for assuming any autority, and because when any of them came to him, he would not so much as rise to receive them. I can hardly contain my self from enlarging upon this subject at this time, but that it will seem to many to be forreign to the argument now in debate, and Mr. *Hobbes* hath little resignation to the autority of matter of fact, by which when he is pressed, he hath an answer ready, that if it were so, or not so, it should have bin otherwise, I shall therefore only refrain my discourse to the time of *William* the Conqueror, and when I have better inform'd him of the State of the Clergy, and Universities of that time, I shall give him the best satisfaction I can to the instance of *Thomas* of *Beckett*, in which both the Clergy, and the Universities will be easily absolv'd from the guilt of adhering to the Pope.

When *William* found himself in possession of *England*, whatever application he had formerly made to the Pope (who was then in *France*) and as some say had receiv'd from him a consecrated Banner with some other relique, beside one single hair of St. *Peter*, for the better success of his expedition, he was so far from discovering any notable respect towards him, that he expressly forbad all his Subjects from acknowledging any man to be Pope, but him whom he declar'd to be so. And there was a President of such a nature in his Reign by *Lanfranke* the Arch B. of *Canterbury*, who had the greatest credit and autority with him, as cannot be parallell'd by the like don in any other Christian State; and impossible to be don, or permitted in any State that was in any degree subject to the Pope, which was the Canonization of a Saint. There being at that time very great fame of *Aldelmus*, who first brought in the composition of Latine verse into *England* and besides his eminent Piety, had so great a faculty in singing, that by the music of his voice he wrought wonderful effects upon the barbarous and savage humor of that People, insomuch as when they were in great multitudes engaged in a rude or licentious action, he would put himself in their way and sing, which made them all stand still to listen, and he so captivated them by the melody, that he diverted them from their purpose, and by degrees got so much credit with them, that he reduc'd them to more civility, and instructed them in the duties of Religion, into which, tho they had bin baptiz'd, they had made little enquiry. He lived a little before the time of *Edward* the Confessor, and the general testimony of the Sanctity of his Life, and some miracles wrought by him (which it may be were principally the effects of his Music) being reported, and believed by *Lanfrank*, *Edicto sancivit, ut per totam deinde Angliam Aldelmus inter eos, qui civibus cœlestibus ascriptierant, honoraretur & coleretur*, as by the authors neerest that time is remembered, &

at large related by *Harps-Field* in his Ecclesiastical History of *England* without any disapprobation. Nor is it probable, that *Lanfrank* who was an *Italian*, born and bred in *Lombardy*, and of great reputation for learning and piety, would have assum'd that autority, if he had believ'd that he had intrenched upon the Province of the Bishop of *Rome*. The truth is, Canonizations in that age were not the chargeable commodities they have since grown to be, since the Pope hath engross'd the disposal of them to himself; and it is very probable, that the Primitive Saints, whose memories are preserv'd in the Martyrologies very erroneously, were by the joint acknowledgment of the Church upon the notorious sanctitiy of their lives, and of their deaths, not by any solemn declaration of any particular autority of *Rome*; otherwise we should find the Records of Old Canonization there, as well as we do of so many new. But of so many of this Nation, who suffer'd in the ten first persecutions under the Roman Governors more then of any other, especially if St. *Ursula*, and her Eleven thousand Virgins be reckon'd into the number, there is no other Record but of the daies assign'd for their Festivities. And in their whole *Bullarium*, which for these latter hundred years so much abounds in Canonizations, the first that is extant is of *Uldricke* Bishop of *Ausburg*, by *John* the Fifteenth *Anno* Nine hundred ninety three, in a very different form, and much different circumstances from those which are now used. Finally, if the Popes inhibition or interposition could have bin of any moment in that time of *William* the Conqueror, he would have bin sure to have heard of it, when he seiz'd upon the Plate & Jewels of all the Monasteries, and laid other great impositions upon the Clergy, which they had not bin accustom'd to, and of which they would have complain'd, if they had known whether to have addressed their complaints.

The two next Kings who succeeded him, and reigned long (for *Henry* the First reigned no less then five and thirty years) wore not their Crowns so fast on their heads, in respect of the juster title in their Brother *Robert*, as prudently to provoke more enemies then they had; and therefore they kept very fair quarter with *Paschal*, who was Pope likewise many years, and were content to look on unconcern'd in the fierce quarrels between the Emperour and him, for he was very powerful in *France* tho not in *Italy*. And *Anselme* the Arch-Bishop of *Canterbury* had great contests with them both upon the priviledges of the Clergy, and had fled to *Paschal* to engage him in his quarrel; yet the Pope pretended to no jurisdiction in the point, but courteously interceded so far with *Henry* the First on the behalf of *Anselme*, that he made his peace with the King: but when he afterwards desir'd to send a Legate into *England*, the King by the advice of the Bishops, and Nobles, positively refus'd to admit him. And whosoever takes a view of the constitution of Christendom, as far as had reference to *Europe* at that time, how far the greatest Kingdoms and Principalities, which do now controul and regulate that ambition, were from any degree of strength and power; that *Italy* was then crumbled into more distinct Governments, then it is at present; that *France*, that is now intire, was then under the command of very many Soveraign Princes, and the Crown it self so far from any notable superiority, that the King himself was sometimes excommunicated by his own Bishops and Clergy, without, and against the Popes direction, and sometimes excommunicated, and the Kingdom interdicted by the Pope, even whilst he resided in *France*, and in Councils assembled by them there, as in the Council of *Clermont*; that *Spain*, that is now under one Monarch, was then divided into the several Kingdoms of *Castile, Arragon, Valentia, Catalonia, Navarr*, and *Leon*, when the Moors were possess'd of a greater part of the whole, then all the other Christian Kings, the whole Kingdom of *Granada* with the greatest part of *Andoluzia*, and *Estremadura*, and a great part of *Portugal* being then under the Dominion of those Infidels; that *Germany* was under as many Soveraign princes as it had names of Cities and Provinces; and that *England*, which hath now *Scotland* and *Ireland* annex'd to it, was then, besides the unsettlement of the *English* Provinces upon the contests in the *Norman* Family, without any pretence to the Dominion of *Wales*, at least without any advantage by it: I say, whosoever considers this, will not wonder at the starts made by many Popes in that age, into a kind of power and autority in many Kingdoms, that they had not before, and which was then still interrupted and contradicted; and that when *Alexander* the Third came to be Pope, who reigned about twenty years, he proceeded so imperiously with our *Henry* the Second upon the death of *Thomas Beckett*, even in a time when there was so great a Schism in the Church, that *Victor* the Fifth was chosen by a contrary party, and by a Council called at *Pavia* by the Emperour there own'd, and declar'd to be

Canonically chosen, and *Alexander* to be no Pope, who thereupon fled into *France*: so that if our King *Henry* the Second had not found such a condescention to be very suitable to his affaires both in *England*, and in *France*, it is probable he would have declin'd so unjust and unreasonable an imposition.

I am afraid of giving Mr. *Hobbes* an occasion to reproch me with impertinency in this digression, tho he hath given me a just provocation to it; and since the *Roman* Writers are so solicitous in the collecting and publishing the Records of that odious Process, and strangers are easily induc'd to believe, that the exercise of so extravagant a jurisdiction in the Reign of so Heroical a Prince, who had extended his Dominions farther by much then any of his Progenitors had don, must be grounded upon some fix'd and confess'd right over the Nation, and not from an original Usurpation entred upon in that time, and when the usurper was not acknowledged by so considerable a part of Christendom; it may not prove ungrateful to many men, to take a short view of that very time, that we may see what unheard of motives could prevail with that high spirited King to submit to so unheard of Tyranny. That it was not from the constitution of the Kingdom, or any preadmitted power of the Pope formerly incorporated into the Laws and customs of the Kingdom, is very evident, by the like having bin before attemted. For tho the Clergy enjoied those great priviledges and immunities which are mention'd before, whereby they had so great an influence upon the hearts of the people, that the Conquerour himself had bin glad to make use of them, and *William* the Second, *Henry* the First, and King *Stephen* had more need of them to uphold their Usurpation; yet those priviledges how great soever, depended not at all upon the Bishop of *Rome*, nor was any rank of men more solicitious then the Clergy to keep the Pope from a pretence of power in the Kingdom. And the Bishops themselves had in the beginning of that Arch-Bishops contumacious and rebellious contests with the King, don all they could to discountenance and oppose him, and had given their consent in Parliament, that for his disobedience all his goods and moveables should be at the Kings mercy: and it was also enacted with their consent (after the Arch-Bishop had fled out of the Kingdom, and was known to make some application to the Pope) that if any were found carrying a Letter or Mandate from the Pope or the Arch-Bishop, containing any interdiction of Christianity in *England*, he should be taken, and without delay executed as a Traitor both to the King & Kingdom; that whatsoever Bishop, Priest, or Monk should have, and retain any such Letters, should forfeit all their Possessions, Goods, and Chattells to the King, and be presently banish'd the Realm with their kin; that none should appeal to the Pope; and many other particulars, which enough declare the temper of that Catholic time, and their aversion to have any dependance upon a forreign jurisdiction. And after the death of *Beckett*, and that infamous submission of the King to the Popes Sentence thereupon (which yet was not so scandalous as it is vulgarly reported, as if it had bin made and undergon by the King in Person) when the same King desir'd to assist the Successor of that Pope, *Lucius* the Third, who was driven out of *Rome*, and to that purpose endeavour'd to raise a collection from the Clergy, which the Popes *Nuntio* appear'd in, and hoped to advance, the Clergy was so jealous of having to do with the Pope, or his Ministers, that they declar'd, and advised the King, that his Majesty would supply the Pope in such a proportion as he thought fit, and that whatever they gave might be to the King himself, and not to the Popes *Nuntio*, which might be drawn into example to the detriment of the King.

The King himself first shewed the way to *Thomas a Beckett* to apply himself to the Pope, till when the Arch-Bishop insisted only upon his own Ecclestical rights and power, in which he found not the concurrence of the other Bishops or Clergy, and the King not being able to bear the insolence of the man, and finding that he could well enough govern his other Bishops, if they were not subjected to the autority and power of that perverse Arch-Bishop, was willing to give the Pope autority to assist him, and did all he could to perswade him to make the Arch-Bishop of *York* his Legate, meaning thereby to devest the other Arch-Bishop of that Superiority over the Clergy that was so troublesom to him, and which he exercis'd in his own right as Metropolitan. But the Pope durst not gratify the King therein, knowing the spirit of *Beckett*, and that he would contemn the Legate, and knew well the Ecclesiastical superiority in that Kingdom to reside in his person as Arch-Bishop of *Canterbury*, who, had bin reputed *tanquam alterius Orbis Papa*, yet he sent to him to advise him to submit to the King; whereupon the haughty Prelate then fled out of the Kingdom, and was too hard for the King with the Pope, who was

perswaded by him to make use of this opportunity to enlarge
his own power, and to curb and subdue that clergy that was
indevoted to him; and so by his Bull he suspended the Arch-
bishop of *York*, and the other Bishops who adher'd to the king
in the execution of his commands; which so much incens'd the
King, that he let fall those words in his passion, that
encouraged those rash Gentlemen to commit that assassina-
tion, that produc'd so much trouble. It must also be
remembred, that the King, when he bore all this from the Pope,
was indeed but half a King, having caused his son *Henry* to be
crown'd King with him, who thereupon gave him much
trouble, and join'd with the *French* King against him: and that
he had so large and great Territories in *France*, that as the
Popes power was very great there, so his friendship was the
more behoovfull and necessary to the King. Lastly, and which
it may be is of more weight then any thing that hath bin said in
this disquisition, it may seem a very natural judgment of God
Almighty, that the Pope should exercise that unreasonable
power over a King, who had given him an absurd and unlawful
power over himself, and for an unjust end, when he obtain'd
from our Country-Man Pope *Adrian*, who immediately
preceded *Alexander*, a Dispensation not to perform the Oath
which he had taken, that his Brother *Geoffery* should enjoy the
County of *Anjoy* according to the Will and desire of his Father,
and by vertue of that Dispensation, which the Pope had no
power to grant, defrauded his Brother of his inheritance, and
broke his Oath to God Almighty, and so was afterwards forced
himself to yield to the next Pope, when he assum'd a power
over him in a case he had nothing to do with, and where he had
no mind to obey. And this unadvised address of many other
princes to the Pope, for Dispensations of this kind to do what
the Law of God did not permit them to do, hath bin a principal
inlet of his Supremacy, to make them accept of other
Dispensations from him, of which they stand not in need, and
to admit other his incroachments from him, which have proved
very mischievous to them. Of the condition of King *John* we
need not speak, whose Usurpation, Murders, and absence of
all virtue, made him fit to undergo all the reproches and
censures which Pope *Innocent* the Third exercis'd him with,
when he usurped upon *France* with equal Tyranny.

  The succeding Kings no sooner found it necessary to expel,
or restrain that power which the Popes had so inconveniently

bin admitted to, and which they had so mischievously improv'd, but the Universities not only submitted to, but advanced those Acts which tended thereunto; as appears by the Writings of *Occam*, and other Learned Men in the University of *Oxford*, in the Reigns of those Kings both *Edward* the First and *Edward* the Third, in which times as much was don against the power of the Pope, as was afterwards don by *Henry* the Eighth himself. And the *Gallican* Church would not at this time have preserved their liberties and priviledges to that degree, as to contemn the power of the universal Bishop, if the University of the *Sorbone* had not bin more vigilant against those incroachments then the Crown it self. So far have the Universities bin from being the Authors, or promoters of those false Doctrines, which he unjustly laies to his charge. And I presume they will be as vigilant and resolute, to preserve the Civil Autority from being invaded and endangered, by their receiving and subscribing to his pernicious and destructive principles, which his modesty is induced to believe may be planted in the minds of men, because whole Nations have bin brought to acquiesce in the great mysteries of Christian Religion which are above reason, and millions of men have bin made to believe, that the same body may be in innumerable places at one and the same time, which is against reason: and therefore he would have the Soveraign power to make his Doctrine, so consonant to reason, to be taught and preached. But his Doctrine is fit only to be taught by his own Apostles, who ought to be looked upon as Seducers, and false Prophets; and God forbid that the Soveraign powers should contribute to the making those principles believed, which would be in great danger to be destroied, if it were but suspected that they affected to have that power, which he would have to belong to them. And such Princes who have bin willing to believe they have it, have bin alwaies most jealous that it should be known, or thought, that they do believe so; since they know there would be a quick determination of their power, if all their Subjects knew, that they believed, that all they have doth in truth belong to them, and that they may dispose of it as they please.

(Pag. 168.) *He saies a Common-wealth hath many diseases, which proceed from the poison of Seditious doctrines, whereof one is, That every private man is Judg of good and evil actions,* which is a doctrine never allow'd in any Common-wealth, the

Law being the measure of all good or evil actions under every Government; and where that Law permits a liberty to the Subject to dispute the commands of the Soveraign, no inconvenience can arise thereby: but if the Soveraign by his own autority shall vacate and cancel all Laws, the Commonwealth must need be distracted, or much weakened.

Mr. *Hobbes* will have too great an advantage against any adversary, if he will not have his Government tried by any Law, nor his Religion by any Scripture: and he could never think, that the believing, that (*pag.* 168.) *whatsoever a man doth against his conscience is sin*, is a Doctrine to civil Society repugnant, if he thought any of the Apostles good Judges of Conscience, who all, upon all occasions and in all actions, *commend themselves to every mans conscience*, 2. Cor. 4. 2. as also, *Our rejoicing is this, the Testimony of our conscience* 2. Cor. 1. 12. and throughout the whole new Testament the conscience is made the Judg of all we do. And if Mr. *Hobbes* had not so often excepted against Divines for being good Judges in Religion, I could tell him of very good ones, who are of opinion, that it is a sin to do any thing against an erroneous conscience, which is his own best excuse, that he will not depart from his own judgment, which is his conscience, how erroneous soever it is. But this liberty of Conscience is restrain'd only to those Cases where the Law hath prescribed no rule; for where the Law enjoins the duty, no private conscience can deny obedience. In case of misperswasion, it looks upon the action as sinful in him, and so chuses to submit to the penalty, which is still obedience, or removes into another Climate as more agreeable to his constitution.

If Mr. *Hobbes* proposes to himself to answer all extravagant discourses or private opinions of seditious men, which have no countenance from public Autority, he will be sure to chuse such as he can easily confute. All sober men agree, that tho faith and sanctity are not to be attain'd only by study and reading, yet that study and reading are means to procure that grace from God Almighty that is necessary thereunto. And himself confesseth, that with all his education, discipline, correction, and other natural waies, it is God that worketh that faith and sanctity in those he thinks fit. So that if he did not think men the more unlearn'd for being Divines, it is probable that there is very little difference between what those unlearned Divines, and himself say upon this point, saving that they may use *inspiring* and *infusing*, which are words he cannot endure as *insignificant speech*, tho few men are deceiv'd in the meaning of them.

If all Soveraigns are subject to the Laws of Nature (as he saies they are) because such Laws are divine, and cannot by any man or Common-wealth be abrogated, they then are oblig'd to observe and perform those Laws which themselves have made, and promised to observe; for violation of faith is against the Law of Nature by his own confession. Nor doth this obligation set any Judg over the Soveraign, nor doth any civil Law pretend that there is any power to punish him; it is enough, that in justice he ought to do it, and that there is a Soveraign in Heaven above him, tho not on Earth.

The next indeed is a Doctrine that troubles him, and tends, as he saies, (pag. 169.) *to the dissolution of a Common-wealth, That every private man has an absolute propriety in his goods, such as excludes the right of the Soveraign*, which if true, he saies, (p. 170) *he cannot perform the Office they have put him into, which is to defend them both from Foreign Enemies, and from the injuries of one another, and consequently there is no longer a Common-wealth.* And I say, if it be not true, there is nothing worth the defending from Foreign Enemies, or from one another, and consequently it is no matter what becomes of the Common-wealth. Can he defend them any other way, then by their own help, with their own hands? and it is a marvellous thing that any man can believe, that he can be as vigorously assisted by people who have nothing to lose, as by men who defending him defend their own Goods and Estates, which if they do not believe their own, they will never care into what hands they fall. Nor is the Soveraign power divided by the Soveraigns consenting that he will not exercise such a part of it, but in such & such a manner, and with such circumstances; for he hath not parted with any of his Soveraignty, since no other man can exercise that which he forbears to exercise himself; which could be don, if he had divided it. And it is much a greater crime in those who are totally ignorant of the laws, to endeavour by their wit and presumtion to undermine them, then that they who are learn'd in the study and profession of the Law, do all they can to support that, which only supports the Government. Much less is the Soveraign power divided by the Soveraigns own communicating part of it to be executed in his name, to those who, by their education and experience, are qualified to do it much better then he himself can be presumed to be able to do; as to appoint Judges to administer Justice to his people, upon all the pretences of right which may arise between themselves, or between him and them, according to the Rules of the Law which are manifest to them, and must be unknown to him; who yet keeps the Soveraign power in his hands to punish those deputies, if they swerve from their duty.

To the Mischiefs which have proceeded from the reading the Histories of the ancient Greeks and Romans, I shall say no more in this place, then that if Mr. *Hobbes* hath bin alwaies of this opinion, he was very much to blame to take the pains to translate *Thucydides* into *English*, in which there is so much of the Policy of the *Greeks* discovered, and much more of that Oratory that disposes Men to Sedition, then in all *Tullies*, or *Aristotles* works. But I suppose he had then, and might still have more reason to believe, that very few who have taken delight in reading the Books of Policy and Histories of the ancient *Greeks* and *Romans*, have ever fallen into Rebellion; and there is much more fear, that the reading this and other Books writ by him, and the glosses he makes upon them in his conversation, may introduce thoughts of Rebellion into young men, by weakning, and laughing at all obgliations of conscience, which only can dispose men to obedience: and by perswading Princes, that they may safely and justly follow the extent of their own inclinations, and appetites in the Government of their Subjects, which must tire and wear out all Subjection, at least the cheerfulness, which is the strength of it, by lessening the reverence to God Almighty, which is the foundation of reverence to the King; and undervaluing all Religion, as no otherwise known, and no otherwise constituted then by the arbitriment of the Soveraign Prince, whom he makes a God of Heaven, as well as upon the Earth, since he is upon the matter, the only author of the Scripture it self; the swallowing of all which opinions, must be the destruction of all Government, and the ruine of all obedience.

Tho most of his reflexions are reproches upon the Government of his own Country, which he thinks is imperfectly instituted; yet he cannot impute the doctrine of killing Kings, whether Regicide or Tyrannicide, to that Government, nor the unreasonable distinction of Spiritual and Temporal jurisdiction, to rob the Soveraign of any part of his Supremacy, and divide one part of his Subjects from a dependance upon his justice and autority. God be thanked the Laws of that Kingdom admit none of that doctrine, or such distinctions to that pernicious purpose. Nor do the Bishops, or Clergy of that Kingdom (however they are fallen from Mr. *Hobbes* his grace) use any style or title, but what is given or permitted to them by the Soveraign power. And therefore this Controversy must be defended by those (who justly lie under the reproch) of the Church of *Rome*, who, it may be, consider him the less, because, tho they know him not to be of theirs, they think him not to be of any Religion.

The power of levying Mony, which depending upon any general assembly, he saies, (pag. 172.) *endangereth the common-wealth, for want of such nurishment, as is necessary to life and motion*, shall be more properly enlarg'd upon in the next Chapter, when, I doubt not, very wholsome remedies will be found for all those diseases which he will suppose may proceed from thence, but tis to be hoped none will chuse his desperate prescriptions, which will cure the disease by killing the Patient.

He concludes this Chapter, after all his bountiful donatives to his Soveraign, with his old wicked doctrine, that would indeed irreparably destroy and dissolve all Common-wealths. That when by a powerful invasion from a foreign Enemy, or a prosperous Rebellion by Subjects, his Soveraign is so far oppressed that he can keep the field no longer, his Subjects owe him no farther assistance, and may lawfully put themselves under the Conqueror, of what condition soever; for tho, he saies, (pag. 174.) *The right of the Soveraign is not extinguished, yet the obligation of the members is*, and so the Soveraign is left to look to himself. There are few Empires of the World, which at some time have not bin reduc'd, by the strength and power of an outragious Enemy, to that extremity, that their forces have not bin able to keep the field any longer, which Mr. *Hobbes* makes the period of their Subjects Loyalty, and the dissolution of the Common-wealth; yet of these at last many Princes have recover'd, and redeem'd themselves from that period, & arrived again at their full height and glory by the constancy and vertue of their Subjects, and their firmly believing, that their obligations could not be extinguish'd as long as the right of their Soveraign Monarch was not. So that there is great reason to believe, that the old Rules which Soveraignty alwaies prescribed to it self, are much better, and more like to preserve it, then the new ones which he would plant in their stead; because it is very evident, that the old subjection is much more faithful and necessary to the support and defence of the Soveraignty, then that new one which he is contented with, and prescribes; which he will not only have determin'd as to any assistance of his natural Soveraign, tho he confesses (pag. 174.) *his right remains still in him; but that he is obliged, (so strictly obliged, that no pretence of having submitted himself out of fear, can absolve him) to protect, and assist the Usurper as long as he is able.* So that the entire loss of any one Battel, acording to his judgment of subjection, and the duty of Subjects, shall, or may put an end to the Soveraignty of any Prince in *Europe.* And this is one of the grounds and principles, which he concludes to be against the express duty of Princes, to let the people be ignorant of.

If Mr. *Hobbes* had a Conscience made and instructed like other mens, and had not carefully provided, that whilst his judgment is fix'd under Philosophical and Metaphysical notions, his Conscience shall never be disturb'd by Religious speculations and apprehensions; it might possibly smite him with the remembrance, that these excellent principles were industriously insinuated, divulged and publish'd within less then two years after *Cromwels* Usurpation of the Government of the three Nations, upon the Murder of his Soveraign; and that he then declar'd in this book (pag. 165.) *that against such Subjects who deliberately deny tha autority of the Commonwealth, then, and so established* (which God be thanked much the major part of the three Nations then did) *the vengeance might lawfully be extended not only to the Fathers, but also to the third and fourth generation not yet in being, and consequently innocent of the fact for which they are afflicted; because the nature of this offence, consists in renouncing of subjection, which is a relapse into the condition of war, commonly called Rebellion, and they that so offend, suffer not as Subjects, but as Enemies.* And truly he may very reasonably believe, surely more then many things which he doth believe, that the veneme of this Book wrought upon the hearts of men, to retard the return of their Allegiance for so many years, and was the cause of so many cruel and bloody persecutions against those, who still retain'd their duty and Allegiance for the King. And methinks no man should be an Enemy to the renewing war in such cases, but he who thinks all kind of war, upon what occasion soever, to be unlawful; which Mr. *Hobbes* is so far from thinking, that he is very well contented, and believes it very lawfull for his Soveraign, in this paragraph of cruelty, to make war against any whom he judges capable to do him hurt.

The Survey of Chapter 30.

Mr. *Hobbes* having invested his Soveraign with so absolute Power and Omnipotence, we have reason to expect that in this Chapter of his Office, he will enjoin him to use all the autority he hath given him; and he gives him fair warning, that if any of the essential Rights of Soveraignty, specified in his eighteenth chapter (which, in a word, is to do any thing he hath a mind to do, and take any thing he likes from any of his Subjects) be taken away, the Common-wealth is dissolv'd: and therefore that it is his office to preserve those Rights entire, and against his duty to transfer any of them from himself. And least he should forget the Rights and Power he hath bestowed upon him, he recollects them all in three or four lines, amongst which he puts him in mind, that he hath power to leavy mony, when, and as much as in his own conscience he shall judg necessary: and then tells him, that it is against his duty to let the People be ignorant, or mis-informed of the grounds and reasons of those his essential Rights, that is, that he is oblig'd to make his *Leviathan* Canonical Scripture, there being no other Book ever yet printed, that can inform them of those rights, & the grounds and reason of them. And how worthy they are to receive that countenance and autority, will best appear by a farther examination of the Particulars; and yet a man might have reasonably expected from the first Paragraph of this Chapter another kind of tenderness, indeed as great as he can wish, of the good and welfare of the Subject, when he declares, (*pag. 175.*) *That the office of the Monarch consists in the end for which he was trusted with the Soveraign power, namely, the procuration of the safety of the People, to which he is obliged by the Law of Nature, and to render an account thereof to God the Author of that Law. But by safety,* he saies, *is not meant a bare preservation, but also all other contentments of life, which every man by lawful industry, without danger or hurt to the Commonwealth, can acquire to himself.* Who can expect a more blessed condition? Who can desire a more gracious Soveraign? No man would have thought this specious

Building should have its Foundation, after the manner of the foolish *Indians*, upon sand, that, assoon as you come to rest upon it, molders away to nothing; that this safety, safety improv'd with all the other contentments of life, should consist in nothing else, but in a mans being instructued and prepar'd to know, that he hath nothing of his own, and that when he hath by his lawful industry acquir'd to himself all the contentments of life which he can set his heart upon, one touch of his Soveraigns hand, one breath of his mouth, can take all this from him without doing him any injury. This is the Doctrine to be propagated, and which he is confident will easily be receiv'd and consented to, since if it were not according the principles of Reason, he is sure it is a principle from autority of Scripture, and will be so acknowledg'd, if the peoples minds be not tainted with dependance upon the Potent, or scribled over with the opinions of their Doctors.

One of the reasons which he gives, why his grounds of the rights of his Soveraign should be diligently and truly taught, is a very good reason to believe, that the grounds are not good, because he confesses, (*pag.* 175.) that *they cannot be maintain'd by any Civil Law, or terror of legal punishment.* And as few men agree with Mr. *Hobbes* in the essential Rights of Soveraignty, so none allows, nor doth he agree with himself, *that all resistance to the rights of the Soveraignty, be they never so essential, is Rebellion.* He allows it to be a priviledg of the Subject that he may sue the King, so there is no doubt but that the Soveraign may sue the Subject, who may as lawfully defend as sue, and every such defence is a resistance to the Soveraign right of demanding, and yet I suppose Mr. *Hobbes* will not say it is Rebellion. He that doth positively refuse to pay mony to the King, which he doth justly owe to him, and which he shall be compell'd to pay, doth resist an essential Right of the King, yet is not guilty of Rebellion, which is constituted in having a force to support his resistance, and a purpose to apply it that way. And as the Law of Nature is not so easily taught, because not so easily understood as the Civil Law, so I cannot comprehend, why Mr. *Hobbes* should imagine the Soveraign power to be more secure by the Law of Nature, then by the Civil Law, when he confesses, *That the Law of Nature is made Law, only by being made part of the Civil Law*; and if the Civil Law did not provide a restraint from the violation of Faith, by the terror of the punishment that must attend it, the obligation from the Law of Nature would be a very faint security to Princes for the obedience of their Subjects. But he chuses to appeal only to the Law of Nature, wch is a Text so few men have read and understand, to support an imaginary Faith that was never given, upon which Soveraignty was founded. For which he hath another reason likewise; for his Law of Nature is always at hand to serve him, when no other Law will. For when you tell him that the Law of Nature forbiddeth the violation of Faith, and therefore that Kings and Princes are obliged to observe the Promises they make, and the Oaths they take; he answers you with great confidence, & great cleerness, that *that rule is only obligatory to Subjects,* for that by the Law of Nature, *such Promises and Oaths taken by Princes, are* ipso facto *void, invalid, and bind not at all.* So that by this omnipotent Law of Nature, which is indispensable and eternal, the Sacred Word of a King, which ought to be as fix'd and unmoveable as the center of the Earth, is made is changeable as the Moon; and the breach of Faith, which is so odious to God and man, is made lawful for Kings, who are the only Persons in the World who cannot be perjur'd, because the indispensable Law of Nature will not permit them to perform what they promise. And now we see the reason why the Law of Nature must only be able to support that Government, which no Civil Law will be able to do: it remains, that tho there may be a very innocent and lawful resistance of some essential Rights of the Soveraign, for recovery whereof he may be put to sue at Law, as hath bin said before, his Soveraign by his right of Interpreting Law, may, as his Institutor here hath don, interpret such resistance to be Treason, and so confiscate the Estate of the greatest Subject he hath, who hath an Estate that he hath a mind to have.

He would be glad to find some answer to the want of President, which he sees will alwaies lie in his way, that there hath not bin hitherto any Common-wealth where those Rights have bin acknowledg'd or challeng'd: but he hath alwaies the ill luck to leave the Objection as strong as he found it; and if he could find no Artificers to assist in the erecting such a Building as may last as long as the Materials, notwithstanding his skill in Architecture from the principles of Reason, his long study of the nature of Materials, and the divers effects of Figure and Proportion, men would rather chuse to dwell in the Houses they have, then to pull them down, and exspect till he set up better in the place. He must give a better evidence then his non-reason, that his Government will be everlasting, before men believe it; and when his Principles from autority of Scripture come to be examin'd, they will be found to have no more solidity, then those which he hath produc'd from his long study and observation. In the mean time he shall do well to get his Doctrine planted in those Countries, and among that People who are made believe, that the same Body may be in innumerable places at one and the same time, where possibly things equally unreasonable may be believ'd. And since men are to be taught, that they ought not to be in love with any Form of Government more then with their own, nor to desire change, which he saies, (*pag.* 177.) *is like the breach of the first of Gods Commandments*, he hath himself raised one unanswerable Argument against the reception and doctrine of his *Leviathan*. His unskilful reproches upon the Universities are sufficiently refuted in the last Chapter.

A man would hardly believe, that the same Person should think it to be of the office of the Soveraign to take care for the making of good Laws, and should so frankly declare, That no Law can be conceiv'd to be good, tho it be for the benefit of the Soveraign, if it be not necessary for the People, for the good of the Soveraign and the People cannot be separated; and yet at the same time determine, that all Laws which establish any Propriety to and in the People, are invalid and void, and that it is an essential and inseparable Right in the Soveraign, to levy as much mony at any time, as he in his own conscience shall judg necessary. And therefore, tho I think I have in several places of this Discourse sufficiently evinc'd the unreasonableness of this Proposition, and the inconsistency of the good and security of the Soveraign with such a Power, I shall here enlarge upon the Disquisition thereof, and of the reasons which induce him to believe, that any kind of restraint of his power of raising mony, by what consent of his own soever, is no less then the dissolution of the Common-wealth: for his power of taking every mans mony from him, and his goods that will yield mony, is his principal contention throughout his Book, besides his liberty to lay asleep, alter, and repeal all Laws according to his will and pleasure. The expence and charge of the preservation and maintenance of the Government being uncertain and contingent, and so not to be provided for by any constant provision or revenue, if by any emergent occasion, upon a suddain Rebellion or forreign Invasion, the Soveraign hath not power to raise what mony he thinks necessary to suppress the one and resist the other, the Kingdom must be lost; and if he may do it in either of those cases, he may do it to prevent either; and it ought to be suppos'd that he will not take more, tho he may take all, then is absolutely necessary for the occasion: and this is the strongest case (and yet is not so strong in relation to an Island, as it is in relation to an In-land Kingdom) he hath, or can suppose, for the support of this power, to every part of which this answer may be applied.

As there is no Soveraign in *Europe* who pretends to this right of Soveraignty, so there was never any Kingdom, or considerable Country lost by want of it, or preserv'd by the acutal exercise of it: and the Laws themselves permit, and allow many things to be don, when the mischief and necessity are in view, which may not warrantably be don upon the pretence of preventing it. The Law of necessity is pleadable in any Court, and hath not only its pardon but justification; as when, not only a Magistrate, but a private man pulls down a house or more, which are next to that house which is on fire, to prevent the farther mischief, the Law justifies him, because the necessity and benefit is as visible as the fire; yet it would not be justice in the Soveraign himself, to cause a mans house to be pulled down that is seven miles distant, upon a fore-sight that the fire may come thither. I am not averse from Mr. *Hobbes*'s opinion, that a man who is upon the point of starving, and is not able to buy meat, may take as much of the meat he first sees, as will serve for that meal; and this not only by the Law of Nature, but for ought I know, without punishment by any Municipal Law, which seldom cancels the unquestionable Law of Nature: but this necessity will not justifie him in the stealing or taking by force an Ox from any man to prevent starving for a month together, how poor soever the man is, or to rob a Poulterersshop, that he may have a second course. Necessity is not a word unknown, or unconsider'd by the Law. No Subject, who will obey the Law, and submit to that power and autority which he confesses to be unquestionable in the King, can run into Rebellion; and if he doth, all other Subjects are bound by the Laws to assist, to suppress it in that manner, and with that force, and under such conduct and command as the Soveraign directs. If this Rebellion prospers, let the Soveraigns right be what Mr. *Hobbes* assigns him, to levy mony, he will never be able to levy it in the Rebels Quarters; and if they extend their Quarters far, they share the Soveraignty with him; for he appoints those who live in those Quarters, and enjoy protection, to assist and defend their Protectors. The case is the same in an actual Invasion, where the Invaders right grows at least as fast as the Rebels; and the power of the Soveraign, be it never so cheerfully submitted to, can levy mony only where he is obeied, and upon those whose hands must fight for him, or give him other assistance; and then the quesiton is, Whether he be not like to be stronger by accepting what they are willing to give, then by letting them know that they have nothing to give, because all they have is his. And yet in both these cases of an actual Rebellion, or actual Invasion, if the King takes any mans mony that he finds (and if he cannot find it, his right to take it will do him little good) not as his own, but as that mans, to be laid out for his own and public defence, and to be repaid by the public, which ought not to be defended at the charge of any private man, there will be little complaint of the violation of the Law, and the right of Property will be still unshaken. But all these mischiefs are to be prevented by the Soveraigns sagacity and foresight; and if he may not levy what mony he pleases, and thinks requisite to make preparations to disappoint all such designs of both kinds, it will be too late indeed to do it after, and the Common-wealth cannot but suffer by the defect of power.

If the mischief be only in apprehension, there is time to raise mony in that way which is provided, and agreed upon for those extraordinary occasions, by asking their consent, who can without any complaint or murmur that can prove inconvenient, give present directions for the paiment thereof. But what if they refuse to give; must the Common-wealth perish, and every man in it, whose defence the Soveraign hath undertaken, and is bound to. If the Soveraign hath taken all they have before, as he may when he will, they may have nothing left to be taken in those necessary seasons, and then what will his obligation to defend them do good? and how are they like to assist him, when they have nothing to defend but his power to make them miserable? It is not good to suspect, that Princes will extend their power, how absolute soever it is, to undo their Subjects wantonly and unnecessarily; nor is it reasonable to imagine, that Subjects who enjoy Peace and Plenty, will obstinately refuse to contribute towards their own preservation, when both are in danger. But since it is necessary to suppose a case that never yet fell out, to introduce a Government that was never before thought of, let us admit that it is possible, that such an obstinate Spirit may rule in that Assembly which have the power to raise mony, that they may peremtorily refuse to give any, and by the want thereof the Commonwealth is really like to be dissolv'd; I say, admit this, (tho the same kind of obstinacy, that is, an obstinacy as natural as this, to perform no function they ought to do, will, and must dissolve the Soveraignty of his own institution) the question shall be, Whether this very disease be worthy of such a cure? whether the confess'd possibility of such a danger be fit to be secur'd and prevented by such a remedy? and I think most wise and dispassioned men will believe, that the perpetual inquietude and vexation, that must attend men who are in daily fear to have all they have taken from them, and believe that they have nothing their own to leave to their Children and Family, is too disproportion'd a provision to prevent a mischief that is possible to fall out; and that the hazard of that is more reasonably to be submitted to, then the danger of a more probable revolution from the other distemper. And when he hath heightened the danger his Soveraignty may be in, by all the desperate imaginations his melancholy or fancy can suggest to him, he will find, that no defect of power can ever make a Prince so weak, so impotent, and so completely miserable, as his being Soveraign over such subjects as having nothing to give, because they have nothing that is their own; nor will the conscience of their Soveraign, that he will not do all he may, bring any substantial Cordial to them: but as he saies, that his Soveraign *may command any thing to be don against Law, because his command amounts to a repeal of that Law, for he that can make himself free, is free*; so they will think, that he that can be undon at the pleasure of another man, is undon already, and that every day is but the Eve of his destruction, and therefore will think of all ways to prevent it; and he knows the effect of fear too well, to think that a man who is in a continual fright can be fix'd in a firm obedience.

His Commentary upon the ten Commandments, which in his judgment comprehends and exacts all his Injunctions contain'd in his *Leviathan*, and his other Theological Speculations, I refer to the consideration and examination of his Friends the Divines, who no doubt will be well pleased to find him a better

Casuist, now he comes to revolve the tenth Commandment in this his thirtieth Chapter, then he was in his twenty seventh Chapter, in his gloss upon the same Text; for there he determines clearly, (*pag.* 151.) that *to be delighted in the imagination only of being possessed of an other mans goods, or wife, without intention to take them from him by force or fraud, is no breach of this Law, Thou shalt not covet: nor the pleasure a man hath in imagining the death of a man, from whose life he expects nothing but damage and displeasure, any sin.* The business he then had, was to find excuses and extenuations for sins; but now having occasion better to consider that Commandement, of which he stood in need, he finds, that the very intention to do an unjust act, tho hinder'd, is injustice, which consisteth in the pravity of the Will, as well as in the irregularity of the act; as if in the former case, all that delight in the imagination of being possessed of another mans Wife, or the pleasure one has in thinking of the death of a man he doth not love, could be without any pravity of the Will. 'Tis true, a purpose and intendment may be more criminal then a mere complacency; but we know more or less do not change the Species of things. And for the best way of inculcating all his useful Doctrines, and setting aside certain daies to infuse (which upon so good an occasion will not offend his severe ear) the same into the hearts of the People, which he conceives to be a duty enjoin'd by the fourth Commandment, I shall defer my opinion till the end of the next Chapter, when upon the view of all his Doctrines by retail, we may better consult upon the method of spreading them abroad. In the mean time he must not take it ill, that I observe his extreme malignity to the Nobility, by whose bread he hath bin alwaies sustain'd, who must not expect any part, at least any precedence in his Institution; that in this his deep meditation upon the ten Commandments, and in a conjuncture when the Levellers were at highest, and the reduction of all degrees to one and the same was resolv'd upon, and begun, and exercis'd towards the whole Nobility with all the instances of contemt and scorn, he chose to publish his judgment; as if the safety of the People requir'd an equality of Persons, and that (*pag* 180.) *the honor of great Persons is to be valued for their beneficence, and the aids they give to men of inferior rank, or not at all; and that the consequence of partiality towards the great, raised hatred, and an endeavor in the People to pull down all oppressing and*

contumelious greatness; language lent to, or borrowed from
the Agitators of that time.

He seems to think the making of good Laws to be incumbent
on the Soveraign as his duty, and of much importance to his
Government; but he saies then, (*pag.* 181.) *that by a good
Law, he doth not mean a just Law, for that no Law can be
unjust, because it is made by the Soveraign Power.* And in
truth, if the use of Laws is not to restrain men from doing
amiss, and to instruct and dispose them to do well, and to
secure them when they do so, they are of no use at all, and it is
no matter if there be any Laws or no. For, to make use of his
own illustration, (*pag.* 182.) *Hedges are set to stop Travellers,
and to keep them in the way* that is allow'd and prescrib'd, and
for hindering them to chuse a way for themselves, tho a better
and nearer way; and Laws are made to guide, and govern, and
punish men who presume to decline that rule, and to chuse
another to walk by, that is more agreable to their own appetite
or convenience. He renews his trouble to find fit Counsellors
for his Soveraign, which he hath so much consider'd before,
and finds the office to be as hard as the Etymology (of which let
the Grammarians and he agree) and saies plainly, (*pag.* 184.)
that the Politics is a harder study, then the study of Geometry:
and probably he believes that he can set down as firm Rules in
the one, as there are in the other. (*pag.* 184) *Good counsel,* he
saies, *comes not by lot or inheritance, and therefore there is no
more reason to expect good advice from the rich or the noble,
in the matter of state, then in delineating the dimensions of a
Fortress*; and is very solicitous, like a faithful Leveller, that no
man may have priviledges of that kind by his birth or descent,
or have farther honor then adhereth naturally to his abilities;
whereas in all well instituted Governments, as well among the
Ancient as the Modern, the Heirs and Descendants from
worthy and eminent Parents, if they do not degenerate from
their vertue, have bin alwaies allow'd a preference, and kind of
title to emploiments and offices of honor and trust, which he
thinks (*pag.* 184.) *inconsistent with the Soveraign power*, tho
they must he confer'd by him: and the Pedegree of those
pretences from the *Germans*, is one of those dreams which he
falls into, when he invades the quarters of History to make
good his assertions.

Lastly, since he reckons the sending out Colonies, and
erecting Plantations, the encouraging all manner of Arts, as

Navigation, Agriculture, Fishing, and all manner of Manufactures, to be of the Policy and Office of a Soveraign, it will not be in his power to deny, that his Soveraign is obliged to perform all those promises, and to make good all those concessions and priviledges which he hath made and granted, to those who have bin thereby induc'd to expose their Fortunes and their industry to those Adventures, as hath bin formerly enlarg'd upon in the case of Merchants and Corporations, and which is directly contrary to his Conclusions and Determinations. And I cannot but here observe the great vigilance and caution which Mr. *Hobbes* (who hath an excellent faculty of employing very soft words, for the bringing the most hard and cruel things to pass) uses out of his abstracted love of justice, towards the regulating and well ordering his poor and strong people, whom he transplants into other Countries for the ease of his own; whom he will by no means suffer to exterminate those they find there, but only to constrain them to inhabit closer together, and not to range a great deal of ground; that is in more significant words, which the tenderness of his nature would not give him leave to utter, and take from them the abundance they possess, and reduce them to such an assignation, that they may be compell'd, if they will not be perswaded, (*pag.* 181.) *to court each little plot with art and labor to give them their sustenance in due season.* And if all this good Husbandry will not serve the turn, but that they are still overcharg'd with Inhabitants, he hath out of his deep meditation prescrib'd them a sure remedy for that too, (*pag.* 181) *War,* which he saies *will provide for every man by victory, or death*; that is, they must cut the thoats of all men who are troublesom to them, which without doubt must be the natural and final period of all his Prescriptions in Policy and Government.

The Survey of Chapter 31.

After he hath form'd such a Kingdom for man, as is agreeable to his good will and pleasure, he concludes this second part of his Discourse, by assigning the one and thirtieth Chapter to the consideration of the Kingdom of God by nature, concerning which, he enlargeth himself with less reservation in the third part of his Discourse which immediatly follows, and therefore I shall make no reflexions upon what he saies concerning it, till we come thither: nor upon his Worship and Attributes which he assigns to God, or rather what are not Attributes to him; in which, under pretence of explaining or defining, he makes many things harder then they were before. As all men who know what the meaning of knowledg and understanding is, know it less after they are told, that it is (*pag.* 190.) *nothing else but a tumult in the mind raised by external things, that press the organical parts of mans body.* And I must confess, he hath throughout this whole Chapter with wonderful art, by making use of the very many easie, proper, and very significant words, made a shift to compound the whole so involv'd and intricate, that there is scarce a chapter in his Book, the sense whereof the Reader can with more difficulty carry about him, and observe the several fallacies and contradictions in it. Of which kind of obscurity Mr. *Hobbes* makes as much use, as of his brightest elucidations, and having the Soveraign power over all definitions: which he uses not (as is don in Geometry, which he saies, is *the only science it hath pleased God hitherto to bestow upon man kind*) as preliminaries or *postulata*, by which men may know the setled signification of words, but reserves the prerogative to himself, to give new Definitions as often as he hath occasion to use the same terms, that when it conduces to his purpose, he may inform his Reader, or else perplex him. And therefore he doth not think himself safe in the former plain Definition which he gives of understanding, (*pag.* 17.) that it is *nothing else but conception caused by speech; by which, speech being peculiar to man, understanding must be peculiar to him also*: but now being in his one and thirtieth Chapter, and to deprive God of understanding, that Definition will not serve his turn, since it cannot be doubted that God doth hear all we say; and therefore we are to be amuzed by being told, (*pag.* 190.) that understanding is nothing else *but a tumult of the mind, raised by external things, that press the organical parts of mans body: So that there being no such thing in God, and it depending on natural causes, cannot be attributed to him.* And now he is as safe as ever he was, and let him that finds no tumult in his mind, that presses the organical parts of his body, get knowledg and understanding as he can.

I am not willing, under pretence of adjourning some reflexions, which would be natural enough upon this Chapter, to a more seasonable occasion, for enlargment upon the third part of his discourse, to be thought purposely to pretermit some of his Expressions in this Chapter, which seem to have somewhat of Piety and of Godliness in them, and to raise hope that his purposess are yet better then they appear'd to be. After all that illimitted power he hath granted to his Soveraign, and all that unrestrain'd obedience which he exacts from his Subject, he doth in the first Paragraph of this Chapter frankly acknowledg, (*pag.* 186.) that *the Subjects owe simple obedience to their Soveraign, only in those things wherein their obedience is not repugannt to the Law of God*, and is very solicitous so to instruct his Subject, that for want of entire knowledg of his duty to both Laws, he may neither by too much civil obedience offend the Divine Majesty, or through fear of offending God, transgress the Commandments of the Commonwealth; a circumspection worthy the best Christian, and is enough to destroy many of the Prerogatives which he hath given to his Soveraign, and to cancel many of the Obligations he hath impos'd upon his Subject. But if the Reader will suspend his judgment till he hath read a few leaves more, he will find, that Mr. *Hobbes* hath bin wary enough to do himself no harm by his specious Divinity, but hath a *salvo* to set all streight again; for he makes no scruple of determining, (*pag.* 199.) *That the Books of the holy Scripture, which only contain the Laws of God, are only Canonical, when they are establish'd for such by the Soveraign power*. So that when he hath suspended obedience to the Soveraign in those things wherein their obedience is repugant to the Law of God, it is meant only till the Soveraign declares that it is not repugnant to the Law of God; with other excellent Doctrine, the examination whereof we must not anticipate before its time; and shall only wonder at his devout provision, (*pag.* 191.) *that Praiers and Thanksgiving to God, be the best and most signficiant of honor.* And whereas most pious men are of opinion, that those Devotions being the most sincere, and addressed to none but to God himself, who at the same time sees the integrity of the heart, ought to be without the least affectation of Word, or elegance of Expression; he will have them (*pag.* 192.) *made in words and phrases, not sudden and plebeian, but beautiful and well compos'd, for else we do not God so much honor as we may*; and therefore he saies, *Though the Heathen did absurdly to worship Images for Gods, yet their doing it in verse and with music, both of voice and instrument, was reasonable.*

I cannot omit the observation of his very confident avoiding that place in the Scripture, (*pag.* 193.) *It is better to obey God then man,* which he could not but find did press him very hard, and was worthy of a better answer, then that it *hath place in the Kingdom of God by pact, and not by nature*; which if it be an answer, hath not that perspicuity in it, which good Geometricians require; and the answer stands much more in need of a Commentary, then the Text, which he will supply us with in the next Edition. However, let it be as it will, he hath, he saies, (*pag.* 193.) *recover'd some hope, that at one time or other this writing of his may fall into the hands of a Soveraign who will consider it himself,* (he acknowledg'd at that time no Soveraign but *Cromwell*) *and without the help of any interessed or envious Interpreter, and by the exericse of entire Soveraignty in protecting the public teaching it, convert the truth of speculation into the utility of practice.*

It is one of the unhappy effects, which a too gracious and merciful Indulgence ever produces in corrupt and proud natures, that they believe that whatsoever is tolerated in them, is justified and commended; and because Mr. *Hobbes* hath not receiv'd any such brand which the Authors of such Doctrine have bin usually mark'd with, nor hath seen his Book burn'd by the hand of the Hang-man, as many more innocent Books have bin, he is exalted to a hope, that the supreme Magistrate will at some time so far exercise his Soveraignty, as to protect the public teaching his Principles, and convert the truth of his Speculation into the utility of practice. But he might remember, and all those who are scandaliz'd, that such monstrous and seditious Discourses have so long escaped a judicial Examination and Punishment, must know, that Mr. *Hobbes* his *Leviathan* was printed & publish'd in the highest time of *Cromwell's* wicked Usurpation; for the vindication and perpetuating whereof, it was contriv'd and design'd, and when all Legal power was suppress'd; and upon his Majesties blessed return, that merciful and wholsom Act of Oblivion, which pardon'd all Treasons and Murders, Sacriledg, Robbery, Heresies and Blasphemies, as well with reference to their Writings as their Persons, and other Actions, did likewise wipe out the memory of the Enormities of Mr. *Hobbes* and his *Leviathan.* And this hath bin the only reason, why the last hath bin no more enquired into then the former, it having bin thought best, that the impious Doctrines of what kind soever, which the license of those times produc'd, should rather expire by neglect, and the repentance of the Authors, then that they should be brought upon the stage again by a solemn and public condemnation, which might kindle some parts of the old Spirit with the vanity of contradiction, which would otherwise, in a short time, be extinguish'd: and it is only in Mr. *Hobbes* his own power to reverse the security that Act hath given him, by repeting his former Errors, by making what was his Off-spring in Tyrannical Times, when there was no King in *Israel*, his more deliberate and legitimate Issue and Productions, in a time when a lawful Government flourishes, which cannot connive at such bold Transgressors and Transgressions; and he will then find, that it hath fallen into the hands of a Soverign that hath consider'd it very well, not by allowing the public teaching it, but by a declared detestation and final suppression of it, and enjoining the Author a public recantation.

We shall conclude here our disquisition of his Policy and Government of his Commonwealth, with the recollecting and stating the excellent Maximes and Principles upon which his Government is founded and supported, that when they appear naked, and uninvolv'd in his magisterial Discourses, men may judg of the liberty and security they should enjoy, if Mr. *Hobbes* Doctrine were inculcated into the minds of men by their Education, and the Industry of those Masters under whom they are to be bred, as he thinks it ncessary it should be; which Principles are in these very terms declared by him.

1. *That the Kings word is sufficient to take any thing from any Subject then there is need, and that the King is Judg of that need.* pag. 106. cap. 20. part. 2.

2. *The Liberty of a subject lieth only in those things, which in regulating their actions, the Soveraign hath pretermitted, such as is the liberty to buy and sell, and otherwise to contract with one another; to chuse their own abode, their own diet, their own trade of life, and institute their children as they themselves think fit, and the like.* Pag. 109. cap. 21. par. 2.

3. *Nothing the Soveraign can do to a subject, on what pretence soever, can properly be called injustice or injury.* pag. 109.

4. *When a Soveraign Prince putteth to death an innocent subject, tho the action be against the Law of*

Nature, as being contrary to Equity, yet it is not an injury to the subject, but to God. pag. 109.

5. *No man hath liberty to resist the word of the Soveraign; but in case a great many men together, have already resisted the soveraign power unjustly, or committed some capital crime, for which every one of them expecteth death, they have liberty to join together, and to assist and defend one another* Pag. 112.

6. *If a Soveraign demand, or take any thing by pretence of his power, there lieth in that case no action at Law.* pag. 112.

7. *If a subject be taken Prisoner in war, or his person, or his means of life be within the guards of the Enemy, and hath his life and corporal liberty given him, on condition to be subject to the Victor, he hath liberty to accept the condition, and having accepted it, is the subject of him that took him.* pag. 114.

8. *If the Soveraign banish the subject, during the banishment he is no subject.* pag. 114.

9. *The obligation of subjects to the Soveraign, is as long, and no longer then the power lasteth, by which he is able to protect them.* pag. 124.

10. *What ever Promises or Covenants the Soveraign makes, are void.* pag. 89.

11. *He whose private interest is to be judged in an assembly, may make as many friends as he can; and tho he hires such friends with mony, yet it is not injustice.* pag. 122. cap. 22. part. 2.

12. *The propriety which a subject hath in his Lands, consisteth in a right to exclude all other subjects from the use of them, and not to exclude their Soveraign.* pag. 128. cap. 24. part. 2.

13. *When the soveraign commandeth a man to do that which is against Law, the doing of it is totally excus'd; when the soveraign commandeth anything to be don against Law, the command as to that particular fact is an abrogation of the Law.* pag. 157. cap. 27. part. 2.

14. *Tho the right of a Soveraign Monarch cannot be extinguish'd by the act of another, yet the obligation of the members may; for he that wants protection, may seek it any where, and when he hath it, is oblig'd (without fraudulent pretence of having submitted himself out of fear) to protect his Protector as long as he is able.* pag. 174. cap. 29. part. 2.

If upon the short reflexions we have made upon these several Doctrines, as they lie scattered over his Book, and involv'd in other Discourses, which with the novelty administers some pleasure to the unwary Reader, the contagion thereof be not enough discover'd, and the ill consequence and ruine that must attend Kings and Princes who affect such a Government, as well as the misery insupportable to Subjects, who are compelled to submit to it; it may be, the view of the naked Propositions by themselves, without any other clothing or disguise of words, may better serve to make them odious to King and People; and that the first will easily discern, to how high a pinacle of power soever he would carry him, he leaves him upon such a Precipice, from whence the least blast of Invasion from a Neighbor, or from Rebellion by his Subjects, may throw him headlong to irrecoverable ruine: and the other will as much ahhor an Allegiance of that temper, that by any misfortune of their Prince they may be absolv'd from, and cease to be Subjects, when their Soveraign hath most need of their obedience. And surely if these Articles of Mr. *Hobbes*'s Creed be the product of right Reason, and the effects of Christian Obligations, the Great Turk may be look'd upon as the best Philosopher, and all his Subjects as the best Christians.